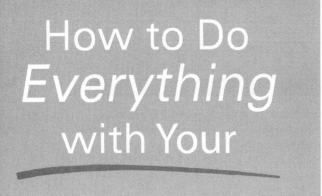

How to Do *Everything* with Your

S0-DTC-177

Treo™ 700p
Second Edition

Derek Ball
Dayton Foster

Mc
Graw
Hill

New York   Chicago   San Francisco   Lisbon
London   Madrid   Mexico City   Milan   New Delhi
San Juan   Seoul   Singapore   Sydney   Toronto

The McGraw·Hill Companies

McGraw-Hill books are available at special quantity discounts to use as premiums and sales promotions, or for use in corporate training programs. For more information, please write to the Director of Special Sales, Professional Publishing, McGraw-Hill, Two Penn Plaza, New York, NY 10121-2298. Or contact your local bookstore.

How to Do Everything with Your Treo™ 700p, Second Edition

1234567890 DOC DOC 019876

ISBN-13: 978-0-07-226249-0
ISBN-10:   0-07-226249-4

Sponsoring Editor
Megg Morin

Editorial Supervisor
Janet Walden

Project Manager
Rajni Pisharody

Acquisitions Coordinator
Agatha Kim

Technical Editor
Michelle White

Copy Editor
Robert Campbell

Proofreader
Ragini Pandey

Indexer
Kevin Brocolli

Production Supervisor
George Anderson

Composition
International Typesetting
and Composition

Illustration
International Typesetting
and Composition

Art Director, Cover
Jeff Weeks

Cover Designer
Pattie Lee

For Devon. The newest of my muses. May your life be full of wonder, amazement, and happiness. Love, Dad.
—*Derek*

For my daughter Avery and my wife Kate, together you bring more joy and happiness into my life than I deserve.
—*Dayton*

About the Authors

Derek Ball is a recognized industry expert in mobile technology and former CEO of Sonic Mobility, Inc. (www.sonicmobility.com), a company focused on delivering solutions for handheld wireless devices such as the Treo. Derek has published twelve other books on technology topics and has traveled the world, speaking at conferences and seminars on emerging technology. In between trips, Derek lives in Calgary, Alberta with his wife, Lesley; daughters Jamie, Carly, and Devon; and golden retriever, Casey.

Dayton Foster is Director of Mobile Solutions for Avocent Corp. Dayton has extensive experience with all aspects of mobile devices including the Treo. He currently lives in Calgary, Alberta with his wife Kate and daughter Avery.

About the Technical Reviewer

Michelle White is a Senior Product Manager at palmOne and was the lead Product Manager for the Treo. She has spent nearly half her career in the handheld and smartphone industry and was responsible for the IBM WorkPad line of handhelds at Palm Inc., Handspring Visor, Visor Platinum, Visor Edge, Treo 90, Treo 600, and most recently the Treo 700p.

Contents

Foreword

A few years ago, I considered myself "retired," having enjoyed 20 great years in high tech. I was keeping myself busy with a couple start-ups when I received a call from a former colleague telling me to "come in, I want to show you something..."

That friend was now working at a small, innovative company called Handspring. That "something" was the Treo 600, and when I saw it, I saw the future.

Without a second thought, I joined the Treo team.

Another chapter was quickly added to this story when Palm and Handspring joined together (there's a whole soap opera there, but that's a different book), and the combined Palm brought more great talent to the Treo DNA.

Now, we have the Treo 700P running on the wicked fast EVDO networks. A flavor of Treo is carried on every major US mobile operator, the world's largest operator in Europe, and more regional operators are added every quarter.

Almost everyone with a Treo uses it to do e-mail and texting and of course talk. But some of the other great things people do with Treo is amazing. One of my friends used hers to tune into live MobiTV and get an update to an airport threat while she was in the middle of the shutdown. Another uses his to tune into live shots of his webcam to make sure all is well with his horse barn.

I love that I can tune into my local NPR station, or get a Yelp restaurant suggestion and directions—letting me feel at home in two different ways—when I'm the road.

So whether it's a Fortune 500 firm rolling the Treo out to its entire sales force, a small business owner running her business from Treo, or the knowledge worker balancing work and life with the freedom of Treo mobility, it's happening with the Treo, and with the help of Derek and Dayton's book, it can happen with you.

–Joe Fabris, Director of Wireless Solutions, Palm, Inc.
(Written on my Treo at the airport on the way to Orlando for the Gartner IT Expo while listening to an MP3 of the White Stripes. Ain't life grand.)

Acknowledgments

Writers are a strange lot; technical writers perhaps even more so. We have had the tremendous opportunity (curse?) to embark upon many book projects in the past. However, as is typical with "selective memory," we often forget what a monumental effort it actually takes to complete a book, not only on the part of the authors, but of all the other people who are involved in the project and without whom no book would ever see the light of day through the bookstore window.

First of all, we want to thank you, the reader. We hope that with this book we can deliver to you information that will help enhance your mobile lifestyle!

There are a great many people we would like to thank who have contributed to this book, but thanks hardly seem to be enough. Megg Morin at McGraw-Hill/Osborne has worked on a three of our books with us and has consistently been amazing. From the initial book proposal, through the writing, editing, and delivering of all the elements of the book, Megg had to deal with our ins and outs and ups and downs. Megg, you are great to work with, and have added an incredible amount of value this book, and all of our previous efforts. We look forward to future projects together!

Special thanks also need to be extended to Agatha Kim for acquisitions coordination (we were one of her last projects before heading out to pursue a graduate degree, and thanks to Carly Stapleton for taking over!); Rajni Pisharody for project management; and Robert Campbell for copy editing this book with skill and finesse. Thank you!

Our technical editor, Michelle White, has been invaluable in making sure our information is as accurate and up-to-date as possible. Thank you, Michelle, for your help in ensuring the quality of this book, and for all of your suggestions and recommendations, which have greatly improved the value of this book for the reader.

There are many other individuals behind the scenes involved in the production of the book whose names we may not know, but whose contribution to delivering this book into readers' hands is no less significant. Your efforts are also appreciated.

And finally, to our wives and kids, who have put up with late nights and family activities we couldn't go to, for encouraging and supporting us through this process. Your love and support made all of this possible. Our deepest gratitude and love.

Introduction

When US Robotics introduced the first Palm Pilot to the world, it began a revolution that would see millions of mobile computing devices in the hands of everyday people. The latest in this extended family, the Treo 700p, has extended that to new extremes.

This remarkable device contains so much power that mobile individuals can now do things that were never before possible with a PDA. Beyond simple contact and calendar management, now people can send and receive e-mail, write documents, build spreadsheets, make presentations, surf the Internet, and so much more, all from a device that easily slips into a pocket.

Palm has gone through many changes recently from the initial merger with Handspring Inc (the maker of the original Treo) and subsequently the splitting off of Palmsource (later acquired by Access in Japan). The future of the Treo continues to grow more and more interesting as the power and battery life of these devices grow, and yet they become smaller and more portable...and with the introduction of integrated wireless technology, more connected! More and more people are adopting this device and integrating it into their mobile lifestyles.

Who Should Read This Book

This book is intended for all Palm OS Treo owners (note that this book does not cover the Windows Mobile version of the Treo as it is a radically different operating system). The major focus of this book is on the Treo 700p model although most of the content is applicable for Treo 600 and 650 users as well. If you're a new Treo owner, this book will help you understand how to get started using your new Treo properly. For the owner who has had a Treo for a while, this book will help you understand how to get more out of your investment.

Whatever your level of experience with the Treo, you will find relevant information in this book to do things with your Treo that you haven't done before.

You can follow along with the information in this book as it walks you through using built-in applications such as Word Mobile and Excel Mobile. In other sections of the book you will find opportunities to read about the potential of the Treo and future devices, and perhaps you will choose to integrate GPS or wireless connectivity into your mobility.

How This Book Is Organized

We have organized this book in sections to enable you to jump right into the area that is most relevant to you. Part I, "Meet Your Treo" introduces you to the basic set up of your Treo and also explains how to use the powerful built-in software that comes with it. You will learn how to get connected with voice, messaging, email, and the Internet.

Part II, "Maximize the Capabilities of Your Treo," switches the focus to more advanced topics such as device security, performing mobile presentations, working with documents and spreadsheets, and using Global Positioning Systems for personal navigation. Part III, "Select Essential Hardware and Accessories for Your Treo" shows you what kind of external devices you can use to expand the functionality of your Treo and how to use the myriad third-party products designed to increase the storage of your Treo, turn your Treo into a navigational tool, and more. The appendices of the book are there to help you troubleshoot some common problems with the Treo, as well as point you to other resources that you might want to investigate for more information on your device.

As you read through the text, you'll see we've included sidebars for points of specific interest, so watch for the sections labeled How To, Did You Know?, Caution, Note, and Tip for special information about the section you are currently reading.

We hope that you will find this book helpful as you learn to live the mobile Treo lifestyle! We use our Treos on a daily basis, and they have almost become an extension of our arms. Our most critical information is never more than a moment away, and we can consolidate many disparate information sources into one location. Your Treo can become as important a productivity tool as it is for us. We use them to find our way around foreign cities when we travel, give presentations while on the road, wirelessly stay connected to the office to manage our infrastructure and data, send and receive e-mail, and so much more!

Part I

Meet Your Treo

Chapter 1

The Treo ... Not Just Another Palm!

How to…

■ Live the mobile lifestyle

■ Live with less paper

Ever since we human beings learned to store information somewhere other than in our heads, we have been working on ways not only to make permanent records of our information but also to take those records with us, wherever we go. Over many millennia, this pursuit has taken us from crude paintings on cave walls, to hieroglyphics on stone tablets, to papyrus, to the printing press, to the day planner, and now to the personal digital assistant (PDA).

No longer are we are satisfied to simply carry our information with us. We are pushing for a new era of portable information. We want our PDAs to do more than was even hinted at by early science fiction writers and television shows like "*Star Trek*." More than ever, we want our devices to become an extension of ourselves, to function as a personal secretary, travel agent, guide, doctor, communicator, and entertainment device.

Palm has been, by far, the most successful in selling PDAs. In fact, Palm PDAs have been so successful that many people refer to any handheld computer as a "Palm," much the same way people use the brand name Kleenex to refer to facial tissue and Xerox to refer to a photocopy.

Recently, many people have been interested in the idea of a device that would merge their cell phone and PDA into a single unit. In response to this market, companies have developed a variety of devices running a variety of operating systems; however, most of these devices have met with limited success. In general, manufacturers took one of two approaches in the endeavor to create a combined cell phone-PDA device. The first approach was to take their existing PDA platform and essentially glue a cellular phone to it. This was less than successful, as evidenced by the low adoption rates of the dozen or so products that took this approach. The second approach was to take a compact cell phone and give it a tiny screen as well as the ability to hold some contacts and do e-mail (as if you could ever truly do e-mail on a keyboard with only nine buttons!).

These two approaches left users very dissatisfied. The end results were too bulky, had poor battery life and inadequate screens, or lacked the necessary input capability to be truly useful.

Initial success in this market was cornered by the BlackBerry devices produced by Research In Motion (RIM). Then a new competitor arrived, leaping into the raging river of this opportunity, the Treo 600. It was actually the fourth in the series of Treo devices from Handspring but the first to truly meet the needs of the end user and deliver mass market appeal and functionality. With its sleek, compact styling, powerful Texas Instruments OMAP processor, abundant memory, and ultra bright and clear touch screen, this device sported an adoption rate unlike any Palm device in recent history. It had a convenient size, so average cell phone users who switched to the Treo 600 didn't feel like they were carrying around and speaking into a brick; yet Handspring didn't make the mistake of making it too small. There was an ample full-color screen and a full QWERTY keyboard for thumb typing.

The Treo 600 proved to be so popular that it was hard to find the unit on store shelves, although increased production as a result of the Palm merger with Handspring quickly remedied this problem. Following on the success of the Treo 600, a new device was launched. Palm had since renamed their company palmOne following the merger with Handspring (and after spinning off a new company called PalmSource that was solely responsible for developing and licensing the Palm operating system). The palmOne Treo 650 had a form factor identical to the Treo 600 but fixed some bugs as well as adding new features such as a better screen, Bluetooth wireless capability, an improved keyboard, and more.

Then, recently the company again rebranded itself as Palm and launched its latest two devices, this time with a twist. Both devices appear physically the same, both are called the Treo 700, but now there is a letter appended to the model number. For the first time, you can choose the Palm device with either a Windows Mobile 5 operating system (the Treo 700w) or the Palm OS 5.4 (the 700p). Given the tremendous differences between the two operating systems, this book focuses specifically on Treo devices running the Palm OS.

In addition to the different models, the Treo comes in many flavors depending upon which carrier (wireless telephone company) you get your device from. The Treo devices support both CDMA (Code Division Multiple Access) and GSM (Global System for Mobile Communications) wireless networks and are often customized as part of the deal with the carrier, or wireless service provider, that is offering the device to its subscribers.

It used to be that a PDA was more of a status symbol than a truly practical tool, but that is changing as the PDA converges with the mobile cellular phone. The latest release of the Palm OS, the operating system that powers the Treo 600, Treo 650, and Treo 700p, is well suited to perform not only the job of a PDA but also that of a true communications tool—handling e-mail, phone calls, voice mail, and Short Message Service (SMS) and Multimedia Message Service (MMS) communication.

The History of Palm and the Palm OS

The lineage that precedes the current Treo models is long and interesting. Without going into too much depth, it can be useful to understand the quantity and quality of engineering that lead up to the leading-edge device you now hold in your hands.

The first commercially introduced version of what has now commonly become known as the PDA was developed not by Palm, but by Apple. Called the Newton, the device featured a touch screen with built-in, space-age handwriting recognition. Unfortunately for Apple, the device was a total flop. Technologists and venture capitalists alike described the PDA market as not being viable.

Luckily for us, Jeff Hawkins didn't agree with them. He first had the idea for his portable computing platform about the same time that the Apple Newton was breaking up on the rocks. He shopped his idea around but was unable to find anyone who would back it. Finally, some risk-taking visionaries at U.S. Robotics got behind Hawkins' project, and the first U.S. Robotics PalmPilot was born. The device had limited functionality, particularly in comparison to today's mobile powerhouses, but it struck a cord with both the technology early adopters and also the all-important executive crowd. The PalmPilot took root and flourished.

U.S. Robotics was acquired by 3COM, which later spun off Palm as its own company. By this time, although there were a few other players, none were achieving the market success of Palm. Microsoft's first entry into the mobile computing space, Windows CE 1.0, was a complete disaster and was generally rejected by consumers. This would not be Microsoft's final challenge to Palm, as the future would show.

By this time Palm had achieved a tremendous milestone. Independent software developers who had been diligently working and deploying software for this mobile miracle had now produced, in aggregate, over 10,000 software applications for the Palm platform. This was very important because no one buys a computer that doesn't have software. With software galore to choose from, Palm owners could count on finding software to help them manage their wine cellars, fly their airplanes, record home inspection data, or pursue just about any hobby or occupation.

Then, Palm hit some challenging times. The future vision that Jeff Hawkins had for the Palm line differed from that of the Palm management team. Jeff Hawkins left Palm to found Handspring, a new mobile hardware platform that would license and use the Palm Operating System (Palm OS).

With its expandability, the Handspring Visor was a leap away from the current Palm hardware. It featured a "Springboard" slot that allowed the user to plug in external expansion modules to turn the Visor into a pager, a bar code scanner, and much more. In fact, this Springboard expansion module was where Handspring first cut its teeth with a GSM phone expansion called the VisorPhone, shown in Figure 1-1. Hawkins' vision extended beyond just plug-in expansion slots. He saw the day when the PDA would merge with your mobile phone to allow you to carry one device instead of two.

FIGURE 1-1   Handspring's first attempt at delivering a telephone on its platform was the VisorPhone.

This was radically different from the vision at Palm, which was to deliver more powerful, but not connected, PDA devices.

Handspring's next-generation devices were called Treo. The first Treos were—as many groundbreaking devices are—not warmly embraced by the targeted end buyers of the devices. The devices were bulky, with a flip-top cover that was inconvenient for answering calls. Consumers told Handspring that they liked the idea, but the implementation was not up to their expectations. Handspring went back to the drawing board and in late 2003 produced the Treo 600 device. This device took all of the feedback from the earlier generations of devices and delivered it in a single, well-engineered, full-featured package.

You might think this is the end of our story (or at least so far), but it isn't. Back at Palm, the company was struggling. The world had told Palm that the market for PDAs that weren't "connected" and able to get data in real time was shrinking. Palm attempted to respond with a new generation of devices, which contained local wireless networking (802.11, or Wi-Fi), and the Tungsten W, a Palm PDA that with a plug-in ear bud could work as a phone. While Handspring was busy hitting the target with their second shot, Palm was shooting wide and missing the target completely with the Tungsten W.

Next came the big surprise. Palm was going to acquire Handspring and bring back into the fold the talent and vision that previously it had lost. Palm spun its operating system division out as a new company called PalmSource and merged Handspring and Palm together into a new company called palmOne. Suddenly Palm's future seemed very bright, with the best-selling PDA platform and the market's hottest converged *smartphone* (the name for a combined cellular phone and PDA device) back under one roof, all running the Palm OS.

As Palm was getting well positioned for the future, Palm's rivals were not sitting still. Microsoft had been very busy revising and improving its Windows CE product into a more viable platform. The latest release, called Windows Mobile 5, is now center stage in high-quality mobile products produced by HP, Toshiba, Dell, and many others. Microsoft has also introduced its competing platform for smartphones, called Microsoft Windows Mobile for Smartphone. In Europe, Symbian took a commanding lead in the connected-device market. And while this was going on, a small Canadian company called Research In Motion (RIM) was becoming the dominant vendor in selling wireless connected e-mail mobile devices ("connected" meaning devices that continually send and receive e-mail through the wireless connection without having to be synced) to large corporate buyers.

As all of these dynamics were shaping up, palmOne released their next iteration of the Treo device, the Treo 650, which improved on many current Treo characteristics by offering a higher resolution, a brighter screen, a better camera, Bluetooth wireless connectivity, an improved keyboard, and much more. The Treo continued to gain market share, and palmOne decided to rename themselves Palm again, acquiring the full rights to the name from Palmsource. Then, the big shock to the world came when Palm loaded their former arch-rival's operating system on the new Treo 700w, making it the first device from Palm to feature a non-Palm OS. Palm insisted that they weren't giving up on the Palm OS as some critics claimed, and backed this up with the release of the Treo 700p, the same device running the Palm OS.

Another interesting development is that Palmsource, the vendor of the Palm OS, was acquired by a Japanese company called Access. Access has indicated that they expect future iterations of the Palm OS to be based upon Linux, which will be a complete rebuild of this popular operating system.

As the future becomes the present, Palm gives consumers the opportunity to choose the platform that will best fit their needs, while stiff competition continues to grow from many other market entrants. For a very long time, there will be a variety of platforms to choose from, which, for the consumer, will help to keep prices low and innovation high. Palm has the largest foundation of all the vendors to work with and it has a tremendous base of loyal customers. The Treo is, without a doubt, one of the leading converged devices on the market today. As a Treo owner, you can be comfortable that you have a well-developed piece of hardware with an outstanding pedigree.

Treo vs. Other Devices

Now that you are a proud owner of a shiny Treo, you might find yourself being approached by owners of other mobile devices who will try to engage you in debate about your device vs. their own. To compare one mobile device to another is to tread into the arena of religion for many PDA users and can be dangerous territory for any author. That being said, we offer a brief comparison here of some of the devices.

Treo vs. Other Palms

Palm is not the only company that uses the Palm OS. In addition to the variety of devices in the Palm lineup, there are many third-party licensees, including Sony, Symbol, IBM, Samsung, and Kyocera. The key differentiator between the Treo and other Palm-based devices is the Treo's focus on being a phone and communications tool. High-end Palm devices, like the Tungsten E2, feature much more advanced screens and more powerful processors than the Treo and thus can perform more intensive number crunching and offer more advanced multimedia capabilities. However, as communications tools, they pale in comparison to the Treo, whose phone and data connectivity is a core component of the system.

There are other mobile phones that feature a Palm OS, such as those offered by Kyocera and Samsung, but they are literally cell phones "glued" onto a Palm handheld with very little integration between the phone and the PDA. They tend to be bulky and to be poor communications tools.

Treo 700p vs. Treo 700w

The closest offerings to the Treo 700p from the Microsoft side of the fence is, of course, the same hardware platform running the Windows Mobile OS, the Treo 700w. Other vendors of Windows Mobile OS competing devices include the Pocket PC Phone Edition (sold by various vendors under different names, including XDA, MDA, and Siemens SX56), and integrated phone-MS Pocket PC offerings from Audiovox, Toshiba, Samsung, and others. (Newer versions of the Pocket PC platform software are called Windows Mobile 5.)

These units are, in general, more bulky than the Treo and have a shorter battery life. They often feature more powerful processors and higher screen resolutions, which can improve software that is processor intensive (like video) or requires more display area (like spreadsheets), but this rarely impacts the core usability of the device and has a negative impact on the battery life.

The Pocket PC/Windows Mobile units sometimes have more available user memory than the Treo 700p because Windows Mobile applications are generally larger and require more space; however, the availability of the Secure Digital (SD) expansion slots on both devices makes extra memory easily available if you find that you require more.

You may find some Pocket PC enthusiasts talking up the multitasking capabilities of their units. The ability for the processor to work on more than one task at a time is an important feature of the mobile environment. Current versions of the Palm OS support only limited multitasking, and this can place some limits on using the tools as connected devices, particularly if you need to connect to your office network using a virtual private network (VPN). The VPN software must run in the background while you are doing other tasks. This has been addressed partially on the Treo, which runs Palm OS 5.4. You can successfully run software, such as a VPN, on these units, as well as have some programs run in the background (for example, e-mail syncing, and MP3 players).

Multitasking—the ability for the PDA to actually be running two or more programs at the same time—can become an extremely valuable feature as you learn to expand your PDA experience beyond the basic built-in applications. For example, with multitasking, you can connect to your wireless provider and download your e-mail in the background while surfing the Web and pasting information from a web site into your mobile word processing application. This complex activity isn't possible on the majority of the Palms currently in circulation.

Applications

There are two categories of applications for Treo, those that come with your device and those that are provided by third parties. A number of applications come bundled with your device, including contact management, e-mail, notes, To Do lists, and calendaring software. Whether you prefer these built-in applications or third-party products will usually depend on what you used before you turned to your smartphone device.

The Treo also comes standard with many other applications, including a version of Documents To Go for working with Microsoft Word and Excel documents and for viewing PowerPoint files as well as PDF files on your smartphone. Who needs a PC when your smartphone can handle all of these applications? At a minimum, these applications allow easy access to your existing files or to file attachments that arrive in your e-mail Inbox. Also, depending on which carrier you purchased your Treo from, you may find some other software goodies preinstalled on your device or on its companion CD.

Where the Palm platform really shines is in the variety of software designed for it; more than 10,000 third-party applications are currently available for the Palm. The large number of Palm applications is a direct result of Palm's early ability to grab market share and the length of time the operating system has been available in the marketplace. This advantage of Palm is slowly decreasing, however, as other platforms such as Microsoft and Symbian are making inroads into Palm-dominated territory.

Expandability

It is important with any mobile computing platform to be able to make it do more than it does out of the box. Expandability of such a device can come through a variety of physical or wireless connections to storage devices or peripherals.

The Treo can currently be expanded through one of three standards. The most common expansion technique is through Secure Digital (SD) or MultiMedia (MMC) cards. The SD or MMC card is a very economical and efficient expansion option weighing in at the size of a postage stamp. All the Treo models from the 600 up sport an SD expansion slot on the top of the device. The small card in the slot when you receive the Treo is a "blank" and doesn't serve any purpose except to keep the dust out of the slot when there is no card inserted.

The second expandability option for the Treo is through the sync/charge port at the bottom of the device. This port is a serial port that can be used to connect your Treo to a variety of devices such as Global Positioning System (GPS) navigation units (discussed in detail in Chapter 14).

With the Treo 650 and 700p models, Palm also added support for the popular Bluetooth protocol for wireless connectivity. What Bluetooth does is allow you to connect wirelessly over a very short distance (usually less than 30 feet) to accessories. The most common uses for Bluetooth are in wireless headsets used for speaking on the phone and for connecting to GPS receivers used for navigation.

The Bottom Line

The Treo device is an ideal blend of portability and power. Its compact size, combined with a large, full-color screen, and quality voice telephone, has made this one of the hottest smartphones on the market today. The devices are flying off the shelves at an unprecedented rate. The fact that Palm OS drives most of the Treo devices on the market means you can run many of the over 10,000 software titles currently available for the Palm platform, giving you immediate access to an amazing portfolio of applications.

With the Treo, you can now perform functions that were literally the realm of "Star Trek" until recently—real-time communication (including voice, e-mail, and instant messaging) and digital photography. The Treo is one of the first truly usable "converged" devices.

The Treo Family

This book focuses specifically on the Treo smartphone device from Palm running the Palm OS. However, there are other devices produced by Handspring prior to the palmOne merger that also carry the Treo moniker. Here is a short pedigree of the roots of the Treo 600.

Treo 180

Handspring's first converged PDA cell phone was the Treo 180. This wasn't the first Handspring phone (the VisorPhone was), but it was the first one that had the cell phone integrated, which is where we will begin. It featured the Palm OS version 3.5, and the address book was conveniently renamed the Phone Book. It featured an integrated flip-top cover, as shown in Figure 1-2.

When the flip-top cover was opened, the Treo 180 would automatically turn the PDA on and open the phone book for you to select a contact to call.

This unit could only pick up e-mail or perform data functions by dialing the Internet like a modem and could manage only minimal data speeds. As such, it was more like the Kyocera and Samsung combined PDA and cell phones. This device was actually produced in two formats. The first format had a standard Graffiti handwriting recognition area and no keyboard. The second format had a small built-in keyboard without the Graffiti entry area. The latter was the winner, and it became the standard for future Treo devices. Even with that, the sales volumes of the Treo were only a shadow of what the Treo 600 and 650 achieved and the Treo 700p is achieving currently. Palm is now expanding their success with the newly introduced Treo 750v in Europe, offered by Vodaphone.

FIGURE 1-2   The Treo 180 was the first Handspring device to feature an integrated mobile phone.

Treo 270

Just like successive generations of aircraft following the Wright brothers' first airplane, which soared only a short distance, time and engineering effort has allowed successive generations of Treo devices to grow into much more. The Treo 270 featured a full-color screen and was the first Treo to take advantage of General Packet Radio Service (GPRS) to provide continuous data connectivity (often referred to as "always-on" connectivity) and therefore constant access to e-mail. For the first time, you really could treat the Treo as a universal communicator. In reviews, it was often compared to the communicator that Captain Kirk used on "Star Trek." The flip-top cover seemed to be an obvious effort to replicate that space-age device. It was still, however, a larger device than what the general consumer wanted to carry around, and, although it was adopted by technology innovators, it never successfully penetrated the mainstream.

Treo 300

Next came the Treo 300, which ran on the Sprint PCS network. It was very similar to the Treo 270, but the advanced Personal Communications Services (PCS) network allowed for even tighter integration of data functions. It was virtually feature-identical to the Treo 270, with 2.5 hours of talk time and over 150 hours of standby time—a convenient feature, depending on how much you used the functions of the Palm organizer.

All of these devices had a common complaint, they were too big to be carried as your every day cell phone. The idea was solid, but the mass market of cell phone buyers weren't buying them, and it was a little early for business executives to be seeking mobile e-mail and web browsing. But the stage was set, and the next model, the Treo 600, hit the market right at the leading edge of demand for mobile connected wireless devices.

Adopt the Mobile Lifestyle with Your Treo

As PDAs have become more popular, many people seem to be carrying them around in their briefcases or pockets, and yet it is amazing that many people also still carry around paper-based day planners and business card files or keep that trusty paper phone book by the telephone (although it always seems to have been moved by someone when you need it most).

In order to get the most out of your smartphone device, it is important to adopt habits that will centralize all of your information in your device. For example, you will never make effective use of your smartphone if you keep some of your appointments in a paper calendar and some in your Treo.

The fact that the Treo is also your cell phone makes it a little easier to have it with you all the time. Many people are already conditioned to carry their cell phones with them everywhere they go, so substituting the Treo for your cell phone is the easiest habit to adopt.

Tips for Adopting the Mobile Lifestyle

Here are some suggestions to help you integrate your smartphone device into your life:

■ Pick one point in the day, usually at the very beginning or very end of the day, entering any business cards that you have picked up into your Outlook Contacts folder or Palm Desktop. This will keep your Treo business contacts completely up-to-date through the HotSync process. (See Chapter 3 for more on HotSync.) Then you can discard the business cards, or, if you feel compelled to keep them, you can place them in a binder to be kept in your office. (Being an old-world guy who has trouble parting with the attractive cards, I keep mine in binders in my office, but I reference them electronically.)

■ Whenever someone gives you personal contact information such as a phone number, resist the urge to scribble it on a piece of paper and stuff it in your pocket or briefcase. We all have drawers of unidentifiable scribbled phone numbers that aren't of much use. These scraps of paper also don't tend to be in your hand when you need to call that person back. Instead, take the extra 45 seconds to put that person's information into your Treo. Then it will be permanently preserved and available to you any time you need it. Also, this information will be backed up on your computer the next time you HotSync your Treo.

■ When you book an appointment or plan an event, even in the distant future, always enter the event into your smartphone calendar immediately. If you do this consistently, you will learn to trust the calendar in your Treo. If you aren't consistent, you will find yourself missing appointments or double-booking as you try to organize yourself with both a paper system (or worse, your memory) and a Treo.

■ If you use your Treo for expense management, use the same diligent technique of entering all your receipts or financial information into your financial management system once a day. You will find more information on useful financial software in Chapter 12.

■ Whenever you think of something you need to do, be it personal or professional, instead of "making a mental note," put it into your Tasks application on your Treo. You can categorize it, prioritize it, and assign a date to it. The latest Treos even ship with a Voice Memo application, allowing you to make a quick dictation to play back later.

■ Every morning when you get up, look at your calendar and To Do list. If there is something that you know is happening that day that isn't in your calendar, enter it. If there is something you need to get done that day, put it on your task list. Not only does this help to keep track of your tasks and appointments, it helps you to feel that you've accomplished something when you look back on your day. Instead of that "where did the day go, and did I actually get anything done?" feeling that sometimes comes at the end of the day, you will be able to look at your list and see at a glance all the activities and tasks that you knocked off.

■ When a special event occurs, such as a birthday or anniversary, record it in your calendar as a recurring event. That way your Treo will become a true personal assistant by reminding you to make a dinner appointment or pick up a gift well in advance of the date!

■ Try to find things that you are already doing that you might be able to do better with the Treo. For example, I work out at the gym regularly and am an avid runner. I use third-party software to help me track my workouts and fitness goals. If you are watching what you eat, check out the diet and nutrition software that is available for the Treo. And if you are an avid wine connoisseur, you can load up databases of different wines, and so on. The amount of software available for the Treo is truly impressive.

■ If you like to listen to music while you are on the go, you can now stream radio right to your Treo. You can also use third-party services like Orb (www.orb.com) to stream your personal music collection to anywhere you are!

■ Headed to the movies but you don't know what is playing? Just jump to your local movie web site right from your Treo. What a timesaver!

Keep Your Treo with You

Making the best use of your Treo also means that you need to keep it with you as you live out your mobile life. The Treo, although small and lightweight, isn't quite small enough to slip into your shirt pocket or the back pocket of your pants like a wallet. It also isn't as small as the tiny mobile cellular phones that are popular these days. However, if you are accustomed to carrying your mobile phone clipped to your belt or in your briefcase, then establishing the habit of keeping your Treo with you shouldn't be difficult.

Your Treo weighs less than a conventional portable CD player and is as easy to carry with you. In fact, you will probably find your Treo works as well or better than your CD player while you run, work out, or perform any such activities. What's more, with MP3 (a popular audio file format) files, you will never again experience that annoying skipping that even the very best "skip-free" CD players are prone to.

For casual walking around, cargo pants with the side pockets can be very useful places for storing your Treo. For more of a business casual appearance, Dockers has released a line of casual pants called "Mobile Pants," which contain a special pocket for holding your Treo. This idea is a good one; unfortunately, Dockers' execution wasn't great. The pocket is a little small. It is possible to squeeze in the Treo, but it can be a little hard to retrieve in a hurry when your phone rings (or vibrates, which presents a whole new social problem). Unless you are standing at just the right angle, the bulge of the Treo is still obvious, and don't you dare sit down! Dockers has the right idea; hopefully, other clothing manufacturers will actually try putting a Treo into the pocket and using it before they tout their clothing as "Mobile" wear! For the business executive, the Treo fits extremely well into the pocket of a suit or sports coat.

One popular method for carrying the Treo is to use the supplied hip holster (which didn't come with all models; so if you didn't get one, don't assume it was missing from the package!) or to get a third-party case with a belt clip. In Chapter 16, we reference case vendors that provide high-quality cases for your Treo.

There are other carrying methods as well, such as the secret agent-style under-the-jacket holster or the multipocketed vest. One of the vests specifically targeted to the PDA owner is the SCOTTeVest (www.scottevest.com). It is a lightweight water-repellent vest that looks rather like a safari vest. It is loaded with pockets for all your wireless toys and has a unique feature, Velcro-enclosed conduits to hold all the wires that connect your devices together and keep the cords tucked safely away. They call this a personal area network, or PAN. The vest isn't something that you could wear to a business function; and for personal recreational wear, the $160 price tag is rather steep. If you like leather, SCOTTeVest has also introduced a leather jacket with the same integrated pockets and PAN features.

Another consideration for the mobile worker who often has to travel with the Treo, and a laptop, are the plethora of cables and chargers needed to carry with them. You can significantly cut down on the number of cables with some third-party products. For example, the iGo Juice product (www.igo.com), shown in Figure 1-3, is a universal charger that can charge your laptop and your Treo from a wall outlet, car power outlet, or the armrest outlet on some airplanes.

Personally, I find I need to give a lot of PowerPoint presentations on the road, and that is one reason why I have had to carry both my laptop and my Treo. Now you can do presentations right from your Treo with products like the Pitch Duo from iGo, the same vendor that sells the Juice product just mentioned. The Pitch Duo connects to any VGA monitor or projector and allows you to show full PowerPoint presentations right from your Treo! More details on this are provided in Chapter 11.

FIGURE 1-3   The iGo Juice makes it easy to travel with multiple devices because you only need one charger.

The sync cable and charger that come with your Treo are bulky to travel with, but there are many third-party cables that are much smaller and easier to travel with. One of these is BoxWave's Mini-Sync charging cable (www.boxwave.com), which is intended to charge your Treo from the USB port on your computer. It also allows you to synchronize your Treo.

Wrap It Up

The Treo is a compact and powerful communication, business, and entertainment tool. It is highly versatile, and there are so many different things that you can do with this "Swiss Army knife" of smartphones that it is difficult to cover absolutely everything in this book. However, we will explore many topics in the chapters to help you get the most out of your Treo, though, from our experience, we cannot cover every way in which you will use your Treo and we are sure you will find many of your own creative ways to enhance your life with this great device!

Chapter 2

Get Started with Your Treo

How to...

- Unpack your Treo
- Turn on your Treo for the first time
- Navigate your Treo using the touch screen and five-way navigation control
- Set up your Treo preferences
- Use the Applications Launcher
- Use the preinstalled Treo applications
- Upgrade from previous versions of Palm
- Synchronize data from your old Palm device to your Treo
- Beam your business card and other useful information

You just purchased a new Treo—or perhaps you've had it for a while—and now you want to find out how to get the most out of this great device. In this book, you will find entire chapters dedicated to specific functionalities like using the phone, camera, and e-mail. This chapter addresses the features and configurations that you will likely need to set up and understand sooner, rather than later. This book is written as a reference book, so you can read it start to finish or jump around from chapter to chapter, depending on what you want to do with your Treo. Let's get started!

Unpack Your Treo and See What's in the Box

When you open the box and take out the contents, you'll notice that your Treo Smartphone comes with the following items.

Here's what's in the box with the Treo 700p:

- Palm Treo 700p Smartphone
- Rechargeable battery
- AC power charger
- USB sync cable
- Headset
- Stylus
- Palm Software Installation CD with User Guide and desktop synchronization software
- User documentation
- Software preloaded on the Treo 700p and on the CD-ROM (the actual software depends on where and when you bought your Treo).
  - Blazer web browser
  - Bluetooth Manager

2

- ■ Calculator
- ■ Calendar
- ■ Camcorder
- ■ Camera
- ■ Card info
- ■ Contacts
- ■ Documents To Go version 8.0
- ■ HotSync Manager
- ■ Memos
- ■ Messaging
- ■ MyTreo
- ■ Phone
- ■ Pictures and Videos
- ■ PocketTunes
- ■ QuickTour
- ■ Tasks
- ■ VersaMail
- ■ Voice Memo
- ■ World Clock
- ■ On the CD
  - ■ Audible
  - ■ Bejeweled
  - ■ Documents To Go (for your desktop)
  - ■ eReader
  - ■ Palm Files
  - ■ Remote File Access
  - ■ Solitaire
  - ■ Traffic for Treo smartphones
- ■ Treo Voice Dialing

Here's what's in the box with the Treo 650:

- ■ Treo 650 Smartphone
- ■ Rechargeable battery
- ■ AC power charger

- USB HotSync cable
- Headset
- Stylus
- Getting Started/Software Installation CD-ROM with User Guide
- Quick Reference Guide
- Software preloaded on the Treo 650 and on the CD-ROM (the actual software depends on where and when you bought your Treo).
- Audible Player
- Blazer web browser
- Camera (photos & video)
- Calculator
- Calendar
- Camcorder
- Camera
- Contacts
- DataViz Docs To Go 7
- Handmark PocketExpress (trial version)
- Handmark Solitaire
- HotSync Manager
- Media
- Media Desktop (Windows only)
- Memos
- Messaging
- Palm Desktop—PC & Mac
- Palm eReader
- Phone
- RealPlayer
- Tasks

Here's what's in the box with the Treo 600 Smartphone :

- VersaMail
- AC charger cable
- Hands-free headset
- USB HotSync cable

- Case (You can learn more about third-party case options for your Treo in Chapter 16.)
- User guide (Note: Not all Treo devices ship with a printed manual. If your Treo did not include a printed manual, the User guide is included in digital format on a CD that is shipped with your Treo.)
- Synchronization and Palm Desktop software CD-ROM (Windows and Macintosh)
- Software preloaded on the Treo 600 and on the CD-ROM (the actual software depends on where and when you bought your Treo).

Here's what's preloaded on the Treo 600:

- Calc
- Calendar
- Camera
- Card info
- CityTime
- Mail
- Memo Pad
- MMS
- Security
- SMS
- Sounds
- To Do List
- Blazer web browser

Here's what's on the CD:

- Zap!
- Klondike
- SplashID
- SplashMoney
- SplashShopper
- Chapura PocketMirror 3.14 (if you choose to synchronize with Microsoft Outlook)

First Steps to Getting Started with Your Treo

After you have unpacked your new Treo and pulled all the included gadgets and connectors out of the box, you will likely want to begin getting familiar with the Treo layout and functionality. But first, plug in your Treo to begin charging the battery.

Charge Your Treo Battery

Before you can get started using your Treo, you will need to charge the battery. Palm recommends at least three full hours of charging, or charging the Treo until the LED is solid green. At this point, you only need to connect your Treo to a power outlet using the charger/sync cable included with your Treo. You don't have to connect the Treo to your PC in order to charge it. It is important, however, to be sure you charge your Treo fully the first time you charge it. This will help ensure you get the maximum life out of your battery.

Information about Your Treo Battery

The Treo 650 and 700p models have a removable rechargeable lithium ion battery, while 600 models have a nonremovable rechargeable lithium ion battery. Your battery life depends on several factors, and one is the type of Treo you have:

- **GSM/GPRS**   A GSM/GPRS Treo provides up to six hours of talk time and up to ten days of standby time.
- **CDMA**   A CDMA Treo provides up to four hours of talk time and up to ten days of standby time.

 The actual talk time varies by Treo model and carrier. See the Palm web site (www.palm.com) for up-to-date statistics.

The Treo battery recharges very quickly, and a car charger or add-on battery pack will help extend your battery life and increase your mobility. The Treo also has features, like auto-off, that well help you get the maximum battery time. If you have a Treo 650 or 700p, then you can also purchase extra removable batteries from Palm.

Get Oriented with Your Treo Hardware

You will quickly be able to get the most out of your Treo by becoming familiar with the buttons, switches, and general layout of your Treo before you get started. This section provides an overview of the parts. Each Treo model—700p, 650, or 600—has a slightly different hardware design, and we will discuss each separately in this section.

Treo 700p Hardware Layout

The Treo 700p is the latest Palm-powered smartphone offered by Palm, and while at a glance it could be confused with a Treo 650 or 600, there are some subtle differences. For a list of button and hardware names and functions, see Figures 2-1 and 2-2 and refer to the following list.

- **(1) Antenna**
- **(3) Status indicator**
- **(4) Phone speaker**
- **(7) 320×320 color screen**

FIGURE 2-1   Components on the front and back of your Treo 700

■ **(8)** SEND **button**

■ **(9) Five-Way Navigator**   This is an excellent hardware design and allows one-handed operation.

■ **(10)** POWER/END **button**   This button ends a phone call and also turns the screen on and off.

■ **(11)** PHONE **button**   Launches the phone application.

■ **(12)** CALENDAR **button**   Launches the calendar application.

■ **(13)** MESSAGING **button**   Launches messaging applications and can be customized to open the messaging application, such as VersaMail or SMS, that you use most often.

■ **(14)** APPLICATIONS **button**   Launches the Applications Launcher screen; much like selecting the programs list on your PC.

■ **(15) QWERTY keyboard**   If you have ever tried to type text on a nine-button cell phone, you know how nice it is to have a full QWERTY keyboard on the Treo.

■ **(16) Phone dial pad**

■ **(26)** MENU **button**   The Menu button allows you to open the application menu for the specific application that you are currently working in.

Side view   4.4 in. (excluding antenna) / 113 mm   0.9 in. 23 mm

Top view   2.3 in. / 58 mm

Bottom view

FIGURE 2-2   Components on the top, bottom, and sides of your Treo 700

■ **(17) Writing stylus**   If you prefer to use the touch screen as well as, or instead of, the five-way navigation tool, the stylus is the best tool for the job.

■ **(18) Digital camera**   Using your Treo camera and digital photography in general is covered in detail in Chapter 7.

■ **(19) External speaker**   The speaker is designed for Handsfree / speakerphone use rather than playing music or other audio, and it is surprisingly loud (especially if you choose a delightfully annoying ringtone).

■ **(20) Removable battery**   The addition of a removable battery allows you to carry extra rechargeable batteries to go longer between charges. Treo add-ons and accessories are discussed in Chapter 16.

■ **(5) VOLUME buttons**

■ **(6) CUSTOMIZABLE button**   You can customize what you want to happen when you press this button in your Treo Prefs. This is discussed later in this chapter.

■ **(2) Ringer on/off switch**   Palm has provided this quick and easy way to turn off the ringer on the Treo; great for when you go into a theater or meeting.

■ **(24) Expansion slot**   Your Treo supports MultiMedia, SD, and SDIO cards; memory cards are discussed in Chapter 15.

■ **(25) Infrared port**   Infrared is a short-range wireless technology that allows you to send data between your Treo and another infrared capable device such as another Palm-powered device or a laptop. Infrared is discussed in this chapter and in much more detail in Chapter 3.

- ■ **(21) Headset jack**   The Treo features a 2.5 mm headset jack. If you want to use other stereo headsets with your Treo, you will need to purchase an adapter, as most are 3.5 mm.

- ■ **(22) Multiconnector**   On the bottom of you Treo, the multiconnector slot is where you plug in a HotSync cable and charging cable.

- ■ **(23) Microphone**

Treo 650 Hardware Layout

The Treo 650 looks similar to other Treo models, but there some subtle differences. For a list of button and hardware names and functions, see Figures 2-3 and 2-4 and refer to the following list.

- ■ **(1) Antenna**
- ■ **(3) Status indicator**
- ■ **(4) Phone speaker**
- ■ **(7) 320 × 320 color screen**

Front   Back

FIGURE 2-3   Components on the front and back of your Treo 650

FIGURE 2-4   Components on the bottom, top, and sides of your Treo 650

■ **(8) APPLICATIONS button**   Launches the Applications Launcher screen; much like selecting the programs list on your PC.

■ **(9) Five-Way Navigator**   This is an excellent hardware design and allows one-handed operation.

■ **(10) MENU button**   The Menu button allows you to open the application menu for the specific application that you are currently working in.

■ **(11) PHONE/SEND button**   Launches the phone application.

■ **(12) CALENDAR button**   Launches the calendar application.

■ **(13) MESSAGING button**   Launches messaging applications and can be customized to open the messaging application such as VersaMail or SMS, that you use most often.

■ **(14) POWER/END button**   This button ends a phone call and also turns the screen on and off.

■ **(15) QWERTY keyboard**   If you have ever tried to type text on a nine-button cell phone, you know how nice it is to have a full QWERTY keyboard on the Treo.

■ **(16) Phone dial pad**

■ **(17) Writing stylus**   If you prefer to use the touch screen as well as, or instead of, the five-way navigation tool, the stylus is the best tool for the job.

■ **(18) Digital camera**   Using your Treo camera and digital photography in general is covered in detail in Chapter 7.

- **(19) SIM tray**   GSM only.

- **(20) Speaker**   The speaker is designed for Handsfree / speakerphone use rather than playing music or other audio, and it is surprisingly loud (especially if you choose a delightfully annoying ringtone).

- **(21) Removable battery**   The addition of a removable battery allows you to carry extra rechargeable batteries to go longer between charges. Treo add-ons and accessories are discussed in Chapter 16.

- **(22) Headset jack**   The Treo features a 2.5 mm headset jack. If you want to use other stereo headsets with your Treo, you will need to purchase an adapter, as most are 3.5 mm.

- **(23) Multiconnector**   On the bottom of you Treo, the multiconnector slot is where you plug in a HotSync cable and charging cable.

- **(24) Microphone**

- **(25) Expansion slot**   Your Treo supports MultiMedia, SD, SDIO cards; memory cards are discussed in Chapter 15.

- **(26) Infrared port**   Infrared is a short-range wireless technology that allows you to send data between your Treo and another infrared-capable device such as another Palm-powered device or a laptop. Infrared is discussed in this chapter and in much more detail in Chapter 3.

- **(2) Ringer on/off switch**   Palm has provided this quick and easy way to turn off the ringer on the Treo; great for when you go into a theater or meeting.

- **(5) VOLUME buttons**

- **(6) CUSTOMIZABLE button**   You can customize what you want to happen when you press this button in your Treo Prefs. This is discussed later in this chapter.

Treo 600 Hardware Layout

On the top of your Treo are the following components, which are shown on both a GSM/GPRS Treo and a CDMA Treo in Figures 2-5 and 2-6, respectively:

- **The ringer switch**   This switch allows you to toggle easily between silent and active modes. For example, if you are going into a movie theater and don't want to turn the phone off, you may want to turn your Treo to Sound Mode Off to avoid bothering other people during the show.

- **Wireless Mode button**   You can use the Palm OS features of your Treo independently of the wireless features and applications, because both the screen and Wireless mode have been designed so that they can be turned on and off separately.

TIP   *You have to hold this button down for a few seconds when turning Wireless mode on and off.*

- **Antenna**   The antenna is used to send and receive wireless data.

FIGURE 2-5
Components on the top of your Treo 600 (GSM/GPRS system)

- **Stylus** The stylus is used for navigation using the touch screen and also doubles as a Reset tool available by unscrewing the pointer of the stylus.

- **Infrared (IR) port** The IR port allows you to wirelessly beam records between Treo and other Palm-powered devices.

- **SD slot** An expansion slot to add memory, software applications, and content.

- **SIM tray** This is where your SIM card is. (See Chapter 5 for more information about SIM cards and wireless connectivity.)

On the left side of your Treo are the volume controls, shown in Figure 2-7, which allow you to adjust the volume level of the phone. Intuitively, the top button turns the volume up, and the bottom button turns the volume down.

FIGURE 2-6
Components on the top of your Treo 600 (CDMA system)

FIGURE 2-7   Volume controls (on the left side of your Treo 600)

The back of your Treo contains the following components, shown in Figure 2-8:

- **Camera lens**   Taking digital photographs with your Treo is covered in Chapter 7.
- **Speaker**   The speaker allows you to hear system sounds and ring tones.
- **Reset button**   The reset button allows you to perform a reset on your Treo.

FIGURE 2-8   Components on the back of your Treo 600

Headset jack

Microphone

Connector

FIGURE 2-9   Components on the bottom of your Treo 600

The bottom of your Treo contains three items, shown in Figure 2-9:

- **Headset jack**   A 2.5 mm jack.

The headset that comes with your Treo features a 2.5 mm jack, but keep in mind that many headphones have a 3.5 mm connector, so if you want to use another headset/ earphones with your Treo, you may need a 3.5 to 2.5 mm adapter.

- **Connector**   This connector is used for synchronizing and for the power supply.
- **Microphone**   The microphone picks up your voice when you are talking on the phone.

The front of your Treo sports the following features, shown in Figure 2-10:

- **Phone speaker**   The phone speaker is at the top, above the screen.
- **Touch screen**   The Treo screen is a 160×160 bright-color, touch-sensitive screen.
- **Keyboard**   The Treo contains a fully integrated QWERTY keyboard, including a backlight so that you can see the keyboard in low-light conditions. Here you'll also find the OPTION, SHIFT/FIND, HOME, and MENU buttons, discussed later in this chapter.
- **Five-way navigation control**   This convenient disc allows for one-handed navigation.
- **Shortcut buttons**   These are quick-access buttons—PHONE, CALENDAR, E-MAIL, and SCREEN.

When we instruct you to press one of the buttons shown in the images of the front of the Treo (or the UP, DOWN, LEFT, RIGHT, and CENTER buttons on the five-way navigation control), we will say simply to press PHONE, CALENDAR, OPTION, SHIFT, and so on.

Phone speaker

Touch screen

Five-way navigation control

Shortcut buttons

Shortcut buttons

Keyboard

FIGURE 2-10   Components on the front of your Treo 600

Turn Your Treo On for the First Time

Turning on your Treo is, of course, only the beginning of a series of steps in getting your Treo up and running. Some other initial steps are covered next, including using the Welcome Wizard.

Turn Your Treo Screen and Wireless On and Off

Your Treo is designed so that you can use the traditional Palm applications, like Contacts / Address Book or Calendar, independently of the wireless features. For this reason, there are separate controls for turning the screen and Wireless mode off and on independently.

- ■ To turn the screen on, press the POWER / SCREEN button, the outside button to the right of the five-way navigation control.

- ■ To turn the screen off, press the POWER / SCREEN button again.

- ■ To turn wireless off or on, depending on the current state, press and hold the POWER / SCREEN button.

Learn How to Navigate the Treo Screen

Navigating the Treo screen is similar to navigating your PC screen. There are two ways to do it, you can use either the five-way navigation control or the touch screen and stylus.

Unlike Windows and other desktop operating systems, the Palm OS is designed so that many of the screens and applications don't have a menu item that allows you to close the application or get back to the Applications Launcher. Press the HOME button, to get back to the Applications Launcher.

Get to Know Your Treo Buttons

There are a few buttons on your Treo that you will want to become familiar with because they allow you to launch the most common functionalities quickly. The appearance of the buttons makes the functionality fairly obvious.

- ■ **PHONE**   This button allows you to access your phone, camera, contacts, and favorites easily.

- ■ **HOME**   This button takes you to the Applications Launcher screens, where you can launch applications, settings, and utilities.

- ■ **MENU**   The Menu button launches the appropriate menu for the application or function that you are currently using. For example, if you are using the Contacts application and you press the MENU button, a menu will appear that allows you to work with your Contact records.

- ■ **CALENDAR**   This button functions as the shortcut for launching your calendar.

- ■ **MESSAGING / E-MAIL**   This button allows you to access your e-mail quickly.

- ■ **POWER / END / SCREEN**   Your Treo automatically turns the screen off to save your battery, and you can use this button to turn your screen on and off.

- ■ **OPTION**   This key isn't as visually obvious as the others; it is the button featuring an ink "blob" at the bottom-left side of the keyboard. This button is used in combination with other keys and is conceptually similar to the SHIFT key on your PC keyboard for typing secondary characters on the keyboard. For example, to type the @ symbol, press OPTION and then the letter I.

Customize Your Shortcut Buttons

You can customize what actions each of these main shortcut buttons does. For example, if you find that you use the Documents application more than you use the Calendar, you can modify your preferences to launch Documents when the CALENDAR shortcut button is pressed. To customize the buttons, do the following:

1. Go to the Applications Launcher by pressing HOME .
2. Find and select Prefs from the Applications Launcher.

FIGURE 2-11   Customize your buttons

3. You will see the screen shown in Figure 2-11, which shows the buttons—the Phone, Calendar, E-mail, Option+Button and Press+Hold the Side Button, and next to each button icon, the application that is launched when you press that button. (The Treo 600 screen is slightly different—to get to the Buttons configuration, select the menu at the top right-hand corner of the screen, and then find and select the Buttons item.)

To change what application a particular button is linked to, select the menu to the immediate right of the button name and choose a new application to associate with that button.

If you are still getting used to your Treo, you may want to leave the default setting in place until you better understand how you will be using your Treo.

Use the Five-Way Navigation Control

Your Treo is equipped with a five-way navigation control, shown in Figure 2-12, which is an exceptional navigation feature that allows you to navigate menu options, onscreen commands, links for web pages, messages, and so on, using only one hand. The five-way navigation control allows you to move between fields and screens. You can do this by pressing the direction arrows on the control to move around. Selected fields and objects will be highlighted or will appear to have a halo around them. To select an item that is highlighted, press CENTER (the button in the center of the control). It works in much the same way as clicking a mouse button.

FIGURE 2-12   Five-way navigation buttons

Use the Stylus and Touch Screen

In addition to the five-way navigation control, your Treo also is equipped with the latest touch screen technology, allowing you to navigate around the interface by selecting menus and tapping on objects and fields with the stylus. The stylus can be found at the top right-hand corner toward the back of your Treo, as shown earlier, in the section "Get Oriented with Your Treo Hardware."

Make a habit of putting the stylus back when you are finished with it. It is very easy to misplace. In fact, you can buy three-packs of styli (yes, oddly enough the plural of stylus is styli) for your Treo just in case you are unlucky enough to lose them as often as some of us do.

Use the Keyboard

The Treo is equipped with an integrated keyboard. Most people use the keyboard by holding the Treo in both hands and using their thumbs to type. If you are not used to using this type of keyboard, it will likely be awkward at first, but you should become proficient with it quickly. Following are a few pointers to get you going.

The Treo 700p and 650 feature a keyboard backlight so that the numbers, letters, and symbols on the keyboard can be read in low-light conditions. The backlight is active any time the screen is on; while the Treo 600 backlight is automatically activated for the first few seconds of use within the phone application and can be manually activated by pressing any button on the keyboard. To turn on the backlight, press OPTION and then the letter P. The backlight will turn off if the keyboard is not in use.

Use Keyboard Menu Shortcuts

On any screen, you can view a menu of possible actions by pressing MENU on the keyboard. You can also choose any of the menu items by pressing the shortcut button that corresponds to the item in the menu.

For example, Figure 2-13 displays a menu that is available within the Calendar application. To delete the selected Calendar event, simply press D on the keyboard. This shortcut functionality helps minimize how often you have to alternate between using the keyboard and using the touch screen.

Enter Lowercase and Uppercase Letters

Here are a few tips on entering upper- and lowercase letters:

- To type a lowercase letter, press the desired button.
- To type an uppercase letter, press SHIFT, and then press a letter button. You don't need to hold down SHIFT while typing a letter.
- To turn Caps Lock on, press SHIFT twice. To turn it off, press SHIFT again. When Caps Lock is on, a symbol appears in the lower-right corner of the screen.

FIGURE 2-13   Calendar application menu

Enter Numbers, Punctuation, and Symbols That Appear above the Letters on the Keys

The OPTION button (which looks an ink blob at the bottom left of the keyboard) functions like the SHIFT key on a standard PC keyboard. Press OPTION, and then press the button with the desired character shown above the letter. You don't need to hold down OPTION while pressing the second letter button.

To turn Option Lock on, press OPTION twice. To turn it off, press OPTION again. When Option Lock is on, the Option symbol appears in the lower-right corner of the screen.

Type Special Characters: Symbols and Accented Characters

As you begin to use the keyboard to type text, you will undoubtedly encounter moments of frustration as you scan the keyboard to type a specific character and can't find it. An example of such a character is an underscore (_). In order to deal with the challenges of the diminutive Treo keyboard, Palm has had to invent some new ways to allow you to type the full character set. The ALT button, to the left of the SPACEBAR on the keyboard, allows you to scroll through related characters until you find the one you are looking for.

Each keyboard character button has an associated set of related characters. For example, you use the A button to type any of these characters: Á À Ä Â Ã Å Æ.

Follow these steps to type an underscore:

1. Launch Memo Pad and choose the New button—or any other application that allows you to input text.

2. Press OPTION and then S.

3. A dash will appear on the screen.

4. Press the ALT key.

   You will see a list of available characters to choose from, as shown in Figure 2-14.

5. The underscore is the second character in the list; select it, and your dash becomes an underscore.

FIGURE 2-14   Typing special characters

The fastest way to find alternate characters is to go to the keyboard help within each application. The keyboard Help lists all of the alternate characters and their corresponding keys. There is also a table in the Treo user guide called "Symbols and Accented Characters" that shows which buttons relate to which special characters.

Cut, Copy, and Paste Text

When you are typing text, especially repetitive text, it is useful to be able to cut, copy, and paste text between fields and screens. On any screen where you are working with text, you can cut, copy, or paste text by highlighting the text (to select text, drag the stylus across the words you want to cut or copy) pressing MENU, and then selecting the Edit menu. Depending on the screen you are on, the Cut, Copy, and Paste commands, as well as a few others, will appear under the Edit menu, as in Figure 2-15.

FIGURE 2-15   Copy text

Use Menus to Navigate

There is a MENU button on the bottom right-hand section of the keyboard. Selecting this button on any screen will bring up a menu related to that screen. Another way to view the menu is to tap the application name in the top left-hand portion of the screen.

Several manufacturers sell external keyboards that attach to your Treo and allow you to enter and edit text using a more traditional PC keyboard. Accessories are covered in more detail in Chapter 16.

Lock Your Phone and Data

Chapter 13 covers security, but we'll also mention it a bit here, since it's an important topic. One of the first things you should consider doing is protecting your Treo and data from unauthorized use. The convenience and power of the Treo can be offset by some of the risks associated with such a small device capable of storing a significant amount of information. Your Treo can be easily lost or stolen, and it is more likely to be left unprotected on a desk or lent to an acquaintance to make a phone call than a larger device might be. If your phone or data (Contacts list, e-mails and attachments, photos, videos, memos, and so on) get into the wrong hands, the consequences could be significant for you and your company.

The good news is that Palm has built some powerful security features into your Treo to help minimize these risks. Your Treo includes several features that help you protect your phone from careless or malicious users and keep both it and your data private. Palm has thought this out well; your Treo can still be used to make emergency calls even if the handset is locked.

Define emergency numbers on your Treo 650/700p. In addition to being able to dial 911 even when the phone is locked, you can predefine up to three additional phone numbers that can be dialed when your Treo is locked. To configure these phone numbers: press the PHONE button, press the Menu button, and choose Options | Phone Lock | Advanced.

Configure Security for Your Treo

The Security settings can be accessed from the Applications Launcher by selecting Security. This is where you can set your Security preferences. Specific fields are explained next, and an image of the Security screen is shown in Figure 2-16.

Password

The Security application on your Treo allows you to configure your Treo' security level. On the Security screen, you can define a password to unlock the device and files. You can also set a Hint question to help remind you of your password in case you forget it. This comes in handy because some of us have a tough time choosing and remembering passwords for all of our hardware, network, and Internet accounts.

Security

Password:
-Unassigned-

Auto Lock Device:
Never

Current Privacy:
▼ Show Records

Lock & Turn Off...   Help

FIGURE 2-16   Security settings screen

Auto-Lock Your Treo

The Auto Lock setting allows you to configure the conditions that automatically lock your Treo. Once your Treo is locked, you will have to enter a password to unlock and use it. Following are your Auto Lock options:

- **Never**   Your Treo will not lock at any time.
- **On Power Off**   Your Treo will lock when you turn the power off.
- **At a Preset Time**   Your Treo will lock at a specific time—for example, at 10 P.M. every day.
- **After a Preset Delay**   This is likely the most secure choice. For instance, you can set it to lock if it's not used for five minutes.

Current Privacy

The Current Privacy setting allows you to define protection for your records. What this means is that you can flag records as Private so that they are either masked or don't appear in your Contacts list at all, until you change the Current Privacy setting to Show Records. For example, if you lend your phone to someone and they select Contacts, they will be unable to view Private records. Your Current Privacy options include the following:

- **Show Records**   Does not hide records flagged as Private.
- **Mask Records**   Private records will appear in the list as grayed-out lines. To view a Private, grayed-out, record, tap it and enter your password.
- **Hide Records**   Private records will not appear in the record list at all. To show Private records when this setting is enabled, either return to the Security screen or within the Contacts screen press MENU, press OPTION, select Security, change the setting to Show Records, and enter your password.

FIGURE 2-17   Making a contact record private

Flag a Record as Private

You can flag a contact record as private by following these steps:

1. Press PHONE.
2. Select Contacts.
3. Select a contact that you would like to flag as private.
4. Choose Edit, and then select Details.
5. Select the Private check box and click OK, as shown in Figure 2-17.

Set Up User Preferences

You may customize your Treo to suit your specific needs and preferences by selecting Prefs from the Applications Launcher. You have control over many of your Treo attributes, including the following:

- **Date & Time**   This is where you define your date, time, and time zone preferences.
- **Formats**   This is where you can define how data is formatted. You can use regional default settings or define each data type separately.
- **Power (650 and 700p)**   This screen allows you to configure options that allow you to minimize battery usage to allow you to go longer between charges. Options include the ability to adjust screen brightness, auto-off, and Beam Receive (infrared).

TIP   *Turn off Beam Receive to maximize battery life. The infrared on your Treo can be activated by bright light. This doesn't cause any problems other than that the infrared turns on when the infrared port perceives that there is another infrared device nearby, but this drains battery power.*

■ **Touch screen**   This is a screen that is also part of the Welcome wizard and allows you to calibrate your touch screen to ensure that your Treo correctly recognizes where you tap the screen.

■ **Default Apps**   Sometimes one application looks for another application to handle data. For example, a mail application might launch a browser when you choose a link in an e-mail message. This is where you define these associations.

■ **Keyguard**   This screen allows you to define the events that trigger the Auto-Keyguard and helps minimize unintentional keyboard button presses.

■ **Sounds & Alerts / Sound**   This screen allows you to define volume levels and the sounds that your Treo will make when specific events occur.

■ **Bluetooth (650 and 700p)**   This is where you define your Treo Bluetooth settings and pairing. Bluetooth is covered in detail in Chapter 5.

■ **Handsfree (650 and 700p)**   If you have a Bluetooth Handsfree set up, this is where you can define the number of rings that will occur before the Handsfree set auto-answers.

■ **VPN (650 and 700p)**   If you have VPN software installed on your Treo, this screen offers some configuration options.

■ **Connection**   This is where you can select and edit the connection options for your Treo.

■ **Network**   This is where you configure your wireless connection and also the screen that you will use to connect to, and disconnect from, the network.

■ **Buttons**   This is where you choose which applications are associated with the buttons on your Treo.

■ **Owner**   This is where you define your personal contact information.

■ **Color Theme (650 and 700p)**   This feature allows you to choose from several color themes for your Treo interface.

■ **Display (600)**   You can determine your screen contrast and brightness here.

■ **General (600)**   Here is where you can define auto-off, sounds, and display colors.

■ **Shortcuts (600)**   Shortcuts are abbreviations for commonly used words. You can use shortcuts to minimize typing. One of the default examples is "me" as the abbreviation for "meeting." After you have defined shortcuts, you can use them when typing by first pressing the FUNCTION key and then typing in the shortcut abbreviation.

Your user guide does a good job of describing what each of these options does, so we will only focus on the ones you are most likely to need set right away. Your preferences are accessed from the Applications Launcher by selecting Prefs.

Safeguard Your Personal Info Using Owner Preferences

The Owner Preferences is where you record information such as your name, company name, phone number, e-mail address, and so on.

2

If you lock your Treo, the Owner Preferences information appears on the screen that requests your password to unlock it, and you must also enter your password to change the Owner Preferences information.

1. Press HOME to open the Applications Launcher.

2. Choose the pick list in the upper-right corner, and then select All.

3. Choose the Prefs icon.

4. For the Treo 650/700p, choose the Owner icon; for the Treo 600, choose the pick list in the upper-right corner and select Owner.

5. If you assigned a password with the Security application, choose Unlock, enter your password, and then choose OK to continue.

6. Type the text that you want to appear in the Owner Preferences screen.

Date & Time

When you set up the Welcome wizard, you set up some of this information, so ideally it should already be correctly set. We mention it here again only because it is important to ensure that your Treo is set up properly and that you know where to go to change your settings. This also ensures that other applications that depend on your Prefs, like the World Clock / CityTime application, work properly.

The Treo 700p and 650 support the ability to use network time instead of requiring you to set the date and time manually. On the Sprint Treo, there is a Date & Time dialog box with a Use Network Time check box. To set your Sprint Treo to use the network time, follow these steps:

1. Start the Applications Launcher by pressing HOME.

2. Choose the pick list in the upper-right corner, and then select All.

3. Choose the Prefs icon.

4. For the 650/700p, choose the Date & Time option on the screen; for the 600, choose the menu in the upper-right corner and select the Date & Time option.

5. Check the Use Network Time check box.

The World Clock / CityTime application has a slick graphical interface that allows you to choose a few different cities around the world so that you can see the current time in those locations whenever you like. You can also tap on the world map to see the current time in other locations.

Configure Your Wireless Connection Information Using Network Preferences

The Network Preferences screen is where your network settings are configured. These settings allow you to connect to your service provider's wireless network. Usually, your Treo ships with your network settings already configured, so you shouldn't have to configure them. (Wireless connectivity is covered in more detail in Chapter 5.)

Once your network settings have been correctly configured, the Network screen is where you will connect and disconnect from the wireless network depending on what you need to do.

Sounds and Alerts

Sound Preferences is where you can define the sounds that your Treo makes and when they are made. This is a handy feature. I wish my home phone had this capability—especially because one ring for everything seems pretty inadequate after the Treo . For example, you can set up your Treo to make different sounds depending on whether an incoming phone call is from a known caller or an unknown one.

Your Treo ships with many different sound files, from which you can pick and choose for various functions. Many Treo users enjoy downloading and using additional tones as well as the default sounds. There are many places on the Web that allow you to download and install new ringtones—and any MIDI file will work with your Treo. One of the many sites that offer MIDI sound files you can download for your Treo's ringtones is http://mididb.com.

Treo 600—Define More of Your Preferences Using General Preferences

The General Preferences screen is a catchall for settings that do not warrant their own categories. Here you can set the auto shutoff interval, the beam receive feature, and define the sounds and screen colors for your Treo. To get to the General Prefs, follow these steps:

1. Start the Applications Launcher by pressing HOME.
2. Choose the pick list in the upper-right corner, and then select All.
3. Choose the Prefs icon.
4. Choose the menu in the upper-right corner and select General.

The General settings that you can change to suit your preferences include the following:

- **Auto-Off After**   The time that elapses before your screen automatically turns off. Setting this to a relatively short time will help preserve your battery life.
- **System Sound**   The volume for system beeps and alerts.
- **Game Sound**   The volume for game sounds.
- **Beam Receive**   The setting for whether you want your Treo to receive beamed information.
- **Colors**   This allows you to change the interface colors by selecting from a set of predefined color schemes.

FIGURE 2-18   The Applications Launcher screen

Keyguard

The Keyguard Prefs screen allows you to define the events that trigger the Auto-Keyguard and disable the touch screen. This helps minimize unintentional key and touch screen input when you are using your Treo as a phone.

- **Auto-Keyguard**   You can set the Auto-Keyguard to automatically disable the keyboard within a specific time period after the power is turned off.
- **Disable Touchscreen When**   You may set your Treo to disable the touch screen when you are on a call or when an incoming call is received.

Launch Applications on Your Treo

The Applications Launcher is a graphical view for browsing and launching your applications and settings; it looks like the screen in Figure 2-18. It is always available by pressing HOME on the bottom of the keyboard. The installed applications are separated into default categories. As you add or remove applications, you can group them in ways that make them easy to find. You can view the application categories by selecting the menu at the top of the screen or by scrolling through the categories by repeatedly pressing HOME.

Installing new applications is easy and can be done several ways, including using the Palm Desktop Quick Install tool combined with a HotSync operation (discussed in Chapter 3) or downloading application files over a wireless Internet connection through e-mail or a web browser on your Treo in much the same way as you would on your PC.

Perform Common Treo Tasks

This section briefly covers some of the most common tasks you will use your Treo for, including managing your contacts, defining your business card, and setting up your favorites.

Manage Your Contacts

Your Contacts can be found under the Phone menu. If you are familiar with Palm-powered devices, Contacts is the new name for what was previously called the Address Book. You can store a lot of information about a contact there, and you can phone or e-mail the contact directly from the contact record.

Add a Contact

You can create a new contact on the fly using your Treo, which is great for storing contact information for people you have just met. If you have several contacts to enter, it may be a tad tedious to enter them on the Treo. Unless you are an adept thumb-typist, it is likely most efficient to enter new contacts into the Palm Desktop software or into Microsoft Outlook on your computer and then synchronize the contact data between the Treo and your computer. Synchronizing your Treo with your PC is covered in detail in Chapter 3. Here are the steps for adding a contact on your Treo:

1. Press the PHONE button to the left of the five-way navigation control.
2. Use the five-way navigation control to select the Contacts list.
3. Choose New Contact.
4. Use the five-way navigation control to move between fields and enter information.
5. On the 650/700p, as an option you can attach a photo to the contact or choose to take a photo with the built-in camera immediately to be attached to the contact record.
6. Optionally, you can place the entry in a category or mark it private. To do this, choose Details.
7. You can also add a note to a contact entry by choosing Note.
8. After you enter all the information, choose Done to save the record.

Quickly Find a Contact

When you are looking for a specific contact, scrolling through the list can be very slow, especially if you have a lot of contacts. Fortunately, your Treo has a feature commonly known as "type-ahead" functionality. You can quickly locate a contact by opening your Contacts list and beginning to type the contact's name. There are three ways to find a contact using the type-ahead functionality:

- Type the first initial and last name.
- Type both the last and first name initials.
- Type the first name.
- Type the last name.

After you have typed a few letters, the Contacts list will jump to the contacts that match what you have typed. Once you are in the correct range, you can also navigate the list using the UP and DOWN buttons on the five-way navigation control.

View or Change Contact Information

Once you have located the contact that you want to view or modify, and it is highlighted on the screen, select it by tapping it on the screen or pressing the CENTER button of the five-way navigation control. This will show the contact details and allow you to select the Edit button to make changes to the contact.

Define Your Business Card

Your business card is a contact record containing your personal contact information that you would like to share with others. Once you have defined your business card, you can "beam" it to other Treo and Palm users. The steps for creating your business card are listed next:

1. Go to your Contacts list by pressing PHONE to the left of the five-way navigation control and then selecting Contacts.

2. Create a new contact by pressing MENU and selecting New Contact.

3. In this new record, enter your own information.

4. While still in Contact Edit view, press MENU.

5. From the Record menu, choose Select Business Card.

6. Your business card is now saved.

Now you can beam your business card to other Palm OS devices. Beaming information is covered in more detail in the section "Beam Data Using Your Treo's Infrared Capability" at the end of this chapter.

Define Favorites

What are Treo Favorites? You are probably familiar with using favorites in your web browser. The Treo extends the concept of favorites even further. In order to make your Treo even easier to use, you may define up to 50 Favorites that can be quickly accessed using a menu or a keyboard shortcut. The types of actions that can be stored as a Favorite are as follows:

- **Dial a phone number**   Essentially the same as putting someone on a speed-dial list
- **Launch an application**   A shortcut to allow you to quickly launch applications
- **Access a web page**   Conceptually the same as storing your Favorites in your PC web browser
- **Address a text message**   Similar to adding someone to a speed-dial list to allow you to quickly send SMS text messages to your friends and family
- **Access your voicemail**   A shortcut that dials your voicemail

Your wireless service provider has likely already preprogrammed some of the items in your Favorites list, such as its support number and your voicemail.

FIGURE 2-19   Your Favorites

Access Your Favorites

You can trigger your Favorites in a couple of different ways:

- **Treo 650/700p**   Your favorites are accessed by selecting the PHONE button and scrolling down using the five-way navigation button. If you have a lot of favorites, they are stored on multiple pages and you can jump to different pages at the bottom of the Favorites screen, as shown in Figure 2-19.

- **Treo 600**   You can see your Favorite buttons by pressing the PHONE shortcut button and selecting Favorites with the five-way navigation control. To scroll through your Favorites, use the number bar at the bottom right-hand corner of the screen. Also, when you are in the phone's Main, Favorites, or Dial Pad view, you can press and hold a Quick Key to launch the Favorite associated with that keyboard button. You can define Quick Keys for each of your Favorites (Quick Keys are optional). Quick Keys can only be letters and are not case-sensitive.

Explore the Applications Installed on Your Treo

In addition to the configuration and preferences utilities installed on your Treo, there are several applications included. Software titles may differ slightly depending on where and when you purchased your Treo. Some of the commonly installed applications are listed and described in the following sections.

Included Treo Applications on All Treo Models

Even though each version of the Palm Treo is different, there are some common applications that are included with each one. This section discusses the applications that you likely have on your Treo, and the next section discusses some software that is more specific to particular Treo models.

Blazer Browser

You can browse the Internet in full color on your Treo using the preinstalled Blazer web browser. The Blazer browser allows you to store Favorites, save web pages for offline viewing, and copy text from a web page. It even gives you the ability to view web pages in Optimized mode. Optimized mode reformats web pages into one column so that information is easier to view on your Treo screen. Web browsing is covered in more detail in Chapter 5.

Camera

The camera application and hardware specifications, as well as tips to get the most out of your Treo camera, are discussed in Chapter 7.

Calc

This built-in calculator application comes in handy and has much more power than I can use. You can choose the type of calculation you need to perform by selecting among several options, including statistics, finance, and weight/temperature. Calculator includes a basic calculator, plus an advanced calculator with scientific, financial, and conversion functions.

Switch Between Basic and Advanced Calculator Modes   To change the type of calculator you want to use, follow these steps:

1. While pressing MENU on the keyboard, press the OPTION button and then select the Toggle Mode menu item. (Toggle mode allows you to toggle between the basic calculator and the advanced calculator.) This will put you in the Advanced Calculator mode.

2. In the Advanced mode, choose the menu near the upper-left part of the screen and select which Advanced Calculator function you would like to use. Your options include the following:

   - **Math**   This option allows you to perform advanced mathematical functions such as exponents, roots, and logarithms.

   - **Trig**   This option allows you to select trigonometric functions such as sine, cosine, tangent, and variants.

   - **Finance**   This option allows you to perform financial calculator functions such as APR and amortization.

   - **Logic**   This option allows you to insert hexadecimal characters in keypad, as well as perform logic functions such as and, not, or, and xor.

   - **Statistics**   This option allows you to perform statistical functions such as sum, factorial, and random number generator.

   - **Weight/Temp**   This option allows you to perform weight and temperature conversions for both the metric and English measurement systems.

   - **Length**   This option allows you to perform length conversions for both metric and English values.

- **Area**   This option allows you to perform area conversions for both the metric and English measurement systems.
- **Volume**   This option allows you to perform volume conversions for both the metric and English measurement systems.
- **Eng(x) (Engineering Notation)**   This option allows you to define an integer for the number of decimal places to display, and then select Eng(c) to round calculations to that decimal place using engineering notation. You can also choose the menu located in the upper-right corner of the screen to select whether you want to display numbers in degrees, radians, or grads.

Calendar

The built-in Treo calendar offers several ways to view your schedule information and allows you to view and edit appointments and schedule new appointments. The calendar will remind you of scheduled events, and when you have HotSync installed and configured, you can synchronize your Outlook or Palm Desktop calendar to make sure you don't forget a thing.

Display Your Calendar   To view your calendar and schedule meetings or events, follow these steps:

1. Press CALENDAR (the button to the left of the five-way navigation control) repeatedly to cycle through the various active views.

2. Use the five-way navigation control to move to another day, week, or month.

3. Choose Go or press MENU. From the Options menu, choose Go to Day and choose a date from the calendar.

The Calendar is covered in more detail in Chapter 10, but here are a few of the things that you can do with it:

- Schedule a new event.
- Add an alarm reminder to a scheduled event.
- Schedule an untimed event. (an event that does not occur at a particular time, only on a specific day—such as a birthday or anniversary.)
- Edit or delete a scheduled event.
- Schedule a repeating event. (a recurring event such as a mortgage payment or weekly sales meeting.)

Customize the General Preferences for Your Calendar   You can define how your calendar should behave by setting your calendar general preferences, which include the following:

- **Start Time and End Time**   The times that your day typically begins and ends. For example, some people may begin work at 6:00 A.M. and end at 4:00 P.M., while others may have a more traditional 9:00 to 5:00 workday.

■ **Event Duration**   This is the typical default event duration, which you can change when you schedule a meeting.

■ **Week Start**   The day of the week that your workweek typically begins. For many of us it is Monday, but you can change it to be whatever you like.

■ **Initial View**   This allows you to define how your Calendar screen looks when you initially launch the Calendar.

By default, you see Day and Month Views, but you can also see other views.
To set your calendar preferences, follow these steps:

■ Treo 700p/650

   1. Press CALENDAR, and then press MENU.

   2. Select the Options menu and Select the Display Options.

   3. Set your preferences.

■ Treo 600

   1. Press CALENDAR, and then press MENU.

   2. From the Options menu, choose Preferences.

   3. Set your preferences for each item.

World Clock (650/700p) and CityTime (600)

The World Clock / CityTime application has a slick graphical interface, shown in Figure 2-20, which allows you to choose four different cities around the world so you can see the current time in those locations whenever you like. You can also tap on the world map to see the current time in other locations. For this application to function correctly, your home city and time must be correctly configured.

FIGURE 2-20   World Clock / CityTime application

Documents—Docs To Go and Sheets To Go

The functionality that you get with Documents and Sheets to go depends on your Treo model.

- Treo 700p   Documents To Go allows you to view and edit MS Word files, view and edit MS Excel files, and view PowerPoint files.

- Treo 650   Documents To Go allows you to view and edit MS Word files, and to view and edit MS Excel files.

- Treo 600   Documents To Go allows you to view Microsoft Word e-mail attachments, and Sheets To Go allows you to view Microsoft Excel e-mail attachments. The preinstalled versions are limited to read-only functionalities. You can purchase a product upgrade that allows you to use your Word, Excel, and PowerPoint files on your Treo, including the ability to modify and create new documents. More detail on this topic is included in Chapter 11.

Tasks / To Do List

Many of us rely on our To Do lists to help us remember what we have to accomplish today, this week, or this year. The To Do List application allows you to keep a list of tasks and keep a record of completed tasks.

E-Mail

Depending on your Treo model, the built in e-mail application will be different. If you have Treo 650 or 700p, then you have VersaMail e-mail software as well as an e-mail solution provided by your carrier, such as Sprint Business Connection. If you have a Treo 600, then you have Mail. The built-in e-mail application on your Treo provides wireless access to an existing e-mail account to allow you to send and receive messages and attachments. More information about setting up and using e-mail on your Treo is included in Chapter 6.

Memo Pad

The Memo Pad allows you to create and store notes on your Treo (for example, directions to your niece's interpretive dance recital). Memo Pad is covered in more detail in Chapter 10.

SMS

SMS (Short Message Service) messages are brief notes, up to 160 characters long, that you can exchange with other mobile phones that have SMS capability. SMS is covered in more detail in Chapter 5.

MMS or Sprint Picture Mail

From a user perspective, MMS and Sprint Picture Mail are very similar. If you have a Sprint Treo, then you will have the ability to send and receive Sprint Picture Mail, and if you have a non-Sprint Treo, then you will have built-in MMS (Multimedia Message Service) capability.

These two technologies are similar in the types of messages and media that can be sent and received. MMS is an enhanced form of SMS messaging that lets you send photos, animations, and ringtones wirelessly with your Treo. In order for you to use this Treo MMS functionality, your wireless service provider must support MMS, and MMS must be enabled on your account. MMS functionality is covered in more detail in Chapter 5.

Games

You may not have based your decision to purchase your Treo solely on its gaming capability, but be warned—the Treo has converted more than a few of us to closet gamers. The bright color screen and sound capability make playing games on the Treo a surprisingly satisfying experience. The Palm operating system is a very popular platform for game engineers, so there is a seemingly perpetual stream of new games arriving on the market, many of which are freeware (free software) or shareware (software that can be tried out and then purchased for a nominal fee). Your Treo likely arrived with a few games on the companion CD, such as *Hanoi Towers*, *Solitaire*, or *Bejeweled*. Third party games, as well as music and movies, are covered in more detail in Chapter 8.

Treo 700p Included Software

Each Treo is uniquely configured with software. The preceding section dealt with software that is installed on virtually every model of Treo, while this section discusses the unique software applications that most likely came with your Treo 700p. We say "most likely" because each carrier has the final say on what software is included on their particular Treos, so not every Treo is configured identically.

- **Media / Pictures and Videos**   This application allows you to manage and view your digital photos and videos; for instance, you can view slideshows and create albums.

- **Pocket Tunes**   This application allows you to play and organize music on your Treo. Music is discussed in detail in Chapter 8.

- **Audible**   This application is media player that allows you to play digital audio books, audio magazines, newspapers, and radio programs on your Treo. This is discussed in more detail in Chapter 8.

- *Bejeweled*   This is a popular game for the Palm platform that is discussed in more detail in Chapter 8.

- **Documents To Go**   This application allows you to create, view, and edit Microsoft Word and Excel files and view MS PowerPoint and Adobe PDF files on your Treo.

- **eReader**   Palm eReader software allows you to read digital books in eBook format on your Treo. Some of the advantages of reading books on your Treo include the ability to define bookmarks and search for words in an eBook. This topic is discussed in detail in Chapter 8.

- **Palm Files**   This application allows you to browse and manage files on an expansion memory card.

■ **Tasks / To Do List** Many of us rely on our To Do lists to help us remember what we have to accomplish today, this week, or this year. The To Do List application allows you to keep a list of tasks and keep a record of completed tasks.

■ **Solitaire** The classic "play against yourself" card game.

■ **Traffic for Treo Smartphones** This application is subscription based and allows you to find out about delays with live traffic information and maps. Only a few major cities are serviced: New York City, Los Angeles, San Diego, San Francisco, Washington DC/Baltimore, Houston, Atlanta, Detroit, Seattle, and Chicago.

Treo 650 Included Software

Each Treo is uniquely configured with software. The previous section "Included Treo Applications on All Treo Models" dealt with software that is installed on virtually every model of Treo, while this section discusses the unique software applications that most likely came with your Treo 650. We say "most likely" because each carrier has the final say on what software is included on their particular Treos, so not every Treo is configured identically, but your 650 likely includes these applications in addition to the applications included on all Treo models.

■ **Palm eReader** Palm eReader software allows you to read digital books in eBook format on your Treo. Some of the advantages of reading books on your Treo include the ability to define bookmarks and search for words in an eBook. This topic is discussed in detail in Chapter 8.

■ **RealPlayer** This popular media player allows the local playback of MP3 and RealAudio files on your Treo. This is discussed in more detail in Chapter 8.

■ **Audible Player** This application is a media player that allows you to play digital audio books, audio magazines, newspapers, and radio programs on your Treo. This is discussed in more detail in Chapter 8.

Treo 600 Included Software

Each Treo is uniquely configured with software. The previous section "Included Treo Applications on All Treo Models" dealt with software that is installed on virtually every model of Treo, while this section discusses the unique software applications that most likely came with your Treo 600. We say "most likely" because each carrier has the final say on what software is included on their particular Treos, so not every Treo is configured identically. If you have a Treo 600, you will likely have these applications on your Treo. Here are some brief descriptions of what each application is for.

■ **SplashID** SplashID is a personal identification organizer that allows you to securely store your personal identification information, including usernames, passwords, credit cards, calling cards, bank accounts, PINs, and other information. The data is stored in a secure, encrypted format, which is accessible on your Treo. A product upgrade is available that also allows you to synchronize and access data on your PC.

■ **SplashMoney** SplashMoney is a personal finance application that helps you manage and track your finances on your Treo, including budgeting and reporting, scheduled transactions with reminders, secure password protection, and other handy features. A product upgrade is available that allows you to synchronize and access your data on your PC.

- **SplashShopper**   SplashShopper is a shopping list application that allows you to keep grocery lists and lists of movies to see, CDs to buy, books to read, and any other lists you might want to track and store on your Treo. A product upgrade is available that allows you to synchronize and access your shopping list data on your PC.

- **Games**   Even if you don't play video games very often, the built-in Treo games can certainly make time go a little faster when you have nothing else to do, such as when you are waiting to board your plane.

- **Zap!2016**   This game is a variation of the classic "shoot all of the spaceships that drop down from the top of the screen without getting shot or crashed into" game. It comes complete with color and sounds, and if that wasn't enough, you also get weapons and power-ups, over 50 different aliens, seven deadly boss enemies, and seven levels with scrolling backgrounds. You navigate your spaceship using the five-way navigation control and fire your weapon using the SCREEN button. The developer of the game has several different games that run on the Palm OS, all of which can be found at www.astraware.com.

- **Klondike 22**   What useful time-saving handheld device would be complete without a game of Solitaire? Klondike allows you to play the most common variation of Solitaire in full color on your Treo.

Upgrade from a Previous Palm OS Device

If you are already a seasoned user of Palm powered handhelds, you may be interested in upgrading your data and applications from your previous Palm-powered handheld to your Treo. This section discusses some differences that you should be aware of and also covers the steps to upgrade smoothly.

Transfer Applications and Data from Your Old Palm

If you are upgrading to the Treo from another Treo or another Palm device and want to transfer compatible applications and data from your previous device to your new Treo, there are a few steps that you need to perform:

1. Perform a HotSync operation of your old device with your old desktop software to ensure that your data is backed up.

2. Install the Palm Desktop synchronization software on your PC (more detailed information about Palm Desktop and HotSync is covered in Chapter 3). The "Palm Desktop and HotSync Manager"software for both Windows and Mac is on the CD that shipped with your Treo and is available for download from Palm (www.palm.com).

3. During the installation process, perform a HotSync operation with your Treo.

    Amid the operation, you will be prompted to enter a username for your Treo. Be sure to use the same username you used on your old device.

If any of the applications you were running on your old device are not compatible with your new Treo, the HotSync Manager may quarantine and not install them.

If you plan on continuing to use your old Palm device, you will need to perform a hard reset to delete the username in order to avoid conflicts because that username is now associated with your Treo. Each device you synchronize with your PC must have a unique name, so the next time you synchronize your old device, be sure to assign it a new username.

Beam Data Using Your Treo's Infrared Capability

Your Treo includes an IR (infrared) port that lets you wirelessly beam information to another Palm-powered device that also has an IR port. You can beam contact records, your business card, and applications to other IR-capable handhelds. The IR port is located on the top of your Treo, between the Wireless Mode button and the ringer switch, behind the small dark shield.

What Is the Range of Infrared on a Treo?

According to Palm, the maximum infrared beam distance with your Palm handheld may vary from 24 in. (61 cm) to 39 in. (1 m). The beam distance variation is dependent on the age and condition of the power supply in your Treo, as well as the power supply in the receiving handheld. For best results, point your IR port directly at the IR port of the receiving unit, while maintaining a beam distance between 3 in. (7.6 cm) and 24 in. (61 cm). In the authors' experience, attempting to beam a contact record between two brand-new, fully charged Treo failed if the Treos were placed much more than 24 inches apart.

Beam Your Business Card to Another Palm-Powered Device

Instead of scrambling to find a pen and paper to give someone your contact information, an easy way to share your contact information is to beam it to the person's Palm device from your Treo . The steps for beaming your business card are shown here:

1. Press PHONE, and then press MENU.
2. From the Record menu, choose Beam Business Card.
3. When the Beam Status dialog box appears, point the IR port on your Treo directly at the IR port of the receiving device.
4. Wait for the Beam Status dialog box to indicate that the transfer is complete.

Beam a Contact Record

In addition to beaming your business card, you can beam any contact record or category. This can significantly reduce the time to get contact information. To beam records, follow these steps:

1. Press PHONE, and then choose Contacts.

2. Choose a record that you want to beam, and press MENU.

3. From the Record menu, choose Beam Contact (Beam on the Treo 600) to send the individual record.

4. When the Beam Status dialog box appears, point the IR port on your Treo directly at the IR port of the receiving device. The device receiving the beamed information needs to be on and in range—18 in. at most—and the user of the receiving device will have to accept the data before transmission proceeds.

5. Wait for the Beam Status dialog box to indicate that the transfer is complete before you move your Treo.

Once the transfer is complete, the user of the device that received the data can either accept or discard the beamed information.

Beam an Application

There are many software developers that program applications specifically for Palm-powered devices such as your Treo. Now Palm users can beam their favorite applications and games to other Palm users. It is a lot less work than searching the Web for a download site. However, not all applications can be beamed. If an application cannot be beamed, a lock icon appears on the Beam screen next to the application's name.

So, just how long does it take to beam an application? Well, for reference, one of the authors beamed a larger-than-average 338KB application to another Treo , and the process took 50 seconds.

To beam an application, follow these steps:

1. Start the Applications Launcher by pressing HOME.

2. Press MENU.

3. From the App menu, choose Beam.

4. Choose Beam from the menu (on the Treo 600, select whether the application you want to beam is located on your Treo or on an expansion card. (Chapter 15 further describes using expansion cards.)

5. Choose the application to transfer.

6. Choose Beam.

7. When the Beam Status dialog box appears, point the IR port on your Treo directly at the IR port of the receiving device.

8. Wait for the Beam Status dialog box to indicate that the transfer is complete before moving your Treo.

Receive Beamed Information

To receive beamed information on your Treo, including business cards, applications, and data, you need to actively accept the data before the download process can begin by following these steps:

1. Turn on your screen.

2. Point the IR port on your Treo directly at the IR port of the transmitting device to open the Beam Status dialog box.

3. When the Beam Status dialog box appears, you can choose a category for the entry to be placed into. The default categories are Business, Personal, Quick List, and Unfiled.

4. On the five-way navigation control, press UP to receive the beam or DOWN to refuse it.

Wrap It Up

Congratulations! If you made it through this chapter, you are well on your way to being able to tell your friends and colleagues that you are a bona fide Treo expert. We covered a lot of ground here, and much of the chapter discussed your Treo from the perspective of the out-of-the-box capabilities utilizing the built-in hardware and software. Hopefully, you are discovering additional uses for your Treo that exceed the reasons why you purchased it in the first place. Many of the topics presented here, and many others, are expanded later in the book. Now that you're warmed up, let's move on to the next chapters, which discuss synchronizing your Treo with your PC, using your Treo phone, and getting connected in the world of wireless data.

Chapter 3

Synchronize Your Treo with Your PC

How to...

■ Install and configure the Palm Desktop synchronization software

■ Synchronize contacts and other data between your Treo and your PC—Windows and Mac

■ Use Palm Desktop applications

■ Use Chapura PocketMirror to synchronize your Treo 600with Outlook

■ Use other personal information manager applications with your Treo

■ Use HotSync conduits with third-party applications

This chapter discusses topics about the synchronization of your Treo data with your personal desktop computer and includes benefits, technical alternatives, and steps for getting set up.

What's on the Treo Companion CD

Your Treo ships with a CD that contains some useful documentation and software. The most important item on the CD pertaining to this chapter is the HotSync software that runs on your PC and allows you to HotSync your Treo with your PC. The CD contains the following items:

■ **Palm Desktop synchronization software** The HotSync software allows you to synchronize data between your PC or Mac and your Treo, as well as install applications and files using your HotSync cable. The Palm Desktop software provides an easy-to-use PIM application for the PC or Mac just in case you don't already have one installed on your computer.

■ **User Guide (PDF)** This document includes general user information about using your Treo.

■ **Acrobat Reader** This software allows you to view the User Guide, but most people already have this software installed.

■ **Applications** These consist of applications such as eReader, Treo Voice Dialing (Treo 650 and 700), and a Documents To Go conversion tool for your desktop PC. The actual software that is on the CD depends on where and when you purchased your Treo.

Connect Your Treo to Your PC

Your Treo works together with your PC to allow you to easily manage data and applications on your Treo. The process of synchronization allows you to enter information on your computer and then efficiently transfer that information to your Treo. Of course, the process works the other way as well, changes that you make on your Treo can be transferred to your PC during the synchronization process. The actual synchronization process is configurable; it is covered in more detail later in this chapter, in the section "Configure HotSync Manager."

Do You Need a PC to Make the Most of Your Treo?

Actually, you don't need a PC to use your Treo. You can use your Treo as a stand-alone unit without ever connecting it to a PC. That said, there are many benefits associated with using a PC with your Treo. It is a good idea to set up your PC to sync with your Treo. Even if you only use your PC to load applications and back up your Treo data, it is a powerful combination that can save you a lot of time.

Before you can synchronize, you need to install the Palm Desktop synchronization software on your computer. Even if you already own a Palm OS device and have installed a previous version, you must install the software that comes on the CD with your Treo.

HotSync Synchronization

The term *synchronization* can be a little bit misleading when we are talking about the way Palm uses the term. If you look up "synchronize" in the dictionary, you will likely find something like

- To occur at the same time; be simultaneous
- To operate in unison

Synchronized swimming, for example, involves two or more swimmers moving in exactly the same way at exactly the same time. But when we are talking about synchronizing your Treo data between your Treo and your personal desktop computer, it does *not* mean that the two are doing the same things at the same time. There is a time lag involved. What we are talking about is roughly as follows: after you synchronize, in what is called a *HotSync operation,* your Treo data on both your Treo and your PC is the same. The data remains in synchronization until you change information on either your Treo or your PC. When you change information on one or the other, the two become out of sync until the next time you perform a HotSync operation, at which time your Treo data on your Treo and your Treo data on your PC are synchronized once again.

To perform this synchronization of Treo data between your Treo and your PC, Palm provides software called HotSync. When you have installed the HotSync software, along with the Palm Desktop software, you use the HotSync software and HotSync charger cable to connect your Treo to your PC. You begin the HotSync process by pressing the HotSync button on the HotSync cable. This is all covered in detail in this chapter.

Treo-to-PC Connection Options

There are several different ways that you can connect your Treo to your PC:

- **Local connection options**   The first time you perform a HotSync operation, you must use one of these methods to establish a username:
  - **Cradle/cable**   This is the most common method. Here, your Treo is physically connected to your PC using a USB or serial port sync cable.
  - **Infrared**   This method allows you to HotSync wirelessly with your PC and requires that your PC have an infrared port. Infrared is discussed in detail in Chapter 5.

■ **Bluetooth** This method (not available on the Treo 600) allows you to sync using a Bluetooth short-range wireless connection between a Treo and a Bluetooth-capable laptop or PC. Bluetooth is covered in Chapter 5.

TIP

More and more handheld device users are going "cradle-less" in favor of synchronizing wirelessly. Bluetooth and infrared technologies are a great way to leave your cables at home and still sync your Treo and PC. Wireless technologies are discussed in detail in Chapter 5.

■ **Direct network connection** This method allows you to HotSync your Treo using another PC connected to the same local area network (LAN) or wide area network (WAN) as your PC. The PC that you connect your Treo to must be running HotSync Manager software, and your Treo must be connected to it using a cradle, cable, or infrared communication.

■ **Remote connection options** It's possible to synchronize your Treo remotely using a wireless connection through your wireless service provider. Some extra hardware and setup effort is required to get this to work properly, however. You'll need both a modem attached to your PC and a phone line for the exclusive use of your desktop computer. If you'll be dialing in to a corporate remote access server (RAS), you'll have to configure the RAS to accept connections between your Treo and your PC.

Considerations When Synchronizing with a Modem

If you are away from your PC for extended periods of time and cannot HotSync your Treo directly with your PC using the HotSync cable, you may need an alternate way to HotSync. One of your options is to perform a HotSync operation remotely using the wireless connectivity on your Treo and a phone-line modem connected to your PC. This method of performing a HotSync operation requires that you have a modem connected to your PC, and here are a few points to consider when evaluating this option:

■ Wireless networks tend to be much slower than wired connections, so if you are syncing a lot of data, the process will be slow.

■ Depending on the service agreement you have with your wireless service provider, you will need to be conscious of how much data you are sending through the wireless network. Data coverage charges can be substantial if you use more than what is specified in your contract.

TIP

Ensure that you are using the correct version of Palm Synchronization software. *It is important to know that not all Treo operating systems are compatible with all versions of the Palm Synchronization software. For example, at the time of writing this book the latest version of the Palm Desktop for Windows was version 414e, which works with both the Treo 650 and 700p models but not with the Treo 600. If you have a Treo 600 and you use a later version of the Palm Desktop such as version 414e, you may encounter problems with syncing photos and videos. Fortunately, Palm allows you to download the correct software for your specific Treo model (www.palm.com/us/support/downloads/).*

Palm Desktop Software

The Palm Desktop software that comes with your Treo is a suite of applications that allows you to manage data on your Microsoft PC or Mac and synchronize data between your PC/Mac and your Treo. There are many similarities between the Palm Desktop for PC and the Palm Desktop for Mac but there are some differences, so there are sections dedicated to each version. The software components include the following:

- **HotSync**   HotSync is the process of synchronizing data between your Treo and your PC. HotSync is initiated from your Treo by pressing the HotSync button on the sync cable. The HotSync button is located on the end section of the HotSync cable that connects to your Treo. The HotSync software must be installed and running on the PC that you are synchronizing data with.

- **Palm Desktop**   The Palm Desktop software includes the following applications and is essentially the tool that you will use if you do not use Outlook. The names of the Palm Desktop applications have evolved across successive versions of the application, and depending on the version of the Palm Desktop you have, the names may be slightly different:

  - **Calendar (formerly Date Book)**   Allows you to schedule and set alarms for single and recurring events, as well as view your calendar information.

  - **Contacts (formerly Address Book)**   Allows you to track your business and personal contacts, including addresses and phone numbers.

TIP *Some of the terminology between the Palm Desktop applications and your Treo phone functions can be a little confusing, depending on which Treo you have. Here are a few clarifications. The Palm Desktop Date Book = the Treo Calendar, and the Palm Desktop Address Book = the Treo Contacts. The data is essentially the same between the corresponding applications, but the naming conventions are slightly different.*

  - **Tasks (formerly To Do List)**   Allows you to view and manage your tasks, including the ability to set priorities and due dates for each task. You can also save a record of complete tasks.

  - **Memos (formerly Memo Pad)**   Allows you to save notes for meetings or other events not associated with the Date Book, Address Book, or To Do list.

  - **Quick Install (formerly Install tool)**   Allows you to manage the applications that are installed on your Treo. Selected applications will be installed automatically on your handheld the next time you HotSync.

  - **Media (formerly Treo Pictures)**   Allows you to automatically download to your PC the digital photos and video (not available on the Treo 600) that you take with your Treo.

- **Treo 600 Specific—Chapura PocketMirror (included on the CD and as part of the Palm Desktop software install)**   Required if you are an Outlook user, this software serves as the synchronization conduit between your Treo and Microsoft Outlook and allows you to maintain your data—contacts, calendar information, tasks, and notes—on both your Treo and in Outlook. Note: the latest versions of the Palm Desktop and HotSync can sync directly with Outlook.

Palm Desktop for Windows PC

This section deals specifically with Palm Desktop for Windows PC. If your computer is a Mac, the Palm Desktop for Mac is discussed in the next section.

Install Palm Desktop Synchronization Software on Your PC

You need to install the Palm Desktop synchronization software on your PC before you can synchronize your PC and your Treo. If you are upgrading from another Palm OS device and have installed a previous version of the Palm Desktop, you must upgrade to the Palm Desktop software version that comes on the CD with your Treo.

Upgrading from Another Palm Device

If you are upgrading to your Treo from another Palm device and have previously installed Palm Desktop or HotSync software on your PC, when you install a later version of the Palm Desktop, you may see the error shown in Figure 3-1.

This error is simply telling you that any software not compatible with your new Treo will not be installed but will be saved in a directory on your PC.

Windows—The Installation Process

The installation process of the HotSync and Palm Desktop software is straightforward and is generally accomplished by repeatedly clicking OK and entering a little information, but there are a few screens that you will want to pay more attention to. These will be discussed in this section.

Before you begin the installation process it is a good idea to connect your Treo to your PC with the synchronization cable. If your PC does not have a USB port, you will need to purchase a serial cable before you can get started.

To begin the installation process, insert and run the companion CD that came with your Treo on your PC. (If you don't have the CD, the software can be downloaded from www.palm.com. If you get stuck on any of the screens or you are not sure what the installation program is asking you for, click the Help button.

FIGURE 3-1   Treo upgrade error

3

The "Give Your Device a Name" Installation Screen   Your username is the key that allows the Treo synchronization software to know which device goes with which set of personal information on your desktop computer. Every Treo has a username associated with it. The username uniquely identifies your device when you synchronize with your PC. The Select User screen looks like that shown in Figure 3-2. To create a new user, click the Create New User button and enter your username, which can be anything you like. If you upgraded from a previous Palm device and are upgrading the Palm Desktop application, your previous user name will be imported and you will likely want to create a new user name for your new Treo. If you want all of your information and data from your previous Palm OS device to be transferred to your new device, select your old username. It is important to note that once you have transferred your username to your new Treo, you must hard-reset your old Treo and give it a new name if you plan to sync it to the same computer. You cannot sync two Treos with the same name.

The "Select an Application to Use for Your Personal Data" Installation Screen   You may or may not see this screen during the installation process. The screen, which looks like Figure 3-3, will appear if you have Microsoft Outlook installed on your PC. If you want to share all of your personal information, such as contacts, tasks, and calendar data, between your Treo and MS Outlook when you perform a HotSync, then choose the Outlook option. If you choose the Palm Desktop option, then your PIM data will be synchronized between your Treo and the Palm Desktop applications. Note that you can change this setting in the Palm Desktop application at any time after you have completed the installation.

If you are not an Outlook user and you don't currently use a PIM (personal information manager application), then the Palm Desktop applications offer a great way to manage your contacts, calendar information, tasks, and notes. If you use another popular PIM application,

FIGURE 3-2   Palm Desktop Installation—Choose HotSync Name

FIGURE 3-3   Palm desktop installation—Microsoft Outlook detected

then there is likely third-party software that allows you to synchronize your Treo with the PIM software that you already use. More information is available on this topic toward the end of this chapter, in the section titled "What If I Don't Use Outlook to Manage My PIM Information?".

Even if you use MS Outlook, there may be situations when you may not want to sync your Treo with your Outlook data. For example, you have different PIM data for personal and company business and don't want to mix the two up. So, you can always use the Palm Desktop application as one PIM and Outlook for the other. In reality, many of us mix up business and pleasure and like to keep everything in one place, but you have the option of keeping your data separate.

The Palm Desktop allows you to manage contact information, tasks, and appointments on your PC and synchronize your data with your Treo. The Palm Desktop is particularly valuable if you do not use another personal information manager (PIM) such as Outlook, Lotus Notes, Act!, GoldMine, or something else. If you use a popular PIM application other than MS Outlook, there are third-party applications that allow you sync your Treo; some are listed later in this chapter, under the heading "What if I Don't Use Outlook to Manage My PIM Information?".

Some of the Palm Desktop functionality will be useful even if you don't need all of it and if you don't currently use personal information manager application. In that case, you will likely find the Palm Desktop exceedingly useful for keeping track of your info.

Palm Desktop Functionality and Applications

The Palm Desktop consists of several useful subapplications, including applications for calendar and scheduling, contact management, a task manager, memos, an application to install applications on your Treo, the ability to view your Treo media, and a VersaMail account setup (VersaMail is discussed along with other Treo e-mail options in Chapter 6). Most of the Palm

Desktop applications are obvious, and the Palm Desktop user guide and help files do a great job of describing how to use them, but there are couple of functions that are worth mentioning here.

NOTE *Your Treo is designed so that any applications or files you install, other than those that were preinstalled when you purchased your Treo, run in RAM (random access memory) and are not stored in ROM (read-only memory). This is only important if you need to hard-reset your handheld, because if you do hard-reset, your installed applications will be deleted. They will be reinstalled the next time you HotSync, however, as long as you have them selected in the Install tool. Any applications or files that are installed on an expansion card will be stored on the card until you remove them—that is, they are not deleted if you hard-reset your Treo, provided you installed the applications using the Palm Desktop Install tool. Applications that were beamed (beaming is covered in Chapter 2) or downloaded directly onto your Treo from the Internet using the Browser may be lost when you perform a hard reset on your Treo.*

Install Applications and Files on Your Treo with the Palm Desktop Quick Install Tool   Applications for your Treo are generally single files with filenames ending in .prc. This makes installing new applications on your Treo easier than installing software on a PC or server. The Palm Desktop software allows you to select applications or files that are stored on your PC to be installed or copied to your Treo the next time you HotSync.

TIP *You can quickly open the Quick Install application by simply double-clicking the .prc (Palm application) file that you want to install on your Treo.*

Treo 650 and 700p—Install Applications or Files on Your Treo Using Quick Install   The latest versions of the Palm Desktop make installing applications and files onto your Treo very easy. The tool also offers the option of installing either into the Treo memory or directly onto a removable memory card. To use the Quick Install tool, simply launch the Palm Desktop and select the tool, as shown in Figure 3-4.

The Quick Install tool offers an easy drag-and-drop interface, shown in Figure 3-5, that allows you to add files to either the Handheld or an expansion card. These files will be synchronized with your Treo the next time you perform a HotSync action.

Treo 600—Install Applications or Files on Your Treo Using Quick Install   The Quick Install tool in the Palm Desktop allows you to select the applications or files that will be installed on your Treo the next time you HotSync.

1. In the Install Tool dialog box, if you have more than one Palm username associated with your PC, make sure your username is selected, and then click Add.

2. In the Open dialog box, browse to select the applications or files to install.

3. Click OK, and then click Done.

The application or file that you have added will be loaded onto your Treo the next time you HotSync.

FIGURE 3-4   Quick Install tool icon

FIGURE 3-5   Palm desktop Quick Install tool

3

If you have an SD card (or cards), you can install and run applications on it. There are a couple of reasons you may want to install and run applications on an SD card. The first is that it allows you to maximize the memory on your Treo, and the second is that if you have more than one SD card, you can swap applications as you need them without taking up unnecessary memory space on your Treo. The steps to install an application on an SD card are as follows:

1. In the Install Tool dialog box, if you have more than one Palm username associated with your PC, make sure that the username you want is selected; then click Add.

2. In the Open dialog box, browse to select the applications or files to install and click OK.

3. Click the Change Destination button.

4. Choose the drop-down menu entitled Install To and select SD Card.

5. If you would like to move an item from one list to the other, click the item and then click the arrow pointing to the other list.

6. On the Change Destination screen, click OK.

7. On the Install Tool screen, click Done.

Palm Desktop Media Application   Not all versions of the Palm Desktop application include the Media application. But if you are running a version that does include the Media application, it is good tool to help you work with your media files. You can find much more information in the Help file for the Palm Desktop, but it is worth discussing the functionality briefly here because it is new and offers some great options to allow you to manage and sync your media files. Here are some of the things that you can do with Palm Desktop Media:

- Add photos to your desktop.
- View your photos and videos.
- Edit your photos and videos.
- Manage your albums, including viewing a slideshow and using a photo for a contact.

Import and Export Data in the Palm Desktop   One of the strengths of the Palm Desktop is its ability to import and export data. This makes it relatively easy to move data between the Palm Desktop, other applications, and the personal information manager software. There are even Palm-only proprietary formats called "archives"—including Date Book Archive (*.dba), Address Book Archive (*.aba), To Do Archive (*.tda), and Memo Pad Archive (*.mpa)—that allow you to easily swap data between Palm Desktop users or offer an easy way to back up your Palm Desktop data.

Note that CSV (comma-separated value) files can be used if none of the other platforms are supported. A full list of supported import and export formats appears at the end of this chapter.

Import Data into the Palm Desktop To import data into the Palm Desktop, ensure that the data you want to import matches one of the supported formats from the preceding list and then follow these steps:

1. In the Palm Desktop application, select the File menu.
2. Select Import.

   A dialog box similar to that shown in Figure 3-6 will open.
3. Select the appropriate choice from the Files of Type drop-down list.
4. Browse to the file you would like to import.
5. Select Import.

It is always a good idea to test an import by importing a small part of the data first, especially if you are about to import a large amount of data. If imported data doesn't import exactly as intended, it could prove a time-consuming task to manually clean up or delete data.

Import Data That Is Not Already in a Supported File Type If you would like to import data that is not already in an acceptable import format, you may still be able to import the data, but it may take a little "massaging." Most applications can export data into a CSV (comma-separated value)

FIGURE 3-6 Palm Desktop Import dialog box

format, which can then be imported into the Palm Desktop. But, before you import thousands of records in this manner, try exporting a small amount of data from the source application and import it into the Palm Desktop to make sure that the data is translated correctly and that you don't end up with phone numbers in the name fields, for example. Another option, although a potentially slow one, is to cut and paste data from one application to the other.

Export Data from the Palm Desktop   To export data from the Palm Desktop, follow these steps:

1. Select the Palm Desktop application you would like to export data from (Contacts, Calendar, Tasks, or Date Book, Address Book, To Do, etc.).

2. Select File | Export to open a dialog box like the one shown in Figure 3-7.

3. Browse to the file location where you want to save the exported data.

4. Enter a filename and select the export format type.

5. Select the range, either All or Currently Selected Records.

6. Click Export.

TIP   *Remember that if you export data in any of the Palm proprietary "archive" types (.dba, .aba, .tba, or .mpa), you will only be able to use the data within a Palm Desktop application, whereas if you export data in a nonproprietary format (.csv or .txt), you will be able to use the data in other applications as well.*

FIGURE 3-7   Palm Desktop Export As dialog box

Use Palm Desktop to Synchronize Your Treo with Microsoft Outlook Microsoft Outlook is a popular e-mail and PIM (personal information manager) application, and Palm allows you to synch your Treo PIM data with your PC. Depending on whether you have a Treo 600, 650, or 700p, the mechanics for syncing vary a little bit. The recent versions (Palm Desktop 4.1.4 or later) of the Palm Desktop for Windows that works with Treo 650 and 700p handhelds allows you to sync your personal information directly with Microsoft Outlook. If you have a Treo 600, you need to use PocketMirror to synchronize your Treo with Outlook.

This section is divided into two sections specifically relating to the Treo 650/700p handhelds and Treo 600 handhelds.

Use Palm Desktop to Synchronize Your Treo 650 or 700p with Microsoft Outlook The Palm Desktop software allows you to sync your Microsoft Outlook data directly with your Treo, including: Calendar, Contacts, Memos, and Tasks. Since MS Outlook does not deal with Photos or Videos, those files are synchronized with the Palm Desktop application.

When you installed the Palm Desktop application, the program should have detected MS Outlook installed on your PC and prompted you to choose whether you wanted to sync your Treo with the Palm Desktop application or with MS Outlook. If you chose to sync with Outlook, then you are essentially already set up, and every time you sync your Treo, your PIM information will be updated between Outlook and the PIM applications on your Treo.

Change HotSync Settings to Sync with Palm Desktop or MS Outlook If, for whatever reason, you now want to sync your Treo with MS Outlook instead of Palm Desktop, or vice versa, it is very easy to do.

1. On your PC, click Start | Programs | Palm | PIM Conduit Sync.

2. Then select either Sync with Palm Desktop or Sync with Outlook, as shown in Figure 3-8.

You can change this setting at any time, but mostly you will just set it and leave it.

Treo 600 Specific—Use PocketMirror to Synchronize Your Treo 600 with Outlook If you have a Treo 600 and use the Palm Desktop and HotSync software that came with your Treo, this section is for you, as it deals specifically with syncing your Treo 600 with MS Outlook.

Configure HotSync settings.

The Palm Desktop software for the Treo 600 includes a conduit that allows you to synchronize the data on your Treo with your Outlook data. This conduit application is called PocketMirror and is produced by Chapura (www.chapura.com).

PocketMirror is an application that runs on your PC and allows you to synchronize data between your Treo and Microsoft Outlook; for instance, you can sync Outlook Contacts, Calendar, Tasks, and Notes with your Treo Contacts, To Do List, and Memo Pad.

NOTE   *Some of the terminology between the Palm Desktop applications and your Treo phone functions can be a little confusing, so here are a few clarifications. The Palm Desktop Date Book = the Treo 600 Calendar, and the Palm Desktop Address Book = the Treo 600 Contacts. The data is essentially the same between the corresponding applications, but the naming conventions are slightly different.*

Once installed, the PocketMirror user interface is accessible within the Microsoft Outlook application. You'll notice two specific additions to the Outlook interface:

- **PocketMirror folder**   In the folders view, you should see a folder called PocketMirror, as shown in Figure 3-9. The PocketMirror folder contains two subfolders:

  - **Archive**   PocketMirror creates a special archive folder in Outlook to store archived handheld items. This means that if you delete a handheld item *and* select the Save Archive Copy on PC option, PocketMirror will move that item out of the Outlook folder it was in and put it into your archive folder.

  - **Conflicts**   Any time the HotSync process encounters data conflicts, it will back up the conflicting data in the Conflicts folder. This means you'll have a backup if a record is inadvertently overwritten during a HotSync operation.

- **Chapura Settings menu**   Shown in Figure 3-10, the Chapura Settings screen lets you manage your Treo user accounts, as well as modify how PocketMirror synchronizes your data.

Change Chapura Synchronization Preferences (Treo 600)   The synchronization settings in the Chapura Settings screen control the way PocketMirror conducts the synchronization process, and can be defined separately for each application. The four Treo applications that PocketMirror synchronizes are Contacts, Calendar, To Do List, and Memo Pad. To change the synchronization settings for a user,

1. Launch Chapura Settings from the Tools menu and select the user.

2. Click the Settings button to open the Change Synchronization Preferences screen.

You can modify the synchronization settings independently for each application (Outlook Calendar, Outlook Contacts, Outlook Tasks, and Outlook Notes) and also define your preferences for System and Install syncing.

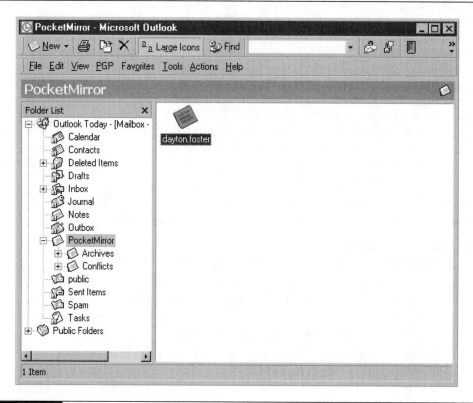

FIGURE 3-9 PocketMirror Folders

Palm Desktop for Mac

The Palm Desktop for Mac and HotSync allows you to sync your Treo PIM data with your Mac using either the Palm Desktop application or the built-in Apple Address Book and iCal applications. An overview of the Palm Desktop was covered earlier in this chapter under the heading "Palm Desktop Software."

Available Mac Conduits

There are several conduits that allow you to sync your Mac applications with your Treo. Some of the available applications are listed here and more information is available on the Palm web site (www.Palm.com).

FIGURE 3-10   Chapura Settings menu

- Personal information managers (PIM)
  - Microsoft Entourage
  - Microsoft Outlook Express
  - MeetingMaker
- E-mail
  - Eudora Internet Suite
  - Microsoft Entourage
  - Microsoft Outlook Express
  - VersaMail

- Microsoft Word and Excel
  - Dataviz Documents to Go (Word and Excel)
  - Blue Nomad Wordsmith (Word only)
  - Personal Finance (Quicken, Money)
  - Pocket Quicken
  - WalletWare Expense Plus
  - SplashMoney
- Database
  - FileMaker Mobile

Import and Export Data to and from Palm Desktop for Mac

Palm Desktop for Mac allows you to import personal information manager information from specific Mac PIM products that are listed next, and you can also import data from other applications by first exporting the data in a comma-delimited format from the PIM application and then importing the file into Palm Desktop.

Supported import formats include

- Address Book Plus
- DateBook Pro
- DayMaker
- DynoDex
- Meeting Maker
- Now Contact
- Now Up-to-Date
- QuickDex
- TouchBase Pro
- vCard/vCal-compatible PIMs

You can also export data from Palm Desktop for Mac so that you can import it into other applications. The format depends on the application that you are going to be importing the data into, so it is a good idea to check product documentation; most applications support comma-delimited formats as an alternative.

Configure HotSync Manager—Windows and Mac

The HotSync Manager allows you to modify your synchronization settings. Even though you may never need to change the default settings, there are situations where you may want to modify them temporarily. Therefore, it's valuable to be aware of these settings.

The HotSync Manager Custom screen can be accessed from the HotSync menu in the Palm Desktop; it looks like this the screen shown in Figure 3-11.

NOTE   *On a Mac the synchronization rules are accessed within the Palm Desktop application by selecting Conduit Settings from the HotSync menu and then selecting a conduit: Address Book, Date Book, Memo Pad, or To Do List. Finally, click the Conduit Settings button to modify your sync settings.*

For each item in the conduit list on the Custom screen, you can change how you want the HotSync application to deal with data. For example, if you select Contacts and click Change, you will see a screen similar to the one shown in Figure 3-12. The Mac screen will look different, but the options are the same.

Here you have four different options:

- **Synchronize the Files**   This is the default setting. Here, data is passed both to and from your Treo and desktop to update data and ensure that both have the most recent version.

- **Desktop Overwrites Handheld**   When this selection is chosen, the desktop always overwrites your Treo data. This means that if you update a record on your Treo, it will be overwritten by the desktop the next time you perform a HotSync operation. This would be a good choice if on your Treo you only read your Address Book information and never modify records. It also results in faster HotSync operations if you have a lot of data.

- **Handheld Overwrites Desktop**   When this selection is chosen, your Treo always overwrites your desktop data. This means that if you update a record on your desktop, it will be overwritten the next time you perform a HotSync operation. This is a good choice if on your desktop you only read your Address Book information and only modify records on your Treo. It also results in faster HotSync operations if you have a lot of data.

FIGURE 3-11   HotSync Manager Custom Settings

FIGURE 3-12   HotSync Manager Change HotSync Action

■ **Do Nothing**   When this option is selected, no data will be synchronized between your Treo and your desktop, and each will have its own data. This option defeats the core benefits of synchronization, but it does have its uses. For example, perhaps you don't have time to sync all of your Address Book data because you have been on the road for a month and have added thousands of records, and you're only interested in moving your digital photographs to your PC during the HotSync process. In this scenario, you could change all of the HotSync Custom conduit actions to move nothing except Treo Pictures.

One-Time Synchronization Options

In addition to configuring your HotSync settings to have them used on a permanent basis, you can use the Change Synchronization Preferences screen to run one-time processes. One-time options are available by clicking the Quick One-Time Action Setup drop-down menu shown in Figure 3-13. This allows you to perform one-time actions without affecting your permanent settings, including the ability to perform actions like Back Up Private Records, Install Applications Only, and Restore from Palm Desktop Files.

Palm Desktop Extensions

Palm Desktop extensions are applications that you can install individually and use within the Palm Desktop window to add more functionality. For example, a particular extension might allow you to record and track your expenses. Buttons for extensions appear on the Launch bar. Each extension runs within the Palm Desktop and may add new buttons or menu items to the interface. Extensions can be downloaded from Palm and other third-party software vendors. Check www.palm.com for information about new extensions.

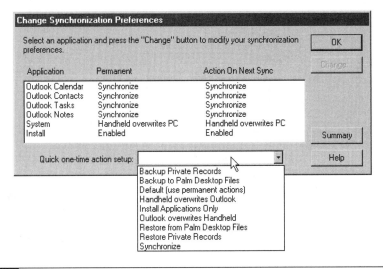

FIGURE 3-13   Quick One-Time Action Setup

Palm Desktop Add-ins

Palm Desktop add-ins are different from extensions because they add functionality to the built-in Palm Desktop applications. For example, an add-in called Delete Duplicates checks for and removes duplicate records in the Palm Desktop software applications.

Add-ins are available from Palm and other third-party software vendors; check the Palm web site (www.Palm.com) for information about new add-ins.

Remove Applications or Files from Your Treo

It may be a little strange that we are dealing with removing applications from your Treo in the sync section, but since we cover adding applications in this chapter, you may also want to know how to remove them. There are several reasons you may want to uninstall applications or delete files. Perhaps you no longer need a particular application, or an application doesn't do what you want, or you need to free up memory on your Treo. Applications are removed directly from your Treo and not through the Palm Desktop. The steps to uninstall an application or file are as follows:

1. On your Treo, go to the Applications Launcher by pressing the HOME button on the keyboard.
2. Press the MENU button.
3. Select Delete.
4. A screen that looks like the following will appear. Select the file or application you would like to remove or delete, as shown in Figure 3-13.
5. Select Delete.

FIGURE 3-14   Treo Delete Application screen

At the top of the screen there is a graphical indicator showing how much available memory you have left on your Treo. If the bar stretches across the entire screen, you'll want to remove some data or applications.

Special Cases to Consider When Removing Applications and Files

Some scenarios warrant discussing a few caveats in regard to removing applications from your Treo. The preceding steps applied to the simplest scenario, where you are removing third-party applications and nonsystem data. Other scenarios you may encounter include the following:

- You want to remove an application that was preinstalled on your Treo when you received it but that doesn't appear in the Delete list.
- You want to delete files that don't show up in the Applications Launcher.
- You uninstalled an application, but it shows up again when you synchronize.

You Cannot Uninstall Built-in Applications

Some of the applications on your Treo cannot be removed, and thus they do not show up in the Delete list. These built-in applications do not affect your memory since they are loaded permanently in read-only memory (ROM).

Uninstall Hidden Files

Use the following information with caution. It is only mentioned here to let you know it is possible. If a file doesn't show up in the Delete list, it may be a "hidden" file. Hidden files can be deleted but only with a third-party application, such as FileZ or zCatalog. The use of these applications is not recommended because removing system files or data may cause your Treo to become unstable and may negatively affect the HotSync process.

3

Why Do Deleted Applications Come Back?

Some of the applications loaded on your Treo may be backed up on your desktop. If an application that you deleted from your Treo is backed up on your desktop, it will be reinstalled the next time you perform a HotSync operation. This is extremely helpful in the event that you have to perform a hard reset on your Treo, because it means that you will only lose the data that has changed since the previous HotSync operation. If you are intentionally trying to delete an application that was backed up, then you will have to remove the application from your PC as well as from your Treo.

To remove the application from the backup folder on your PC, follow these steps:

1. Navigate to the Backup folder in your Palm application folder.

2. The Backup folder is usually found in the Palm or Palm folder. For example, on my Windows PC, it's in C:\Program Files\Palm\dayton\Backup.

3. If your PC is a Macintosh, you can locate the Backup folder using the Find function under the File menu.

4. Find the file or program you would like to delete—it will likely end with either a .prc (a Palm application file) or .pdb (a Palm database file) extension—and select File | Delete.

Add Functionality to Your Palm Desktop

The Palm Desktop functionality may be expanded through Palm Desktop Extensions. This set of add-on features, such as expense management, is available from Palm and other third-party software vendors. More information about specific products is available on the Palm web site (www.palm.com).

Third-Party Sync Tools for Microsoft Outlook—Microsoft PC

Some Treo users may find that built in HotSync software doesn't sync all of the MS Outlook data that you need. Fortunately there are some software developers that have our best interests at heart. Or at least they are willing to sell us tools to help us overcome specific problems.

PocketMirror Professional XT—Treo 650 Only

Chapura has been making software for Palm users for quite a while now, and their PocketMirror XT software (about $50) offers some specific extra features that enhance what the Palm HotSync software offers. These are specific functions that will not be of interest to everyone, but they are great if you need them. Look for this package at www.chapura.com.

- **Global Address List**   PocketMirror XT can transfer names and e-mail addresses from a Global Address List as well as Personal Contacts to your Treo.

- **Microsoft Outlook 2007**   PocketMirror synchronizes Microsoft Outlooks Contacts, Calendar, Tasks, and Notes folders with your Treo 650 Address Book, Date Book, To Do List, and Memo Pad.

- **Integration with MS SharePoint**   Transfer SharePoint Contacts and Calendar folders from Outlook to your Treo.
- **"DataFix" technology**   The DataFix feature detects corrupt records and invalid data on your Treo and corrects them when possible or removes them and replaces them with the Outlook version. It also removes any corrupted archived records from the Treo.

KeySuite—Treo 600/650/700p

This product is also by Chapura (about $70 and offers a free trial version). It is designed to enhance synchronization between your Treo and MS Outlook. It eliminates the need to reorganize, rename, and revise information in Microsoft Outlook Calendar, Contacts, Tasks, and Notes. This package is found at www.chapura.com. The product allows you to

- Sync folders, including Public Folders and Subfolders
- Link Contacts
- Use more fields
- On your PC, keep information separated by folders
- On your Treo, keep Outlook folders as separate categories, instead of lumped together in the "unfiled" category

Third-Party Tools to Sync My Treo with My Mac

Most users who don't already use a third-party PIM application on their Mac will find the Palm Desktop to be a fantastic tool. Some users, however, may find that the Palm Desktop for Mac application is a little lacking for their needs. Fortunately, there are some third-party tools to help you better match your Treo to your Mac.

The Missing Sync for Palm OS

This software (from www.markspace.com) costs about $40 and offers some expanded sync functionality over HotSync and iSync, including

- **Address Book**   Sync instant messages, addresses, birthdays, and contact photos; choose to sync contact groups and categorize them.
- **Calendar**   Simulate iCal calendar colors on your Treo and choose specific calendar events to sync.
- **Photos**   Includes a free version of the SplashPhoto photo viewer.
- **Music**   Sync iTunes playlists to your Treo.

- **Backup and restore**   Mac Palm BackupDemand allows you to restore your Treo to a previous state.
- **Support for other conduits**   Documents to Go, FileMaker Mobile, LifeBalance, PocketQuicken, and SplashID. There is also a Mac OS X-compatible conduit for iAnywhere AvantGo.

iSync by Apple

iSync software by Apple (www.apple.com/support/downloads/isync.html) is a free download and allows you to synchronize your Address Book contacts, iCal calendar, and To Do information with your Mac. If you have a .Mac account, you can also use iSync to synchronize your contacts, calendars, and Safari bookmarks over the Internet. iSync also allows you to use an SD card as a USB drive, which can come in handy.

What if I Don't Use Outlook to Manage My PIM Information?

This section relates specifically to Windows PC users; similar information for Mac users is discussed in the preceding section, "Third Party Tools to Sync My Treo with My Mac." Your Treo ships with the Palm Desktop and an application conduit that allows you to sync your Treo with MS Outlook. But what if you use a different PIM? If you use another popular personal information manager application, you can probably find third-party software that allows you to synchronize. Some of the sync options will vary slightly, depending on which model of Treo you have as well as the version of Palm Desktop / HotSync that you are using. Following are some examples:

- Intellisync (www.intellisync.com) offers conduits for
  - Microsoft Outlook
  - Outlook Express
  - ACT!
  - Lotus Notes
  - Schedule+
  - Novell Groupwise
  - Day Timer Organizer
  - Meeting Maker
  - Oracle Mobile Sales
  - SalesLogix

- Lotus (www.lotus.com) has a product called EasySync Pro that allows you to sync with
  - Lotus Notes
  - Lotus Organizer
- CompanionLink (www.companionlink.com) offers conduits for
  - ACT!
  - GoldMine
  - Lotus Notes
  - MS Outlook
  - Schedule+
  - TeleMagic

Use the HotSync Conduit with Third-Party Applications

When you install an application on your Treo that uses or stores files and data, it will likely use a "conduit" application to transfer the data between your Treo and your PC. The term "conduit" refers to software that allows data to be transferred to and from both your PC and your Treo during a HotSync operation. Many third-party applications install a conduit on your PC when you install software on your Treo. You can modify your conduit settings for this through the HotSync manager. Each conduit will have different application-specific items that allow you to define how you would like the synchronization to occur.

To help explain third-party conduits, it may be helpful to use an example. One third-party application that has its own conduit is the application we used to take screenshots of Treo screens for the first edition of this book. The software, called ScreenShot5, is produced by LinkeSoft (www.linkesoft.com).

After you install the application using the Treo Install tool, the conduit appears in the HotSync Custom settings list. You can get to the Custom settings by launching the HotSync application on your PC (not on your Treo). You can then browse to the HotSync Custom settings by clicking the HotSync icon in your toolbar and selecting the Custom menu item. You can also browse to the HotSync Custom settings in the Palm Desktop by selecting the HotSync menu at the top and choosing Custom. The Custom settings screen is shown in Figure 3-15.

The ScreenShot-specific conduit appears at the top of the list. To view and change the settings, click Change. Figure 3-16 shows the conduit-specific synchronization items that you can change. For this particular application, you can choose where you would like the screenshot images to be stored when you HotSync and what format you would like the images saved as. Again, the types of things that you can modify are specific to each application conduit.

FIGURE 3-15   HotSync Conduit Custom settings

FIGURE 3-16   HotSync Conduit Custom settings for the ScreenShot conduit

Supported Palm Desktop Import and Export File Formats

Your Treo is capable of importing and exporting several file formats. The supported Palm Desktop import and export file formats according to Palm are listed here:

Export Formats

- Contacts
  - Contacts Archive (*.aba)—Palm proprietary
  - Address Archive (*.aba)—Palm proprietary
  - Comma-Delimited (*.csv, *.txt)
  - Tab-Separated Values (*.tab, *.tsv, *.txt)
- Calendar
  - Calendar Archive (*.dba)—Palm proprietary
  - Date Book Archive (*.dba)—Palm proprietary
- Tasks
  - Tasks Archive (*.tda)—Palm proprietary
  - To Do Archive (*.tda)—Palm proprietary
- Memos
  - Memos Archive (*.mpa)—Palm proprietary
  - Memo Pad Archive (*.mpa)—Palm proprietary
  - Comma-Separated (*.csv, *.txt)
  - Tab-Separated Values (*.tab, *.tsv, *.txt)
  - Text (*.txt)

Import Formats

- Contacts
  - Address Archive (*.aba)—Palm proprietary
  - Comma-Delimited (*.csv, *.txt)
  - Tab-Separated Values (*.tab, *.tsv, *.txt)
  - vCard File (*.vcf)—Microsoft Outlook proprietary
- Calendar
  - Date Book Archive (*.dba)—Palm proprietary
  - vCal File (*.vcs)—Microsoft proprietary
- Tasks
  - To Do Archive (*.tda)—Palm proprietary

- Memos
  - Memo Pad Archive (*.mpa)
  - Comma-Separated (*.csv, *.txt)
  - Tab-Separated Values (*.tab, *.tsv, *.txt)
  - Text (*.txt)
- Date Book formats
  - Date Book Archive (*.dba)—Palm proprietary
  - vCal files (*.vcs)—Microsoft Proprietary
- Address Book formats
  - Address Book Archive (*.aba)—Palm proprietary
  - Comma-Delimited (*.csv, *.txt)
  - Tab-Separated Values (*.tab, *.tsv, *.txt)
  - vCard files (*.vcf)—Microsoft proprietary
  - CSV files (Lotus Organizer 2.*x*/97 mapping)
- To Do List formats, To Do Archive (*.tda)—Palm proprietary
- Memo Pad
  - Memo Pad Archive (*.mpa)—Palm proprietary
  - Comma-Separated (*.csv, *.txt)
  - Tab-Separated Values (*.tab, *.tsv, *.txt)
  - Text (*.txt), vCal

Wrap It Up

The combination of a Treo and a desktop Windows or Mac PC offers many benefits, and ultimately, performing routine HotSync operations can make your life easier. This chapter covered some of the benefits and also reasons why it is a good idea to synchronize your Treo data with your PC regularly, not the least of which is that it offers a great way to back up your Treo data.

In addition to ensuring that your personal information is the same on both your desktop PC and your Treo, synchronization also allows you to copy music, pictures, applications, and information back and forth between your PC and your Treo. This is especially valuable when files are too large to transfer quickly to your Treo using a wireless data connection or when data entry is too time consuming using the Treo keyboard. Once you are set up to synchronize, your Treo and your PC make a great combination to help you get the most out of your Treo.

Chapter 4

Make Calls
with Your Treo

How to...

- Dial a number from your Contacts
- Configure your phone display and sounds
- Use speed dial for one-button calling
- Set up custom ringtones and pictures for specific callers
- Prevent accidental calling with the Keyguard

The Treo is a very high-quality telephone and communication tool. I am sure that as a new Treo owner, one of the first things you did was make a phone call. One of the strengths of the Treo is that you are able to pull it out, turn it on, and make your first call without the need to consult the manual or read a book. This is the hallmark of user-friendly technology. Some parts of the Treo are just that simple, but some of the other things you may choose to do are not quite as obvious.

The Treo is capable of much more advanced calling features, and in this section of the book we will help you make better use of the more advanced phone capabilities of your Treo including custom ringtones, picture display, conference calls, speakerphone, speed dial, hands-free calling, and much more. If you are already comfortable with all the basic calling functions of your Treo, skip the following "Use the Basic Phone" section and go right to the advanced calling.

I want to make sure with this book that we aren't rewriting the Treo instruction manual. I will spend very little time on the basic functions of the Treo, assuming that you have read the manual, and what I will present here will only be refreshers. If you have lost your Treo manual, you can download it from the Palm site at www.palm.com/us/support/.

Use the Basic Phone

As long as you have wireless service where you are, using the Treo as a telephone is very straightforward. This section will familiarize you briefly with the basic controls to use while you are on a call.

Dial a Call

Often, the initial comment we hear when people first look at our Treos is about how small the keyboard is. Then follows the question, "How do you make a phone call on that?" There are actually seven different ways you can dial a call on a Treo.

Keyboard

You can use the number buttons on the keyboard to dial a number when you are in phone mode (pressing the leftmost hard button beside the navigation control). The number pad is embedded within the standard keys on the keyboard. In order to make them stand out for easy dialing, they are highlighted in a blue or black color. In phone mode, you don't have to press ALT (which is blue or black in color, depending on the Treo model you have) to access the numbers; you can just type them directly and then press RETURN to dial the number.

The Dial Pad

Luckily for those of us with big fingers, in addition to the hard keyboard, the Treo features a "soft" keyboard right on the screen that you can easily tap out a number on with your fingers. It's shown in Figure 4-1. Note that if you have an older Treo 600 or 650 version, your screen may look slightly different.

In phone mode, the soft Dial Pad will automatically appear when you press the leftmost button beside the navigation control (this button has a small picture of a telephone on it).

 Some of the Treo versions may behave differently depending on the carrier and model number of your Treo. For example, if you are using the Orange version of the Treo 600, pressing the left button will not bring up the Dial Pad. Instead, it will open a bitmap explaining how to dial your phone from the hard keyboard. You will also find some additional differences on an Orange Treo, such as that the default configuration for the navigation control is slightly different than what is mentioned in these chapters.

You can then type in your number and press the Dial soft button to initiate the call.

The Recently Called List and the Call Log

When you are in phone mode, you can also use the five-way navigation control to perform a variety of actions. With the Treo 650 and 700p models, you can navigate to the Call Log or Contact List right from the soft buttons on the screen. On the Treo 600, pressing the CENTER button will open up the list of numbers that you most recently dialed, as shown in Figure 4-2. This list can be opened on the Treo 700p by pressing the green button to the top left of the navigation control.

The Treo features both hard and soft keyboards.

FIGURE 4-2   The list of most recently dialed numbers makes it easy for you to connect to a number that you called recently.

 Look Up a Number on the Fly

Have you ever wished you could look up a number for someone on the fly? There are many web sites now that will provide directory assistance in your local area. In your web browser, you can go to www.anywho.com to look up a person or business in the U.S. AnyWho also has a link to other lookup services online for many other countries around the world at www.anywho.com/international. Once you find who you are looking for, the person's number will show up as a hyperlink (underlined). Tap the link with the stylus, or select it with the five-way navigation control and press the CENTER button.

In addition to the browser-based service, there is a free utility called Directory Assistant that you can load on your Treo to look up U.S. phone numbers. You can download a free copy of Directory Assistant at http://home.triad.rr.com/rlwhitt/palm/#da.

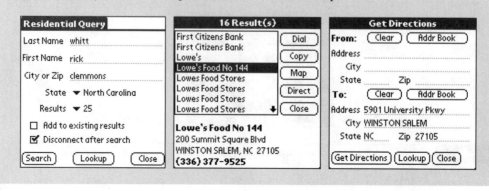

You may also find convenient lookup software preinstalled on your Treo, depending on which model you have and which carrier it came from. For example, the Treo 700p from Sprint comes with a version of the Handmark Express software called On Demand. Among its many useful functions you will find a 411 Directory Assistance application that will allow you to look up entries in the phone book.

The first two entries on the menu are Call Log and Dial Pad. Dial Pad will simply return you back to the numeric Dial Pad to place your call manually. The bottom ten entries on the list will be the names or numbers of the last ten telephone numbers you called. If the number is in your contact list, then the name of the person or company you called will be displayed followed by a letter in parentheses to show if you called them at home, at work, on their mobile, or another way. Highlighting the number with the five-way navigation control or tapping it with the stylus will cause that number to be dialed. On the 700p, pressing the green SEND button will also dial any number that is highlighted.

The Call Log entry displays a chronologically sorted list of all of your calls, starting from the most recent, as shown in Figure 4-3.

Each entry will show you who the call was with (by name if the number you called is in the Contacts list, or by number if it is not), if it was incoming or outgoing (as shown by the direction and color of the small arrow to the left of the name), and the date of the call. You can select any number on this list and a pop-up window will give you the option to dial this number. You can choose to make minor changes to the number (as by adding a 1 in front of it if you need to make it a long distance call) and press the Dial soft button to make an immediate call to that person. On the Treo 600 only, if the person isn't already in your contact list, you also will see a soft button labeled Add Contact, which will take you to the new contact window, discussed in detail in Chapter 2.

When a call is highlighted in the Call Log, you can press the Details soft button to see a detailed accounting of the call, as shown in Figure 4-4. The information you can see includes the duration of the call, and if you were roaming at the time or not.

FIGURE 4-3   The Call Log will allow you to see a list of all your calls, allowing you to dial any number you've communicated with or see the details of a specific call.

Name: Dayton Foster (M)
Number: 403-561-3433
Date: 6/20/06
Time: 9:59 pm
Roaming: Yes

FIGURE 4-4   You can view the detailed information from any call that is still in your Call Log.

This call log can get quite large if you use your Treo frequently, so it is useful to empty it from time to time. You can delete a particular entry out of the call log by selecting it and then opening the menu and choosing Delete Record. You can clear the entire log at once by selecting the Purge menu item.

> **NOTE**   *Push-To-Talk (or "walkie-talkie" style) communication between mobile phones has recently become very popular. The current models of Treo in North America do not support this feature; however, Orange in the UK released a Treo 650 version with Push-To-Talk functionality.*

Dial from Contacts

You can also dial any phone number that is in your Contacts application. From within the phone application, you can launch the Contacts application by selecting it from the Favorites soft buttons on the Treo 650 and 700p, or on the Treo 600 by pressing the five-way navigation control in the appropriate direction. Then you can type in the first few letters of a person's name (first or last) or just type the person's initials, so if you wanted to dial "Michelle White," you could type in "mich" or "mw" or "white." Any of these would pare down your Contacts list and probably turn up Michelle quickly. Because this feature is so compelling and useful, there is a preference setting under the Options menu called Phone Display Preferences where you can switch the mode by which the phone begins to dial when in the Phone application main view. Out of the box, the Treo is configured to "Typing dials phone number,"

so people can get used to just dialing with the keyboard. However, many people change this setting to "Typing starts Contacts search," since most people have all of the numbers they want to dial in their Contacts list.

The Contacts application is covered in more detail in Chapter 10.

Speed-Dial from Favorites

You can also dial using the Favorites application, which is discussed in the section "Use Advanced Calling Features" of this chapter.

Dial Through Hyperlinks

If someone sends you an e-mail with a phone number, or if one shows up in a web page, SMS, or MMS message, it will appear with an underline beneath it. This indicates it is hyperlinked and if you tap it or select it with the five-way navigation control and press the CENTER button, your Treo will automatically dial the number for you!

Use "On Call" Controls

When you are actively engaged in a call, the controls that appear on the Treo will be different, as shown in Figure 4-5.

Some of the things you can control during a call include the following:

- **Volume**   The volume up and down buttons on the side of your Treo allow you to change the volume of the speaker or earbud while in the middle of the call. Note that these are not soft buttons but hard controls on the left side of your Treo. This is very useful if you find you are having trouble hearing the person you are speaking with, or if the call is too loud, making it uncomfortable for your ear.

- **Hang Up**   This self-explanatory button will disconnect the current call.

- **Speakerphone**   This button will turn your Treo into a speakerphone by increasing the volume of the speaker significantly so that it can be heard by everyone in the immediate proximity. The microphone sensitivity will also be turned up to enable everyone who hears the call to speak and participate. Pressing this same soft button again will return you to regular phone mode, allowing you to hold the Treo up to your ear to continue the call in private.

FIGURE 4-5   The options available to you when you are in the middle of a call include Hang Up, Speakerphone, Mute, and show the Dial Pad.

■ **Hold**   This button will put a caller on hold, permitting you to take or place a second call (if your plan with your wireless service provider, the company who provides your phone service, supports this). Once a call is on hold and you have a second call, you can actually conference the two (or more) calls together. Again, this is a feature that must be supported by your carrier and your calling plan.

■ **Mute**   The button with the picture of a microphone allows you to mute your call so that the other party on the call cannot hear what you are saying. You will know the call is muted because the microphone will show a red *X* through it. Pressing this button again will unmute your call and allow the other party to hear you.

■ **Dial Pad**   The small button that looks like a little telephone dial pad will open up the full Dial Pad screen, allowing you to enter keystrokes. This is important for voicemail systems and Interactive Voice Response systems that require you to press numbers on your phone to initiate actions.

While in the middle of a call, you can continue to use your Treo as a regular PDA to make notes, look at documents, and perform other functions. To return to the call in progress, simply press the PHONE hard button to the far left of the five-way navigation control.

Change Volume and Vibrate Settings

The volume of the Treo ringer can be controlled either from the hard controls or from the preferences for the phone as shown in Figure 4-6.

The hard controls are the volume controls on the left side of the Treo. Pressing the UP or DOWN button will increase or decrease the volume of the ringer as appropriate (as long as you are not on an active call, in which case they will not change the ringer volume; they will change the speaker volume for the call). On the screen, you will see a graph showing the current setting for the ringer.

One of the most beloved features among Treo users is the ringer switch on the top. This allows you to immediately switch your Treo from ring to vibrating. How often have you been embarrassed by your phone ringing in a meeting or restaurant? While other devices often make

FIGURE 4-6   Ringer volume can be set with the physical buttons on the side or through the Sound Preferences in the options menu.

you go through the pain of turning off your ringer in some obscure menu, Palm has made this incredibly easy with the simple switch right on top!

Alternatively, you can also set the ringer volume by selecting Sound Preferences from the Options menu on the main telephone window, as shown in Figure 4-6.

Use Advanced Calling Features

Learning to use your Treo to make and receive calls is quite intuitive; however, once you have mastered that, it is time to start learning how to do some of the more advanced functions that can really make the most out of your Treo investment!

Speed-Dial a Favorite Number

The Treo has a very useful feature called Favorites. In addition to being able to define shortcuts to your most frequently used applications and web sites, it also is where you can set up specific contacts as speed-dial numbers. With the touch of a single button you can instantly be connected to up to 70 of your most frequently called numbers (50 on the Treo 600).

Favorites are accessed from the phone Dial Pad screen. If you have a Treo 650 or 700p, you will see the first four of your favorites displayed in the bottom area of your dial pad. Using the navigation control and pressing down will scroll the list of favorites so that your dial pad disappears and the screen is full of your favorites as shown in Figure 4-7. For Treo 600 users, you get to your favorites by pressing the TOP button of the navigation control.

Roaming	R	
	10:20 pm	6/21/06

Contacts	Call Log
Voicemail 1	Web
Camera	SprintTV
GetGood	Get BC
Get Ringers	Get Games
Get Apps	Get Images
pTunes	Email

1 2 3 4 5

FIGURE 4-7   The Favorites feature of the Treo allows you to create one-button access to your favorite phone numbers, messaging numbers, applications, and web pages.

See All the Numbers for a Contact in My Favorites

When the focus is on a specific speed-dial Favorite, you can press the SPACEBAR and the Treo will display all the phone numbers associated with the contact in your Contacts list. This means that instead of just having one number for the speed dial, you can access all the numbers. In order to enable this feature, the speed-dial Favorite must have been set up using the "lookup" feature.

Speed-dial favorites show up with a small phone beside them and a name. On the right side of each favorite button, you may also see a letter or number representing a key on the keyboard. To speed-dial a number, you can press and hold the key on the keyboard from the Phone screen to immediately begin dialing that number. You can also press the soft button on the interface of the Favorites screen to do the same. The Favorites screen only shows you fourteen of your favorites at a time (ten on the Treo 600), but at the bottom of the screen you will see five boxes numbered 1 through 5. Each of these boxes represents a different page of favorites. The page you are currently on is highlighted. You can move from page to page by tapping any page number with your stylus, or you can use the navigation control to move left or right through the pages.

To create a new speed-dial number, you can tap on any empty speed-dial button. This will open the Add Favorite screen, as shown in Figure 4-8.

The Type drop-down is where you will select the type of Favorite you are creating. This will default to be a speed dial, but you can change this to create a link to an application, web page, messaging number, call log, e-mail, or more.

The Label field is the label that you want to appear on the favorite soft button so that you can recognize it on the Favorite screen. There is a button labeled Lookup that will let you select a contact from your list of Treo contacts to fill in the label and number.

FIGURE 4-8   The Add Favorite screen is where you will create your new speed-dial number.

The Number field is the field that you want to speed-dial when this favorite is selected.

The Quick Key field is where you will select a single key from the keyboard that you want to define as the Quick Key for this favorite. This means that when the phone interface is up, if you press and hold this key on the keyboard, it will automatically speed-dial that number. For example, in Figure 4-7, you can see a speed dial defined as "Voicemail" with a Quick Key of "1." Pressing and holding 1 when the Treo is turned on will initiate the speed dial of a call to my voicemail box.

The More button on the bottom-right opens up a screen of extremely useful features, as shown in Figure 4-9.

The extra digits option is a feature that is extremely valuable for many uses. It allows you to choose specific digits that you want dialed in after the number is called. Two examples of how this might be used include the following:

- **Entering a password**   Some numbers when you call them require you to enter a password. For example, when you call your voicemail account, you might be prompted to enter your pass code and then press #. You can define a set of extra digits to perform this automatically. If your pass code was 7124, you could define extra digits of 7124# and then select the Dial Extra Digits Automatically check box to automatically authenticate with your voicemail system when you speed-dial the number.

- **Routing a call through an automated attendant**   Many organizations now use an automated attendant to answer calls. This is when the organization's telephone automatically picks up your call and tells you to press a specific button to connect to a department, or to dial the extension of the person you are trying to reach. If you wanted to speed-dial someone at an office number with an automated attendant, you could use the extra digits to dial their extension. For example, if you wanted to call someone at 555-6134 and then connect to extension 214, you would define extra digits of "214." The two commas are there to create a delay to allow the automated attendant to answer and get ready for the extension. Each comma creates a one-second pause before dialing the next digit. You can also use a "p" for a three-second pause.

FIGURE 4-9   The More Options screen allows you to define dialing of extra digits as part of the speed dial, as well as, on some models of Treo, define custom ringtones and a picture ID for this phone number.

The Ringtone and Image boxes are only available on older Treo models. Newer models allow you to set these options in the Contacts area. If you see these options in your window, then your device will allow you to define custom ringtones or picture IDs for calls from this number, as discussed in the following sections.

Two final things to be aware of for speed dialing are how to edit a defined speed- dial number and how to organize your Favorite numbers. To edit a favorite, use the five-way navigation control to highlight the button, and then use the stylus, or the MENU button, to open the menu and select the Edit Favorites Button menu item.

On the same menu, you will also see the Edit Favorites Pages menu item. Selecting this item will open the Edit Favorites Pages screen, as shown in Figure 4-10.

To move a defined Favorite button, tap and hold your stylus on the button. Then, without lifting the stylus from the screen, drag the button to the space where you want that button to appear. If that space is already occupied, your Treo will bump the existing button one button down. If the space you wish to move your Favorite to is on another page, then you can drag and hold your button on the icon at the bottom of the screen representing another page and wait. The Treo will then open that Favorites page and allow you to drop your button into any space on that page.

Tap the Done button when you are finished organizing your Favorites.

Manage, Set, and Download Ringtones

One of the fun and useful things about the Treo is the ability to set different ringtones for different types of callers. The advantage of this is that you can tell from the sound whether the person calling is your spouse, your boss, or someone else you know. Then you can choose whether to take your phone out of the case and answer, or not! You can also choose from a vast library of free ringtones to further personalize your Treo.

The standard format for ringtones is called MIDI, which is an acronym for Musical Instrument Digital Interface. The MIDI standard is convenient and compact, but it sounds mechanical on the

FIGURE 4-10   The Edit Favorites Pages screen allows you to reorganize your Favorites buttons into whatever order you like.

FIGURE 4-11   The Sound Preferences window lets you change the audible tones for the phone, including the volume, vibration, and ringtones.

Treo in comparison with popular sound formats such as MP3. With third-party software (discussed later in the section "Download New Ringtones"), you can use other sound formats for your ringtones, such as the popular MP3 format and .WAV files.

Set Ringtone Preferences

Ringtones are managed through Sound Preferences. You can navigate to Sound Preferences in two different ways. The first is by opening the menu and selecting Sound Preferences under Options. The keyboard shortcut for this is to press MENU and then W. This opens up the Sound Preferences window on the Treo 700p, as shown in Figure 4-11.

Note that this window will look somewhat different on the different Treo versions, but the functionality is largely the same. The older Treo versions split the functionality of this window into two windows, as shown in Figure 4-12.

FIGURE 4-12   The older Treo version provided the split the Sound Preferences into two windows that you navigate between by selecting Volume or Tones on the screen.

The second way to get to this interface is to choose the Preferences icon from the Application Launcher and then choose Sounds & Alerts from the available selections. On the Treo 600 this is done from the drop-down menu in the top-right corner of the screen.

For the Treo 700p, the Application drop-down box must have Ring Tones selected, or on the Treo 600 and 650, Phone selected to see the options for the phone; otherwise, you will be setting sound preferences for other Treo applications.

The Sound Preferences (ringtone options) screen lets you set a different ringtone for the following notification types:

- **Known Callers**   These are callers who are in your Contacts list on your Treo.
- **Unknown Callers**   For callers who aren't in your contact database.
- **Roaming Calls**   For calls that come in while you are roaming.

On the Treo 600 and 650 you can also select:

- **Voicemail**   This tone gets played when a new voicemail is received.
- **Service**   This tone sounds when your Treo successfully connects to your service provider for your phone service.

These options can also be changed on the Treo 700p, but this is done under the Phone Alerts selection of the Application drop-down. You will find the ability to set different tones for Voicemail, for In and Out of Coverage (called Service on the earlier Treos), and also for when the signal fades from your carrier.

Manage Ringtones

On the bottom-right corner of the Sound Preferences (ringtone options) screen, you will see a button labeled Manage. Tapping this button will open the Manage Sound screen, as shown in Figure 4-13.

This is the entire list of MIDI ringtones stored on your Treo. Selecting any tone in the list will cause it to play (or on the Treo 600 tapping the Play button after selecting a tone will accomplish this).

FIGURE 4-13   The Manage Sound screen lets you listen to ring tones, send them to others, or record your own.

The Send button will allow you to send the currently selected ringtone to another user either by beaming it, through Bluetooth (if your Treo is equipped with this), via e-mail, or through MMS.

The Details button (Edit button on the Treo 600) will open a window where you can change the name of the tone or choose to delete the tone.

Set Caller-Specific Ringtones

In addition to setting a ringtone for a specific type of caller, you can set a distinct ringtone for any caller you would like to identify immediately. You might set it to play "Hard to Say I'm Sorry" by Chicago when your spouse calls, "Take this Job and Shove It" by Johnny Paycheck when your boss calls, or whatever makes you happy!

The technique for doing this varies depending upon which Treo model you have. With the Treo 700p, you can open up any contact in your Contacts application; there you will find a field where you can select which of your ring tones you want to play if you receive a call from that caller.

To do this with your Treo 600 or 650 is rather nonintuitive. Instead of assigning a custom ringtone in the Contacts application, you have to do it in your speed-dial favorites. Thus, you are limited to a maximum of 50 numbers (the maximum number of speed-dial numbers you can define) for which you can define custom rings.

As discussed earlier, you will need to be on the Edit or Add Favorite screen to change to a custom ring for the specified number. Once on that screen, you can press the More button to open the More Options screen that was shown to you earlier in Figure 4-9. On this screen, the Ringtone drop-down allows you to select a custom MIDI ringtone to play when a call comes in from this number.

Download New Ringtones

You can easily download new ringtones to your Treo from third-party web sites. One popular web site for free MIDI ringtones is www.mididb.com. You can navigate to this web site using the built-in Blazer Web Browser, as discussed in Chapter 5. At this web site, you can select from a number of categories of music to find your favorite ringtone (although you have to wade through a number of advertisements). Once you have the song picked out, simply click the link in the web browser to begin downloading the song to your Treo. You will then be able to see the details of the file and confirm the download, as shown in Figure 4-14.

There may also be a web link in your Favorites from your carrier with links to their own database of downloadable ringtones. These may be free or may have a cost associated with them, so be sure to check your contract with your carrier before downloaded content, or you might get a nasty surprise on your bill!

FIGURE 4-14 New ringtones can easily be downloaded to your Treo through the web browser.

Record a Ringtone

On the Treo 650 and 700p you can also record your own ringtone right from the ringtone manager. You simply select New and press the record button to record up to one minute of your own sounds!

Associate a Picture with a Specific Caller

Another fun feature of the Treo is its capability to have a picture of a caller (or any other image that will jog your memory) show up in your screen when that person calls you. It can be a photo you've taken with the Treo, or you can sync pictures from your desktop over to the Treo to use. For example, when my coauthor Dayton calls me, on the screen a picture pops up of Dilbert talking on the phone.

As in the case of the ringtones, you set up this feature differently depending on which model of Treo you have. With the Treo 700p and 650 you select the picture in the Contacts folder as discussed in Chapter 10 of this book.

If you have the Treo 600, you can set up this picture ID function in the Favorites area the same way you set up a ringtone. In the same More Options window discussed in the ringtones section, you can select the check box to tell the Treo you want it to display a picture for this phone number. A button will appear labeled Select Image. When you tap the button, you will be able to select an image from the images taken by the camera. After selecting the image you want, a "thumbnail" (smaller version) of the image will appear next to the Image check box on the More Options screen. Tapping this image will allow you to select a different image.

If you want to use a picture other than the one taken with the camera, you can do this by moving the image on your PC to the Treo Pictures folder. When you installed the Treo software on your PC to enable syncing, you should have had a shortcut placed on your desktop automatically to Palm Desktop (or with earlier Treo models, Treo Pictures). On the 650 and 700p Palm has changed where pictures are stored. They are no longer in the Treo Pictures folder, since it was buried in the Palm Desktop User ID. They are now stored in the "My Pictures" Palm or Palmone Photos folder inside a user name folder. Putting an image in this folder will cause the image to be uploaded to your Treo on the next HotSync. Once on your Treo, you will be able to select it as a picture ID image.

When you place a figure into the Treo Pictures Transfer or My Pictures Palm folder, it should be uploaded to your Treo on the next HotSync. If it doesn't appear, check the Treo Pictures conduit settings in the HotSync manager to ensure it is set to Synchronize. For more information on setting custom conduits, refer to Chapter 3.

Prevent Unauthorized Calls with Call Barring

Call Barring is a feature from your wireless service provider that allows you to set restrictions on what kinds of calls you are allowed to make and receive. This service is not available from all service providers, so you will need to check with the carrier that you specifically connect with. The purpose of call barring is to allow you to stop unauthorized calls from reaching your Treo.

The types of calls you have control over will vary, depending on how your wireless service provider has decided to configure the service. Call-barring options are divided into two categories: outgoing and incoming. Some of the most common call-barring options include the following:

- Outgoing
  - **None** No outgoing calls are barred. Anyone using the phone can call anywhere in the world.
  - **All** No outgoing calls are allowed. The Treo cannot make any outgoing calls, even local.
  - **International** You cannot make calls to international numbers.
  - **International Except Calls Home** You cannot make calls to international numbers except for the number on record with the carrier as your home number.
- Incoming
  - **None** No incoming calls are barred. Anyone can call this Treo.
  - **All** You will not be able to receive any incoming calls on this Treo.
  - **Only When Roaming** You can receive calls when you are on your home network, but not when you are roaming on another service provider's network. For example, if your service provider is Cingular, you can only receive calls when your Treo is connected to the Cingular network. When you are roaming on the T-Mobile network, you will not be able to receive any calls.

In addition to these standards, various carriers will have different call-barring options. For example, if you purchased your Treo from Orange in the UK, your phone will come preconfigured to bar calls outside the UK or from Premium Numbers.

Call-barring options are set at the service provider and are usually protected by a password that has been set up by your carrier. If you do not know what that password is, you will need to call your carrier to get the password in order to make any changes to your Call Barring preferences.

To access your Call Barring preferences, from the main phone screen navigate to the menu. From the menu, under the Options menu item you will see an option called Call Barring. Selecting Call Barring will open the Call Barring screen, the Treo 600 version of which is shown in Figure 4-15.

| FIGURE 4-15 | The Call Barring preferences allow you to restrict what kinds of calls can be made or received on your Treo in order to prevent unauthorized use of the device. |

From this screen you can select the changes you want to make to your call-barring options. The first time you enter this screen, your Treo will contact your service provider automatically to download what your service provider's call-barring options and settings are. On subsequent visits to this screen, it will not. If your service provider has made changes in their call-barring settings that aren't reflected on your phone, you can select the Get Status button to update the cached information on your Treo. The Password button allows you to enter your carrier-provided password to authorize the call-barring changes you are making.

Prevent Accidental Calls with Keyguard

Have you ever had your phone ring, and picked it up, only to hear some background noise, maybe a car driving, and someone talking in the distance? I have had many of these calls. Someone sits on their phone, which causes some buttons to be pushed, and suddenly they are placing a call to someone and they don't even know it. In addition to being annoying to the person being called, this is costly to the caller as this eats through your airtime minutes and runs down your battery.

To prevent this, the Treo has a Keyguard feature. What the Keyguard does is prevent accidental dialing of your Treo. If you push any buttons on your Treo, you will see a small message that appears in the bottom of the screen.

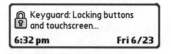

This message tells you that the Keyguard is active and that you must push the CENTER button in the middle of the navigation control in order to unlock the phone. The Keyguard will activate automatically after the phone has been off for 30 seconds. You can turn the Keyguard off or change its settings in the Preferences application under the Keyguard option, as shown in Figure 4-16. On this same screen, you can also disable the screen of the Treo so that you can't accidentally tap the screen and disconnect your call.

FIGURE 4-16   The Keyguard preferences will let you adjust the behavior of the Keyguard feature.

If you want to manually turn Keyguard on and power off the screen, you can do so by pressing the OPTION button (the blue button on the bottom-left of the keyboard) and the SCREEN button (the button to the far right of the five-way navigation control) at the same time.

One step beyond Keyguard is to implement a Power On password, which will challenge you to enter your password when your Treo is started up. This feature is covered in detail in Chapter 13.

Forward Your Calls

Call forwarding is a fairly standard phone feature from most wireless service providers, yet making it work has often been extremely difficult on mobile phone handsets. Often, this feature is never utilized by mobile phone users because of the challenge of having to remember obscure codes to begin or end forwarding, and advanced call-forwarding features, such as "transfer only when busy" or "transfer on no answer," are even more cryptic.

Luckily, the Treo makes this process remarkably easy to accomplish. If you want to set a call-forwarding number, you can do so on the Phone Preferences screen (referred to as Call Preferences on earlier Treo models), which is shown in Figure 4-17.

FIGURE 4-17   Forwarding calls is an easy feature to implement on the Treo.

The process to call-forward your phone is different on the Treo 700p than earlier models. On the 700p you open the Phone Preferences screen by navigating to the Phone Preferences menu item under the Options menu. The first drop-down lets you select which phone number you want to forward your calls to, or turn off the feature. The Edit option allows you to add new numbers to your list of possible call forward destinations. Options to do different things when busy or after a "no answer" condition don't currently exist.

On the Treo 600 and 650, the Call Preferences screen is opened by navigating to Call Preferences under the Options menu in the main phone interface. The first time you open this screen, your Treo will connect to your carrier to determine how your call-forwarding information is currently set. Very likely, your phone will be set to only call-forward when busy, or when there's no answer or no service. The number that you will see it call-forwarding to is for your voicemail on your phone (if your service plan includes a voice-mail option, that is; otherwise, these options will likely be set to "Don't Forward Calls").

The first drop-down selection field on the screen is labeled Forward All Calls. There are three options in this list, the first of which is Don't Forward Calls. When this option is selected, calls come to your Treo. The second thing you will see in the list are phone numbers. These are phone numbers that your Treo is aware of that you might want to forward all your calls to. Often, one of them is your voicemail number. Selecting that option means that no calls will come to your Treo; instead, they will all go directly to voicemail. This is useful if you are in a meeting and don't want your Treo vibrating or ringing and distracting you. I have added to my list my home phone and my office main phone line, allowing me to direct calls to those two locations when I choose. The final option in your list is Edit Numbers. When you select that option, the Edit Number dialog box will open.

This dialog box will display the entire list of numbers that you have entered as possible call-forwarding numbers. You can select any number in the list and edit it, or delete it. You can also add new possible call-forwarding numbers to the list by pressing the New button and filling in the number. All numbers you enter in this list will appear in the drop-down selection boxes in the Call Preferences screen as numbers that you can call-forward to.

In addition to the Forward All Calls option, you can select settings for what you would like to have happen with your call if your phone is busy, you don't answer it when it rings, or your Treo is off or not in a wireless service area. You can set different options for all three if you choose.

FIGURE 4-18   The Call Waiting feature issues a visual and audible alert to let you know a second call is coming in while you are on another call.

Manage Two Calls

Call waiting is a feature that you may, or may not, have on your calling plan with your service provider. If you are already on a call when another call comes in, you will hear an audible sound (if your ringer switch isn't set to vibrate) and a visual alert will show up on the screen of your Treo, as shown in Figure 4-18.

When the second call comes in, you can choose to answer it or ignore it with the buttons on your screen. If you ignore it, the call will either ring until the caller hangs up, or will transfer to whatever number you specified for your Call Forwarding When Not Answered option (discussed earlier). If you answer it, you will see on your screen both of the calls that you are currently connected to, as shown in Figure 4-19.

The call you are currently speaking with is shown as Active while the other call is shown as On Hold. The Active call will have a color phone icon next to it, while the On Hold call will have its icon grayed out.

FIGURE 4-19   When you are connected to two calls, you will see both calls on the screen of your Treo.

How to ... Block Your Outgoing Caller ID

If you don't want the people you are calling to be able to see your phone number on their phones when calling them, you can block your outgoing caller ID on the Call Preferences screen by checking the Block Outgoing Caller ID check box. This feature must be supported by your service provider and your particular Treo model in order for you to be able to do this. Some service providers charge a fee for this service.

There is a row of buttons on the bottom that will allow you to disconnect the Active call (or calls), switch to speakerphone mode, swap calls (puts the Active call On Hold and makes the previous On Hold call Active), or conference the calls (makes both calls active so all three parties can hear and speak with each other).

Remember that when you have two calls going, your wireless carrier will be charging you for the airtime for both calls, even if one of the calls is on hold!

If you do not want to have Call Waiting as a feature on your Treo, you can disable the feature in the Call Preferences screen by checking the Disable Call Waiting check box (if this is supported by your particular Treo model).

Customize the Look of Your Phone

One thing that almost every user likes to do with their phone is find some way to make it distinctively their own. In addition to custom ringtones, you can set up custom wallpaper to personalize the main screen of your phone. You can also use third-party software to change the appearance of the phone dialer and Favorites screen.

To change from showing the standard dial pad to showing a picture for your wallpaper, you can go to the Phone Display Preferences under the Options menu and change the Show Dial Pad drop-down to Show Wallpaper. A small image of default wallpaper will appear. Tapping this image will allow you to select from any photo or image on your device for your wallpaper as shown in Figure 4-20.

If you are moving an image to your phone to use as wallpaper, make sure that you resize it first. Your Treo will resize the image if it isn't quite right, but this will slow down your device performance. For the Treo 700p and 650, you should make your images 320×240 pixels. For the Treo 600, make them 160×120.

FIGURE 4-20 You can personalize your phone by selecting an image to be your custom wallpaper.

One third-party application that can really customize your phone is called Skinner from 79b Media (www.79bmedia.com). The Skinner application comes with three free "skins" to change the appearance of your phone.

You can also create your own skins with the Desktop Skinner application, and many free skins can be downloaded directly from the 79b Media web site.

Use External Headsets

Sometimes you may not want to hold your Treo up to the side of your head to make a call, and you don't want to use the speakerphone due to privacy concerns or background noise. In these situations, you can use an external headset. Another advantage of the external headset is that you can use your Treo to play games, take notes, or do other things, while in the middle of a call.

The Treo comes with an earbud-style headset that you can use right away. Since it's not the highest-quality headset, you may want to consider upgrading it to a better one if you use it frequently.

To use an external headset, simply plug it into the bottom headset jack of your Treo. The external speaker will automatically turn off, and all sound will now come through your headset. The microphone on the standard headset is built into the cord and will hang at the side of your face when the earbud is in your ear. On the microphone, there is also a small button that you can push to answer an incoming call or disconnect the call you are on.

Fortunately, the Treo uses the most common standard headset jack, a 2.5 mm headphone plug. This is a big advantage because you can buy headsets from a very large number of vendors. (Some of the vendor headsets that we tested for this book are detailed in Chapter 16.)

The Treo 650 and 700p models also support Bluetooth, which allows you to use wireless headsets. This is very convenient. For details on how to connect a Bluetooth headset, refer to Chapter 5.

One third-party headset mentioned in Chapter 16 is the retractable earbud from Zip Linq (www.zipling.com). Personally, I ruin three or four earbud-style headsets a year. This is because when you are not using them, they seem to miraculously tie themselves into knots in the glove box of your car. Headset cables that aren't in use seem to always be in the way. The Zip Linq retractable cable automatically winds the cord around a small, spring-loaded spool that conveniently tucks the cord away and reduces the headset to a very manageable size that is easy to store and carry around.

Set Dialing Preferences

Depending on which part of the world you live in, you will have different dialing preferences options you will want to set on your Treo. These dialing preferences allow you to adapt how the Treo behaves in certain dialing conditions. These preferences are really only relevant in North America; thus, the first check box on the Dial Preferences screen, as shown in Figure 4-21, is labeled North American Dialing.

In some regions in North America, you must dial the area code for your call even if it is a local call. You may have a lot of your contacts in this region with only seven-digit numbers, but due to changes from the carrier, you must dial a ten-digit number to reach them. If this is the case, on the Treo 700p you can elect to add additional digits whenever the dialer encounters a seven-, six-, five-, or four-digit number. These shorter ones are ideal if you are dialing someone at work and,

FIGURE 4-21   Dialing preferences can be set for North American customers to modify how numbers that are dialed out of your contacts list are handled.

for their phone number, you only have their extension listed. On the Treo 600 and 650, you can check the second check box that appears in the options window to add the three-digit area code for your region to the front of all seven-digit numbers. For example, if you live in Vancouver, you need to prefix all your seven-digit numbers with 604.

The other check box on the screen allows you to force the Treo to always dial a 1 in front of the area code. This is useful if you store the numbers in your Contacts list without the 1. The Treo will automatically add this for you. If it is a local call, most carriers are sophisticated enough to recognize this and drop the 1 (and area code, if applicable) when placing the call.

4

Wrap It Up

With the information in this chapter, you should now be comfortable using the advanced features of the Treo to maximize your voice communications with call forwarding, speed dialing, conference calling, and other sophisticated features. No more are you limited to just "dial" and "answer" functions!

Chapter 5 Connect Wirelessly

How to...

- Configure your Treo for wireless data
- Connect to the wireless cellular data network
- Connect your Treo using Bluetooth (Treo 650 and 700p models)
- Use Bluetooth to make your Treo 650 or 700p into a wireless modem for your laptop
- Connect your Treo using infrared
- Browse the Web
- Use Multimedia Messaging Service (MMS)
- Use Sprint Picture Mail
- Use Text Messaging
- Use third-party wireless applications
- Find helpful Treo-specific web sites

The most useful and, arguably, the most interesting features of your Treo involve wireless connectivity. Obvious examples include using the phone, sending and receiving e-mail, and browsing the Web, but there are many other things you can do using the wireless capabilities of your Treo. This chapter includes topics such as configuring your Treo for wireless connectivity, and using Multimedia Messaging Service (MMS), Sprint Picture Mail, and Text Messaging / Short Message Service (SMS). It also contains a listing of other wireless options and third-party wireless applications designed for your Treo.

Wireless and Nonwireless Modes

Your Treo essentially uses two independent modes: Organizer mode and Wireless mode (phone, Text Messaging, e-mail, web browsing). While the Wireless mode is turned off, you can still use all of the functions that don't require wireless connectivity, such as the organizer, contact list, calendar, music, and so on. One reason that you may want to leave the Wireless mode off when not using it is that it significantly improves how long you can go without recharging your Treo battery. Another advantage of being able to turn the Wireless mode off is that you can continue to use the nonwireless features on an airplane where Wireless mode may interfere with the airplane navigation systems.

Multitasking: Use Nonwireless Applications While Talking on the Phone

You have complete access to all of your other applications, except those that use the serial library during a call, such as another wireless application. Therefore, you can view your calendar, enter an appointment, write a note, create a To Do item, take a picture, or enter contact information in your address book, all while talking on the phone. Being able to multitask in this way is even more valuable if you are using a phone headset or are using the speakerphone functionality (covered in Chapter 3), so that you can continue talking on the phone while working on your Treo. The caveat to multitasking on your Treo is that you cannot simultaneously make voice calls and use wireless data. For example, you can't talk on the phone and browse the Internet at the same time.

NOTE   *On most Treo models, if you receive a phone call on your Treo while you are using it to browse the Web or read your e-mail, you will receive an alert on the screen that allows you to choose between answering the call and sending it directly to voicemail. Whatever wireless functions you were using when you received the call will be disconnected until you have finished using the phone. The exception is that if you have a Treo 600 or 650 on a CDMA network (Sprint/Verizon, Alltel, etc.), while you are using wireless data all incoming calls will go straight to voicemail.*

Turn the Phone and Wireless Data Off

The state of the Wireless mode determines whether you can connect to a mobile network to make and receive phone calls and use other wireless services like e-mail or web browsing.

- **Treo 650 and 700p**   To turn the phone on, press and hold the POWER/END button.
- **Treo 600**   To turn the Wireless mode on, press and hold the Wireless Mode button, until you hear a series of ascending tones indicating Wireless mode has been activated.

When Wireless mode is on, your Treo connects to a mobile network, allowing you to use the phone and Internet features (your wireless service provider must support data services, however). Press and hold the Wireless Mode button again to turn off Wireless mode. A series of descending tones will sound. When Wireless mode is off, your Treo does not have a connection to any mobile network. You can still use the organizer and other Palm OS features. This is ideal for airplane flights and for maximizing battery life, since leaving the connection open uses more battery power.

Get Connected

One of the most compelling reasons why many of us purchase the Treo in the first place is the wireless data capability. This section covers wireless data topics such as ensuring that you have the appropriate contract with your wireless service provider (WSP), browsing the Internet, and sending MMS and Text Messaging messages using your Treo.

Using Wireless E-Mail, Web Browsing, and Data Applications on Your Treo

Your Treo is essentially two devices in one: a cell phone and a wireless computer. The wireless computer component of your Treo requires different wireless services than the phone. It is important to understand that a WSP (the company you pay to use your Treo phone) tends to view wireless voice and wireless data services as separate. Ideally, both your service contract and Treo were set up correctly when you purchased your Treo and you are immediately able to use the mobile phone and take advantage of advanced features like Text Messaging and MMS (used for taking and sending digital photos and downloading ringtones, for example), e-mail, and the Internet. However, not all WSPs offer data services, and some WSPs, though they do offer them, do not automatically include such data services in your phone plan.

Make sure that your service contract includes data services and that they have been activated. Some providers separate data services into Internet, MMS, and Text Messaging functions, so you should make sure each one is included in your plan in order to take advantage of all the features offered by your Treo. Some of the brand names for data services are listed in the next section.

 Your Treo does not need or utilize WAP service, so if your WSP offers it as an optional charge, decline it.

Brand Names for Wireless Data Services

When dealing with a WSP—also known as a *carrier*—it is helpful to be aware that each has its own names associated with its wireless data services. Examples include the following:

- Cingular: Data Connect
- Fido-GPRS: GPRS Access
- Rogers AT&T: GPRS Data Access
- Sprint PCS: 1xRTT- PCS Vision
- Nextel: Web Plan
- Verizon: NationalAccess, BroadbandAccess, or PDA/Smartphone E-Mail
- T-Mobile: Wireless data and text/instant messages

What if My WSP Does Not Offer Wireless Internet Service?

Although this has become rare, some WSPs offer wireless data but not wireless Internet. If your WSP does not offer wireless Internet service for your Treo, you may also need an Internet service provider (ISP). Confusing? Well, the reason for this is that some WSPs offer data services (the ability to send/ receive data wirelessly) but do not act as a gateway to the Internet. In such cases, you may need to use a separate ISP to access the Internet with your Treo.

Another solution is to change your service contract to another WSP that offers full voice, data, and Internet service. However, this may not be a realistic option if you live in an area where coverage is only offered by a WSP, or if you are locked into a long-term contract, or if your Treo is "SIM-locked" and thus permanently linked to a particular WSP.

How Do I Know if I Am Connected to a Wireless Network?

There are a series of icons that appear on the upper right-hand corner of your Treo screen that indicate the current state of wireless connectivity. Each carrier has a different set of icons, so check your user guide to find out what each icon means. Fortunately, most of the icons are relatively obvious.

Of course, the easiest way to check whether you have Internet access is to launch the Blazer Web Browser to see if you can view a web page. To launch the built-in Blazer Web Browser:

1. Open the Applications Launcher screen by pressing the HOME button.

2. Find and launch the web icon, which looks like a globe.

3. The browser is likely already set up to go to the Palm web site or carrier portal, but you can choose another web site that you know will be there by selecting the globe icon at the top of the screen (Treo 700p/650) or the WWW button on the bottom of the screen (Treo 600) and entering a web site address.

If you are unable to connect to the Internet, there are two things to check:

- ■ Your wireless service contract, to ensure that you have wireless data and Internet service.

- ■ Your network settings, to ensure that your Treo is correctly configured for wireless data.

Configure Your Wireless Network Settings

Your network settings are specific to your WSP (the company that provides your wireless connectivity, such as Sprint, Cingular, or T-Mobile). In fact, your Treo may already be configured for wireless data connectivity. To check the settings or enter new information, access the Network Preferences screen shown in Figure 5-1. To do this, follow these steps:

1. Press the HOME button to open the Applications Launcher. Keep pressing the HOME button until you see the System screen.

2. Find and select Prefs.

3. Select the network button on the screen. (On a 600, select menu in the top right-hand corner of the screen.)

4. From the menu list, select Network.

FIGURE 5-1   Treo network settings

If the network data is blank and you don't have the information, you will have to contact your WSP to get the necessary information. Many of the WSPs list some of this information on their support web sites.

Browse the Web

Once you are connected to the data network and to the Internet, you can use your Treo to browse the Internet. The Internet originated in the 1960s but has only become a commonplace facet of our culture in the last 10 or 15 years, revolutionizing communication and the sharing of ideas and information. The Web has also significantly altered commerce. Many companies and retail outlets would not consider doing business without a web site and e-mail. Entire books have been written about the impact that the Internet has had on the world, and needless to say, the ability to browse the Web on a Treo can be tremendously useful.

Use the Blazer Web Browser

Your Treo was shipped with a built-in web browser called the Blazer Web Browser, which you can use to surf the Internet. Several third-party browsers are available for your Treo. A list of available browsers is shown later in this chapter. For many users, however, the Blazer browser not only provides great functionality but also has the added benefit of residing in read-only memory (ROM), thus preventing it from using up any user-available memory as third-party web browsers would. The section "Blazer Web Browser-Supported Media Types" at the end of this chapter describes the technical, download, and media capabilities of Blazer.

Blazer Browser Basics

The Blazer Web Browser on your Treo provides an easy way to access and view web pages. The first generation of mobile web browsers was somewhat limited. Many of the first browsers designed for mobile devices required adherence to WAP (the Wireless Application Protocol) and could not handle features like JavaScript or frames. This meant that many web sites were either not accessible at all, or were less than perfectly user friendly. The Treo Blazer Web Browser belongs to the latest and greatest of mobile browsers. Now you can use your Treo to view all web sites, including sites with security and even advanced features like JavaScript and frames.

Use Blazer to View a Web Page

To view a web page with the Blazer Web Browser, follow these steps:

1. Ensure that the phone is on.
2. Select the HOME button to open the Applications Launcher.
3. Find and select the Web icon (Blazer on the Treo 600) from the list of applications.
4. Your Blazer browser likely is configured to open the Palm web site, or your carrier's web site, by default. If a page doesn't load automatically, choose the Home icon at the bottom of the screen.

5. To view a specific web page in Blazer, select the address field and begin typing, www.google.com, for example. (On the Treo 600, select the globe icon and enter a web site URL address that you would like to view.)

View Web Pages in Wide and Optimized Modes

Most web pages are not properly formatted for the smaller screens on mobile devices. Web pages are generally designed for much larger displays—at least 800×600 pixels—and layouts do not take into account the idiosyncrasies of mobile devices and the latency of wireless networks. The Blazer Web Browser, in addition to some other mobile browsers, has implemented ways to improve your wireless web browsing experience. An innovation that drastically improves wireless browsing is the Blazer Web Browser Optimized mode.

Optimized Mode   The Blazer Web Browser uses patent-pending technology designed to optimize web pages for your Treo screen. Most web pages are formatted for viewing on a much larger PC screen than your Treo screen.

The default Blazer browser mode is called Optimized mode, which reformats web pages into one column to make best use of your Treo screen real estate. This means that viewing web pages in Optimized mode reduces the amount of scrolling you have to do to see information on the screen. A side effect of this feature is that web pages with rich graphical content tend to look a little like Picasso portraits.

Wide Mode   Depending on the type of web page you are viewing and how you want to interact with the page, you may also view web pages in the Blazer Wide mode. An example of a page that you would likely want to view in Wide mode is a page that includes an image of a map that is wider than 160 pixels. Wide mode means that no formatting of web pages is done on your behalf and the page is presented the same way it would look on a desktop PC. But, because your Treo screen has a 160×160 pixel screen and web pages are generally designed for much larger screens, you will have to scroll around both vertically and horizontally to see all of the content on a particular web page.

Change Between Optimized and Wide Modes   You can choose to view a web page in either Optimized or Wide Page mode by simply toggling between the two settings. The settings can be found under the Blazer Page menu (in the Blazer application, press the MENU button and select Options), as shown in Figure 5-2.

FIGURE 5-2   Blazer Optimized mode menu item

Move Around a Web Page with Blazer

When viewing a web page using Blazer, you can navigate the links and menus in much the same way you would using a desktop PC browser. To follow a link to another web page, you can do either of the following:

- Tap the link on the touch screen with your stylus.
- Navigate the screen with the five-way navigation control—move around until the link is highlighted and select it by pressing the center of the five-way navigation control. Using the five-way navigation control for navigation can be a challenge until you get used to how the cursor moves around the screen (use left and right instead of up and down). Once you get the hang of it, it's a great way to navigate the Web using only one hand.

Create a Bookmark

Blazer Bookmarks are similar to the favorites concept in PC-based web browsers. Bookmarks allow you to store web site addresses and quickly access pages without retyping the URL. Blazer allows you to store up to 100 Bookmarks. To create a Bookmark, follow these steps:

1. Browse to the web page you want to bookmark (for example, www.google.com).
2. Press Menu.
3. From the Page menu, choose Add Bookmark.
4. Now, whenever you want to view www.google.com, all you have to do is switch the view to Bookmarks and select the Google bookmark. This saves a lot of thumb typing, especially when dealing with long web site addresses.

Save a Web Page for Offline Viewing

Occasionally, you may want to save a web page to your Treo. For example, here are a couple of common scenarios:

- You want to capture and save the information on the web page for reference purposes (such as a symphony orchestra concert schedule).
- You don't have time to read a particular web page, and you want to save it so you can read it at a later time without having to download it again.

To save a particular web page, do the following:

1. Browse to a web page using the Blazer browser, or if you are already looking at the page you want to save, press the MENU button.
2. From the Page menu, select Save Page.

3. A dialog box will appear called New Saved Page Bookmark, where you can type in a Name and a Description for the page to help you identify it later. The Preview at the bottom allows you to see how the Bookmark will look after you have saved the page. Obviously, keeping the Name and the Description text short so that it is visible and helpful when later looking for the Bookmarks is beneficial.

4. After saving the page, you can access it at any time from your Bookmarks view.

View Bookmarks or Saved Pages

After you have created Bookmarks and saved web pages, you can access them both on the Bookmarks view in Blazer, as shown in Figure 5-3. You can access your Bookmarks view from the Blazer main screen by pressing the icon that's second from the left at the bottom of the screen, or by pressing the MENU button and selecting Bookmarks View from the Page menu.

Saved web pages, as opposed to bookmarked web pages, are indicated in the Bookmarks view by a small triangle in the upper-right corner of the bookmark.

Edit or Delete Bookmarks   You may edit or delete bookmarks as your needs change by following these steps from the Bookmarks view screen:

1. Press the MENU button.

2. From the Bookmarks menu, choose the Edit Bookmarks option.

3. Choose the bookmark you want to edit or delete.

4. Enter the desired changes to the bookmark, including Name, Description, or URL.

5. Select OK.

Arrange Your Bookmarks and Saved Pages   Blazer allows you to store up to 100 bookmarks and saved web pages. The Bookmarks view consists of ten pages containing ten bookmarks. Because you have ten different pages of bookmarks to work with, this enables you to organize your bookmarks in any way that makes sense to you so that you can find what you are looking for quickly. For example, one page may include financial web sites, one page may include weather sites, or you may put a list of Hot Dog Eating Contest web pages, and associated sites, on one bookmark page—the point is, you can arrange your bookmarks into whatever groupings makes sense to you. To arrange your bookmarks, follow these steps:

1. From the Bookmarks view, press the MENU button.
2. From the Bookmarks menu, choose the Edit Bookmarks option.
3. Type a title for this page—Hot Dog Eating Contests, for example.
4. Use your stylus to drag and drop bookmarks into different positions on the current bookmark page.
5. You can move a bookmark to a different page by dragging and dropping it on the appropriate page icon.
6. When you are finished arranging your bookmarks, select OK.

Download Files from a Web Page

The Blazer browser allows you to download files that you can use on your Treo, such as applications, images, sounds, documents, and others. Any file that is downloaded to your Treo is automatically associated with the application that can open and use the file.

To download a file from the Internet, whether an application, image, or another type, follow these steps:

1. Browse to the page that contains the link to the file you want to download.
2. Highlight the link using the five-way navigation control, or tap the screen and press CENTER on the five-way navigation control to begin the download process.

Remember that large files may take several minutes to download over the wireless network. For large files, you may want to download them onto your PC and then load them onto your Treo using HotSync. If you have a Treo 700p, it is capable of faster networking speeds than previous Treo models, so the download speeds will be significantly better.

Navigate Web Sites with Split Pages—Frames

Some web sites use a type of navigation and screen layout called *frames*. A web page that uses frames splits the web page content into multiple separate areas on the screen, and each area has its own set of scroll bars. Blazer allows you to "zoom in" to a specific frame on a web page to make it easier to view the content. To zoom in to one particular framed area, follow these steps:

1. Load the web page that contains frames in the Blazer browser.
2. Tap the screen inside the area frame that you want to get a better view of. (Don't tap on a link, or you'll end up jumping to wherever that link is pointed.)

3. Tap the magnifying glass icon located in the button bar on the bottom of the screen. Note that the magnifying glass icon appears in the button bar only if the current page you are viewing consists of frames.

4. After you tap the magnifying glass icon, only the selected frame will be visible. To return to the full-page view, tap the icon again.

Copy Text from a Web Page

Chapter 2 covered how to cut, copy, and paste text on your Treo in order to move and copy text between applications and documents. The same basic logic applies here as well.

1. Use your stylus to highlight the text you want to copy.

2. Press the MENU button.

3. From the Edit menu, choose the Copy option.

4. Now, browse to the application, document, e-mail, and so on where you want to paste the copied text.

5. Place the cursor where you want to paste the text.

6. Press MENU again.

7. From the Edit menu, choose the Paste option.

View Your History of Previously Viewed Web Pages

The Blazer Browser stores a record of the web pages you have visited previously. This provides an easy way to help you find pages quickly. You can even add a page in your History list to your Bookmarks by selecting the web page from the list and tapping the Bookmark button.

Send a Web Page Address to Another Person Using Text Messaging

If you find a web page that you would like to share with a friend or business acquaintance, you have a few different options. You can copy the web page address (for example, www.webpage.com) using the steps outlined in the section "Copy Text from a Web Page" in this chapter and paste it into an e-mail, or you can send it using Text Messaging, which is covered in greater detail in the section "Text Messaging (SMS)" later in this chapter. If you are not familiar with Text Messaging, you may want to read that section before continuing with this one. Assuming that you know all about Text Messaging, here are the steps to send a web page address to another person using Text Messaging:

1. Using Blazer while viewing the web page you want to send to another person, press the MENU button.

2. From the Page menu, select Send Page Address.

3. Your Treo will create a new Text Message containing the web page address.

4. Enter the phone number of the person you want to send the address to, along with any text or smiley faces that you like, and select Send.

Find Text on a Web Page

Sometimes scrolling around a web page looking for a particular word or phrase, especially on a page with a large amount of text, can be a slow and tedious process, not to mention hard on the eyes. Fortunately, Blazer comes equipped with a search tool to allow you to quickly find what you are looking for. The steps to search a page are as follows:

1. In Blazer, if you haven't already, load/view the web page you want to search.

2. Press the MENU button, and from the Page menu, select Find Text on Page.

3. In the dialog box, type the word or phrase you're looking for and select Find.

*When searching for text in a web page, the text you enter for Blazer to find can be incomplete. For example, if you are searching for the word "Nostradamus," typing **ostra** in the Find dialog box would probably find the Nostradamus text because "ostra" is likely unique; but, in general, the more precise you are in your search, the better your chances of finding the information you want.*

Dial Your Phone Using a Phone Number on a Web Page

This handy feature leverages two unique capabilities of your Treo. It combines using information from the Web to directly dial your phone, and it does it seamlessly. Phone numbers displayed on web pages show up as underlined hyperlinks, as shown in Figure 5-4. When you select the link, a dialog box pops up, as shown in Figure 5-5; just select the Dial button on the screen, and the phone number is dialed. Isn't that a nice way to combine the wireless Web with a wireless phone?

Online phone directories make this feature even more convenient. Most phone companies offer their phone directories online, so you can easily use your web-browsing capabilities to dial your phone for you. Call me lazy; it's still a great feature.

Configure Your Blazer Preferences

The types of browser settings you can define include establishing your default home page, defining whether or not images are shown on web pages, and how you want Blazer to handle cookies and memory management. These topics, and a few others, are covered next.

FIGURE 5-4 Phone number link

FIGURE 5-5   Dial phone link

Set Your Default Home Page

Your Home page is the web page that opens when you launch Blazer and when you tap the Home button in the Blazer button bar. To set your Home page, follow these steps:

1. Launch Blazer.
2. Press the MENU button on the keyboard.
3. From the Options menu, select Preferences.
4. Select the Home Page field and enter the URL for your Home page.
5. Select OK.

Set a Limit on Memory for Storing Recently Viewed Pages

Blazer, like any other web browser, stores web page information so that when you return to a web page at a later time it doesn't need to download all of the images and text again. Blazer simply reuses the information that was stored the first time you viewed the page. This allows the pages to load faster. The place where web page files and information are stored on your Treo is called the *web cache*. Memory management can be an issue on resource-constrained devices such as your Treo. So, within Blazer you can decide how much memory you want to allocate to Blazer. To view and change the cache size, follow these steps:

1. Launch Blazer.
2. Press the MENU button on the keyboard.
3. From the Options menu, select Preferences.
4. Select the Advanced button. The Advanced Preferences page should appear, as shown in Figure 5-6.

FIGURE 5-6   Blazer cache

5. Next to Set Limit on Memory for Storing Recently Viewed Pages (Cache), you will see the amount of memory currently set aside for the Blazer web page cache. You can change the number if you want:

- If you are running out of memory on your Treo, you will want to reduce this number.

- If you find that you do a lot of web browser work and memory is not a problem, you may want to increase the number.

6. Select OK.

To ensure that the web browser cache is taking up minimal valuable memory on your Treo 650 or 700p, you can set the cache to be deleted every time Blazer exits. This is configurable on the Menu | Options | Preferences | Advanced tab.

Set a Proxy Server—Advanced

Many Internet accounts require that your Treo connect to a proxy server. If this is the case, you can define the proxy setting by selecting the Set Proxy button. The information needed to define your proxy includes the following:

- **Proxy Server address**   Usually an IP address in the form of 10.10.10.1.
- **Port number**   The default is 80, but you may change it if necessary.

This information needs to be provided by your Internet service provider, so contact your Internet service provider or IT administrator to find out what settings to use.

Set Whether Blazer Should Accept Cookies

Selecting the Accept Cookies check box allows some web sites to store personalized information on your Treo. Some sites do not work properly unless you select this option.

5

NOTE

If you are a savvy web user, you may already know that web cookies are files that some web sites send to your browser for storage. These files are intended to make your browsing experience better by allowing the web site to store information about you or your preferences on your Treo. Some web sites require that your browser accept cookies.

Other Web Browsers for Your Treo

Your Treo ships with the Blazer Web Browser already installed. The Blazer is a great browser, and it is worth mentioning that you also have other browser options. This section lists a couple of the more common browsers and discusses the difference between online and offline browsers.

NOTE

When considering third-party web browsers, it is important to pay attention to the amount of memory a particular browser application requires to install and run. Some third-party browsers use significantly more memory than others, and this means that you will have to be more conscious of memory management and that you may experience decreased performance.

Types of Web Browsers—Online and Offline

Two types of web browsers are available for your Treo. The Blazer Web Browser is what is known as an "online" browser. This means that the browser accesses the Internet in real time using the wireless network to download web pages.

Web browsers of the second type of are called—what else?—"offline" browsers. Offline browsers are designed to allow you to download web pages from your PC during the HotSync process and then save them on your Treo so that you can view them at any time without needing to connect to the Internet. There are a couple of significant advantages to the offline variety, stored Internet pages and information are immediately available without requiring a live connection to the Internet, and viewing pages is obviously faster because they're stored locally on your Treo. For example, you can download web pages using HotSync in order to browse them later on an airplane where you can't use your wireless connection. Offline browsers are also advantageous for storing pages you need to access on a regular basis. Many online browsers also allow you to save web pages for offline viewing. Need both an online and offline browser? Nothing says you can't use both.

Some of the online browsers available include the following:

- Xiino, formerly PalmScape (www.ilinx.co.jp)
- EudoraWeb (www.eudora.com)
- PocketLink (www.mdevelop.com)

The following are a few of the offline browsers available:

- AvantGo (www.avantgo.com)
- Plucker (www.plkr.org)
- HandStory (http://handstory.com)

Use Bluetooth on Your Treo 650 or 700p

Palm added Bluetooth technology to the Treo 650 and 700p models, but unfortunately, the Treo 600 does not have a Bluetooth radio. Bluetooth wireless technology is a short-range wireless standard and specification sometimes called a PAN (personal area network) that is intended to replace the multitude of cables that connect digital devices together. Palm, among many other product manufacturers, has built Bluetooth into their products. In doing so, Palm produced the Bluetooth-enabled Treo in compliance with the industry standard. However, it is important to keep in mind that each product manufacturer tends to integrate Bluetooth in its own unique way, although you can usually get two Bluetooth devices from different manufacturers to "talk." These are some of the technical details of the Bluetooth standard:

- Bluetooth is an open standard governed by the Bluetooth Special Interest Group (SIG).
- The majority of mobile devices are Class II devices that have a range of up to 33 feet.
- The most commonly supported Bluetooth specifications are Bluetooth versions 1.1 and 1.2.
- One of the advantages of Bluetooth is that it requires very low power. It uses less than 1 milliwatt, which is important for your Treo battery.
- Bluetooth operates in the 2.4 GHz frequency band, also known as the Industrial Scientific Medical Band (in case you were wondering).

As Bluetooth is a short-range wireless network, the most common uses for Bluetooth on mobile devices such as your Treo include using Bluetooth headphones to talk on the phone and listen to audio without wires; printing to a Bluetooth-capable printer; connecting to a PC to transfer files or to synchronize; and connecting to keyboards, mobile phones, and Global Positioning System (GPS) kits.

Bluetooth Terminology

Many technologies have specific terminology to describe unique concepts, and Bluetooth is no exception. In this section, we will discuss some of the Bluetooth concepts and terms that are important to understand. Many of these concepts will be discussed in more detail later on.

- **Authentication** Verification of a numeric passkey, a similar concept to a password, needed before a connection can be made.
- **Authorization** The process of approving a connection or activity before it can proceed.
- **Bonding** The process of creating a trusted connection between two Bluetooth devices; after a bond is created, the two devices are "paired."
- **Device address** The unique electronic address of a Bluetooth-capable device.
- **Device discovery** The wireless process of searching for other Bluetooth devices; your Treo must be enabled for discovery to allow other Bluetooth devices to find your Treo and to allow your Treo to find other devices within range.

■ **Device name**   The name that is provided by a Bluetooth device when it is discovered by another Bluetooth device. You can configure your Treo with whatever device name you want—for example, Michelle's Treo.

■ **Devices in range**   During discovery, a Bluetooth-capable Treo searches an area of no more that 33 feet. It is also important to know that some Bluetooth devices have less range. Check your product documentation for specifications.

■ **Devices not found**   You will see this error message when no Bluetooth devices are discovered within the 33-foot range.

■ **Discoverable mode**   In order for another Bluetooth device to find and connect to it, your Treo must be in discoverable mode.

■ **Pairing**   If you intend to use two Bluetooth-capable devices together on a regular basis, it is a good idea to pair the devices so that you don't have to reenter authentication information every time you want them to connect. For example, if you plan to use a Bluetooth-capable printer with your Treo on a regular basis, pairing allows you to save the device name, passkey, and other information to enable the devices to automatically connect when you need them to. Some types of Bluetooth devices such as Bluetooth headsets require pairing in order to connect at all.

■ **Personal identification number (PIN) or passkey**   A PIN can be required to authenticate incoming connections in the process of pairing two Bluetooth devices. This helps prevent unauthorized Bluetooth devices from connecting to your Treo without your knowledge.

■ **Profile (service)**   In Bluetooth, a *profile* is the technical definition of how a device manufacturer must implement Bluetooth wireless technology for a particular user scenario. For practical user purposes, profiles and services are essentially the same thing. In order for two Bluetooth-capable devices to connect and function, both devices must offer the same profile. This topic is covered in more detail next in this chapter, under the heading "Bluetooth Pairing vs. Bluetooth Profiles."

Bluetooth Pairing vs. Bluetooth Profiles

The concepts of pairing and profiles can be a little confusing, but they each serve a specific purpose. Pairing, also known as bonding, is a concept that was introduced to create a first-time recognition of which devices are allowed to communicate with each other. The initial pairing process is required to allow each Bluetooth device to recognize the other and begin communicating. It is a security feature embedded in Bluetooth that effectively prevents a nonauthorized Bluetooth device from connecting to your Treo. Now, profiles are different: every Bluetooth-capable device such as a printer, laptop, or headset supports specific Bluetooth profiles. A profile is a unique way to describe the Bluetooth functionality of different devices. The Bluetooth wireless technology is used for many different types of applications, and it is necessary to describe how the different devices and their applications should connect and function together. This description is called a profile. The supported profiles will be listed in the user manual for each device. For example, a Bluetooth mouse that supports the HID (Human Interface Device) profile will not work with your Treo because Treos do not currently support HID. It is important to ensure that whichever Bluetooth device you want to connect your Treo to supports at least one profile that is the same as your Treo.

The Treo 700p features a handy security feature, the ability to leave the Treo in discoverable mode for a short time period. When you set the device visibility to Temporary, your Treo will remain discoverable for only two minutes.

Make a Bluetooth Connection with Your Treo 650 or 700p

One of the most common uses of Bluetooth on a Treo is the use of Bluetooth headphones and headsets. The process of connecting your Treo to another Bluetooth-capable device is essentially the same regardless of what kind of Bluetooth device you want to connect your Treo to. For example purposes, we will go through the process of connecting a Bluetooth headset to your Treo. If you don't have a Bluetooth headset and want one, Palm (www.Palm.com) offers a model that matches perfectly with their Treo so you won't have to worry about incompatibilities.

Connect a Bluetooth Headset to Your Treo 650 or 700p

Bluetooth headsets are a great idea, and you will know what we mean if you have ever used a wired headset and had the unfortunate experience of getting the cord caught on something as you moved around.

To begin this process, you need to ensure that the Bluetooth radio is turned on. If the Bluetooth radio is on, the Bluetooth icon will be shown at the top of most of the screens, as shown in Figure 5-7.

Ensure that your Treo Bluetooth is on and visible/discoverable. If your Bluetooth radio is off, follow these steps to turn it on:

1. Press the HOME button to view the applications screen (you may need to press the HOME button more than once to bring up the Application screen).

2. Find and select the Bluetooth icon.

3. Ensure that the On button is selected, as shown in Figure 5-8.

4. Also, ensure that your Treo is visible by selecting the Visibility drop-down list and selecting the Visible option. (On a Treo 650 this is accomplished by changing the Discoverable option to Yes.)

FIGURE 5-7   Bluetooth icon

FIGURE 5-8   Turn Bluetooth on.

TIP   *If you initiate a Bluetooth pairing session from your Treo 700p/650 instead of the Bluetooth device that you want to connect to, your Treo does not need to be in discoverable mode. This feature helps minimize security risks.*

Palm Treo Bluetooth Headset Example

Depending on the brand and model of Bluetooth headset you will be using, the steps to put it into discoverable mode may be different, so it is important to read your product documentation. For example purposes we will discuss the Palm Treo Bluetooth headset that can be purchased directly from Palm (www.palm.com). To pair your Treo with a Palm Treo Bluetooth headset, follow these steps:

1. Put the headset into discoverable mode. To do so, press the multifunction (MF) key for eight seconds until the blue indicator light illuminates and stays on. Don't release the button when the light begins to flash, keep pressing it until the light is solid.

2. Initiate pairing:

   a. On your Treo, launch the Bluetooth screen, if you haven't already (Applications | Bluetooth) and select the Setup Devices button at the bottom of the screen to launch the screen shown in Figure 5-9. There, select the Hands-free Setup button.

   b. Click the Next button to start your Treo searching for Bluetooth devices in the area with the objective of finding the Bluetooth headset. If your headset is not in discoverable mode, your Treo will not be able to find it.

   c. Once the headset has been "found" it will show up on a Discovery Results page. Select the Treo Headset in the "Select a handsfree device" list and select the OK button.

   d. You will be prompted to enter a passkey. The passkey for your particular headset will be on your user documentation. If you don't have the user documentation, try entering four zeros—0000—as the passkey. If all has went as it should, your Treo will now be paired and connected to your headset.

FIGURE 5-9   Bluetooth—Set up Devices

To check to see if your Treo is paired with your Palm Bluetooth headset, press the Multifunction key and the headset will test the connection with your Treo.

More about Bluetooth: Configuring and Connecting

Your Treo user documentation covers a lot of ground regarding Bluetooth, so we'll just talk about the things you are most likely going to need to configure.

■ **Change the Bluetooth Device Name on your Treo**   You want to use a different name for Bluetooth than your Treo device name. To change it, open the Applications Launcher by pressing the HOME button and then Find. Select the Bluetooth icon and then the Device Name field. Type in a new name and select OK. That's it. Now that name will show up when another Bluetooth device detects your Treo.

If you know that the Bluetooth device that you want to connect to is within the 33-foot range and you still get the Devices Not Found error message or no devices show up in the Bluetooth browser, the device may not be in discoverable mode. If it is in discoverable mode, there is a small possibility there is interference from other radio devices using the same radio frequency. Devices such as microwave ovens, some cordless telephones, and certain wireless LAN products, among other things, can interfere with Bluetooth. If you can, turn off these devices and try the discovery again.

■ **Put your Treo into discoverable mode**   It is a good idea to leave discoverable mode turned off on your Treo to help avoid unwanted connections. However, if you need to turn discoverable mode on, open the Applications Launcher by pressing the HOME button and find, select the Bluetooth icon, and change the Discoverable drop-down list to Yes, as shown in Figure 5-10.

FIGURE 5-10 Set Bluetooth to discoverable mode

Synchronize Your Treo 650 or 700p with Your PC Using a Bluetooth Connection

More and more Treo users are taking wireless to the next level. Not only can you use your Treo as a wireless device to connect to carrier networks but you can also connect your Treo to your PC using wireless technology. For this purpose we are talking about Bluetooth technology. Some technical details and technology-specific jargon are discuss earlier in this chapter, so let's get right to the steps of setting up a Bluetooth sync connection between your Treo 650 or 700p and a Bluetooth-capable PC. Follow these steps:

1. As discussed earlier, ensure that the Bluetooth functionality is turned on for both your PC and your Treo.

2. On your Treo, press the HOME button to get to the Application screen. You may need to press the button more than once.

3. Find and select the Bluetooth icon.

4. Select the Set Up button at the bottom of the screen.

5. Select the HotSync Setup button and follow the directions to create a connection between the two.

Once the Treo and PC are configured to connect to one another, follow these steps to begin the HotSync process using Bluetooth.

1. On your Treo, press the HOME button to get to the Application screen. You may need to press the button more than once.

2. Find and select the HotSync icon.

3. Select the Local option.

4. The drop-down list should now include the name of your PC. Select your PC name.

5. Select the HotSync icon/button in the middle of the screen to begin the HotSync process.

Connect Your Treo Using Infrared

Infrared is a short-distance, line-of-sight wireless technology with a maximum data transmission rate of 1.15 Mbps (megabits per second) with a maximum infrared (IR) transmission distance of 7.8 in. (20 cm).

Use Infrared to HotSync Your Treo with Your PC or Mac

A great use of infrared technology with the Treo is synchronizing your Treo with a laptop that is equipped with an infrared port. We will use that example here because connecting your Treo to any infrared-capable device is similar.

If your PC isn't equipped with an infrared port, there are third-party USB infrared ports that you can add to most PCs that have a USB port. To see what is available, USB Gear (www.usbgear.com) offers several options.

To connect your Treo with your PC using an infrared connection, ensure that your PC has an infrared (IR) port with the driver installed and that HotSync Manager software is active. On a Windows PC you should see the HotSync icon in your toolbar on the bottom right of your screen. The steps to HotSync using infrared are divided into Windows and Mac sections.

HotSync Using Infrared with Your Windows PC

Follow the steps below to set up your Treo to sync with your Windows PC using an infrared wireless connection.

1. On your Windows PC, click the HotSync Manager icon in the taskbar in the lower-right corner of your screen. Make sure that Infrared has a check mark beside it; if it doesn't, click it to add the check mark.

2. On your Treo, open the Applications Launcher (press the HOME button).

3. Find and select HotSync.

4. Select Local.

5. Select the menu below the HotSync icon and select "IR to a PC/Handheld."

6. Line up the IR port of your Treo with the IR port on your PC no more than a few inches apart. Technically, you can place them up to 30 inches apart, although closer is better.

7. On your Treo, while still in the HotSync application, select the HotSync icon to begin synchronization.

8. Synchronization may take a few minutes depending on how much data is being synchronized.

HotSync Using Infrared with Your Mac Computer

Follow the steps below to set up your Treo to sync with your Mac using an infrared wireless connection.

1. On your Mac, find and select the HotSync Manager icon in the Palm folder.
2. Select the HotSync Controls tab and select the Enabled option.
3. Select the Connection Settings tab, and ensure that the "On" box next to IR port is checked.
4. On your Treo, open the Applications Launcher (press the HOME button).
5. Find and select HotSync.
6. Select Local.
7. Select the menu below the HotSync icon and select "IR to a PC/Handheld."
8. Line up the IR port of your Treo with the IR port on your PC no more than a few inches apart. Technically, you can place them up to 30 inches apart, although closer is better.
9. On your Treo, while still in the HotSync application, select the HotSync icon to begin synchronization.

Synchronization may take a few minutes, depending on how much data is being synchronized.

Web Sites with Content Dedicated to the Treo

A comprehensive list of web sites dedicated to Palm-powered—and Treo—specific topics is shown in Appendix B at the end of this book. Many of these web sites include news and user forums where you can search, view, and post opinions and questions about your Treo. It can be a great way to learn how other Treo owners use their Treos. Often, web sites are great places to find out about new applications and accessories for your Treo . Some of the most enlightening information available on these sites comes from other Treo users who describe the products they have tried. Of course, any posted opinion should be taken with a grain of salt, since it is just an opinion. That said, if 200 people say a product is great and one person says it isn't, it's pretty easy to determine the level of user satisfaction.

Treo-Friendly Web Sites

While the majority of web sites are formatted for PC screens, many web sites have a specific set of pages designed for viewing on wireless smartphone devices. The primary difference is that there is less screen content in order for it to fit more easily on the screen, as well as less graphical content (fewer pretty pictures and image buttons) to help reduce the time it takes to download a page to your Treo. The following is a short list of web sites that have been designed for your Treo and other smartphone devices:

- **Financial**   CNN Financial (www.cnnfn.com/pushthis/avantgo/channel.html)
- **News**   USA Today (www.usatoday.com/palm/)

- **Phone** InfoSpace Yellow Pages (www.infospace.com/info.avant/yellow.html); InfoSpace White Pages (www.infospace.com/info.avant/index_ppl.html)
- **Sports** FOX Sports (www.foxsports.com/palm/)
- **Technology** ZDNet (www.zdnet.com/zdnn/feeds/palmpilot/pageone/)
- **Travel** MapQuest! (www.mapquest.com/avantgo/)
- **Weather** The Weather Channel (http://harvest.weather.com/3com/avantgo/)

Eventually every popular web site will offer pages designed for wireless smartphone devices, and while not every web site is at that stage now, many offer customized pages for smartphones. Often, there is a link on the main page of a web site that allows you to link to pages designed for your Treo. Keep this in mind as you browse the Web with your Treo. It can drastically improve your Treo web-browsing experience. Appendix B has a much larger list of Treo-friendly web sites.

Multimedia Messaging Service vs. Sprint Picture Mail

In this chapter you will see sections devoted to MMS and others devoted to Sprint Picture Mail. It is important to know that both technologies offer similar functionality. So, what is the difference? Basically, Sprint Picture Mail is Sprint's version of MMS. If you have Sprint Treo, then the sections specific to Sprint Picture Mail are for you, and if your Treo is on another wireless network, then the sections on MMS pertain more closely to your Treo.

Use MMS—Multimedia Messaging Service

If your Treo is hosted on the Sprint Network, Sprint has implemented this functionality using slightly different technology called Sprint Picture Mail, which is discussed in the next section. MMS has been gaining popularity as an easy way to share short messages consisting of images, text, and sounds.

In order for MMS to work, both the sending and receiving devices must be MMS capable. The types of content you can send in an MMS message include the following:

- **Ringtones** MIDI up to 16-voice polyphony, Standard or SP-MIDI format, and up to 64KB per sound file
- **iMelody** Up to 64KB per sound file
- **Sound clips** Up to 30 seconds playback time, 64KB per sound file
- **Pictures**
  - **JPEG** Up to 640×480 pixels, 64KB-per-image files
  - **GIF** Up to 640×480 pixels, 64KB-per-image files
- **Video clips** Up to 64KB per file

Note that not all Treos ship with MMS software installed. For example, Sprint Treo smartphones do not ship with MMS. That said, Sprint Treos do ship with a similar service called "Picture Mail" that allows you to send MMS-type messages, as is discussed in this chapter.

MMS vs. E-Mail

Depending on the type of e-mail account you have, you can send the same content with e-mail that you can with MMS. So why use MMS? The primary answer is that MMS is *designed for* mobile devices, while e-mail has been *adapted for* mobile devices. The result is that MMS is easier and faster to use. E-mail and MMS are based on similar technologies, with the primary difference being that MMS messages are sent straight to the receiving smartphone, while e-mail messages are sent to the receiving person's e-mail account. So, e-mail is not downloaded until the e-mail server either "pushes" the message to the recipient's smartphone or the recipient's smartphone checks the e-mail server for new messages. This means that there will be a delay between when an e-mail is sent and when the recipient receives it. This is less of an issue when you use MMS to send a message.

Of course, all of this depends on both the sending smartphone and the receiving smartphone having MMS capability. At this point, MMS has not yet been as widely adopted as e-mail, so e-mail is still the most common way to send content-rich messages.

Get Ready to Send an MMS Message

You will have to have MMS enabled on your Treo and in your service contract with your WSP before you can send an MMS message. To do this, you may have to contact your mobile service provider to add MMS to your account. Of course, there is an extra monthly service charge for MMS.

 You cannot use your Treo phone and send an MMS message at the same time.

Send an MMS Message

To send an MMS message, perform the following steps:

Treo 700p   On the Treo 700p, Text Messaging (SMS) and MMS are sent and received using the same application, called Messaging. The only difference between the two is whether or not the message includes an attachment. If the message contains only text, then it is a Text Message.

1. Access the Applications Launcher screen. To get there, press the HOME button, and then choose the Messaging icon.

2. Select New.

3. Type in the address of the person you want to send the message to using a phone number or an e-mail address. If the contact is in your contact list, when you begin typing the Treo will try to match it.

4. Type in text for your message (you can also select Quick Text, and add a "smiley" if you want) and then select the Add Media button.

5. Select the Media icon and select an option from the list:

   a. Attach from device

   b. Attach from Online (depending on your Treo, you may or may not see this option)

   c. Take new picture

   d. Take new video

6. Whatever type of file you want to attach, you have the option of either attaching an existing file or capturing a new one to attach to the message.

7. After you have attached the media and are happy with the message, select Send.

Treo 650   On the Treo 650, Text Messaging (SMS) and MMS are sent and received using the same application, called Messaging. The only difference between the two is whether or not the message includes an attachment. If the message contains only text, then it is a Text Message.

1. Access the Applications Launcher screen. To get there, press the HOME button, and then choose the Messaging icon.

2. Select New.

3. Type in the address of the person you want to send the message to using a phone number or an e-mail address. If the contact is in your contact list, when you begin typing the Treo will try to match it.

4. Type in text for your message (you can also select Quick Text, and add a "smiley" if you want) then select the Add button.

5. Select one of the icons that represent the photo, sound, or video functions.

6. Whatever type of file you want to attach. you have the option of either attaching an existing file or capturing a new one (sound, photo, or video) to attach to the message.

7. After you have attached the media and are happy with the message, select Send.

Treo 600

1. Access the Applications Launcher screen. To get there, press the HOME button, and then choose the MMS icon. An MMS window should appear.

2. From the MMS list view, choose New.

3. Address the new message by either using your Contacts list or by entering the phone number or e-mail address of the recipient in the To field.

4. Press the DOWN button on the five-way navigation control.

5. Type in the message's subject text.

6. Press DOWN to highlight the image icon, and then press the CENTER button of the five-way navigation control.

7. Choose the type of file you want to add to the message.

8. Follow the onscreen steps to insert the file.

9. Select Preview to view your message as the recipient will see it.

10. Select Send.

The Treo comes equipped with preconfigured templates. Select the Inbox pull-down menu and choose the last item, Templates. Four templates will appear from which you can choose, each with animated graphics and sound.

5

Use Sprint Picture Mail

If your Treo is hosted by Sprint, it uses the CDMA wireless network. The CDMA wireless network does not currently support MMS, but Sprint has included Sprint Picture Mail, which allows you to do some of the same things you can do with MMS. As with MMS, you may have to pay additional fees for Picture Mail service. If you're not sure if your Sprint contract includes Picture Mail service, either check your contract or contact Sprint directly to find out.

Send a Picture Using Sprint Picture Mail

You can share a picture with someone who uses a Treo or PCS Vision Phone, or you can send pictures to someone by e-mail. In order to use Picture Mail, you need a Picture Mail web site account. The first time you use Picture Mail, you will be prompted to set up a Picture Mail account with a password. In the Password field, enter the password of your choice, between four and eight characters long. You will receive confirmation that your account is set up, after which you may begin uploading and sharing your Treo photos.

Reduce the Size of a Photo Before You Send It Using Sprint Picture Mail

Your photos are sent, and received, in less time if you send smaller image files. Picture Mail allows you to reduce the size of your photos before you send them. To reduce the photo size prior to sending it, follow these steps:

1. Launch Picture Mail from the Applications Launcher screen.

2. Choose Pictures view and select the picture you want to send.

3. Choose Share.

4. In the To field, type the e-mail address or phone number of the recipient. (The recipient must have a Picture Mail account to receive the message.)

5. In the message area, you can type text to send with the photo or select from the Canned Message list to select an appropriate predefined phrase and save yourself some typing.

6. Select Share.

When you choose Share, your photo will be uploaded to the Picture Mail web site and sent to the recipient's Picture Mail account. The recipient can view the photo and message using any web browser by logging in to his or her user account on the Picture Mail web site.

Receive Sprint Picture Mail

You can set your Treo to download any new messages automatically or have it display an alert to notify you that a new message is available for you to download. When you receive the alert telling you of a new Picture Mail message, you can choose from the following options:

- **Go To** This downloads the message immediately.
- **Snooze** This closes the alert but will remind you of the message again in five minutes.
- **OK** This closes the alert without downloading the message.

Access Your Sprint Picture Mail Inbox

You can access your Picture Mail account at any time using your Treo. The steps for accessing your account are listed here:

1. If Picture Mail is not currently running, press the MENU button on the keyboard to open the Applications Launcher, and then find and select the Picture Mail icon.

2. Once Picture Mail is running, choose the web icon. This will open your Inbox.

3. With your Inbox displayed, you can choose from several options:
   - **Share Inbox** Enables you to share all of your photos in your Inbox.
   - **Save Inbox As** Copies your photos in your Inbox into a new album.
   - **Move All Pictures** Transfers the photos in your Inbox to an existing album.
   - **Back** Returns you to the Camera application on your phone.
   - **Album List** Displays a list of all of your photo albums in your Picture Mail account.

One of the advantages of your Picture Mail account is that you may access it any time using any web browser. This allows you to view and manage your photos from, essentially, anywhere you can access a web browser. The web site address is www.picturemail.sprintpcs.com.

Customize Your Sprint Picture Mail Settings

There are several Sprint Picture Mail configuration settings that you can change to suit your needs. The settings that can be changed are listed here:

- **Default Name**   The default name assigns a name to the next series of pictures that you take, such as MingsBDay001, MingsBDay002, and so on.
- **Category**   This setting allows you to set the default category of the pictures you take from now on.
- **Picture Size**   This setting lets you set the default size for the pictures you take with your Treo. There are two size options: Large (640×480 pixels) and Small (160×120 pixels).
- **Play Capture Sound**   This setting lets you determine whether or not your Treo will play a sound when you take a picture.
- **Confirm Before Deleting**   This instructs Sprint Picture Mail to ask whether you're sure you want to delete a picture before deleting it.
- **Confirm Before Saving**   With this setting, Sprint Picture Mail prompts you to confirm whether or not you want to save a picture before it is stored on your Treo.
- **Backup Settings**   This allows you to back up your Treo image database on your computer.

You may access any of these settings by following these steps:

1. If Picture Mail is not currently running, press the MENU button on the keyboard to open the Applications Launcher, and then find and select the Picture Mail icon. From any Picture Mail view, press MENU.
2. From the Options menu, select Preferences.
3. Change any of the settings and select OK.

Third-Party MMS Applications

There are some software vendors that offer MMS applications for your Treo. This is especially important if your Treo, including those sold by Sprint, does not have a built-in MMS client.

Pixer MMS

Pixer MMS allows you to send photos, animations, and picture messages to e-mail boxes and mobile phones from your Treo using MMS. More information about the software is available on the Electric Pocket web site (www.electricpocket.com), and the product is available for sale from Handango (www.handango.com).

Text Messaging (SMS)

If you have not personally used Text Messaging (also known as SMS messaging), you may have heard about it. Text Messaging is extremely popular in Asia and Europe and is beginning to catch on in North America.

What Is Text Messaging?

Text Messaging is basically a mechanism for delivery of short, text-only messages using mobile wireless networks. Text Messaging offers a store-and-forward method of transmitting messages to and from mobile devices like your Treo. Text Messages are short messages that you exchange with other mobile phones and devices that have Text Message capability. Messages longer than 160 characters are split into multiple messages. You should refer to your service plan for per-message costs and availability on your wireless network.

A Text Message (text-only) is sent from the sending wireless device and is stored in a central short message center, which then forwards it to the intended recipient's wireless mobile device. So, in case the recipient is not available, the short message is stored and can be sent later.

What's So Great about Text Messaging?

So why would you use Text Messaging? As with many technologies, there are specific functions that make Text Messaging more valuable than its conventional competition. For example, Text Messaging is well suited for exchanging small messages like "See you at 8:45 tonight at the theater" because Text Messaging is much less expensive than calling someone using your Treo phone to give them the exact same message. In fact, calling the person to give them the exact same message almost invariably takes more time and costs more.

Many Text Message users think it an excellent technology for "chatting" (done using Chat view). If you have ever used instant messaging applications on your PC, the concept is very similar. With Text Messaging, you type and send short text messages (and appropriate smiley face icons) back and forth with another Text Messaging user while the conversation is visible on the screen in a single thread. This provides a more interactive feel to your messaging.

One of the advantages of Text Messaging, similar to e-mail in this regard, is that all of the major wireless mobile networks support Text Messaging, so it is becoming a universal standard that can be used across a wide variety of wireless mobile devices and networks.

What You Need to Send and Receive Text Messages

Text Messaging does not require a specific account as e-mail does, but a few things need to be in place for Text Messaging to work properly. The Treo is Text Message-capable right out of the box, but all of the following points need to be true for both your Treo and the wireless device that you will be exchanging Text Messages with. In order for Text Messaging to work, both the sending and receiving mobile devices must

- **Be Text Message-capable** Not all of the available wireless mobile devices and cellular phones are capable of sending and receiving Text Messages.

- **Be hosted on a Text Message-capable wireless network** Not all WSPs have made the necessary technical upgrades for Text Messaging.

- **Have Text Messaging included in their service contracts** This is not necessarily part of the default wireless contract.

NOTE   *The size limit of SMS is 160 characters if Latin alphabets are used (English, French, German, Spanish, and so on). If non-Latin alphabets like Chinese, Korean, or Arabic are used, the limit is shortened to 70 characters.*

Send a Text Message

If you have a non-Sprint Treo, you can use your Treo to easily send and receive Text Messages, as long as the items cited in the preceding section are all true. To create and send a Text Message, follow these steps:

Treo 650 or 700p

1. Press the PHONE button.
2. Find and select the Messaging button. You may need to scroll down to see the button.
3. Select the New button at the bottom of the screen and begin constructing your message.

    Here are some of the options that are available to you:

    a. Select a recipient from your Contact list.
    b. Add QuickText to a message (QuickText is preconfigured messages that you can create and add to a message to help minimize typing. Your Treo includes default QuickText items such as "In a meeting," but you can edit and create your own entries).
    c. Add a "smiley" to your message.
    d. Add a picture or sound (note that when you choose to add an attachment to a Text Message, it automatically becomes an MMS message, so the recipient's device must support this format and your service plan must include MMS service.

Treo 600

1. Ensure that your Wireless mode is turned on. (This was covered earlier in the chapter, in the section "Turn Wireless Mode On and Off.")
2. Press the HOME button to view the Applications Launcher screen.
3. Find and select the SMS icon.
4. Your SMS Inbox will open. If you have any messages, they will be listed here.
5. Select the New button at the bottom of the screen.
6. A new SMS screen, like that shown in Figure 5-11, will open. You can then begin typing your message.

NOTE   *The "To" address information that you need to send an SMS message is the recipient's phone number or Internet e-mail account address. The phone number must be in the international format. For example, in North America, the recipient's number would take the form of 1-555-555-5555.*

5

FIGURE 5-11 Compose Text Message

7. Type the full phone number or e-mail address of the recipient or, if the intended recipient is in your Contacts list, start typing the first initial and last name (without spaces). Afterward, press the DOWN button on the five-way navigation control and choose the recipient's phone number or e-mail address from the list that appears.

8. Type your message (including any smiley icons if you feel it adds to the mood of the message).

9. Select Send.

> TIP
>
> *Use QuickText and Emoticons—the Text Messaging / SMS application on your Treo gives you a time-saving feature called QuickText. QuickText allows you to select a message from a preexisting list of phrases. This enables you to quickly insert common text with emoticons (also called smiley face icons). You can even edit your QuickText list and add new messages that you can reuse by selecting the QuickText button and then selecting Edit QuickText from the menu. Or you can add emoticons to spice up your messages or help set the tone of a message.*

Receive Text Messages

While your phone is on and you are in an area of wireless coverage, you will automatically receive any SMS messages sent to you. You can configure your Treo to instantly notify you when new text messages arrive, through a ringtone and vibration or an onscreen alert, whichever you prefer.

- When you receive an alert notifying you of a new SMS message, choose the Go To button. Once you are viewing the message, of course, you can reply as well.

- To dismiss an alert, choose OK, and the message will be saved in your SMS Inbox.

- If you want to be reminded of the new message again in five minutes, choose Snooze.

Use Links in Text Messages

Palm has done a great job of allowing you to combine the various functions across applications on your Treo. For example, you may use content in SMS messages to launch other applications and utilize different functions on your Treo. When you receive an SMS message containing a telephone number, e-mail address, or web site URL, you can dial the number, send an e-mail message, or go to the web page by tapping on the linked text. To see this in action, follow these steps:

1. Open the Applications Launcher by pressing the HOME button on the keyboard. Find and select the SMS application to launch it.

2. Select an SMS message from the list.

3. Select the e-mail address, phone number, or web site URL that appears as underlined blue text.

4. Your Treo will automatically launch the appropriate application from the selected link. In other words, if you tapped a phone number, your Treo phone will activate.

What Other Wireless Functions Can You Use Your Treo For?

This section is designed to provide a brief listing and overview of some of the ways you can use your Treo. One of the great things about Palm-powered devices, like your Treo, is that the Palm developer community is extremely active, and new products (and therefore new uses) for your Treo are constantly being introduced. Chapter 1 explained why the Treo is much more than just an updated PalmPilot, with its wireless capabilities putting it in an entirely different league.

Use Your Treo as a Wireless Modem for Your PC

The Treo user guide covers this topic in detail, so we won't rehash exactly how to set this up, but we will mention it because it is a great capability. The development of faster wireless networks such as EDGE and EVDO have helped make it feasible to use your Treo as a wireless modem for your laptop to allow you to use your laptop to access the Internet anywhere that your Treo has wireless connectivity. You also have the flexibility to connect your Treo to your laptop using the USB cable, or if you have a 650 or 700p, you can also connect the two using Bluetooth.

One thing to keep in mind is that to leverage this capability, you will likely have to sign up for a dial-up network plan from your WSP.

Download and Install Applications Wirelessly

Many applications have a small enough file size that you can download them wirelessly and install them directly to your Treo without the HotSync installer. In fact, many software developers offer shareware and freeware applications that you can download from reseller and company web sites.

Shareware is software you can download and use without needing to immediately pay. It is a great way to try out software before you buy it. If you decide you want to use the software on a regular basis, simply purchase a license key, usually online, with your credit card. Most shareware applications are functionally limited to encourage you to pay for the software in order to get the fully functional version.

There are several web sites that resell applications for your Treo. Many of these sites allow you to pay for, download, and install applications and games to your Treo, and do it wirelessly. A prime example of a web site that lets you do this is Palm (www.Palm.com).

Some applications require a conduit application that runs on your PC to facilitate application data synchronizing during HotSync. Any conduit applications need to be installed locally on your PC.

Use Your Treo to Connect to a Virtual Private Network

Remote workers and telecommuters have used virtual private network (VPN) technology with PCs for years to allow them to securely access company computer networks over long distances. You may have heard of a wide area network (WAN), which is a generic term for a computer network that is spread out over a large area—possibly over the entire world. This is really what we're talking about when we talk about VPNs. The most useful characteristic of a VPN is that it uses public networks, such as the Internet, to connect a remote user to a corporate network—and it does it securely. This is important because organizations and, increasingly, individuals are concerned about Internet security, so anything that can help minimize the risk of using the Internet is a good thing. Fortunately, there are software vendors that know that a wireless mobile device such as your Treo presents unique security challenges and have chosen to develop technology to address these problems and allow you to use your Treo on a VPN. VPN tools for your Treo are covered in more detail in Chapter 13.

Computer System and Network Management Tools

This topic is aimed directly at information technology professionals, network security people, and anyone responsible for managing computer systems and networks—even if it is just your home network. Tools for remote management of computer systems have been available for years. Technologies such as Citrix, Terminal Services, remote access servers (RAS), and many others allow IT people to remotely access computers, servers, and networking hardware. These technologies are all designed for use while connected to traditional wired infrastructure—cable or phone lines. Now, the availability of truly next-generation wireless devices, such as the Treo, prompts the comment, "Would it ever be great if I could manage my servers and networks with my Treo!" Well, there have been some companies that have answered that question while overcoming the idiosyncrasies of the relatively small screen, the relatively slow wireless networks, and concerns about wireless security.

SonicAdmin (www.Avocent.com)

Avocent has been delivering mobile systems management software for a few years now and has an impressive customer list, including a major national defense contractor, branches of the U.S. military, and several Fortune 500 companies. With its product, SonicAdmin, you can use your Treo to securely connect to your back-end computer systems and network hardware to diagnose and fix problems or do routine maintenance using a wireless connection.

The software includes an embedded client that runs on your Treo and a server component that runs in your computer network. The types of things you can manage include the following:

- Integration to allow mobile management of the following third-party applications:
    - MS Exchange
    - RSA SecurID
    - NetIQ AppManager
    - OpalisRobot
    - TelAlert
- Management of Windows systems, including the following:
    - User management
    - Event logs
    - DNS management
    - Print service management
    - File Explorer functionality, and even e-mail files from a remote computer
    - Services and server processes
    - Server and device management: log off, shut down, or force-reboot servers
    - Power to external devices, including servers, switches, and so on
    - The command-line interface and VT100 terminal emulation to manage Telnet or SSH devices

Mobile TS (www.ddhsoftware.com)

Mobile TS is a useful application that allows you to connect your Treo to Windows desktops and workstations using the Windows Terminal Services or Remote Desktop capabilities built into many Microsoft Windows operating systems.

GPS, Navigation, and Maps

Being wireless means that if you get lost, you don't have the option of following your network cable to find your way back to the office, but the good news is that your Treo makes a great compass, map, and helpful navigation tool. You can convert your Treo into a stand-alone tool for GPS, as is covered in detail in Chapter 14, and use it to display maps and driving directions. You can even load maps of entire continents on your Treo to help you find your way around. One such application is Mapopolis Navigator for Palm OS 5.0 GPS Bundle (www.mapopolis.com). Mapopolis Navigator costs approximately $249 and makes your Treo the ultimate in-car navigator. The bundle comes with a mouse-type GPS, a Y-cable, and the Navigator for Palm OS 5.0 software with U.S. maps on CD. It allows you to plot your course and have it guide you with visual and audible prompting, and you will never again have to figure out how to refold the road map!

Stock Market Applications

It isn't difficult to imagine that your Treo mobile connectivity capability offers a great way to keep you in the loop with changing information. Certain information is very time-sensitive, and the ability to receive real-time information updates can be extremely valuable. Some application vendors also provide software that keeps you abreast of changes in the stock market.

Charts

Charts, by Tawacentral, is an application for displaying price charts, retrieving delayed quotes, and viewing the fundamental financial data of stocks traded on North American and worldwide markets.

With this program, stocks can be organized into separate watch lists for easier management of your portfolio. Using Charts is as simple as entering one or more stock symbols and performing a HotSync operation, which downloads all the necessary information from the Internet and uploads it to your smartphone.

Chart MA Stock

Chart MA Stock graphs share prices, volumes, and MA lines from any exchange. Download historical data when you HotSync your Treo. You can specify stocks for a period of time and graph them with moving averages. You can also reanalyze stocks using different periods, scales, and MA values.

Chart MA can be downloaded from Handango (www.handango.com), and product information can be found at the Pen Systems web site (www.pensystems.com).

TTY—Teletypewriter for the Deaf

A TTY, which stands for *teletypewriter*, is a special device that lets people who are deaf, hard of hearing, or speech-impaired use the telephone to communicate by allowing them to type text messages back and forth instead of talking and listening. Many people use TTYs, not just those who are deaf. A TTY is required at both ends of the conversation in order to communicate, however. If you use a TTY device, you can use your Treo to facilitate communication between you and someone who also uses a TTY device. One company that manufactures TTY devices that you can use with your Treo is Ultratec (www.ultratec.com). TTY-specific adaptor cables to connect the TTY to your Treo are available from Hitec (www.hitec.com).

Other Wireless Topics Worth Mentioning

Wireless technology is changing rapidly and will continue to do so for quite some time. It doesn't make sense to try and learn everything about wireless just to make the most of your Treo. There are a few wireless connectivity topics you may want to be aware of with regard to your Treo.

Roaming

Roaming is the term WSPs use to describe the situation where you are outside of your primary coverage area but are still connected to a wireless network. Your ability to "roam" outside your coverage area is dependent on the relationships between WSPs in other areas and on the details of your service contract. You can roam and use another carrier's wireless network as long as your WSP has a roaming agreement with the other carrier to allow your Treo to connect to that carrier's network. There are two main reasons why roaming is important:

- **Dollars and cents—or euros, francs, yen, and so on**   You pay your WSP for your service, but if you move into an area where you are using another WSP's network, someone has to pay for that service. Therefore, there must be a business agreement between the two WSPs so that the WSP providing your roaming can bill *your* WSP, who in turn bills you. So to cover the associated extra accounting costs, many WSPs charge you more when you are roaming.

- **Performance in dollars and cents**   In areas where normal service is not available, some carriers may resort to a "backup plan" and allow you to use a dial-up connection to access the Internet. The performance of dial-up is slower, and there may be an added fee for using the service. So, if you don't want to use this dial-up option when roaming, be sure to disable any automatic Internet connections you may have set up, such as checking your e-mail.

Blazer Web Browser-Supported Media Types

This section is primarily intended for individuals with prior technical knowledge about web technologies and also serves as a reference if you are experiencing difficulties viewing specific web sites. (You can view and use most web sites using the Blazer browser.) What follows is a list of what is, and is not, supported on the Blazer Web Browser version 3.0.

The following Blazer markup languages are supported:

- HTML 4.01
- XHTML 1.1
- XHTML Mobile Profile
- cHTML (iHTML)
- WML 1.3
- DHTML
- DOM

The following Blazer style sheets are supported:

- Cascading Style Sheets as called for in the WAP2 specification:
    - CSS1
    - CSS2

NOTE *The Treo web browser will show content regardless of CSS support.*

The following Blazer scripting languages are supported (WML script is not, however):

- ECMAscript (JavaScript 1.5)
- DeviceID (lets a web site store cookies effectively)

These Blazer image formats are supported:

- GIF
- Animated GIF
- JPEG
- PNG
- WBMP

NOTE *Blazer version 3.0 does not support BMP-formatted images.*

The Blazer Web Browser supports cookies and session cookies are cleared 10 minutes after you exit the browser or 25 minutes after your last interaction with the application.

NOTE *Desktop PC browsers are generally configured to clear session cookies immediately when you exit a web application or web page. But, due to the unique nature of browsing the web using the Treo, some tweaks have been made so that usability is maximized. For example, you may need to take a phone call or check the calendar and then return to the browser. If so, it makes sense to have session cookies kept around for a longer period of time. Of course, all of this is done behind the scenes, so you don't have to worry about it.*

The following points should be noted when it comes to downloading particular file types supported by the Blazer Web Browser:

- Some download file types have a size limit. This means you won't be able to download these specific file types if they are too big. Specifically, MID/MIDI files cannot be larger than 64KB.

■ You can only download files from the web browser if that file type is supported by an application on your Treo (including third-party applications). For example, you can download any MIDI file less than 64KB and use it as a ringtone. You can also download any .prc (Palm OS application) or .pdb (Palm OS database) file, and it will be installed on your Treo.

■ Out of the box, the web browser in Treo allows you to download these file types: JFIF, JPE, JPEG, JPG, MID (less than 64KB), MIDI (less than 64KB), OPRC, PDB, PRC, TXT, and VCF.

Blazer can't access web pages containing any of the following elements (they're not supported):

■ Java applets

■ Plug-ins (Flash, Shockwave, audio, video, and so on)

■ BMP

■ WML script

You can download other file types with the help of third-party software. For example, if you install Documents To Go from DataViz, you will be able to download .doc (Microsoft Word) and .xls (Microsoft Excel) files and open them directly in Documents To Go on your Treo.

TIP   *With the help of third-party applications such as Sprint TV, MobiTV, Real Player, and others you can stream media over the Internet using a wireless connection. Some of the primary benefits of this approach are that you can view/listen to music, radio, TV, or video without needing to download it to your PC and then sync it to transfer it to your Treo, and that you don't need to use up as much valuable memory on your Treo. Streaming media are discussed in detail in Chapter 8.*

Wrap It Up

Your Treo offers powerful wireless connectivity capabilities. Network capability is no longer restricted to corporate networks and desktop PCs. As software and hardware vendors (as well as generally inventive people) continue to recognize the vast possibilities of mobile devices and networks, your options will continue to grow. So, in addition to your Treo being an excellent mobile phone, it is capable of many other valuable tasks, as diverse as playing games in real time with other Treo users, navigating the nation's highways, browsing the Web, checking your Palm stocks, and managing your network systems from anywhere.

Chapter 6

Send and Receive E-Mail

How to...

- Select the right e-mail software for your needs
- Set up your Treo to send and receive e-mail
- Use the built-in mail program (VersaMail)
- Use third-party e-mail software
- Customize your e-mail

We decided to create a separate chapter just on Treo e-mail because there are enough options and choices for setting up and using e-mail that the topic can get confusing quickly. This chapter identifies the three general types of e-mail accounts, discusses your software options, and guides you through the steps to get each up and running—or rather, get you up and e-mailing.

E-Mail—The Killer Wireless Application for Your Treo

E-mail has revolutionized the way we communicate, and in many cases e-mail has even altered the way we do business. Extending e-mail into the wireless realm has enabled us to be connected no matter where we are. Of course, not everyone thinks that this is a good thing, but for many of us it offers freedom from the constraints of the office environment while still allowing us to be involved and in touch. The Treo lets you send and receive e-mail in many different ways, and perform tasks usually relegated to the desktop, such as managing contacts and viewing attachments. Regardless of how many other applications you use on your Treo, or how often you play games or listen to MP3s, you will likely use e-mail almost as much as you use your Treo phone.

Get Connected

Your wireless service provider, the company you are paying to use your Treo as a phone, classifies e-mail as data. Not all mobile phone contracts include data service by default. If you know that your contract includes data service, then great! If you are not sure, you may want to take a look at your contract to find out, or give the company a call. In order for your Treo to send and receive e-mail, you must have data service included with your Treo phone plan. This topic is covered in more detail in Chapter 5.

Understand Your E-Mail Options

Several different technologies and configurations allow you to send and receive e-mail on your Treo, so it's important that you understand the available options and what their differences are before you get started. If you already have an e-mail account, or many e-mail accounts, your options are relatively straightforward because you don't have to consider all of the available options. The four major types of e-mail accounts you can use with your Treo are POP3, corporate (Exchange and Lotus Domino), IMAP, and web-based e-mail. Each type is described in more detail later in this chapter.

Understand E-Mail Account Types

The type of e-mail account you have determines the type of software you will need to run, as well as how to configure your Treo to send and receive e-mail. Generally, e-mail accounts fall into one of four categories:

- **Corporate e-mail such as MS Exchange/Outlook or Lotus Domino**   If you have an e-mail account through your employer, chances are it's one of these, but this isn't always the case.

- **POP3 (Post Office Protocol 3) e-mail such as Eudora, Outlook Express, and Entourage**   If your Internet service provider (such as EarthLink, AT&T WorldNet, BellSouth, Shaw, Telus, Comcast, O2, Orange, SBC, or Verizon) hosts your e-mail account, then it is likely a POP3 account.

- **IMAP (Internet Message Access Protocol)**   This is a method of accessing electronic mail or bulletin board messages that are kept on a mail server. IMAP permits a "client" e-mail program on your Treo (or PC) to access remote e-mail message stores as if they were local. For example, e-mail stored on an IMAP server can be manipulated from a home desktop computer, a workstation at the office, or a notebook computer while traveling, without the need to transfer messages or files back and forth between these computers. Many of the corporate e-mail account types support IMAP e-mail. Some IMAP e-mail software options are listed later in this chapter, in the section "IMAP E-Mail Application Options for Your Treo."

- **Web-based e-mail such as Hotmail, Yahoo!, Netscape, Lycos, and Excite**   You typically use these types of e-mail accounts by going to a web page and logging in to your account to send and view e-mail.

> **NOTE**   *Yahoo! can be either POP3 or web-based e-mail, depending on your account type. Yahoo! offers free web-based e-mail, so if you didn't pay anything to get your Yahoo! e-mail account, then it is a web-based account. But, if you paid to upgrade to Yahoo! Premium, you may use your account with POP3 software on your Treo.*

Find Out Your E-Mail Account Type

You need to find out what type of e-mail account you have (POP3, IMAP, corporate—Exchange or Domino—or web-based e-mail) in order to choose the correct Treo software and configure it properly so that you can use e-mail.

Ask for Help

Asking for help is a lot like asking for directions (for some of us it is more difficult than for others). Nevertheless, asking the proper people the right questions can save you a lot of time and frustration. The fastest way to find out information about your e-mail account is to call up the Support desk of the organization that provides your e-mail. Usually, just introducing yourself, explaining why you're calling, and asking whether your e-mail account is a POP3 account will start you down the right path. If, on the other hand, the company you work for provides your e-mail, great! Go bug the e-mail or systems administrator; you may even be able to persuade her to set up your Treo for you—something well worth the price of a soy latte if you find that a little bribery is necessary.

Use Online Support Resources

If you're more of a figure-it-out-yourself type of person, many service providers have excellent online knowledge bases that can supply you with all the information you need. So, if you know the company that provides your e-mail, go to their web site and find the Support section. Palm also has an excellent Support and FAQ section at www.palm.com.

Don't Already Have an E-Mail Account?

If you don't already have an existing e-mail account, your options are a little simpler because you don't have to worry about corporate e-mail solutions like Exchange or Lotus Domino. With corporate e-mail out of the picture, your remaining options are POP3 and web-based e-mail.

Set Up a New POP3 E-Mail Account

POP3 is a common e-mail standard that is widely supported, so it is relatively easy to find a service provider that offers POP3 e-mail accounts.

If You Have a Home Internet Connection   If you already have an Internet service provider that provides your home with Internet access, the company supplying your connection can likely set you up with a POP3 e-mail account. In fact, the cost is often included in your Internet fees. Contact the company to find out how to get set up, and then get the POP3 set-up information covered later in this chapter, in the section "Set Up a POP3 Account."

If You Don't Have a Home Internet Connection   If you do not have a home Internet connection, there are organizations that provide free POP3 e-mail accounts. As with most things, you get what you pay for, so if you choose to use a free provider, don't expect high reliability or top-notch service. Examples include www.HotPOP.com and www.gmx.co.uk, but a quick Internet search will produce several others. The most reliable POP3 option is to purchase e-mail service from a web-hosting company. The cost of POP3 service is reasonable ($20 per year in North America) and will vary between providers, so shop around and make sure you find a provider that is reasonably priced and that will provide quality customer service when you need it. E-mail is transported on the Internet, so the physical location of the company hosting your POP3 account is relatively unimportant. Having said this, though, service may be slower if your e-mail server is located on a different continent.

Set Up a New Web-Based E-Mail Account

The fastest and simplest way to set up an e-mail account is to use web-based e-mail. To do this, just use your Treo web browser to open a web page and log in to view and send e-mail using the web page. Before you decide whether web based e-mail is right for you, take a look at the following sections, which describe some of the advantages and disadvantages of using it.

Advantages of Web-Based E-Mail There are pros and cons associated with each of your Treo e-mail options. Here are some of the best features of web-based e-mail:

- **It is cost-effective** In fact, web-based e-mail is usually free.
- **It is easy to set up** Just fill out a form and you're registered.
- **It is easy to use** Web-based e-mail typically has simple user-friendly interfaces.
- **It is accessible** Web-based e-mail can be accessed easily from any device with a web browser, including your home, office, or neighbor's PC. (Note that POP3 e-mail can also be accessed from other computers and devices, but it's not nearly as easy to set up.)

Disadvantages of Web-Based E-Mail While web-based e-mail is the easiest option to set up, there are some limitations you should be aware of:

6

- **Screen size** Browsing web pages that are generally designed for a much larger screen can be trying. (Note that an increasing number of web-based e-mail providers provide specific pages that are formatted for mobile devices such as your Treo.)
- **Slow speed** Browsing web pages on most wireless networks can be too slow for many users, so you may want to first try out web-based e-mail to make sure it's not too slow for you. Many users don't find speed to be a problem, however.
- **Having to check for e-mail** One of the advantages of POP3 e-mail is that you can set up the client software to check for new messages at timed intervals and alert you when new messages are received. When you use web-based e-mail, you have to log in to your e-mail to see if there is anything new. This means that important e-mail may go unnoticed for long periods of time until you check you account.

Some examples of organizations that offer free web-based e-mail include the following:

- Yahoo! Mobile Mail: www.yahoo.com
  (mobile site: http://mobile.yahoo.com/mail)
- Hotmail Mobile: www.hotmail.com
  (mobile site: http://mobile.msn.com/hm/folder.aspx)
- Ultimately, you may need to try a few different e-mail options to find the best one for you.

Verizon Wireless Sync Service

If your Treo is hosted on the Verizon network, then you have a Treo e-mail option that is not available to others, called Verizon Wireless Sync Service. The service is fee based and involves installing and configuring a Verizon Wireless Sync application on your Treo. More information is available directly from Verizon (www.wirelesssync.vzw.com).

Use the Included E-Mail Application on Your Treo

Depending on which Treo you have, Palm includes free e-mail software: on Treo 650 and 700p devices you get VersaMail and on Treo 600 devices you get Palm Mail. This software allows you to use your Treo with your POP3 e-mail account. Depending on when and where you purchased your Treo, e-mail software may already be installed on your Treo. GSM versions come preinstalled with e-mail software, while some Sprint CDMA Treo users may need to download it for free from the Palm web site at www.palm.com. If you have a Treo 600, you can also purchase VersaMail software from Palm for around $30.

Use VersaMail for Your POP3 or IMAP E-Mail Account

VersaMail is included with Treo 700p and Treo 650 devices and is available for purchase for use on Treo 600 devices from the Palm web site (www.palm.com). There are several different versions of VersaMail for the Palm platform, and most are similar. The steps to configure and use VersaMail in this section were done largely with version 3.5.1, but they are similar for other versions of VersaMail.

Configure VersaMail

The VersaMail application is designed for use with an existing POP3 or IMAP e-mail account. (The different types of e-mail accounts are discussed earlier in this chapter.) Before you can begin using VersaMail to send and receive messages through your e-mail account, you must first configure VersaMail for your Treo. If you have more than one e-mail account that you want to use on your Treo, you will have to set up each account individually in VersaMail.

 If you are going through these steps and the Windows menu sequence (Start | Programs | palmOne | VersaMail Setup) doesn't give you the VersaMail Setup option, then you may have a more recent version of the Palm Desktop software. So, launch the Palm Desktop application on your PC and select the VersaMail Setup icon to begin the setup process.

There are four methods to set up an existing e-mail account in VersaMail, so you should choose the most appropriate method for your current setup:

If You Have Not Already Installed the Palm Desktop and HotSync Manager Software on Your PC

If you have not already installed the Palm Desktop and HotSync Manager software on your PC, when you choose to do so, the last screen of the installation program asks you if you want to set up VersaMail and walks you through the process. If your e-mail account is one of the "Common" providers, your will need your username and password, but if your e-mail account is hosted with a more obscure e-mail provider, you will need more information from your provider, such as e-mail server names and authentication security passwords. If you have already installed the Palm Desktop and HotSync Manager software on your PC, then the options that follow are more appropriate.

Set Up a VersaMail Account on Your Treo Using Your Windows PC

There a couple of different scenarios to transfer e-mail settings from your PC to your Treo using HotSync: your account is already configured on your PC or you need to set up a new account. Both options are discussed here.

If your PC runs Microsoft Windows and your e-mail account is already configured on your PC—for example, if you use MS Outlook to send and receive messages from your e-mail account—you can transfer the e-mail account settings to your Treo using HotSync by following these steps:

1. Connect your Treo to your PC with a HotSync cable. (Note: you can also HotSync using a Bluetooth or Infrared connection as is discussed in Chapter 3.)

2. On your Windows PC, select Start | Programs | palmOne | VersaMail Setup.

3. Select your Treo username from the drop-down menu.

4. Select the option to sync with an e-mail account detected on your PC, and select the account from the list.

5. Step through the setup screens and sync your Treo with your PC when you are prompted to do so. This will transfer you e-mail account info to the VersaMail application on your Treo.

If your PC runs Microsoft Windows and you have a new e-mail account that is not configured on your PC—you need to set up the e-mail account on your PC and then synchronize the information with your Treo. To do this, follow these steps:

1. On your PC, select Start | Programs | palmOne | VersaMail Setup.

2. Select your username from the drop-down menu.

3. Select the Create New VersaMail account option.

4. Select the option to sync with a mail service from the list.

5. Choose your mail service from the list.

   a. If your mail service is included in the list, all you will need is your e-mail username and password.

   b. If your mail service is *not* included in the list, select the Other option. You will need quite a bit more information about your e-mail account to continue with the setup, including

      i. The names of the incoming and outgoing mail servers for this account.

      ii. Whether the account requires Extended Simple Mail Transfer Protocol (ESMTP); if it does, you will need the username and password for ESMTP.

6. Select Next.

7. Enter your account information:

    a. Enter a name for the e-mail account. This is descriptive name to help you to remember which account it is.

    b. Enter your e-mail account username and password. Note: If you chose the Other option in Step 5, enter the names of the incoming and outgoing mail servers and if the account requires Extended Simple Mail Transfer Protocol (ESMTP), enter your ESMTP username and password.

8. After your account setup is complete, you can access additional account settings by selecting Advanced Settings. You can also test the account settings by selecting the Test My Settings option.

9. Select Next.

10. You can set up another account or select Finish to exit the setup.

11. Perform a HotSync operation to transfer your e-mail account information to your Treo.

The VersaMail application on your Treo will now be configured for e-mail.

Set Up an E-Mail Account In VersaMail Directly on Your Treo

If your home Computer is a Mac or you feel comfortable configuring your e-mail account directly on your Treo, follow these steps:

1. Before you begin, you will need some information about your e-mail account, including

    a. Your e-mail address.

    b. Your user name, which is usually the part of your e-mail address before the @ symbol.

    c. The name of your e-mail provider (for example, EarthLink).

2. If your e-mail provider is not on the VersaMail "common" provider list, you may need some additional information such as the following (don't get overwhelmed by these acronyms; you don't need to know what these settings are for, but it is important that you have the correct information from your e-mail provider):

    a. The Internet names of your provider's e-mail servers: both incoming (POP3/IMAP) and outgoing (SMTP).

    b. The incoming e-mail server port number and whether the server requires SSL or APOP authentication.

    c. The outgoing e-mail server port number and whether the server requires SSL or ESMTP.

3. On your Treo, launch the VersaMail application by pressing the HOME button to open the Applications Launcher and find and select the VersaMail icon.

4. The first time you launch VersaMail, a setup wizard will walk you through the setup process; if this is not the first time you have run the VersaMail application, press the MENU button | Accounts | Account Setup | New, as shown in Figure 6-1.

FIGURE 6-1   VersaMail—Account Setup

5. On the first page of the new account setup, enter a name for this e-mail account to help you remember what it is, such as "Work Mail."

6. On Choose your e-mail service provider from the list, as shown in Figure 6-2:

a. If your e-mail account is a Microsoft Exchange ActiveSync account that syncs with Microsoft Exchange Server 2003, you will need additional information such as the e-mail server network name port number and whether the server requires a VPN connection, as well as whether or not VersaMail needs to go through a proxy, and if so, the name of the proxy server. You will likely want to recruit some help from your friendly IT people regarding this setup.

b. If your service provider is not in the list, then choose Other and make sure that you have the information discussed in Step 1d.

7. After you have completed the screen, press Next.

FIGURE 6-2   VersaMail—Choose Your Provider

FIGURE 6-3 VersaMail—User Password

8. On the screen shown in Figure 6-3:

   a. Enter your account name, which is usually the part of your e-mail address before the "@" symbol. For example, if my e-mail address was dfoster@somemail.com, my username is likely "dfoster."

   b. Enter the password for your e-mail account, and press Next.

9. If you chose your e-mail provider from the list, then you are finished; if you chose Other, then you still have some work to do and you will see a screen similar to Figure 6-4.

   a. Confirm your e-mail address.

   b. Enter the outgoing e-mail server name (POP3 or IMAP server).

   c. Enter the incoming e-mail server name (SMTP server).

10. You may have to edit the Advanced settings for your e-mail account if it requires further authentication/security such as SSL, APOP, or ESMTP, so it is important to find out from your e-mail administrator what information you need.

FIGURE 6-4 VersaMail—Other Mail Servers

If your configuration settings are all correct, then you will now be able to send and receive e-mail using VersaMail on your Treo. The downside is that if your e-mail is not working after you have set it up, the error messages are sometimes not very helpful, so you will need to check all of your information. Sometimes it is even easier to delete the account and start over. Fortunately, it doesn't take very long.

Use VersaMail

Once VersaMail is configured and you are able to send and receive messages, there are a few handy features that you should know about. We are assuming that this is not the first time that you have ever used an e-mail application, so we won't go over the basic compose, send, and receive actions in VersaMail.

Set Up Auto Sync in VersaMail

With Auto Sync you can configure your Treo to automatically check for new e-mail, calendar events, or contacts. The alternative if you have not turned on Auto Sync is to press the Send/Receive button every time you want to check for new mail, contacts and calendar events on the mail server. Also, you can configure Auto Sync to alert you with a sound or vibration when new message arrive.

TIP *Calendar and contacts sync is only available if Exchange Active Sync is selected. With POP3 and IMAP only e-mail sync is available.*

To configure Auto Sync follow these steps:

1. In VersaMail (to launch VersaMail press the Home button and in the application launcher find and select the E-mail / VersaMail icon).

Press the MENU button | Options | Preferences | Signature | select the Attach Signature checkbox. You should see a screen that looks like Figure 6-5. If you are not using a POP3 or IMAP e-mail account you won't see the Contact and Calendar check boxes on the screen.

FIGURE 6-5   VersaMail—Auto Sync configuration screen

2. Here you can define how often you want VersaMail to check for new data, start time and end time, days of the week (which days and hours you want Auto Sync to run). If you are using Exchange Active Sync you can also define when you want the Calendar and Contacts to sync.

3. Once you have set your preferences, press OK.

To kick off the process, you will want to manually select the Sync action by selecting the Get or Sync button in VersaMail.

VersaMail Message Menu

The VersaMail Message menu allows you to perform several actions on your messages. The menu, shown in Figure 6-6, allows you to perform common tasks on messages, including moving messages and marking messages read or unread. You will likely get very familiar with this menu as you use VersaMail.

The VersaMail Preferences Screen

After you have configured e-mail and defined your Auto Sync preferences you can likely leave the default settings in VersaMail and be happy with it. That said; there are a few preferences that you should at least know about in case you want to change them. The VersaMail Preferences screen is accessed by pressing the MENU button and then selecting Options | Preferences in VersaMail. It looks like Figure 6-7.

- **General—Display options**   Here you can define sort parameters and other display options for your e-mail.

- **General—Deletion**   Here you can define whether you want to confirm deletions and how often you want your deleted items (trash) permanently deleted.

FIGURE 6-6   VersaMail Message menu

FIGURE 6-7 VersaMail Preferences screen

- **Delivery—Incoming** Here you can define how you want incoming mail to be handled, including whether you want to automatically download attachments and the maximum message size that you want to automatically download, among other things.

- **Delivery—Forwarding** On this screen you can define how you want VersaMail to treat messages that you forward from your Treo: Forward original from server vs. Forward a copy from device.

- **Delivery—Auto Sync** This is discussed in the previous section called "Set Up Auto Sync in VersaMail."

- **Delivery—Alerts** Here you can define whether you want an audible alert to be generated when you receive new messages or there is a failure.

- **Message—Reply Options** This screen allows you to define how you want messages that you are replying to to be treated, including whether you want the original text from the message included.

- **Message—Signature** This screen is discussed in the next section, called "Define an E-Mail Signature."

- **Advanced—Connections** Here you can define your time-out interval and how long you want the modem to wait before ending.

- **Advanced—Server** This feature may or may not be important to you, but in order to save memory on the Treo, you may want to delete messages after you have read them. This screen allows you to set a flag so that messages are not deleted from the e-mail server when you delete them on your Treo.

FIGURE 6-8   VersaMail—Attach Your Signature

Define an E-Mail Signature

An e-mail signature is predefined text, usually consisting of your name, company, contact information, or anything else that you want to send with every e-mail without having to type it every time. To define your e-mail signature, follow these steps:

1. Start VersaMail (to launch VersaMail, press the HOME button and in the application launcher find and select the VersaMail icon).

2. Press the MENU button and select Options | Preferences | Signature. Select the Attach Signature check box.

   You should see a screen that looks like Figure 6-8.

3. Enter your signature text and select Done.

Now, whenever you compose a new e-mail, the signature will be included in the message by default.

About Palm Mail on the Treo 600

If you have a Treo 600, your Treo likely shipped with the Palm Mail application. This e-mail service is no longer supported. Since the creation of Treo Mail, Visto Corporation has managed the back end of the Treo Mail system. In early 2004, Palm decided to transition the entire Treo Mail service management to Visto. Therefore, you may want to consider VersaMail version 2.7 or above, or one of the other e-mail options discussed in this chapter, to send and receive e-mail on your Treo 600.

Third-Party POP3 E-Mail Application Options for Your Treo

If Palm Mail or VersaMail is not exactly what you need, there are third-party e-mail applications that allow you to use your Treo with your POP3 e-mail account. The following list outlines the various POP3 e-mail client software options for your Treo. Specific product information is available from the product web sites, and an updated list of products is available on the Palm web site at www.palm.com.

- SnapperMail (www.snappermail.com)—also supports IMAP accounts
- Corsoft Aileron (www.aileron.com)
- Eudora for Palm OS (www.eudora.com)
- VersaMail (www.versamail.com)—also supports IMAP accounts
- Iambic Mail (www.iambic.com)—also supports IMAP accounts

IMAP E-Mail Application Options for Your Treo

The Internet Message Access Protocol is a method of accessing electronic mail or bulletin board messages that are kept on a mail server. IMAP permits a "client" e-mail program on your Treo or PC to access remote e-mail message stores as if they were local. For example, e-mail stored on an IMAP server can be manipulated from a desktop computer at home, a workstation at the office, and a notebook computer while traveling, without the need to transfer messages or files back and forth between these computers. Many of the corporate e-mail account types support IMAP e-mail, such as the following:

- GoodLink (www.good.com)
- VersaMail (www.palmone.com/us/software/versamail)
- SnapperMail (www.snappermail.com)
- Iambic Mail (www.iambic.com)
- ChatterE-mail (www.e-mailtreo.com)

Corporate E-Mail Options—Microsoft Exchange and Lotus Domino

If your e-mail account is hosted and managed by the company you work for, there is a high likelihood that it's either Microsoft Exchange or Lotus Domino. The configuration of an e-mail application on your Treo depends largely on how your corporate e-mail infrastructure is set up. VersaMail and other e-mail applications can use Domino and MS Exchange e-mail provided that IMAP, POP3, or Microsoft ActiveSync is enabled on the mail server.

Set Up Your Treo to Use a Corporate E-Mail Account

If the organization you work for uses Microsoft Exchange or Lotus Domino, then the first thing you should do is contact your organization's e-mail administrator or Help Desk to find out whether the company already has an e-mail solution for handheld devices running the Palm operating system. If you are not the first one in your company to get a shiny new Treo, then chances are your company already has the necessary software and the understanding of how to get your Treo e-mail set up. If you don't find the help you need within your Information Technology (IT) staff—or if you are the IT staff—then refer to the following sections on using Exchange and Lotus Domino e-mail on your Treo.

Push E-Mail

Traditional e-mail is non-push. But what the heck does that mean? Well, to explain it properly, we should probably explain "push" e-mail first. Push e-mail is sent to your Treo without requiring any effort from you or your Treo besides turning the wireless mode on. E-mail simply shows up when you are not looking because it is pushed to your device from the e-mail server. Non-push e-mail, on the other hand, requires you or your e-mail application to actively request to send or receive e-mail before your Treo will connect to the e-mail server to send any pending e-mail, and to check for new e-mail. The free Palm Mail application is a non-push e-mail application. If you would prefer a push application, there are several third-party applications to consider.

NOTE   *Push e-mail applications use a software component that interacts with the e-mail server.*

Software That Allows You to Use Corporate E-Mail Systems

Several vendors provide third-party e-mail applications that allow you to use your Treo with your corporate e-mail account, as listed here. Specific product information is available from the product web sites, and an updated list of products can be found on the Palm web site at www.palm.com.

- Visto MessageXpress (www.visto.com/treo)
- GoodLink (www.good.com)
- Infowave SymmetryPro (www.infowave.com)
- Basejet (www.basejet.com)
- Notify Technology NotifyLink (www.notifycorp.com)
- Seven (www.seven.com)
- Sprint PCS Business Connection (Sprint customers only; http://businessconnection .sprintpcs.com)

Wrap It Up

Only a few short years ago, mobile devices and networks were designed specifically to allow users to make and receive wireless phone calls. The Treo offers a quantum leap forward in mobile technology. Palm has extended tried-and-true mobile phone technologies to allow us to send and receive e-mail from virtually anywhere. The promise of a true mobile office has never been closer.

Arguably, getting the e-mail functionality set up on your Treo for the first time may not be the easiest part of configuring your Treo but armed with the information presented in this chapter, you should be well on your way.

6

Chapter 7

Take and Send Photos

How to...

- Take a photo
- Record video (not available on the Treo 600)
- Send photos and video to others using e-mail, Sprint Picture Mail, MMS, Bluetooth, and Infrared
- Download your Treo photos and video to your PC—Windows and Mac
- Use third-party software to edit your photos
- Personalize your Treo with wallpaper and photo caller ID
- Use third-party software to manage your photos
- Share your photos with others online
- Create your own photo blog
- Print your photos

Clearly, if your Treo does not feature a camera, then this chapter won't contain a lot of useful information for you, but most Treos do include a camera application, and many also include a camcorder. One of the most significant recent advances in consumer electronics, in addition to your fantastic Treo, has been the evolution of digital photography. And as if your Treo doesn't let you do enough already, it also allows you to take digital snapshots and video (not available on the Treo 600), save them, and send them to others.

Technical Information about Your Treo Digital Camera and Camcorder

The Treo camera is not intended to capture monumental sweeping mountain landscapes to hang on your wall or to record your wedding reception for generations to enjoy—although you certainly can do that if you like. The camera is really intended as a fun way to take snapshots anywhere and share them with friends. Your built-in Treo camera features include the following:

Treo 700p—camera technical specs

- 1.3 megapixel capability 2× digital zoom
- Maximum resolution of 1280×1024 (alternate settings are VGA 640×480 and QVGA 320×240)
- Video clip and audio recording capability at a 352×288 resolution (alternate settings are QCIF 176×144 resolution)
- Automatic light balance
- Frames Per Second capture rate

Treo 650—camera technical specs

- VGA lens with 2× digital zoom
- 0.3 megapixel capability
- Maximum resolution of 640×480
- Automatic light balancing
- Video capture and audio recording capability at a resolution of 176×144

Treo 600—camera technical specs

- Single-focus VGA lens
- 0.3 megapixel capability
- Maximum resolution of 640×480

TIP

Your Treo screen resolution is lower than the photo resolution your Treo camera can take. This means that your resulting photos will be of a higher quality when viewed on your PC or printed than what you see on the screen when you take the photo or when you view your photos on your Treo.

Take Photos with Your Treo

If you are the type of person that likes to press every button and simply play around with your new electronic toy before reading about its features and how they work, then you may already have taken some photos of your pets, office, friends, and so on. But if you haven't yet ventured into the world of Treo digital photography, here's your chance to get started. To take a photo in the simplest way possible, follow these steps:

1. Choose something to be your photo subject, taking care to ensure that the object is in bright light (the more light there is, the better your result will be).

2. Press the PHONE button.

3. Find and select the Camera button on the bottom of the screen (you may need to scroll down to see the button).

4. The screen now becomes your camera view finder, and you will be able to see what the camera is "seeing"—this feature also means that you don't have to hold the camera up to your eye to see where the camera is pointing. You can hold it any way you want as long as you can see the screen. (Ensure that the Camera button, not the Video button, is selected as shown in Figure 7-1. Note that the screen shown is from the Treo 700p, and if you have a different model it will look different.)

FIGURE 7-1 Camera button

5. Point the camera at your target, which should be at least 18 inches from your Treo.

6. When your target is framed on the screen (while holding the camera as still as you can), press the CENTER button of the five-way navigation control or tap the Capture button on the screen.

After the image has been captured, it will be accompanied on the screen by three button options to choose from: Save, Delete, Recorder, and Send. Save and Delete, shown in Figure 7-2, should be relatively obvious functions; the other two are covered in the next section.

Tips for Taking Photos with Your Treo

You probably aren't surprised that your Treo doesn't produce photographs like a Hasselblad 501 or an eight-megapixel digital SLR. But, it has been our experience and that of many others that there are steps you can take to help ensure you produce high-quality digital photos with your Treo. In fact, there are a few web sites where Treo users showcase their Treo photos, clearly showing that if you understand your Treo camera, you can take some great photos. You can find these web sites by typing **Treo camera** into the Google search engine (www.google.com). Of course, if you already have a good working knowledge of photography, some of these suggestions will seem basic. Nevertheless, they are very important for maximizing the quality of your photos.

Use Good Light

Your Treo doesn't have a flash, so your subject's light source is one of the most important factors to consider when taking photos with your Treo. (Note that the term "subject" is just an artsy way of saying "that thing you're taking a picture of.") Of course, in many situations, the source and location of the light are beyond your control. For example, it usually isn't very practical to wait for the sun to move across the sky so that the daylight illuminating your squirrel subject is

FIGURE 7-2 Save, Delete, Recorder, and Send buttons

coming from *just* the right angle. Low lighting will be obvious on the screen because you will see little blue pixels on the screen. A couple more tips are listed next.

Ensure the Main Light Source Is Behind You, Not the Subject   Often, if you take photos of people with the sun shining behind them, your resulting photos are more like silhouettes of the people than detailed likenesses. A photo will turn out better if the sun is behind you when you take it because the sun will be facing your subject and will provide more of the light your Treo needs to capture the image.

Move the Camera Until You Don't See Washed-Out Areas   When looking at the screen in camera mode, you may notice that areas of high contrast, as well as very bright or reflective areas, will seem washed out or whiter than they should. Often, moving the camera slightly to change the angle of the shot will allow the camera to recompose the image so that it reflects more accurately what the scene looks like.

Keep the Treo Still While Taking a Picture

Keeping your Treo still while you snap your shot is another very important aspect of taking good photos. If you can, steady your arm on a table, tree, or parking meter, and your shots will improve. You will notice that even a little bit of movement will cause blurring in the photo. Of course, if you *want* a little blurring in your photos for artistic effect, that's easy enough to do.

Take a Picture Within Two Seconds of Launching the Camera

Some users who have taken a picture within two seconds of launching the camera (before the screen has had time to compose the image) have reported that their picture quality is improved. The success of this technique seems to depend on the user and the individual Treo. You may find it doesn't make much difference at all, but it's worth mentioning here as an addition to your bag of Treo tricks.

Take Multiple Pictures of the Same Subject

If you have the time, it is always a good idea to take a few photos of the same subject from different angles and distances. One of the best things about digital photography is that you can simply delete any photos you don't want, and it doesn't cost you a thing—unlike film photography, where you have to pay for the film to be developed before you can find out whether that photograph of your thumb is worth keeping or not.

Treo Camera Features and Functions

The camera functions that are presented in this section are largely unavailable on the Treo 600. The scenario presented above in the section called "Take Photos with Your Treo" is the simplest way to take a photo, and there are some other features that you should be aware of to help you get the most out of your Treo camera. Details on how to use the features that are not terribly

FIGURE 7-3   Zoom button

obvious such as Sprint Picture Mail and Sprint Online Album functionality are covered in detail in your Treo user guide, but they are listed here because all Treo users should certainly know about them.

- **2x zoom**   Your Treo is equipped with a digital zoom that allows you to get twice as close to your target without physically moving closer. The zoom options surround the Onscreen Capture button, as shown in Figure 7-3. You can toggle between the zoom modes by in the camera application, by either pressing the on screen buttons above and below the onscreen camera button: 2x and 1x; or you can use the 5-way navigation button to select the appropriate zoom.

- **Record a voice or sound caption**   After you have taken a photo, you have the option to record a short sound clip to be linked to the photo. A caption may be something like: "This is Dave crumpled on the ground after his four-year-old hit him in the shin with a hockey stick." The Record button option will appear immediately after you take a photo, as shown in Figure 7-4.

Options to send a photo are covered in more detail later in this chapter, under the heading "Send a Photo to Others." The list includes:

- Sprint-specific options
  - Send a photo as part of a Sprint Picture Mail message.
  - Send a photo using Sprint Online Services.
  - Upload a photo to a Sprint Online Album.
- Verizon-specific options
  - Send a photo as part of an MMS message (MMS, the Multimedia Messaging Service, is discussed in more detail in Chapter 5).

FIGURE 7-4   Record Sound button

Of course, in addition to the send options that you can perform from within the camera application, you can e-mail photos using the e-mail application on your Treo, and you can move the photos to your PC and send them to others from there. Some of the options to send files directly from the Treo are discussed later in this chapter, and e-mail is discussed in Chapter 6.

Configure Your Treo Camera Settings

There are a few camera configuration settings that you should be aware of. You can access and change the camera settings from within the camera application by pressing the MENU button on the Treo keyboard. You will see a screen much like the one shown in Figure 7-5.

- **Effects**   You can choose a few different effects for your photos, including black and white and sepia. Sepia is an effect that is designed to make your photos look aged, as if they were stored in a photo album for decades.

- **Prompt sound**   This setting allows you to select a sound, or even record your own, that plays before you take a photo. To use this feature, when you are ready to take a photo press the CAPTURE button or the center of the five-way navigation button to start the sound; then click the button again to take the photo. This feature can be useful if you want to get the attention of your subject before you snap a photo, but keep in mind that it will slow down the process because you have to press the button twice. We found the Bach Partita clip was especially effective, as the subject looked around to find out who was playing the violin behind him or her only to have their unsuspecting face being captured on a Treo.

- **Shutter sound**   You have the option of turning the shutter sound off. This is a good idea if you are trying to hide the fact that you are taking a photo with your Treo, as the shutter sound tends to give it away.

- **Resolution**   If your Treo is capable of taking photos in different resolutions, it is an important feature because depending on how you want to use a photo, you may want to set a different resolution. Lower resolutions mean smaller file sizes, which means that you can store more photos in memory and they will be easier to upload, download, or send to someone else—but at the cost of reduced photo quality.

FIGURE 7-5   Photo settings

■ **Date stamp**   It is often useful to date-stamp your photos so that you have a record of when the photo was taken. The downside is that the date will appear as part of the photo.

■ **Review photos**   This setting allows you to define whether you want to review your photos before saving or deleting them. If this setting is off, the photo will be automatically saved and after you have taken a photo, the application will take you back to the camera ready screen. A benefit of turning the Review photos setting off is that you can take successive photos at a quicker pace.

■ **Auto Naming**   You have the option to change the auto-naming format for your photos. This feature may be a little limited, on our Sprint 700p at least, as all you can do is define a five-letter name that will be saved in front of a sequential number. For example, we wanted to name some photos with the prefix "TechEdTradeShow" because that is where they were taken, but we were limited to "trade," so we ended up with photo files named trade01.jpg, trade02.jpg, etc. Still, it is handy to help you categorize your photos.

Save a Photo or Video

When you take a photo, it is automatically saved, unless of course you select to Delete it. There are a couple of things that you should know about saving a photo.

Use Treo Albums to Organize Your Photos and Videos—Treo 650 and 700 specific

By default, the Treo Camera application stores your photos on your Treo in a file directory called the "Palm album." If you have an expansion memory card inserted into your Treo, then a Palm album directory will be created on the card and your photos will be stored there. If you want to store your photos in a different location, you can create a new album and include the name and location. This is a great way to group your photos so that you won't have to scroll through 160 or more photos to find the ones you want.

To change or add an album, simply select the albums MENU button on the camera application screen, as shown in Figure 7-6, and select the album you want or select the New Albums option, as shown in Figure 7-7.

Use a Memory Card to Store Photos

Removable memory cards are discussed in more detail in Chapter 15, but we discuss the basics relating to storing photos and videos here. Your Treo is equipped with a memory card slot that allows you to use removable Secure Digital (SD) or MultiMediaCard (MMC) memory cards.

FIGURE 7-6   Camera/Camcorder albums

FIGURE 7-7	New Album option

There are many memory card standards, so when you're looking to buy a memory card for your Treo, make sure you buy an SD or MMC card. Examples of memory cards that don't work with your Treo are Compact Flash and SmartMedia. Again, your Treo is designed for use with SD and MMC cards only.

Your Treo has limited available on-device memory for files, applications, and pictures, so the ability to expand memory is extremely useful. Memory cards are available at very reasonable prices; 4GB cards are currently available for around $100, and we can expect the capacities to continue to rise and prices to continue to drop. You can create albums in the Camera and Camcorder applications that are stored on a memory card. The steps to do this are discussed in the previous section called "Use Treo Albums to Organize Your Photos and Videos."

Some newer DVD players have the ability to show images that have been stored on recordable DVD/CD discs. This means that if your PC is equipped with a DVD or CD burner, you can burn your photos to a recordable DVD/CD and play them back on your TV using your DVD/CD player.

Treo 600-Specific Camera Options

The camera application on the Treo 650 and 700p are very similar, but there are a few options that are specific to the Treo 600; some of the more useful ones are listed here.

On a Treo 600 you cannot store newly captured photos directly to your SD memory card. Initially when you take a photo with your Treo, the photo will be stored locally on your Treo. Once the photo is taken, you can move it to your SD card. On a Treo 650 or 700p you can create a new photo Album that resides on a removable memory card so that every time you save a photo or video to that Album it will automatically be saved to the memory card.

Rename a New Photo Before You Save It—Treo 600 Specific

Your new photo is assigned a default name, something like Picture009_05Feb04, which may not be very useful in identifying the photo from a list later on without looking at it; but you have the option to rename the photo before you save it. To rename the file, simply select the text in the upper-left corner and type in a new name.

File a New Photo—Treo 600 Specific

You can file your photos in folders to help better organize them. Palm uses the term *category* to allow you to define groups that help you organize your information. Categories are conceptually similar to files, folders, organizational units, shopping carts, and other organizational types you've run across in the past. Categorizing and renaming photos when you save them may not seem like a big deal when you only have a few photos, but later on when you have hundreds or thousands of photos, you'll be thankful you took the time to get organized now. For more information on photo naming, see the section "Define a Default Picture Name" later in this chapter.

To save the photo to a specific category, follow these steps:

1. Immediately after you have taken a photo, select the menu in the top-right corner of the screen and select the category this photo should be filed in. If you want to create a new category, simply follow these steps:

    a. Select the Edit Categories option from the menu.

    b. Type in a name for the new category.

    c. Press OK.

2. Press the Save button.

Now you will be able to easily locate your new photo later on both your PC and on your Treo.

Define a Default Picture Name—Treo 600 Specific

A default picture name on your Treo looks something like Picture009_05Feb04. This naming scheme tells you what day a photo was taken, but you may want a little more information to help you identify pictures later. One option is to name every photo immediately after you take it; another option is to set the default name to something useful for a series of pictures. For example, you may want a series of photos that you will be taking at Dave's 42nd birthday party to begin with the name "DavesBDay." To change the default name, follow these steps:

1. Launch the Camera application (as described in the earlier section "Take a Quick Series of Photos").

2. From any Camera view, press MENU on the keyboard.

3. From the Options menu, choose Preferences.

4. At the top of the Preferences screen, there is a field called Default Name. In this field, you can type the name of the next series of photos that you are going to take—for example, "DavesBDay," as shown in Figure 7-8.

Now, every subsequent picture will have a name beginning with the new default name and the number of the photo. You can change the default name at any time to better reflect the name of your next series of photos.

Define the Default Category for New Photos—Treo 600 Specific

Your categories are conceptually similar to file folders, and they allow you to organize your Treo files, including your photos, in a way that helps you store them in logically organized groups. This helps you find things more quickly when you need to.

FIGURE 7-8   Treo 600 default picture names

7

When you take a new photo and save it without changing the category, it is saved into the default category. You can change the category by selecting an alternate category for the photo from the Category menu. If you like, you can also change the default category. This enables you to create a more appropriate category name than "uncategorized" and speeds up the process by immediately saving your photos in the most appropriate category so that you can easily locate a particular photo later on. To change the default category, follow these steps:

1. Launch the Camera application by pressing the PHONE button and selecting the Camera Onscreen button (you may have to scroll down to see the button).

2. From any Camera view, press MENU on the keyboard and choose the Preferences menu option.

3. Select the Category pull-down menu and choose the category that you would like to be the default category for new photos. You can add a new category by selecting the Edit Categories option from the list.

4. Select OK, and if you edited your categories, select OK on the Preferences screen as well.

Configure Your Default Picture Size—Treo 600 Specific

Your Treo is capable of taking two different sizes of digital photos: large—640×480 pixels, and small—120×160 pixels. The default size for newly captured photos is the larger format of 640×480 pixels, but there may be times when you prefer to use the smaller format—for example, if you want to conserve the amount of Treo memory that's used to store your Treo photos or if you want to send your photos using wireless connectivity applications like e-mail, MMS, or Sprint Picture Mail. The smaller format creates smaller file sizes that are easier to transmit over relatively slow wireless networks. Smaller files sizes also mean that the recipient of a message containing a photo will be able to download and view it faster than if it were a larger image file.

Be aware that the smaller image size results in a smaller file size and also a lesser-quality image. So, you should choose the appropriate photo size for what you intend to do with it.

You can toggle between the larger and smaller photo sizes at any time by configuring your camera preferences. The steps are listed here:

1. Launch the Camera application (as described in the earlier section "Take a Quick Series of Photos").

2. From any Camera view, press MENU on the keyboard.

3. From the Options menu, choose Preferences.

4. Select the Picture Size drop-down menu, shown in Figure 7-9, and choose the size you want. Select OK.

Define Your Backup Settings—Treo 600 Specific

Your Treo picture backup setting is very straightforward, you either want your pictures copied from your Treo to your PC during a HotSync operation, or you don't. The trade-off is that if you do back up your pictures to your PC every time you perform a HotSync operation, the process will take longer. This is more important if you are performing a HotSync operation remotely instead of through a HotSync cable connected directly to your PC. But if you don't back up your pictures to your PC and you lose your Treo or have to perform a hard reset, your pictures will be unrecoverable. This warning is also written on the Backup Settings screen, which is shown in Figure 7-10.

To change your backup setting (the default setting is to back up your pictures during a HotSync operation), follow these steps:

1. Launch the Camera application (as described in the earlier section "Take a Quick Series of Photos").

2. From any Camera view, press MENU on the keyboard.

FIGURE 7-9 Select picture size

| FIGURE 7-10 | Backup Settings |

3. From the Options menu, choose Preferences.

4. On the Preferences screen, select the Backup Settings button.

5. If the Backup Pictures During HotSync Process check box is checked, it is set to back up automatically during a HotSync operation. Check or uncheck the box according to how you want HotSync to deal with pictures.

6. Select OK on the Backup Settings screen, and then select OK on the Preferences screen.

Obviously, you can change this setting at any time, depending on your circumstances—for example, you may want to perform a HotSync operation using the wireless network because you are traveling and are away from your office PC. If you are interested in synchronizing the new contacts you have made but are less worried about the hundreds of photos you have taken, you may want to turn off the Backup Pictures During HotSync Process setting to ensure that the HotSync operation takes significantly less time—and if you pay a user fee on the amount of wireless data you send, you will save money by not backing up your pictures until you are back in the office and can synchronize locally to your PC.

Take a Quick Series of Photos—Treo 600 Specific

There may be times when you want to take a sequence of photos in a row during a relatively short period of time. For example, a sequence of a friend jumping off of a balcony holding only a Mickey Mouse umbrella in one hand and a frothy pink beverage in the other. These photos may be followed by a sequence of photos of the same friend getting his ankles adjusted at the hospital. The Treo 600 does not have an adjustable frames per second capture rate, but there are a couple of Treo settings that you can change to allow you to minimize the interval between successive photos. (Translation: they let you take a bunch of photos in a row quickly.) When selected, these two settings slow down the repeated picture-taking process and interrupt the pattern of taking several pictures in a row.

- **Play Capture Sound/Shutter Sound**   This setting produces a camera sound effect, and it delays the process by a second or more.
- **Confirm Before Saving**   The screen containing your photo and the Save, Don't Save, and Send buttons that pops up by default after you take a photo is a more significant interruption than the camera sound setting because it requires an action from you that may take several seconds to complete, such as selecting the Save option and readying the camera for the next photo.

To change both of these default settings, follow these steps:

1. Launch the Camera application by doing one of the following:
   - Press the HOME button, and then find and select Camera.
   - Press the PHONE button and press the RIGHT button on the five-way navigation control.
2. From any Camera view, press MENU.
3. From the Options menu, choose Preferences.
4. Uncheck both of the following settings:
   - Play Capture Sound
   - Confirm Before Saving

With these two settings disabled, you can take a series of photos much more quickly than before.

View a Photo or Video on Your Treo

Depending on which model of Treo you have some of the terminology is a little different as are the steps to perform similar actions.

View a Photo on Your Treo 650 or 700p

You may view your saved photos on your Treo at any time by following these steps:

1. Launch the Camera application by selecting the PHONE button and finding the Camera shortcut (you may have to scroll down to see the button).
2. In the Camera application, select the Pictures and Videos button on the bottom left of the screen (it looks like a stack of paper), as shown in Figure 7-11.

FIGURE 7-11   Pictures and Videos button

FIGURE 7-12   Treo 600 Pictures list

3. Select the album where the photo you are looking for is, or select All Pictures & Videos to browse thumbnails of your pictures and videos.

4. Select the photo or video that you want to view by either selecting it on the touch screen or use the five-way navigation buttons to highlight and select it.

View a Photo on Your Treo 600

You may view your saved photos on your Treo 600 at any time by following these steps:

1. Press HOME to open the Applications Launcher screen.

2. Find and select the camera icon.

3. Choose the Pictures view icon at the bottom of the screen to see a list similar to that shown in Figure 7-12.

4. Scroll down until you see the photo you want to view and select it by either tapping the touch screen or pressing the CENTER button on the five-way navigation control.

5. From Pictures view, you can browse to the previous photo in the list by selecting the Prev button or skip to the next photo by selecting the Next button.

Record Video and Sound with Your Treo

Video functionality is not available on the Treo 600. To begin recording video and sound with your Treo 650 or 700p, follow these steps:

1. Launch the Applications screen by pressing the HOME button.

2. Select the Camcorder icon, or the Camera icon—either works, and if you have a 650, you may not have a camcorder icon. This can also be accessed from the PHONE menu.

3. By default, your videos will be stored in the Palm album on your device; if you have a removable memory card in your Treo, a Palm album will be automatically created on the memory card, but you can change which album you want the video stored in.

4. When you are ready to record, point the Treo camera lens at your subject while watching the Treo screen so that you can see what you will be recording.

5. Press the center of the five-way navigation button to begin recording.

6. When you have finished recording, press the CENTER button again.

Immediately after you have finished recording your video, you can access a few options directly from the screen: you can view, save, delete, adjust the sound volume, or send the video. The send options are discussed earlier in this chapter.

The video recording screen shows the approximate remaining recording time based on available memory on your Treo or memory card. Remember that this is only an approximation.

Modify Your Camcorder Settings

The Treo Camcorder is very easy to use and offers some customizability, including the ability to configure the following settings:

- **Effects**   This control allows you to configure the color palette before you record a video. Your options include Normal (color), Black and White, and Sepia. The Sepia effect, in our opinion, is more effective for photos than video, but if you want a vintage-looking effect, you may like it. It is important to know that you cannot change an effect after you have recorded the video without using a third-party video editing software tool on a PC, and even then you may be limited.

- **Shutter sound**   This setting determines whether a sound is played when you start and stop recording.

- **Microphone**   This setting allows you to turn the microphone on and off.

- **Resolution**   This allows you to define the resolution of videos, the options are 352×288 and 176×144 (in the 650 and 700p). The main reason that you may want to change this is that the smaller resolution will have smaller file sizes, so you will be able to store more video in memory or on a storage card.

- **Review videos**   This setting allows you to define whether you want to review videos before saving them.

- **Auto-naming**   The default file naming is a little vague, so you may want to define a new naming convention for a series of videos, for example: "staff," which will be the prefix for the next videos you take, resulting in filenames beginning, for instance, staff_070706_001.

The Camcorder Video Settings can be accessed by launching either the Camcorder or the Camera, ensuring that the Video icon is selected in the application, and pressing the MENU button.

Tips to Improve the Quality of Your Treo Video

There are a few simple tips that will help you get the most out of your Treo camcorder functionality:

- *Pay attention to the light conditions.* Your video will look best when there is a lot of light on the subject, so if you are using the camcorder inside, turn on additional lights or open blinds, if you have those options. Another good tip that any photographer should know is that is important to have a major source of light, such as the sun, behind the videographer so that it is shining on the subject. This will help ensure that your subject doesn't end up looking like a silhouette, as this is what can happen if there is bright light behind the subject.

- *Keep the Treo as still as you can while you are recording.* We have likely all seen video shot by a shaky camera person. It can be hard to watch and even cause a little motion sickness in some viewers.

- *Ensure that the lens is clean.* It is important to use a clean, soft cloth to wipe the lens so that your videos can be as clear as possible.

- *Keep any sound source at least a foot away from the Treo.* Whether you are recording your own voice as you narrate the video or recording someone else, try to keep the Treo at least 12 inches away from the sound source to minimize sound distortion.

Transfer and Send Your Treo Media

Once you have taken a photo with your Treo, you can send it to others using a variety of methods. Immediately after you have taken a photo, you can choose to send the photo to someone else. The options that you have available to you vary slightly depending on what carrier network is hosting your Treo and which model you have. Of course, you can also attach a photo to an e-mail or MMS/Sprint Picture Mail message at any time.

There are many reasons it is a good idea to transfer photos, and any other files, from your Treo to a PC; common reasons include

- File backup
- Manipulation of files, for example photo editing with PC-based software
- Sending files using PC-based e-mail software

The most common methods to transfer or send files from your Treo to a PC include

- **HotSync**   When you perform a HotSync operation your Treo with your PC, your photos will be copied to your PC. Setting up your Treo and PC (Windows and Mac) to synchronize data using the Palm HotSync software is discussed in detail in Chapter 3.

- **E-mail**   You can e-mail files to any e-mail address using an e-mail application running on your Treo. E-mail is covered in detail in Chapter 6.

- **MMS or Sprint Picture Mail**   Multimedia Messaging Service or Sprint Picture Mail are non-e-mail messaging alternatives that allow you to send an image as a part of the message. Both MMS and Sprint Picture Mail are discussed in detail in Chapter 5, but there is also a section later in this chapter.

- **Bluetooth** (not available on the Treo 600)   Bluetooth is a short-range wireless technology that allows you to connect your Treo 650 or 700p to other Bluetooth-capable devices and transfer files. Bluetooth technology is discussed in detail in Chapter 5.

- **Infrared**   Bluetooth is a short-range, line-of-sight wireless technology that allows you to connect your Treo to other infrared-capable devices and transfer files. Infrared technology is discussed in detail in Chapter 5.

- **Removable Memory Card**   Your Treo is equipped with a removable memory card slot. You can save your files to the card and then remove the card to insert it into another compatible device or card reader. Memory cards are covered in detail in Chapter 15.

Sprint-Specific Message Send Options

Sprint offers a few options that are not available on other carriers. These options include Sprint Picture Mail and Sprint Online Services. You may or may not value these options, but it is nice to be able to choose whether or not you want to use them.

> TIP   *Your Sprint Picture Mail account requires some initial setup, and the first time you try to send a photo or video, you will have to set up an account with Sprint. The setup process is simple and involves entering your Treo phone number, if it isn't detected automatically, and a four- to eight-character password.*

Upload to Sprint Online Albums

Once you have set up a Sprint PCS Picture Mail account, you have access to a personal online album that resides on the Sprint PCS Picture Mail web site (https://pictures.sprintpcs.com). Once set up, your online album allows you to store and view pictures on your Sprint-hosted web site.

To upload a photo from your Sprint Treo to your Sprint Picture Mail online album web site, follow these steps:

1. Select the HOME button to view your applications.
2. Select the Pics & Videos application icon.
3. Select the album that contains the photos that you want to upload from your Treo to your online album.
4. Select the Upload to Online Albums option.
5. Browse to the photos or videos that you want to upload.
6. Finally, select Upload.
7. If all goes well and you are in a coverage area, your selected media will be uploaded to your Picture Mail online album for you to view and share with others.

Send Media with Sprint Picture Mail

If your Treo is a Sprint device, Sprint has included an application called Sprint PCS Photo Mail that allows you to send messages consisting of photos, videos, text, and sound files, including media you record or capture on your Treo and other files that are stored on your Treo. One advantage of Picture Mail is that you don't need an e-mail account to send messages and media to others.

This type of messaging is different than e-mail or text messaging because the media is not sent directly to them. What happens is this: Your message is uploaded to the Sprint PCS Photo Mail web site (www.sprint.com/photomail), where a private Guest Book is created for the recipient. The recipient then receives a message that encourages him or her to use a web browser to access this private Guest Book so that he or she can view the photos or videos that you "sent." The site also allows recipients to enter comments if they like.

The types of files that you can include in a Sprint Picture Mail message include

- Photos
- Videos
- Text messages
- Voice memos

To create and send a new Picture Mail message on your Sprint Treo, follow these steps:

1. Press the Messaging button (the button that looks like a mail envelope).

2. Select the New button.

3. Select the To field and enter the e-mail address or mobile phone number of the person you want to send the message to. As you begin typing, any matches from your Contact list will appear in a drop-down menu, so you can select an appropriate match to minimize typing. The quickest way to do this is to enter the first initial and last name of the contact, with no spaces in between.

4. Select the Add Media icon and select one of the options:

   a. **Attach from device**   This option lets you browse and attach a photo or video that is stored on your Treo.

   b. **Attach from Online**   This option lets you attach a photo or video from your online album. The Sprint Online Album is discussed next in this chapter.

   c. **Take new photo**   This option prompts you to take a new photo with the built-in Treo camera, which will then be attached to the message.

   d. **Take new video** (not available on the Treo 600)   This option lets you to capture a new video with the built-in camcorder, which will then be attached to the message.

5. After you have attached your media, enter the text that you want to accompany the media and select Send.

Send Media Using MMS—Non-Sprint Treos

MMS is covered in detail in Chapter 5, and we will only touch on it here. If your Treo is correctly configured for MMS and you are in a wireless coverage area, the steps to send one of your stored photos using MMS are as follows:

1. Launch the Camera application by selecting the PHONE button and then selecting the Camera button on the screen (you may need to scroll down to see the button).

2. Press the Pictures view (the second icon on the bottom of the screen that looks like a list).

3. Select the photo you want to send either by tapping the touch screen or by using the five-way navigation control to highlight the photo.

4. Press the Send button on the screen.

5. A menu will appear with the choices Mail and MMS.

6. Select MMS, and then select OK.

7. Type in the phone number or e-mail address of the person to whom you want to send the photo. If the recipient's e-mail address is stored in your Contacts list, you can begin typing the recipient's name, and the rest of the field will fill in as your Treo finds the match in the Contacts list.

8. Select the Send button (or select Send Later if you are not currently connected to the wireless network and want to delay sending the message until your next connection).

Set Your Treo Wallpaper

You can set your Treo wallpaper to be a photo that you have taken with your Treo or one that is saved on your Treo. The steps to set the wallpaper vary depending on which model of Treo you have.

Set Your Wallpaper on a Treo 650 and 700p

1. Press the PHONE button.

2. Press the MENU button (above the mail button).

3. Select Options.

4. Select the General Preferences (650) or Phone Display Options (700p) menu item.

5. If you see the Show Dial Pad menu on the screen, select the Show Dial Pad menu and change it to Show Wallpaper.

6. Select the current wallpaper photo or image that is shown to the right of the Show Wallpaper menu.

7. Then browse to the photo that you would like to use as your wallpaper.

It is important to know that when you set your wallpaper to be an image, you will no longer see the dial pad on the screen when you press the PHONE button. On the 700p, press the SEND button to bring up the option to select the dial pad. On the 650, to bring the dial pad up onto the screen, press the PHONE button twice, and when the menu pops up, select the Dial Pad option.

Set Your Wallpaper on a Treo 600

Your Treo 600 has a default view that appears when you press the PHONE button. Many Treos are set to show the dial number pad when you press PHONE, but you can change the view to show an image instead. Your Treo background is called your wallpaper. There are two ways to change your wallpaper. The first method is as follows:

1. Launch the Camera application (as described in the earlier section "Take a Quick Series of Photos").
2. Select the Pictures view and choose the image you want to use as your wallpaper.
3. Press MENU on the keyboard.
4. From the Picture menu, choose the Set Wallpaper option.
5. A confirmation message will appear; select Yes.

The second method for changing your wallpaper is described here:

1. Press PHONE on the keyboard.
2. Press MENU on the keyboard.
3. From the Options menu, choose the Display Preferences screen.
4. Choose the menu at the top of the screen and select the Show Wallpaper option.
5. Choose the image you want to use and select OK.

Use Your Treo Pictures for Picture Caller ID

As long as your phone plan includes caller ID, you can use your Treo pictures, or any picture, to help you identify, at a glance, who's calling you.

Set a Picture for Caller ID on a Treo 650 or 700p

The Treo 700p allows a little more flexibility with this feature than previous Treos; for instance, you can take a picture of a contact and associate it with the contact's information right from the contacts application on your Treo.

TIP

If you are using a third-party application, such as GoodLink, to store your contacts, this feature won't be available to you.

FIGURE 7-13   Contact Picture

To set a picture for caller ID on a Treo 700p, follow these steps:

1. On your Treo, press the PHONE button and select Contacts.

2. Browse to the contact that you want to work with, or choose the New Contact button.

3. Once you are looking at the contact record, choose the Edit button.

4. Choose the Picture icon, as shown in Figure 7-13.

5. A pop-up menu will appear on the screen allowing you two options: Photo or Camera, as shown in Figure 7-14.

   a. If you choose Photo, you can browse to a photo that is saved on your Treo and will be used for caller ID for this contact.

   b. If you choose the Camera option, the Camera application will launch and you can immediately take a photo that will be associated with this contact. This is very handy if the contact happens to be standing in front of you and enjoys having his or her photo taken.

FIGURE 7-14   Contact Camera or Photo Option

Set a Picture for Caller ID on a Treo 600

1. Identify a picture you want to use to identify a contact when he or she calls.

2. Go to your Favorites by pressing the PHONE button and then selecting Favorites with the five-way navigation control.

3. Select an empty Favorite by tapping on the screen or select the CENTER button on the five-way navigation control.

4. In the Type menu, select Speed Dial.

5. Fill in a name in the Label field.

6. Type in the phone number of the person.

7. You can type in a Quick Key to speed up dialing this person, if you like.

8. Select the More button. This allows you to define advanced settings for this Favorite:

   ■ **Ringtone**   You can define a different ringtone sound that will be played when this person calls you on your Treo. To change from the default ringtone, select the menu and then select another ringtone.

   ■ **Image**   You can define a specific image to appear on the screen when this caller calls you. To do this, check the box beside the image text and press the Select Image button. After your picture list appears, browse to the image you want to use to identify this caller. (You can change the category to view by selecting the menu at the top right-hand corner of the screen and choosing the appropriate category.)

Edit Your Treo Photos Using Third-Party Software

A significant difference between digital photography and film photography is that you don't have to be an expert or own thousands of dollars of film equipment to edit your digital photos. Your Treo produces photos and allows you to send them to others and copy them to your PC, so there isn't anything you *have* to do to your photos to enjoy them. But, if you wanted to edit and work with your photos, what would you use?

Imaging software has come a long way in the past few years, and this has lead to a proliferation of image-editing software on the market. While choice is rarely a bad thing, it can also present an overwhelming number of alternatives. Most software office suites that include word processing and spreadsheet applications also include some kind of image-editing program, so you may want to find out if you already have something you can use.

Although many of the built-in tools may be fine for rudimentary image manipulation, you may want a different option. Your choices may be somewhat different depending on whether your computer runs a Windows or a Macintosh operating system; but either way, there are lots of choices available, including these:

- The latest versions of the Palm Desktop software that ships with the Treo 700p and 650 includes the ability to edit photos on your PC with features such as:

  - Crop
  - Resize
  - Rotate
  - Enhance
  - Remove red eye
  - Add text and draw on images

- Adobe Photoshop Elements 4 (www.adobe.com) is available for around $90. This program is a trimmed-down version of the more powerful and much more expensive Photoshop versions and is available for both Windows XP and Mac; you can download a trial version to try it out before you buy it. Elements allows you to do a lot of things to help you enjoy and share your iPAQ digital photos, including

  - Removing red eye automatically as you download
  - Creating composites
  - Creating slideshows with pan and zoom effects, voice narration, and multiple music tracks
  - Ordering prints online with one click
  - Viewing photos on your TV
  - Sharing your photos online
  - Easily isolating objects from backgrounds
  - Organizing your photos

- Adobe Photoshop (www.adobe.com) is comparatively expensive—around $900—but if you need more than red-eye reduction and slideshows, you may enjoy this full professional image editing standard for both Mac and Windows. Photoshop is an industry standard for graphic designers and professional photographers and is a powerful application. Be aware that it can be challenging to learn, but you likely won't be limited by the software capabilities.

- Paint Shop Pro (www.corel.com) is a powerful image editing application for Windows that offers a lot of functionality and costs around $100. (You may know that this was formerly a Jasc product.) You can download a trial version before you buy and view an extensive list of its functionality on the Corel web site.

- Microsoft Digital Image Pro (www.microsoft.com) is Microsoft's consumer digital imaging and editing software and is available for around $100.

- Digital Image Viewer (www.proaxis.com/~rwi/imagevw.htm) is a free program. With it, you can manage images from one location, performing operations such as viewing, resizing, deleting, renaming, creating slide shows, editing, and dragging a photo to a favorite program.

- Artizen (www.supportingcomputers.com) is an image manipulation tool (about $40) that offers a large number of image effects and works with JPEG, GIF, BMP, and ICO formats.

- Easypicture (www.virieu.com/easypicture) is a photo editor (about $40) that offers the photo managing, editing, and JPEG compression tools you need to get photos from your camera to your web page.

This is a small selection of some of the more popular imaging products that are on the market, but there are many more you can find by doing a web search for "image editing software" or a similar search phrase. If you have time to try a few to see what works for you, great. If you don't, you can't go too wrong with Adobe or Corel products.

Add Special Effects to Your Treo Photos

You can apply a ton of effects to your Treo photos. Some are just plain fun, and some add more of an artistic flavor. Of course, as with anything, beauty is in the eye of the beholder. Most image-editing software packages have special effects or filtering options. Be sure to look through the user's guide or help documentation of any software that you choose to make sure you're aware of all its functionalities. Even if you don't use the effects very often, they may still come in handy at critical times.

Use Fractal Effects

"So, what the heck is a *fractal*?" you ask. There are a lot of definitions on the Internet, and most are verbose mathematical descriptions. Let me say that fractal effects are less than subtle, so you may want to try them out to see they are useful to you. An example of a fractal effect is shown in Figure 7-15.

FIGURE 7-15   Fractal effect

Many high-end image-editing applications feature fractal effects, such as Fractal Explorer (www.eclectasy.com/Fractal-Explorer/index.html). This program allows you to generate polynomial and iteration sets such as Mandelbrot, Julia, and Newton fractals, as well as (just in case you have an aversion to Julia fractals) orbital fractals.

Make a Treo Photo Look Like an Oil Painting

Oil Painting Assistant (www.mxac.com.au/oilpaint.htm) is a software program that works with BMP format images to show you how your photos might look as oil paintings. Since your Treo produces JPEG files, you will need to use an image-editing application to convert your photos to BMP format first.

Sharpen Your Treo Photos

Though some great photos may be blurred beyond the point of no return, they may also be photos that can't be easily re-created—the fantastic back-flip Grandma did off the garage roof onto her BMX bike, for example—where you want to minimize the blur as much as possible. For such episodes, inexpensive software tools are available that allow you to sharpen your digital photos. The success rate of these products is reported to be good, but you may want to try them out yourself to ensure they meet your expectations.

Focus Magic

There is a product called Focus Magic (www.focusmagic.com) that allows you to improve the quality of photos. It is available for both Windows and Mac platforms, and you can try the software before you buy it. A brief explanation of the product, taken from the Focus Magic web site, describes the product:

> Focus Magic has forensic strength technology to recover detail that is not visible to the naked eye. Unlike the Sharpen or Unsharp Mask filters, which increase the contrast at the edges of an image, Focus Magic reverses the formula by which the image got blurred. This forensic strength technology gives you as much of the original "in focus" image as possible.

Unshake 1.4

Unshake (www.hamangia.freeserve.co.uk/Unshake/) is a freeware tool for Mac and Windows that is designed to improve blurred, and "shaken," photos by programmatically determining the form of the blurring and deducing what the photo would have looked like if it had not been blurred. The author of the software originally developed the software for his own use but now shares it for free with others (as long as they don't use it professionally). Isn't the Internet great? This Doctor doesn't even know us and he is willing to share his work. There is a scientific explanation on the web site that explains in detail how the software works. I always say "you don't have to study the roots of a tree to pick an apple." (If for some reason the web site link does not work, there is a good chance you will be able to find it by searching a web site search engine such as Google (www.google.com). To run this program, you will need to use software called the Java Runtime Environment, which can be downloaded from Sun Microsystems at http://java.sun.com/getjava.

Corel KnockOut

Corel KnockOut (www.corel.com) allows you to perform complex masking on your images. This allows you to preserve fine image details by improving blurred or out-of-focus edges, hair, smoke, water, glass, and shadows.

Harm's Tile 99 Graphics

Harm's Tile 99 Graphics (www.users.qwest.net/~sharman1/) is a freeware graphics application that allows you to create tiles and retouch your photos. It includes a set of filters and effects, and supports BMP, JPG, and GIF file formats.

Adjust the Color of Your Treo Photos

Most middle- to high-end image-editing applications allow you to adjust the color of your photos, while some are dedicated to image color manipulation. One example is Color Pilot (www.colorpilot .com), which describes itself on its web site as "Software for quick and easy color correction using the natural language of color. Correct digital camera or scanned photo images."

7

Reduce Photo Size

Your Treo produces image files in JPEG format, which is the most popular format for digital photographic images. This is why it's easy to find image-editing software that allows you to edit your Treo photos.

Using an image-editing application, you can resize your photos from the larger Treo size of 640×480 pixels down to half that size (320×240 pixels). JPEG images do not scale up very well, however—that is, you will find that if you increase the size of a JPEG image using an image-editing application, you probably won't be happy with the results. But JPEG images *do* scale down well. One way to improve your images is to reduce the size using image-editing software.

TIP   *Most image-editing applications have an option called Unsharp Mask. You should use this feature whenever you downsize a JPEG image. By applying this filter after you have reduced the size of an image, you will reduce some of the blur and sharpen the edges. You can usually find out if your image editor has this feature by looking in the application's Help files.*

Other Software Available for Your Digital Photos

Although your Treo camera is primarily a tool for sharing fun photos with friends (and it does a fantastic job at this), it is also a great way to get into digital photography for very little money. In fact, the camera is really a free gift that Palm threw into the deal when you bought your Treo . Digital photography is a booming business driven by both professionals and hobbyists alike. The digital nature of your Treo photographs means that the types of things that you can do to, and with, your photos on your PC is really only limited by your imagination. There is a wide variety of software and tools that let you do some very imaginative things to your photos, as well as practical tools that allow you to manage them. This section provides a list of some of the different types of software available that allow you to manage your Treo photos on your PC. Where appropriate, also included is whether or not the software works on Windows or Mac platforms.

 Digital photography can be addictive.

Organize Your Treo Photos

When you get to the point where you've collected a large number of photos over a long period of time, you may discover that organizing your photos to quickly find what you want is a bit of a challenge. These same statistics state that families are taking over 1000 digital photos per year. Organizing thousands of photos like this becomes unwieldy very quickly. Luckily, there are software applications that provide some help in this endeavor. These software applications allow you to view, track, and manage digital photos. Generally, the way they work is that they automatically scan your existing photo directories and create a database. Then you simply add information about the files in the program, select one or more images, and assign keywords such as "family," "reunion," and "vacation" to them. According to your keywords, you can quickly search and locate the photos you want to view.

- **Palm Desktop**   The latest versions of Palm Desktop software that comes with your Treo includes an application called Media that allows you to organize your photos into albums and create slide shows. It is a good idea to check out this application before you spend money on another application. It just might do what you need.

- **Photo Manager by ModTech (www.mt-ac.com)—Mac and Windows**   This application allows you to create musical slide shows and add animated clips, effects, and captions. Once you have created your slide show, you can upload it for free (for 30 days) to www.photoshow. net; publish it as HTML for your web site; burn it to a CD, VCD, or DVD-ROM; or make a self-running executable file or a screen saver.

- **Adobe Photoshop Album (www.adobe.com)—Windows only**   Adobe has been the leader in digital imaging products for a very long time. This application allows you to see all of your photos, access your entire collection of photos (even your video and audio clips) in one place, no matter where they're stored, and locate photos by date. You can locate photos by the date they were taken using the sliding timeline or Calendar View, which lets you review your photos by day, month, week, or year. You can also use keyword tags and even touch up your photos.

Make a Digital Photo Album or Slide Show

The digital world, in some respects, does a fine job of emulating the nondigital world. We have been sharing, reminiscing, and embarrassing each other by showing off our family photo albums for decades. The idea of an old-fashioned photo slide show has been significantly updated.

Even though the idea of sitting around watching Uncle Wally's holiday slides as he explains in stunning detail exactly what each slide is about is already pretty darned exciting, now you can combine sound and animation with your photo slides and run the whole thing on your PC.

There are two primary methods of putting your photos into a photo album or slide show format: doing so locally on your PC, or on the Web. (The online approach is discussed in more detail later in this chapter, in the section "Publish Your Treo Photos on the Web Using an Online Picture-Hosting Web Site.") Here, however, I will discuss a couple of options that allow you to easily put your Treo photos together into a digital photo album on your personal computer.

TIP *You can create slide shows directly on the Treo 700p. Not only can you organize them in a slide show, but you can add music and timing to make a true multimedia experience. Now you can unleash those photos and share them more often. Who needs a PC when you have a Treo?*

Third-Party Software for Creating Digital Photo Albums and Slideshows

What would we do without software? (Besides spend more time outdoors.) There is some great software on the market that allows you to create digital slide shows easily to show off your digital photos. Here is a short list of a few of the vendors that provide software to create digital photo albums and slideshows (as always, there are others that we have not had time to cover):

- ■ **Palm Desktop** The latest versions of Palm Desktop software that comes with your Treo includes an application called Media that allows you to organize your photos into albums and create slide shows. It is a good idea to check out this application before you spend money on another application. It just might do what you need.

- ■ **Adobe Photoshop Elements (www.adobe.com)—Windows** Discussed earlier, in the section "Edit Your Treo Photos Using Third-Party Software."

Back Up Your Photos

Many people unexpectedly lose documents and other information from their PCs and handhelds. This may happen for a variety of reasons, such as hardware or software failure or "pilot error," but, if you are not in the habit of backing up your PCs and handhelds, you permanently lose your files. This can be a painful experience. It is even more important to back your digital photos up. The most common way to back up your photos is to copy or move them to a writable CD/DVD, a Zip drive, or a tape drive. Another way is to copy your pictures to a few different computers or network hard drives so that if one fails, you have a backup. There are even online services that allow you to back up your files using the Internet. There are too many to recommend one or two, but if you use an online search engine with a phrase like "online backup service," you will likely be able to find something to suit your needs.

■ **Simple Star PhotoShow (www.simplestar.com)—Windows and Mac** The Deluxe version of Simple Star costs about $40, but Simple Star offers an Express trimmed-down version for free. The application allows you to create and share multimedia shows using your own photos and music. You can choose photos, a soundtrack, and transitions and effects, and then drag and drop animated clip art and captions to create PhotoShows. These can then be shared online, burned to CD-ROM, used as a screen saver, or published to a web site.

■ **SmoothShow Slideshows (www.smoothshow.com)—Windows** This application is about $20 and offers a free trial, so you can check it out before you buy. SmoothShow 3 allows you to export your shows as digital movie files (AVI or MPEG) for making DVDs, VCDs, streaming video web sites, or other video applications. There are also web templates, pan and zoom effects, unlimited overlays, and digital video transitions.

■ **SWF 'n Slide by Vertical Moon (www.verticalmoon.com)—Windows and Mac** At about $50, SWF 'n Slide is a program that allows you to take both digital images and music and create a slideshow. Your final slideshows are rendered in Flash (SWF) format, which is an easy standard format to e-mail, web-publish, or burn onto a CD-ROM.

■ **Paint Shop Photo Album 5 (www.corel.com)—Windows** At about $49, Paint Shop Photo Album makes it easy to enhance and edit your photos. It can fix photo imperfections, add a fancy frame or photo border, or, for the antique look, add a sepia tone, frames, photo edges, and borders to your photos. You can give yourself or your friends a slim new look with Photo Album's unique Thinify tool, and you can also add captions and sound.

Publish Your Treo Photos on the Internet

Yet another great thing about digital images, like your Treo photos, is that they are easy to share with others by publishing them on a web page. This way, your friends and family, and the general public, if you like, can view your Treo photos from any PC or device using only a web browser. You can easily put your photos up on a web page and then e-mail all of your friends the web site address, allowing them to appreciate your photos with no more effort than clicking the site's link.

There are two primary ways to publish your digital photos on the Internet: using a picture-hosting service and publishing your pictures on your own web site. The easiest way is to use an online picture-hosting company, but that doesn't mean you can't set up your own web site, if you don't already have one. Both options are discussed next.

Publish Your Treo Photos on the Web Using an Online Picture-Hosting Web Site

Besides sending your photos by e-mail, MMS, or Sprint Picture Mail to friends and family, another easy option is to post your photos on the Internet using an online photo album service. This option is especially effective in that it allows you to share a bunch of photos at one time with many people (after all, it's pretty inefficient to e-mail the 439 photos you took at the Montreal Jazz Festival to 60 of your best friends when you could simply send them a web link and let them browse through the photos themselves). You can also show off your photos from anywhere you happen to be, as long as you have access to a web browser. Some online picture-hosting sites are listed here, but there are many others:

- Sprint Online Albums—if your Treo is hosted on the Sprint network, then you can use this service. It is discussed in more detail earlier in this chapter, under the heading "Upload to Sprint Online Albums."
- PictureTrail (www.picturetrail.com)
- Flickr (www.flickr.com)
- Photo Navy (http://pnavy.com)—free
- PhotoIsland (http://pacific.photoisland.com)
- FotoTime (www.fototime.com)
- Snapfish (www.snapfish.com)
- EZPrints (www.ezprints.com)—free

7

> **TIP**   *If you decide to create an online picture-hosting service, remember to only copy your photos to the web site—don't move them. You don't want to risk permanently losing your photos if anything should happen to the service company or their servers.*

Use Your Treo to Publish Your Own Photo Blog

A *blog* is basically a journal that is available for others to read on the Web. The term blog evolved by slightly modifying the word "weblog." Apparently, the term weblog was just too difficult to pronounce and took far too long to type, so blog and blogging were born. The term sounds far less thoughtful and intelligent than what it actually means. The activity of updating a blog is "blogging," and someone who keeps a blog is a "blogger." Blogs are typically updated every day using software that allows people with little or no technical background to update and maintain their very own blog. Postings on a blog are almost always arranged like a diary, in chronological order with the most recent additions at the top of the list. Another feature of most blogs is that they include links to other web sites to help feed the discussion topic; these sites may include other Blogs, news sites, band web sites, book stores, and whatever else the author finds interesting.

Seems pretty straightforward, right? Well, the concept is simple, but the interesting fact is that blogging has become somewhat revolutionary in the world of publishing. Blogging levels the literary playing field by making it tremendously easy to share thoughts, ideas, rants, opinions, and photos with the general public. Historically, in order to be "published," you first had to convince a publisher and printer that your writing was indeed worth publishing and that there was an audience that would pay money to read your words. But now, artfulness and monetary value are just icing on the cake. Now, anyone, even you and I, can publish our thoughts, ideas, rants, opinions, and photos on the Internet for the entire world to see—if we choose.

Create Your Treo Photo Blog

Once you have an idea of your blogging options and have decided on one, the next thing you will want to do, if you haven't already, is to take some pictures with your Treo. Here are some common steps that you may want to follow to get your photo blog on the web. A common example would look something like this:

■ *Arrange your pictures and thoughts*. Example: holiday, school trip, business trip, or a two-hour unicycle tour of your neighborhood back alleys wearing a Darth Vader mask and taking pictures of spray paint graffiti, etc.

■ *Find and choose a blog hosting site*. A list of blog sites is included at the end of this chapter, and a short cross-section of your options is discussed under the heading "Blog Hosting Options—Where to Put Your Blog?"

■ *Learn how to post your blogs*. Understand the technology; understand how to publish your text and images to the blog server—this is largely dependent on understanding how your chosen blog service works.

■ *Post and update your blog.*

■ *Invite your friends and family to look at your blog on the Internet.*

Blog Software for Your Treo

There are several options that allow you to post your pictures and thoughts on the web in blog format. There are more traditional blogging sites that allow you to post using a web browser, and now there are applications designed specifically for the Palm Operating System to allow you to blog right from your Treo; they include SplashBlog by Splash Data (www.splashdata.com) and HBlogger by NormSoft (www.normsoft.com).

■ **HBlogger by NormSoft (www.normsoft.com)**   This product runs on your Treo and allows you to create new entries and either save them or post them immediately. You need to be signed up on a supported blog site to which your posts will be uploaded. Some of the features include

■ Support for popular blog sites, including Live Journal, Blogger, Movable Type, DeadJournal, Blurty, NeedlessPanic, GreatestJournal, TypePad, and Weblogs

■ Capability to include images in your posts

■ Capability to upload images to your post from your Treo memory card or your Treo image database

■ Support for multiple accounts

■ Capability to post to several Blogs at the same time

- Capability to retrieve available blog list and download a list of journals/blogs available for a given user
- Capability to mark your post with attributes, including public/private, mood, no comments, picture, etc.
- **SplashBlog by Splash Data (www.splashdata.com)** This product was purchased by Six Apart (www.sixapart.com), which also runs Movable Type and other Blog products.

Blog Hosting Options—Where to Put Your Blog?

There are many hosted blog sites that provide free and/or paid accounts for your photo blog. Here are some representative sites:

- Live Journal (www.livejournal.com)
- Movable Type (www.sixapart.com/movabletype)
- DeadJournal (www.deadjournal.com)
- Blurty (www.blurty.com)
- NeedlessPanic (www.needlesspanic.com)
- Caleida (www.caleida.com)
- GreatestJournal (www.greatestjournal.com)
- TypePad (www.typepad.com)
- Weblogs (www.weblogs.com)
- CamBlog (www.camblog.com)—a specialty hosting site specifically designed to allow you to create a photo blog using cell phone cameras like your Treo
- Fotopages (www.fotopages.com)—a site dedicated to enabling you to set up your photo blog
- Blogger (www.blogger.com)—a popular blog hosting site
- Blog-City (www.blog-city.com)—offering support for blog photo albums

Many other Blog solutions will show up in a quick web search.

Publish Your Treo Photos on Your Own Web Site

This section is not intended to provide detailed instruction on how to set up your own web site. There are many, many resources that describe exactly how to publish images and content on the Web. You can find informative web sites to help get you up to speed, and most bookstores have web publishing guides and reference books.

Following are some great McGraw-Hill books about HTML and web publishing, whether you are just getting started or are more experienced with web pages. All are available at bookstores or online at either (http://books.mcgraw-hill.com) or Amazon (www.amazon.com).

- *Web Design: A Beginner's Guide* by Wendy Willard (2002)
- *HTML and Web Design Tips and Techniques* by Kris A. Jamsa, Konrad King, and Andy Anderson (includes some advanced topics as well as basics, 2002)
- *Schaum's Easy Outline HTML* by David Mercer (2003)

The key point to understand about publishing your photos on the Internet is that it is *not* difficult. If you are willing to put some time into learning the basics, you can do it. The most important thing you need is a company to host your web site. Essentially, the web-hosting company provides a web server to load your photos and web pages onto so that others can view them on the Web. There are a lot of options, many of which are free or available at a low monthly cost. If you have a home Internet connection, chances are that the company that provides the service also provides web-hosting services.

Creating web pages has also become very easy if you have the right tools. Web page-editing tools have become so simple to use that you no longer have to learn HTML in order to publish pages and photos on the Web. There are a lot of choices when it comes to WYSIWYG (pronounced "whiz-e-wig"—What You See Is What You Get) HTML editors. In fact, most office document applications allow you to save a document as a web page (in HTML). Some examples of web page authoring tools include the following:

- Virtual Mechanics SiteSpinner (www.virtualmechanics.com), about $50
- Macromedia Dreamweaver (www.macromedia.com)—Windows and Macintosh, about $400
- Microsoft FrontPage (www.microsoft.com)—Windows, about $150

NOTE   *Some versions of Microsoft Office include FrontPage, so you may already have it.*

- Evrsoft 1st Page 2000 (www.evrsoft.com), free

By no means are these the only options you have to create web pages easily. There are hundreds out there. If you are so inclined, you can even create web pages using pure HTML code by employing a simple text editor like Notepad—although this is not the easiest way to get going if you are just getting started with web technologies.

Print Your Digital Photos

As you are likely aware, digital photography offers many practical advantages over traditional film photography. One advantage is you can select which photos you print, if any, allowing you to keep the cost of taking and printing pictures down. It is becoming more common to not print photos at all. Many people choose to keep photos in digital format and show them only on a computer monitor or projector rather than in printed form.

> **TIP** *If you have a Sprint Treo, you can use Sprint Online Services to upload and print your digital photos. Visit the Sprint web site to find out more about the service (www.sprint.com).*

What you do with your photos depends on how you want to use them. When you want to print a digital photo, you have several options, and you are not limited to one—you can use all of them, depending on your needs:

- Purchase a photo-quality printer to print your own photos at home. There are some fantastic home photo printers that work very well with your Treo.

- Take digital media storage such as memory cards, CD/DVD, USB drives, and so on to a photo printing shop. This works in much the same way taking film to be developed does.

- Use an online photo printing service that uploads your digital photo files, prints your photos, and sends them back to you. There are so many companies offering this type of service that you may want to do a quick web search to find one that suits your needs. A few are listed in this chapter.

Many of the same sites that offer photo hosting also offer printing services, including

- www.snapfish.com

- www.shutterfly.com

- pix.futureshop.ca (Canada)

- www.photobox.co.uk (United Kingdom)

Wrap It Up

Ten years ago, not many of us would have imagined that mobile technology would have evolved as it has. Even fewer of us would have imagined that our cellular phones would be capable of taking digital photographs or video and sound. As a matter of fact, I'm not sure I had even heard of digital photography ten years ago. The Treo was not designed as a dedicated, high-quality digital camera or camcorder, and likely not many Treo owners based their purchasing decision solely on the camera or camcorder capabilities; however, it's a nice bonus to an already great device. This chapter covered a lot of ground, with discussions ranging from photographing dos and don'ts to digital editing and presentation software. One of the many things you can do with your Treo photos is to create your own photo blog. Happy imaging!

Part II

Maximize the Capabilities of Your Treo

Chapter 8

Enjoy Music, Movies, and Games

How to...

- Listen to music
- Listen to streaming media
- Listen to the news and other radio programs
- Watch movies and videos
- Play games

Use Your Treo as an MP3 Music Player

In addition to being able to use your Treo as a cell phone and an organizer, you can also use it for the Internet, playing games, sending SMS (Short Message Service) or MMS (Multimedia Messaging Service) messages, and taking pictures. On top of this, you can play music on your Treo. Many of us have, or used to have, Sony Walkmans—or similar versions of portable radios, tape players, or CD players—and you can easily make your Treo into a music player as well. You are carrying around your Treo anyway, so why not use it to listen to your favorite music? One of the advantages of listening to MP3s as compared to listening to CDs or tapes on a portable device is that with MP3s there is virtually no skip or sound interruption if you are moving while you are listening to your music—for example, if you are listening to music on your Treo while jogging.

Learn about Sound File Formats

There are several types of files that can be played by electronic devices such as your Treo. Standards have evolved to help software and hardware manufacturers agree on formats that can be generated and played on a variety of different platforms. Many of the standards use similar technologies, and of course it is important to understand what file types your media software can play so that you can convert files to other formats. The most common file types for digitally recorded and played music are MP3, Ogg Vorbis, WAV, and streaming audio/video. These technologies are discussed briefly here, and much more information is available on the Web if you want to find out more. Later in this chapter, there is brief discussion on converting your CDs to files that you can play on your Treo under the heading "Convert Music CDs to Files That You Can Listen to on Your Treo."

WAV Files

WAV files are noncompressed audio files that can be played by a computer like your Treo or PC. Most CD-burning software, which allows you to convert your music CDs so that you can store and play them on your PC, converts audio files to WAV format. WAV files are noncompressed, so the sound quality tends to be better than compressed audio files like MP3 and Ogg Vorbis. The drawback, though, is that WAV files can be very large—many megabytes—so storage space can be a problem on memory- and processor-restricted devices. That is why the MP3 and Ogg Vorbis files are more popular for devices such as your Treo.

MP3 Files

MP3 files are sound files that can be played by computer hardware running the necessary software to read and play the files. MP3 technology evolved primarily because of the need to reduce file sizes to make file transmission over the Internet faster and more efficient. This technology also minimizes how much memory is needed to store music files on your Treo. MP3s allow for smaller file sizes based on sophisticated file compression technologies. Music that you buy on CDs at your local music store is uncompressed and therefore requires a lot of memory, which is fine because the files are conveniently stored on a CD and are not taking up memory on your Treo or PC.

When uncompressed music from a CD is converted to an MP3 file, compression is applied that can reduce the file size to 10 percent of the original. How is this possible? The MP3 compression technology is mathematically complex, so we won't go into too much detail, but if you're interested, there are some great books and web sites devoted to the more technical aspects of MP3 technology. For the most part, most of us just want to listen to music and not worry about the technicalities.

Uncompressed files that are on your music CDs store more data than our brains can realistically process. For example, if two notes that are played simultaneously are very similar, our brains may hear only one note. Or if one note is much louder than another, our brains may only perceive the louder of the two. MP3 compression removes any data from the file that you are not likely to notice as missing. This allows for much smaller file sizes. There are different levels of compression, and obviously the more data that is removed from a sound file, the more the quality is reduced; so there is some trade-off.

One of the advantages of MP3 files is that additional information, such as the name of the artist, the track title, the album title, the recording year, the genre, and even personal comments, is stored at the beginning or end of an MP3 file. This is very useful for storing and tracking your MP3 collection.

Ogg Vorbis

Ogg Vorbis is a compressed audio format similar to MP3. (See the preceding section, "MP3 Files," for more information on audio compression; the same general principles apply to both Ogg Vorbis and MP3.) Ogg Vorbis is designed to provide better audio quality than MP3 while producing smaller file sizes. One of the advantages of Ogg Vorbis is that the technology used to create the audio files is not restricted by patents and therefore is royalty-free to users. More information about Ogg Vorbis can be found at the Vorbis web site (www.vorbis.com).

Audio/Video File Formats

There are many types of file formats. To make things more confusing, some of the file types are used for both music and video, but some of the formats you may see include MPEG/MPG, VCD, DIVX, and AVI files, among others. Some of these files are more common for video, which is covered in more detail later in this chapter.

Streaming Audio

Most music and audio files are stored in memory and played from memory. Even when you download music such as an MP3 file from the Internet, the entire file must be downloaded and saved before you can play it. Wouldn't it be great if we could begin to play the music before it is fully downloaded? Well, that is essentially what "streaming" media is all about. When you select a file to listen to, or watch in the case of streaming video, the file starts playing a few seconds after you begin downloading it, and as long as your Internet connection is steady, it will keep playing. If you have heard of Real Player or Macromedia Flash, these are examples of technologies that leverage streaming media.

So, the question is: How does streaming audio sound? Generally speaking, especially over relatively slow wireless connections, it tends to work better for talk radio than for streaming music. As connection speeds improve, however, streaming media will continue to improve. The best way to find out what streaming audio sounds like on your Treo is to try it out for yourself. Fortunately, you can use Pocket Tunes (www.pocket-tunes.com) to play streaming audio on your Treo using the SHOUTcast (www.shoutcast.com) service. See the section "Use Pocket Tunes to Play Music on Your Treo" later in this chapter for more information.

What Audio/Music Player Software Is Included with Your Treo

Your Treo likely arrived preloaded with a media player so that it can play audio right out of the box. The most common configurations for each Treo model include:

- **Treo 700p**   Pocket Tunes; Audible is included on the CD
- **Treo 650**   RealPlayer; Audible is included on the CD
- **Treo 600**   The Treo 600 does not ship with music playing software. Fortunately there are several options inexpensive and free options, including Pocket Tunes and Real Player, both of which are discussed in this chapter.

Listen to Music Files on Your Treo

Treo 700p and 650 models arrive preinstalled with music player software, but the 600 does not, so you will need to install a third-party music player before you can listen to music files on it.

Use a Stereo Headset to Listen to Music with Your Treo

If you have tried to connect a stereo headset jack to your Treo, you may already know that most stereo headset cords don't fit into the Treo jack. This is because your Treo earphone jack was designed primarily for hands-free phone usage with the included phone headset. The Treo jack is a 2.5 mm size, and most stereo headsets are 3.5 mm, so you will need a 2.5 to 3.5 mm adapter. Fortunately, Palm sells an adapter to allow you to use a 3.5 mm stereo headset with your Treo. This is called the "Treo Stereo Headphone Adapter." Also, Palm sells Treo stereo headphones that have a 2.5 mm connection so that you can use the stereo headset without an adapter.

Use Third-Party Applications to Play Music

There are several music players for your Treo. The most common applications are included in this list and are covered in more detail later in the chapter:

- **Pocket Tunes (www.pocket-tunes.com)** In the U.S., NormSoft's Pocket Tunes is a gift when you register your Treo with Palm. With Pocket Tunes, you can play compressed audio files—MP3 or Ogg Vorbis—or uncompressed WAV files on your Treo.

- **RealPlayer for Palm (www.realnetworks.com)** This application supports the local playback of MP3 and RealAudio content on your Treo that is played from a Secure Digital (SD) memory card or a MultiMediaCard (MMC).

- **AeroPlayer (www.aerodrome.us)** AeroPlayer can be downloaded for free to try for 14 days. If you want to play MP3 files after the 14-day trial period has passed, you have to purchase a registration code; but if you only want to play Ogg Vorbis files, you can continue to use the software for free. AeroPlayer allows you to play both video and music files on your Treo.

- **MMPlayer (www.mmplayer.com)** MMPlayer can play several types of files on your Treo. A notable difference between MMPlayer and many other video-capable players is that MMPlayer is able to play standard video formats, such as MPEG and AVI formats; some other video players require that videos be converted to a proprietary format that can only be played by that specific player.

8

> NOTE *If you purchased your Treo in the U.S., Palm will give you Pocket Tunes MP3 player software for free just for registering your Treo on the Palm web site (www.palm.com).*

Pocket Tunes and RealPlayer are discussed in greater detail later in this chapter (see the sections "Use Pocket Tunes to Play Music on Your Treo" and "Use RealPlayer to Play Music and Other Audio on Your Treo").

Convert Your Music CDs for Playback on Your Treo

This topic can be a little complicated but it can be boiled down to one thing, the music player(s) that you use on your Treo can play only specific file types and you may need to convert files on your PC to play them on your Treo.

On the Treo 650, Palm ships the Real music client, and the Rhapsody desktop software converts files to the correct file type for that player. The Treo700p Palm ships Pocket Tunes, which can play WMA files when you upgrade to the Deluxe version. With this package, you can use iTunes on your PC to rip a CD to MP3 format directly. To offer an example, the next section talks about ripping CDs using Windows Media Player, which is free from Microsoft. Many of the media players that you can install and use on your Treo allow you to play WMA files, but there are at least two reasons that you may want to convert your newly ripped WMA music files or other file types before you put them on your Treo:

- Your Treo media player may not support a particular file type, so you'll need to convert the file to a format that your media player can play.

- You want to reduce the song file size so that you can get more songs onto a memory card for your Treo.

You should know the types of media files that the media player on your Treo is capable of playing. For example, RealPlayer plays RM or RMJ files, while most other players do not. Another popular group of media player-specific file formats includes the Apple music file types such as AAC, AIF, AAIF, and AIDD.

Many web sites allow you to download music and video for free, and many more that allow you to purchase media for download. Although you can usually find music already in a file format you can play on your Treo, what if it isn't? You'll need to convert it.

The process of converting files is fairly simple. The first step is finding the correct conversion tool. There are a lot of file conversion tools available on the Web. Many of these are shareware and offer free trial periods before you have to purchase the software. It is always a good idea to try out software before you enter your credit card number to be sure you are getting software that will work for what you need.

NOTE *Digital Rights Management (DRM) and license protection is a hot topic in the press, mainly because there has not yet emerged a clearly better way to protect copyrighted digital files. Obviously, media companies that make their money from selling movies or music have a vested interest in ensuring they get paid for all of the hard work that goes into producing the entertainment that we enjoy. Generally, if you rip your own music CD, the resulting files will be unprotected. However, you may find that when you purchase music on the Internet, DRM protection is in place that will prevent you from converting or burning the media onto a CD/DVD. If you get protection or licensing errors when you try to burn or convert files, this is likely why.*

Rip Your Music CDs for Playback on Your Treo Using Windows Media Player

There are many tools that are available for you to convert your music CDs to MP3 files that you can playback on your Treo. We will discuss this process using Windows Media Player, as it is common and is free from Microsoft.

If you don't already have the Windows Media Player installed on your PC, you can obtain it for free from the Microsoft web site, www.microsoft.com/windows/windowsmedia/default.mspx. Windows and Mac versions are available.

TIP *Mac users, you can use iTunes on your Mac to convert your music CDs to MP3 files.*

You probably have music CDs, or even video DVDs, that you would like to play on your Treo. The process of converting CD/DVD files to files that your Treo media player is capable of playing is essentially the same, although the software that you will use will likely be different. We will discuss only music CDs here to help keep it simple.

NOTE   *Ripping is MP3 jargon commonly used when talking about encoding. Basically, ripping is the process of extracting raw audio files from a music CD and is the first step in making a digital file. When you rip a CD, the result is a bunch of WAV files that are generally larger than you would like. The next step is to convert the WAV file to a digital format that is smaller and playable on your Treo. This is accomplished with an encoder. Programs that allow us to rip CDs are also known as CD grabbers or digital audio extraction (DAE) tools.*

To rip tracks from an audio CD using Windows Media Player, follow these steps:

1. Insert the CD you want to rip into your PC CD drive.

2. On your PC in Windows Media Player, select File | CDs and Devices | Rip Audio CD, as shown in Figure 8-1.

3. The Rip tab will be displayed, as in Figure 8-2, with all of the songs checked. If you only want to rip certain songs, uncheck the ones you don't want to rip. You can also select and deselect all tracks by clicking the check box at the top of the check box column.

4. Once you have selected the tracks that you want to rip, click the Rip Music button, as shown in Figure 8-3.

5. By default, the music files are ripped to the My Music folder on your PC and displayed in the Library feature in the Windows Media Player. The labels for the files will likely be default names, so you may want to rename the files with the name of the artist and album so that you can easily find the songs when you want to play them. If you are connected to the Internet while ripping a CD, Windows Media Player will name the files by artist and album for you.

8

FIGURE 8-1   Windows Media Player's Rip CD menu

FIGURE 8-2   Windows Media Player's Select All Songs screen

FIGURE 8-3   Windows Media Player's Rip Music button

Windows Media Player rips your music CD into a format called WMA, which is short for "Windows Media." The Windows Media Player Mobile player can play WMA, ASF, WMV, and MP3 files, so you can move your newly ripped WMA music files to a memory card and play them on your Treo. The process of moving your music from your PC to your Treo is covered in the section "Transfer Music and Other Media onto Your Treo." Since the WMA files are relatively large in size, you may want to convert them to reduce the file size so that you can get more songs onto a memory card.

Encoded Files to MP3-Encoded Files

Once you have ripped your music CD to WMA files using Windows Media Player, as discussed previously, you can either move the WMA files to your Treo for playback or convert them. The most common digital media type is MP3, so we'll focus on converting WMA to MP3.

There are so many types of encoders out there that we hesitate to recommend one over the other, but many are available for you to try before you buy. Some great online resources to help you find WMA-to-MP3 encoders include:

- www.wmatomp3.com-http.com
- www.mp3-converter.com

8

Transfer Music and Other Media onto Your Treo

Some of the music software that will run on a Treo requires you to have a memory expansion card, either SD or MMC, to transfer music from your PC to your Treo. Expansion cards are covered in Chapter 15. There are two primary methods of transferring music from your PC to your Treo. The first method is to use the Palm Desktop and the Install tool. The second, and faster, way to transfer music files is to use a USB card reader to copy files onto your SD or MMC card.

Transfer Music to Your Treo Using the Palm Desktop

Chapter 3 discusses using the Palm Desktop and synchronizing your Treo with your PC. Once your Treo and PC are set up to HotSync and your memory card is ready to go, follow these steps to transfer your music:

1. Open the Install Tool by selecting the Install button in the Palm Desktop application or by choosing the Install Tool (Start | Programs | Handspring or PalmOne or Palm | Palm Desktop). In newer versions of Palm Desktop, this tool is called Palm Quick Install.

2. Click and drag the files you wish to transfer into the Install Tool window. The files will appear in the Expansion Card area of the window.

3. Select Done.

4. If it is not already connected, connect your Treo to your PC using the HotSync cable and press the HotSync button on the cable, and the music files will be transferred to the correct location on your memory card.

Transfer Music to Your Treo Using a Card Reader

Once you have an SD or MMC memory expansion card, an invaluable tool is an SD/MMC card reader. Card readers are available in many places, and you can find them for less than $20 online or in specialty stores. (SanDisk is one of many manufacturers, and you can find it at www .sandisk.com.) The SD/MMC card reader attaches directly to your PC and allows you to swap your SD/MMC card from your Treo to the card reader to quickly transfer pictures, music files, applications, and other files to and from your Treo without needing to HotSync. If you have an SD/MMC memory expansion card and a card reader, follow these steps to transfer your music from your PC to your Treo:

1. Once your card reader is connected to your PC, insert your SD/MMC memory card into the card reader.

2. On your PC, select Start | My Computer and double-click the drive that represents your memory card. This will vary depending on how many drives you have on your PC.

3. Open the AUDIO folder. If this is the first time you are using your memory card, you will have to create an AUDIO folder by choosing File | New | Folder on your PC.

4. Click and drag your music files (.ogg or .mp3 files) into your open AUDIO folder.

5. Palm suggests that you right-click the drive that represents your card reader and choose Eject before removing your card from the card reader. If you do not "eject" your memory card before removing it, the files on the card may be damaged.

6. Place the memory card into your Treo and select the files that you want to play on your Treo.

Use Pocket Tunes to Play Music on Your Treo

One of the most popular software applications for your Treo is Pocket Tunes by NormSoft (www.pocket-tunes.com). The product is offered in two versions—Basic for about $15 and Deluxe for about $35—and is available as a 15-day trial so that you can try it out. The Basic version is included with many Treos and has an icon in the Applications Launcher called "pTunes." Also, if you want to use stereo headphones to listen to music with your Treo, you will need a 2.5mm to 3.5mm stereo headset adapter; for more information, see the section "Use a Stereo Headset to Listen to Music with Your Treo " in this chapter. The main screen in the Palm version of Pocket Tunes, as shown in Figure 8-4, is very intuitive, as are the menus allowing you to work with your music files.

The basic version allows you to play MP3, Ogg Vorbis, and WAV files and also allows you to listen to streaming audio downloaded over your wireless Internet connection.

The basic version includes:

■ Support for MP3, Ogg Vorbis, and WAV files
■ Graphic equalizer

FIGURE 8-4   Palm Pocket Tunes interface

- Windows Media Player integration (MP3 only, no WMA)
- Skin support
- Background playback
- Playlists
- Tag-Based Song Browsing

The Deluxe version adds these features:

- Play music from subscription services
- Play purchased music
- Play WMA files (Windows Media)
- Streaming audio and ShoutCast
- Crossfade
- Bookmarks and Auto-Bookmark

Create Pocket Tunes Playlists

You can create a custom playlist that includes what songs to play and the order in which to play the songs. To create a new playlist, follow these steps:

1. If Pocket Tunes isn't currently running, press HOME on the keyboard to open the Applications Launcher; then find and open Pocket Tunes.

2. Select the menu button | Actions | Manage Playlists to open the Manage Playlists screen shown in Figure 8-5.

FIGURE 8-5 Pocket Tunes Manage Playlists screen

3. Select the New button to open the New Playlist screen.

4. Type in the name of this playlist at the top of the screen and then select Add Song.

5. Select a song and continue adding songs until your list is complete.

6. You can use the Up and Down buttons to reorder the list.

7. When you are finished, select Save List.

Now you can select the playlist at any time, and the same songs will be played in exactly the same order. You can always create, delete, and edit your playlists at any time.

Play Songs in the Background with Pocket Tunes

Pocket Tunes will play music in the background even when you switch to another application, so you can listen to music while you work with other applications on your Treo. At any time, you can enable or disable background playback from the Background Preferences screen shown in Figure 8-6.

FIGURE 8-6 Pocket Tunes Background Playback setting

Crossfade Your Songs with Pocket Tunes Deluxe

Crossfade is a fancy word that means that you can seamlessly fade from one song to the next (not available in the Basic version). It is only available in the deluxe version of Pocket Tunes. You can change your crossfade settings by following these steps:

1. Select the MENU button, and then select Crossfade Prefs.

2. To enable crossfading, select the Enable Crossfade check box, and set the desired crossfade duration by selecting a duration from the pop-up menu.

The duration setting in Step 2 is the number of seconds that Pocket Tunes will overlap and fade from one song to the next. The gapless setting means that Pocket Tunes will seamlessly blend two song files together without leaving any gap.

According to Pocket Tunes, this feature requires a certain amount of additional memory on your Palm device in order to prepare the audio information for crossfading. Longer crossfade durations require more memory. The Crossfade screen displays your available memory and the amount of memory required for crossfading; in addition, it displays a message indicating whether you have enough memory.

8

Create Bookmarks in Pocket Tunes Deluxe

With Pocket Tunes Deluxe, you can create a bookmark to save your place when you are part of the way through an audio file and want to return to the same place later on (not available in the Basic version). This is particularly useful when you are listening to e-books or recorded radio broadcasts. Bookmarks are only available in the deluxe version of Pocket Tunes. Follow these steps to create a bookmark in Pocket Tunes:

1. In Pocket Tunes, press the MENU button and select the Add Bookmark option from the Tools menu.

2. In Bookmark Name dialog box, enter the name of your new bookmark and select OK. If you don't type in a new name, the default is that the title of the song will be used. If you want Pocket Tunes to always use the title of the song, then uncheck the Always Ask for Name check box.

Jump to a Bookmark in Pocket Tunes Deluxe

Once you have defined a bookmark, you can jump back to the same place in the audio file by following these steps:

1. Select Bookmarks on the Tools menu in Pocket Tunes.

2. Select the bookmark you wish to go to, and then select the Go button.

You can also rename or delete a bookmark by selecting the bookmark and then selecting the Rename or Delete button, respectively.

Use the Pocket Tunes Deluxe Auto-Bookmark Feature

Pocket Tunes has an auto-bookmark feature that allows you to automatically create bookmarks. When the auto-bookmark feature is enabled, Pocket Tunes will automatically create a new bookmark whenever you press the Pause option and then open a new audio file. This allows you to easily jump between different audio files without losing your place. You can enable the auto-bookmark feature by selecting the Auto-Bookmark option from the menu in Pocket Tunes.

Change Your Pocket Tunes Advanced Preferences

There are several settings that you can change to customize Pocket Tunes. You can access these settings by selecting the Advanced Preferences option from the Prefs menu. There are several options that you can change, and some examples are listed here:

- **Stop playing on low battery**   By default, Pocket Tunes will pause music playback when you get a low-battery warning. This allows your Treo to go to sleep and prevents it from draining the battery.

- **Stop playing after x minutes**   You can set Pocket Tunes to automatically stop playback after a predefined period of time has passed.

- **Start playing on startup**   Pocket Tunes can be set to automatically start playing the last song you were listening to the next time you start up your Treo.

Playing SHOUTcast Stations with Pocket Tunes Deluxe

The Basic version of Pocket Tunes doesn't allow you to use SHOUTcast, so you will need to upgrade to the Deluxe version, which is about $35, to use SHOUTcast. The easiest way to listen to SHOUTcast stations is to visit www.shoutcast.com on your Treo web browser, look for a station that you want to listen to, and select the Tune In button. If your Treo prompts you to open or save the file, choose Open. If your Treo prompts you as to whether or not you want to accept the file, select Yes. Pocket Tunes will then load the station and begin playing it.

You can also tune into a SHOUTcast station from the Choose Songs screen in Pocket Tunes. To do so, select the SHOUTcast option from the menu in the upper-right corner of the screen. On the screen, you will see a list of all the SHOUTcast stations you have listened to. You can add a new station manually by selecting the New button. Pocket Tunes will ask you for the SHOUTcast web site address or URL, and you can also enter the URL for a static (nonstreaming) MP3 or Ogg Vorbis file.

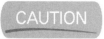

Streaming media can use a lot of bandwidth because it transmits a significant amount of data. You will want to ensure that your service contract allows for unlimited (or a lot) of data to avoid a surprise bill at the end of the month, because when you use more data than is specified in your contract, there can be expensive overage charges.

You can also use Pocket Tunes to play SHOUTcast stations from premium services such as Di.FM (www.di.fm). Many of the premium stations require a username and password. In order to access these stations, use the Pocket Tunes Choose Songs screen to add a SHOUTcast URL. The URL for the station should look something like this: http://username:password@10.10.10.10:8096.

Some SHOUTcast stations require a high-bandwidth connection. Look for the Kbps (kilobits per second) setting for these stations. If your current connection is 64 Kbps or lower, then you may have trouble playing these stations on your Treo wireless Internet.

Use RealPlayer to Play Music and Other Audio on Your Treo

RealPlayer (www.realnetworks.com) allows you to play MP3 and RealAudio (.rm, .rmj) content from your SD or MMC memory expansion card. (Real Player cannot currently play music files that are stored in the internal Treo memory. You must use a memory card.) To transfer music files from your PC (Windows and Linux only) to your Treo, you will need to install the RealPlayer plug-in software on your PC. As with the other applications that allow you to play music files on your Treo, music files must be stored on the SD or MMC memory card—playing files from internal memory is not supported.

If you have ever used RealPlayer media player software on your PC, you know that PC-based RealAudio will play streaming audio. This is not the case on the Treo. Files must be downloaded or moved and stored locally on a memory expansion card; streaming audio is not yet supported on the Treo.

Play Files Using RealPlayer

The steps for playing music and other media files with RealPlayer are listed here:

1. Select the Real icon from the Applications Launcher screen.
2. Select Songs to bring up a list of available tracks.
3. Select the desired song to begin playback or use five-way navigation control to select a song.
4. Press the CENTER button to highlight the first track and use the UP and DOWN buttons to scroll.
5. Choose Select to play the song.

You will notice that information about the song is displayed in the light green status area, and you can tap the Information icon to view extra information about the song.

Create a New Playlist in RealPlayer

You can create a custom playlist that includes what songs to play and the order in which to play the songs. To create a new playlist, follow these steps:

1. If RealPlayer isn't currently running, press MENU on the keyboard to open the Applications Launcher.
2. Find and open RealPlayer, and then select Playlists.
3. Select New, name the playlist, and select Add.

8

4. From the list of available songs that appears, select the check boxes next to the songs you wish to add to your playlist.

5. Select Done to return to the Edit Playlist screen, select Done to return to the Playlist screen, and select Done to return to the list of available playlists.

6. Select Done again.

Use Your Playlist in RealPlayer

Once you have created your own custom playlists, you can play them at any time by following these steps:

1. If RealPlayer isn't currently running, press MENU on the keyboard to open the Applications Launcher.

2. Find and open RealPlayer, and then select Playlists.

3. Select the desired playlist.

4. Select the first song in the list to begin playback in the RealPlayer.

Listen to Nonmusic Audio on Your Treo with Audible and AudibleAir

Music is not the only type of audio that you can listen to using your Treo. There is a wide variety of audio that you can store and listen to on your Treo, such as

- Audio books
- Audio magazines
- Audio newspapers
- Downloadable radio

Audible software (www.Audible.com) is included with Treo 700p and 650 and is a service that allows you to download non-music audio content to your desktop PC so that you can transfer that content to your Treo. An Audible.com membership allows you to download more than 18,000 audio books and programs to listen to on your Treo. With Audible, you can download audio versions of digital audio books, newspapers, magazines, etc., and store the files on memory cards or in your Treo memory.

While Audible requires you to download files to your PC and then sync to transfer the files from your PC to your Treo, AudibleAir allows you to wirelessly download audio directly to your Treo. AudibleAir allows you to wirelessly download audio books and subscriptions and configure schedules for automatic delivery so that you can automatically get new sections of the audio programs you are listening to. For example, you can set up your Treo to download the *New York Times* or other subscription programs every morning.

Download MP3 Files from the Internet to Your Treo

In addition to being able to copy and move files between your desktop PC and your Treo, you can download music directly from the Internet using the wireless Internet capabilities of your Treo.

 Some clever hackers have figured out ways to embed viruses into MP3 and movie files, so it is very important to use antivirus software on your Treo if you are going to be downloading media files directly to your Treo over the wireless Internet. More information about securing your Treo is covered in Chapter 13.

There are many web sites where you can download MP3 and Ogg Vorbis files. Just do a search on your favorite Internet search engine. Be aware that there are royalty and legal issues when downloading protected music.

Convert Music CDs to Files You Can Listen to on Your Treo

Recent technology makes it extremely easy to convert your CDs to MP3 files. Many third-party add-ons for Mac and Windows that are designed to play your CDs on your PC can also convert your CD music into MP3 files and/or Ogg Vorbis files. Examples are Cdex (http://cdexos.sourceforge.net) and dBpowerAMP (www.dbpoweramp.com). If you want to convert your CD files to MP3 files, you can search the Internet for software that allows you to do the conversion on your PC. Remember to look for software that converts WAV format to MP3 format because your CD music is WAV format.

Some Great Ways to Use Your Treo as a Music Player

As you have probably already figured out, your Treo is an ultimately portable and useful device that is capable of many, many things. Well, now that you can use your Treo as a music and audio player by storing music on memory expansion cards, essentially what you have is a portable CD collection. Now, instead of hauling your CDs between your house, car, office, and weekend cottage, you can store all of your favorite music on SD or MMC memory cards and play music on your Treo wherever you happen to be.

Obviously, your Treo is a great personal entertainment center, but you can also use your Treo to play music through your car or home stereo as well.

Play MP3s Through Your Car Stereo

There are several ways to play your Treo music through your car stereo. Most of your options for your car stereo apply to your home stereo as well.

Use an RF Modulator (Radio Frequency Modulator)

This option likely has the highest "Cool!" factor. It allows you to wirelessly connect your Treo to your car stereo using the FM capabilities of your car stereo, as well as a little device that you plug into the earphone output jack of your Treo. (Note that you will need a 2.5 mm to 3.5 mm adapter to plug the RF modulator into your Treo.) Once the RF modulator is hooked up to your Treo, you tune your car radio, or any FM radio, to one of the digitally tuned FM stations supported by your modulator. For example, the Arkon (www.arkon.com/sf.html) SoundFeeder FM Modulator allows you to use eight different FM frequencies: 88.1, 88.3, 88.5, 88.7, 107.1, 107.3, 107.5, and 107.7 MHz. So there is a very good chance that you will find a frequency that a radio station in your area is not using. Some users have reported great success with this approach, but others have reported that it can be difficult to get static-free sound. An RF modulator solution is relatively inexpensive (about $30-40). Here are two vendors that manufacture and sell FM modulators:

- RadioShack (www.radioshack.com), product name iRock
- Arkon (www.arkon.com/sf.html), product name SoundFeeder

Upgrade Your Car Stereo

Obviously, replacing your car stereo is not always practical, but it is valuable to mention so that you know it's an option. If your current stereo does not already have a 3.5 mm input jack, there are some models that do have the necessary input jack to allow you to plug your Treo directly into your car stereo using an inexpensive patch cable. You can buy this cable from a store such as RadioShack. Virtually all car stereo producers now have this feature. Connecting your Treo to your home stereo may be more practical than connecting it to your car stereo, since many home stereos have input jacks; however, you may need an adapter cable or two to make the connection.

Use a Cassette Adapter

If your car has a cassette tape player, then you can easily use a CD car adapter designed to allow your portable CD player to work via your tape deck. The adapter costs about $15-25, and here's how it works: The CD car adapter has a connector that fits into your car stereo tape deck and simulates a cassette tape. The adapter also has a cable that you plug into a portable CD player so that you can hear your CDs through your non-CD-equipped car stereo. You can plug the cable into your Treo using a 2.5 mm to 3.5 mm adapter and hear music on your Treo through your car stereo. Adapters are generally available at electronics stores, and RadioShack is usually a good place to start.

Make Your Car Stereo into a Speakerphone

Using a speakerphone while sitting in your car is useful, and perhaps more importantly, is a great way to impress your friends and colleagues. There are no manufacturers that make products specifically for this purpose, but the same technology that allows you to use your Treo to play music and sound through your car stereo speakers also works great for converting your car stereo into a speakerphone. Basically, the way it works is that your Treo' hands-free microphone acts as the input for your voice, and your car stereo becomes the speaker half of the speakerphone.

If you have already read the "Play MP3s Through Your Car Stereo" section of this chapter, you are aware of RF modulator technology that allows you to wirelessly connect your Treo to your car stereo using the FM capabilities of your car stereo and a little device that you plug into

FIGURE 8-7   Altec Lansing

the earphone output jack of your Treo. (Note that you will need a 2.5 mm to 3.5 mm adapter to plug the RF modulator into your Treo.) Once the RF modulator is hooked up to your Treo, you tune your car radio, or any FM radio, to one of the digitally tuned FM stations that is supported by your modulator. An RF modulator solution is relatively inexpensive, about $30-40.

So once your RF modulator is hooked up to your Treo and you make or receive a phone call on your Treo , the voice of the person you are speaking to is played through your car stereo, and your voice is picked up by the phone microphone. (When you are using your Treo and car stereo as a speakerphone in this way, remember to use the speakerphone option, which is covered in Chapter 4.) There are some great car-mount kits that allow you to mount your Treo to your dash for easy and accessible operation—and to keep your Treo near the stereo. These options are covered in Chapter 16.

Altec Lansing inMotion iMT1 Speaker System for Treo 650

Altec Lansing makes an audio docking station for the Treo 650. The system is ideal for conference calls or playing music or other audio on your Treo, as shown in Figure 8-7. The station:

- Charges your Treo when it is docked in the system.
- Battery powers for up to 24 hours of playback.
- Can be used with any audio player such as CD and DVD players.
- Has a built-in microphone for conference calls.

Play Video and Movies on Your Treo

All Treo handhelds, with the exception of Treo 600, can capture and play back video clips. Your Treo is also capable of playing other video/movie files using third-party software. In fact several of the media players you can use to play music files also allow you to play video. A few of your video options are listed here

- **The Core Pocket Media Player for Palm OS (http://mytreo.net/downloads/ author-Gr_Kov.html)**   This freeware allows you to play media files: DivX, XviD, MP3, Matroska, MP4, and others.

- **AeroPlayer (www.aerodrome.us)**   AeroPlayer is a free download for you to try for 14 days. AeroPlayer is mentioned in the music section of this chapter, but it also allows you to play video files on your Treo.

- **MMPlayer (www.mmplayer.com)**   MMPlayer is one of your Treo music player options, and it can play several types of files on your Treo. A notable difference between MMPlayer and many other video-capable players is that MMPlayer is able to play standard video formats, such as MPEG and AVI formats, while some other video players require that videos be converted to a proprietary format that can only be played by those specific players.

- **Kinoma (www.kinoma.com)**   Kinoma, which costs about $30, is optimized specifically for the Treo and allows you to view MPEG-4 video, listen to AAC audio (unprotected iTunes audio), and view JPEG photos. You can Zoom, Rotate, and Pan movies and photos.

Watch TV with Sprint TV (Sprint Only)

If your Treo is on the Sprint wireless network, then you have the option of signing up for the Sprint TV service. There are multiple packages with various pricing levels, so much as you do with your home cable TV, you can choose which package includes the type of programming that you want to watch. You can also subscribe to individual channels. Your choices include SIRIUS radio, sports, news, fashion, weather, and even cartoons and comedy. You can get more information on Sprint TV at the Sprint PCS web site (www1.sprintpcs.com).

Watch TV on Your Treo with MobiTV

MobiTV (www.mobitv.com) is a subscription-based wireless TV service for your Treo that costs about $10 per month. The service features more than 20 channels, a graphical channel guide, and support for beaming.

Play Games on Your Treo

Like the drive-in movie and penny candy, the days of playing Pong on your TV and going to the video arcade to plug fistfuls of quarters into arcade games are long gone. Fortunately, your Treo is equipped with a bright-color screen and stereo sound, which makes it an excellent choice for gamers. The Palm OS operating system also happens to be the platform of choice for many mobile game-development companies, which means that there is a huge selection of games available for your Treo. Many of the games that are available are shareware and freeware, so you can be a gamer without spending a fortune on new games as they come out.

This section provides only a short list of games to give you an idea of what is available on the market. It is tempting to create a catalog of games, but the list in this book is only provided to give you some idea of what is out there. There are many extensive download and review sites on the web, and we recommend that your check these out:

- Palm (www.palm.com)
- Handango (www.handango.com)
- Handmark (www.handmark.com)
- Tucows (www.tucows.com)

Another great resource that will tell you what games are available and what other Treo owners think of the games is the Treo fan site discussion boards. A full list of sites is available in Appendix B, but here are a few examples:

- Treo.com (www.treo.com)
- Treo Central (www.treocentral.com)
- Everything Treo (www.everythingtreo.com)

Card Games

Your Treo allows you to play a game of cards without the cards—it ships with a version of Solitaire and other games. One of the standouts is CardSuite because it includes enough games to keep you from getting bored.

CardSuite

CardSuite by Glavark (www.glavarkcom), $20, is a collection of 10 card games and 70 Solitaire games, including the following:

- **Card games**   Euchre, Hearts, Cribbage, Spades, Gin Rummy, Rummy, Blackjack, Crazy Eights, Whist, and President
- **Solitaire games**   Klondike, FreeCell, Spider, Pyramid, and Memory

Board Games

What could be better than a board game without the board? Good question. I don't know, but there are some great Treo games that are based on familiar traditional board games. A small cross section is listed here, but there are many others:

- **Backgammon 3.1, freeware**   Available on several web sites for download. Search on the full name in an Internet search engine. Even if you don't know how to play, you can learn to using your Treo by watching the Treo play against itself. Then play in the beginner mode, or challenge yourself with the advanced mode. This application lets you play backgammon with a friend or against the computer.

- **Chess Tiger (www.ChessTiger.com), $19** If you are a chess player, this game has enough options to keep you entertained for a long time, including a training mode, different board sizes, and over 100 different skill levels.

- **Trivial Pursuit Handheld Edition for Palm OS (available from www. handmark.com), $30** A digital version of the classic game, with more than 1,600 multiple choice and true/false questions. There are two modes of play, Classic play (the original game) and Flash mode (a quick-fix Trivial Pursuit game). There is multiplayer support of 2-6 players over Bluetooth and IR (infrared). A multiplayer lobby offers a meeting place for a networked game, including chat among players.

Puzzle Games

Games can be categorized differently, depending on who is doing the categorizing. Generally speaking, puzzle games tend to be slower-paced and involve problem solving and strategy.

- **Astraware Sudoku (www.astraware.com/palm/sudoku/)** This costs about $20 and is a very popular logical puzzle game with a 9×9 grid. Within the grid are nine boxes each with nine cells, and the object of the game is to fill in the numbers 1–9 in each row, column, and box, but they must only appear in each one once. The game features six levels of difficulty, pencil marks in a choice of styles, optional completion and tracking of pencilmarks, a notepad, and an advanced hint system. After registration the game allows you to add additional prebuilt puzzle packs. These extra packs are available free from www.sudokuoftheday.com; the unlocked version of Astraware Sudoku includes a puzzle creator, which generates billions of Sudoku puzzles, and a puzzle solver, which allows you input Sudoku from a newspaper or book.

- **Bejeweled (www.astraware.com), free trial; full version, $15** This is a popular game that seems to be on the top of many Treo owners' installed games lists and may have been included with your Treo. It offers the following features:

  - High-quality gray or color graphics and animation

  - Sound effects

  - Two modes: Easy (for relaxation) and Timed (for a frantic game)

  - Ability to export high scores to the Astraware Bejeweled Internet High Score Table

  - Instructions and tips to get you started

  - Automatic hints to help you play

- **Plumber Pete (www.palmstorm.com), free trial available at www.palm.com; full version, $6** This game offers a new twist on thinking against the clock. The objective of the game is to fix pipelines by rotating the pipe pieces into their correct positions, all while trying to keep water from leaking out of the pipes.

Action Games

This category is a little open to interpretation because one gamer's backgammon is another gamer's "action" game.

- **Sea Strike by Island Labs (www.islandlabs.com), shareware; full license, $15**   This game is based on a popular web-based game; and as you can tell by the title, it is centered on the life and times of a military submarine. Along the way, you defeat enemy subs while avoiding depth charges, mines, and bombs. Also, in true-to-life fashion, you must catch fish in order to replenish your oxygen before you run out.

- **3D Master Thief FREE Demo Mission 1.3 by Cascata Games (www. cascatagames. com), freeware**   The Phoenix Gemstone worth a reputed $24 million has been stolen by the Russian Mafia, the Kombati. Your mission is to steal it back for a billionaire collector. Break into the Kombati Stronghold and find the hidden vault room, where you will find the gemstone protected by armed guards. You will be paid handsomely if you succeed.

- **Roids 1.2 by Flippinbits (www.flippinbits.com), shareware**   In case your life doesn't have enough stress already, your job in this game is to save the world. Hoards of aliens are heading this way with an even greater number of asteroids to block their way.

- **3D Air Hockey for Palm OS by Paul Ellams (available at www.handmark.com or www.handango.com), $8**   This game is slightly more portable than an air hockey table and almost as much fun.

Software to Help Your Game

Your Treo is also great for assisting you with nonvideo games. An example of software that can really help out—if you spend your time outdoors wearing plaid pants and spiked shoes—is software that you can use to improve and track your golf game.

IntelliGolf 7.0 for the Treo (Birdie edition) by Karrier Communications (www.intelligolf.com), $30, includes support for GPS and Bluetooth and is the only golf software to include all seven Ss of golf. In case you, like me, don't know what those seven Ss are, here is a list of what they stand for:

- Scoring
- Shot tracking
- Satellite GPS
- Sidegame wagers (30+)
- Statistics and graphs (250+)
- Signature courses (18,500+)
- Sharing of information between handhelds

IntelliGolf for the Treo software comes complete with the software that resides on your Treo and PC synchronization software—everything you need to improve your game, except Tiger's swing.

Wrap It Up

This chapter discussed some of the fun things you can do with your Treo. This is the kind of stuff that your boss doesn't need to know about. Palm has done a great job of designing the Treo in a small package that allows you to play music, watch video, watch TV or other mobile content, and play games (whenever you aren't working on spreadsheets, swapping messages with the Chairman of the Board, or explaining the benefits of the United Nations, that is). After all, you work hard; you should have a little fun, too.

Chapter 9

Keep Your Treo Running at Its Best

How to…

- Back up your Treo
- Manage your battery life
- Charge your Treo on the road
- Use third-party application launchers
- Navigate faster
- Optimize text input
- Protect your Treo from damage

An important part of being a Treo owner is making sure that your device is set up to maximize its efficacy. This can involve many factors, including adjusting settings for the operating system, managing the battery, and acquiring third-party software and accessories to improve how the Treo works. There is no shortage of great ways to improve how your Treo works for you. In this chapter, we explore some of the ways that we optimize our Treos, and you can decide for yourself which of these will add value to you.

Back Up Your Treo

A very real hazard of integrating a mobile device like the Treo into your lifestyle is the risk that something could go wrong with your device and that you could lose all of your data. This could happen because your battery runs so low that memory integrity cannot be maintained, because of a bad piece of software you have loaded that forces you to hard-reset your device, or because of some other combination of bad luck. It is worthwhile to mention here that all Treos after the 600 have persistent user storage and loss of battery power will not cause you to lose data.

NOTE   *Some people have begun talking about the risk of viruses getting onto your handheld device and not only damaging the data on your device, but potentially getting into your PC and perhaps your work or home environment through the device. We want to provide our opinion that although this is technically feasible, it is highly improbable, and the first viruses are likely to be limited in scope and damage. Don't be talked into buying antivirus software for your handheld until such a risk actually shows up as a clear and present danger.*

The only incidents of mobile viruses seen to date have been on the Symbian and Windows Mobile platforms—the Palm OS that your devices uses has so far been safe from the criminals who develop these malicious applications.

To help protect yourself, it is essential to ensure that your Treo is backed up regularly. The Treo is equipped with some built-in backup capabilities, and there is third-party software that can help you perform more extensive and sophisticated backups, depending on what your needs are.

Perform a HotSync Backup

Every time you synchronize ("HotSync") your Treo (as described in Chapter 3), the Treo performs a full backup of everything about your device. All installed applications are backed up, as are preferences, favorites, and more. Your contact information, calendar, tasks, and notes will be synced with Palm Desktop, Outlook, or your third-party personal information manager (PIM). This synchronization will back up your PIM information. If you have a failure of your Treo and lose your data, you can restore it simply by performing a HotSync operation of your device.

Back Up Using Third-Party Software

The major drawback of HotSync-based backups is that they require you to be connected to your PC. If you are a traveler, don't sync frequently, or need to ensure you can recover your device while away from your PC, then you will require software that will back up your data to a storage card.

One such product is BackupMan from Bits 'n Bolts software (www.bitsnbolts.com), which we use to back up our Treos to Secure Digital (SD) cards. BackupMan allows you to recover your entire device from a compact SD card in the event of failure while you are traveling.

With BackupMan, you can also schedule your Treo to back up its data automatically on a daily or hourly basis, as shown in Figure 9-1. There are many people who use Treos in business environments where the data on their devices changes frequently. Imagine you are a doctor and you use your Treo to keep patient notes and dispense prescriptions. As you go through the day, you can't keep running back to your PC to sync in order to protect your critical data. With BackupMan, you can schedule your Treo to back itself up to the storage card every hour throughout the day. That way, you are never in danger of losing more than the past hour's work.

With BackupMan, you need to make sure you have an SD card that is large enough in capacity to handle each backup set. You can also limit the number of backup sets to store on the card. We usually keep only two backup sets so that we have the most recent backup and the backup immediately before that.

FIGURE 9-1   BackupMan allows you to back up your Treo on a scheduled basis to an external storage card.

BackupMan will also install itself onto the card so that in the event of a total hard reset of your Treo, you can load BackupMan directly from the card and then restore the backed up information from the card.

 Back Up an Orange Treo Wirelessly

A unique feature of some of the Orange brand Treos is the ability to back up your device over the air. You can initiate this service by selecting the Orange Backup application and selecting which of the databases on your device you want to back up.

When you initiate the backup, as shown in the following illustration, all of your critical data will be backed up wirelessly. If your Treo should ever be hard-reset, erasing all of your data, you can initiate a restore over the air to bring your Treo back to the same state it was in when you performed your last backup.

Another very useful feature of BackupMan is that you can restore only individual files. Let's say that you performed some action that ended up messing up the data inside one of your applications. A real-world example of this is that when I first received my Treo, I inserted the SIM card that had previously been in my Sony Ericsson t68i. I had already synchronized my Treo, and after inserting the SIM card I was prompted and asked if I wanted to copy the contacts of my SIM card into my Contacts application. When I answered yes, it copied the contacts from my SIM card in a format that was completely inconsistent with the way that I manage my contacts, creating many duplicate records and junk data in my Contacts application. Had I had BackupMan installed (and a recent backup set), I could simply have restored my Contacts-related files and returned to the state I was in before I ruined my data. Instead, I had to spend time cleaning the junk data manually—data that had now been synchronized back to my Outlook folders, creating junk data in them as well.

The most recent version of BackupMan allows you to encrypt your backups (for data security purposes) and also to perform only partial backups of your Treo.

For a full listing of vendors that provide backup software for your Treo, refer to Chapter 16.

Maximize Your Battery

One of the biggest thorns in the side of the mobile community has been the battery life of mobile devices. As we equip these devices with more powerful processors, more memory, brighter-color screens, and embedded cellular phones, more and more demands are placed on the batteries of these units.

With the newest Treo models using persistent data storage, loss of data is generally a nonissue; however, if you have a Treo 600, you need to be aware that you could lose your data if your battery gets too low.Great strides have been made to counteract the increasing demand for power, but you still need to be very aware of your device usage and take appropriate steps to get the most out of your battery. Although the Treo should, when the power gets low enough, switch into a "safe mode" that won't allow you to turn it on but will still protect your data, you shouldn't rely on this. If your battery gets low enough, you could find yourself having to reload all of your applications and data back on to your Treo.

Keep an Eye on Your Battery

On the main phone and application screens of your Treo, you will see an icon in the top-right corner that shows you the approximate strength of your battery:

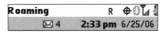

If the battery is at or near full strength, the battery icon will appear solid. As the battery strength drops, the icon will show the battery as being less than full. How full the battery appears is roughly proportional to the battery strength left. If your Treo is plugged into a power source, the icon will show a bolt of electricity over the battery to show that it is charging, as you can see in the preceding illustration.

If you would like to see a reading of your battery strength as a percentage of total battery strength, you can tap the battery icon to see the top bar replaced with a percentage number. If you would like to know more details about your battery, the BatteryGraph application discussed in the following section is available to help you with this.

You can also adjust some simple settings to help maximize your battery life. Select the Power option in the General section of the Preferences application to see some options that you can configure, as shown in Figure 9-2.

The most important battery conservation setting is Auto-off After. This allows you to specify the time period after which you would like to have your Treo go to sleep when there is no activity from you. The options range from 15 Seconds to 3 Minutes. The longer the delay, the more battery power that will be consumed in an idle period. You will notice that there is no option to disable the Auto-off feature. This is because, inevitably, at some point we all forget to turn our devices off and then are upset because our battery is completely drained as a result. On the Treo, some reasonable Auto-off setting is mandatory.

Another place you can squeeze out some battery savings is in the screen brightness. There is a slider bar at the top of the window to adjust the brightness. Turning down the brightness will consume less battery power if you find you are running through your battery too quickly. If you find you use your Treo in low light situations primarily, such as indoors at your place of work, you may find you don't need the maximum brightness.

TIP *You can quickly jump to the screen brightness controls by pressing the OPTION-P buttons on your keyboard. If you are in a very dark place like a movie theater and you power on your Treo, you will find the screen is so bright it will disturb those around you. You can quickly drop the brightnss by 50 percent by pressing the OPTION-MENU buttons*

You can also set the screen to dim the backlight after a certain period of time on a call, and this will conserve battery power as well. The shorter you are comfortable setting this, the better. Your options range from 30 seconds to 5 minutes (default is 2 minutes), on 700p only.

FIGURE 9-2   In the Power preferences there are some settings that you can adjust to help reduce your battery consumption.

Also, many people don't use the beaming feature of the Treo on a regular basis. If this is your situation, you can turn off the beam receive option so that no power is used to keep monitoring for an incoming infrared beam. Just remember if you are trying to receive a beam from someone in the future that you may have turned off this option, which means that beaming to you won't work!

Next we explore some third-party applications that will help you manage your battery most effectively.

BatteryGraph

The built-in software for telling you the status of your battery is very limited on the Treo. If you travel or use your Treo intensively throughout the day, you may want to get more detail on your battery to help you gauge your usage pattern and know when you need to plan to recharge.

BatteryGraph is a free (for noncommercial use) application you can download for your Treo that will log your battery status in a database every time you turn your Treo on or off. This data can then be graphed so that you can see how your battery performs over time, as shown in Figure 9-3.

You can also set alarms to warn you when your battery drops below acceptable levels. Two different levels of alarms can be created. You can download your own copy of this utility from http://palm.jeroenwitteman.com/.

BatteryGraph will help educate you about your usage, but it doesn't directly reduce your battery consumption. For that, we look to some other third-party applications.

Radio Control

The Treo does not come equipped with a scheduler that allows you to turn the radio on and off at scheduled times. Many people don't receive phone calls at 2:30 in the morning! If you would like your Treo to automatically power the radio on or off at a certain time, you can download a free utility called Radio Control, shown in Figure 9-4. This battery-saving (and possibly sleep-saving) utility was written by a dedicated Treo user, Chris Hobbs. It can be downloaded at http://clanhobbs.org/treo.

FIGURE 9-3   BatteryGraph is a free tool to help you gain more visibility into your power usage on your Treo.

Radio Control

Wireless Mode
after soft reset: On / Off

Radio On: Never
Radio Off: Never

Clear

FIGURE 9-4   Radio Control allows you to schedule when the radio of the Treo turns on and off, conserving battery power.

With Radio Control, you can also set the Treo radio to automatically turn on after a soft reset. By default, when you soft-reset the older Treo models the radio will turn off. I have personally missed many calls when I have forgotten to turn my radio back on after a soft reset. If you have a Treo 650 or 700p this shouldn't be a problem.

Recharge Your Battery

In addition to the standard charger that comes with your Treo, there are some other charging solutions worth considering, from car chargers to the solar panels.

What Palm Offers

Many of the charging accessories you might be interested in can be purchased directly from Palm. These include the following:

- **Combined charging and HotSync USB cable**   A cable that charges your Treo from the USB port on your laptop and syncs at the same time
- **Cradle**   A device that also charges a second battery (650 and 700p only)
- **Car charger**   A separate cable solely for charging your Treo from your car

iGo Everywhere / iGo Juice

For the person traveling with a laptop and a Treo, the iGo Juice (www.igo.com) is a great accessory that allows you to charge your laptop and your Treo at the same time. With exchangeable tips, a wide range of laptops, phones, and PDAs can be charged. This one is a true must-have for the road warrior.

Zip Linq

The ZIP-LINQ retractable sync cable (www.ziplinq.com) advertises the ability to both sync and charge your Treo from the USB port of your computer. After testing a number of these cables, we found that they did charge the Treo; but unfortunately, we were not successful in actually HotSyncing through the cables. These cables are also sold under different brands, including BoxWave (www.boxwave.com) and JAVOSync (www.javoedge.com), among others. An excellent small charger for travelers, but it appears not to live up to its full billing.

Solio Solar Charger

A very interesting offering for charging your Treo is the Solio Universal Charger (www.solio.com), which will charge your Treo directly from the sun! This product is great for hikers, backpackers, pilots, and others who use their Treos for GPS navigation or may not be near a power outlet regularly.

General Power Tips

Here are some general bits of advice to consider to make your Treo battery life last as long as possible:

- *Turn down your brightness*. As discussed earlier, the bright screen is a major consumer of battery juice.

- *Keep your battery charged*. The lithium-ion batteries in your Treo can be charged at any time, so make sure you plug it in every night instead of letting it run down as you might have done with much older rechargeable devices.

- *Watch out for hot and cold temperatures*. Don't leave your Treo in your hot car in the summer, as excessive heat can damage your battery. Cold temperatures won't generally damage your battery, but they will drain some of the stored energy.

- *Turn off features that you don't use*. Turn off features like beaming and Bluetooth to minimize their drain on your battery

- *Watch out for tricky applications*. Some applications regularly activate to perform functions, such as e-mail apps that check the server on a regular basis. These applications can be real battery thieves, so beware.

Work More Efficiently

We carry a Treo for a number of reasons, one of which is that we want to be able to have access to information and communication at our fingertips. This means being able to get to what we need on the device efficiently. There are a number of tools that can improve the standard navigation of the Treo.

Launch Applications

The more applications you load on your Treo, the more challenging it can become to navigate quickly to what you need. There is a combination of built-in and third-party products that can speed your launching of applications.

Favorites

The Favorites screen was introduced in Chapter 4 as a way to create speed-dial shortcuts for your favorite phone numbers. The Favorites screen can also be used to create shortcuts to launch your favorite applications. To create an application shortcut, open the Favorites screen and select an empty favorite button to open the Add Favorite screen, as shown in Figure 9-5. (For a refresher on how to add speed-dial shortcuts, refer to Chapter 4.)

In the Type drop-down, select Application and then choose which application you want to launch in the Label field. You can also define a hard keyboard key that will launch this application when you press and hold the key.

Hard Buttons

Another way to launch your favorite applications quickly is to link them to the four hard buttons on the front of your Treo to the left and right of the five-way navigation control. By default, the buttons will launch the Phone, Calendar, and Mail applications from left to right. The rightmost button will power the screen off on older Treos, or switch to the Application Launcher on the newer 700p model. Pressing and holding the OPTION button and then pressing one of the hard buttons will launch a different application.

You can configure which applications are launched by the hard buttons in the Preferences application. Selecting Buttons from the drop-down will open the Buttons Preferences screen shown here:

Every button is displayed with a drop-down arrow beside it. You can select the application you would like the button to launch by choosing it in the list. If you ever want to return to the default application associated with the button, just tap the Default button on the bottom.

FIGURE 9-5   You can add applications to your Favorites screen to make shortcuts to your favorite programs.

The HotSync button, also on the bottom, allows you to change which application is launched when the button on the HotSync cable is pressed. By default, this launches the HotSync application, but there is rarely a reason you would want to change this.

Hi-Launcher

For those of you who would like to navigate your Treo in the same way you do your desktop computer, Hi-Launcher from RaNo Software (www.hilauncher.com) will let you build a custom menu that pops up from the bottom, as in Figure 9-6.

You can choose any key to open the Hi-Launcher menu and then select the application or function that you would like to jump to. You can create your own entirely custom menu, including submenus, splitter bars, and links to applications or links to special functions such as the screen brightness control. You can also set the colors for each menu background and font to help make it easy to read.

Today

The Today application is *the* product for people familiar with Microsoft's Windows Mobile platform (and is great even if you have been a Palm user from the beginning). It gathers information from your other applications and presents it in a consolidated format on your screen using a style that is very familiar in the world of the Pocket PC.

You can see in an easy-to-read format the current date and time, any upcoming appointments you have, if you have unread e-mail, the number of active tasks you have to complete, and more, depending on how you have it configured. It also serves as a mini-application launcher, allowing you to put icons for your most common applications on a bar at the bottom. Tapping the icon launches the program. In addition, the very top of the screen shows you a system summary of your battery strength and available memory.

FIGURE 9-6   The Hi-Launcher menu provides an easy way to navigate among applications and functions on your Treo.

This is another free Palm application developed by a dedicated Palm user. You can read more about the application and its author and download your own copy at http://today.get.si.

Treo Butler

The Treo Butler is an application with a few tricks up its sleeve to help you use your Treo more efficiently. It offers the following functions and features:

■ The ability to change the function of the Volume buttons to act as controls for scrolling the screen or switching between applications.

■ The ability to disable the LED function or show if there is voicemail pending (on some carriers).

■ The ability to launch your Favorites applications from anywhere, not just the Phone application.

■ An alarm clock to wake you up or remind you of appointments.

This application is not free, but it isn't terribly expensive if you like what it does for you. You will need to pay $4.50 to register the application. You can try it out for free, though, to see if you like its functionality before paying for it. It can be downloaded from PalmGear at www.palmgear. com—in the Search area, select the Palm OS Software check box and search for Treo Butler.

Enter Text Faster

I find typing on the Treo keyboard to be very easy, even given its small size. The thing that I find tricky when I am typing away is pausing to hit the right key combination to get a capital letter or a special character. There is a free utility called KeyCaps600 that makes it extremely easy to type capital letters or special characters without having to use multiple keys to do it. There are two versions, one for the Treo 600, and one for the 650 and 700p—make sure you download the correct version!

You can configure the application to give an uppercase instead of a lowercase letter by holding the key for a moment longer. Tapping the key twice will give you the special character on the key instead of the lowercase letter. You can customize what kinds of keystrokes trigger these reactions, as well as how long a delay you want before a different type of character is initiated.

This application is free and can be downloaded from www.geekandproud.net/software/keycaps600.php. It is one of the applications that we highly recommend as a productivity improver for the Treo.

Never Miss an Alert

One complaint of all-in-one mobile devices such as the Treo is that sometimes you miss an important alert. You don't realize there is a voicemail waiting for you, or an appointment reminder went off, but because you were going over a bump in your car at the time you didn't feel the vibration, and the sound was lost because the stereo was too loud. For just that reason, PDAapps (now owned by Intellisync, but you can still use the web address www.pdaapps.com) created TreoAlertMgr, which will keep alerting and reminding you until you acknowledge the alert. You can have your Treo play a sound, vibrate, and flash the screen (or any combination thereof) when an alert comes in. Luckily, you can also schedule this to occur only during certain hours so that if an SMS message arrives while you are sleeping you don't have to deal with your Treo having a fit until you respond!

Protect Your Treo from Damage

Your Treo is a very hardy and well-built device, but that doesn't mean it is indestructible. I am a true road warrior and am very hard on my devices. A common joke in the office is "If you want to see how tough a device really is, give it to Derek for a week. If it survives, it's a good unit."

No matter how hard you try not to, someday you will drop your Treo, or it will fall off your belt or face some other kind of trauma. There are a number of things you can do to improve your odds of not damaging your device—from nonslip grips to cases and screen protectors.

Use Better Grips

One unfortunate thing about the design of the Treo is that the sides of it are made of the same polished metal that the whole case is formed out of. Other device manufacturers have been learning that putting rubber grips on the sides of their devices makes them easier to hold and less likely to be dropped.

Although Palm overlooked this detail, you do have the option of adding third-party grips that can be applied to the Treo to provide the same benefit. The leading provider of these grips is called Egrips (www.egrips.com).The Egrips product is applied to your Treo with a light adhesive. It provides you with a sure grip on your device and keeps it from sliding around on the dash of your car as well. These grips should be considered "consumables" because they wear out over a period of several months and need to be replaced. In addition to being functional, they are also a fun way to personalize your Treo, as Egrips come in a variety of cool patterns, including Tiger Skin and more! If your company deploys Treos to its staff, you can have custom designs made incorporating your corporate logo. Without a doubt, these Egrips are one of the absolute "must-have" accessories for your Treo.

Use Better Cases

Depending on which Treo model you own, you may or may not have received a case with your unit. Treo owners are lucky that the case that ships with the product (if you did get one) is of much higher quality than cases shipping with many competing products. However, a different case is another way of personalizing your Treo and serves the added benefit of providing extra protection in the case of a fall or bump.

You can choose from many different kinds of cases, and the number to choose from continues to grow on a daily basis as the Treo gains mass popularity. Different cases have different general features that may help you narrow your selection. Selecting a case is always a matter of personal preference, so you should consider what is most important to you from the following list:

- **Pouch/holster vs. always covered**   Some cases are pouch or holster types. This means that when you want to use your Treo, you take it out of the case and hold the "naked" Treo in your hands. The other kinds of cases always stay on the Treo, so they keep it covered at all times. The latter style usually offers more protection for the device. Most of the time when I drop my Treo, it is while I am fumbling to get it out of a case when a call is coming in. The drawback of an always-on case is that it does add to the bulk of the case.

- **Flip style vs. nonflip style**   For the cases that are always on, you generally find two different fundamental styles. One type allows you to hold the Treo up to your head and take a call without having to open or flip up any cover. The other type has a flap that folds over the front of the Treo and must be opened before you can take a call. The flip style usually affords the most protection to the device; but for some people, having to open the cover to answer the phone is an annoyance that they do not want to deal with. One other bonus of the flip style is that pockets are often located in the flip cover to hold extras such as additional storage cards, credit cards, business cards, and so on.

- **Cutouts**   A case should have holes and openings cut in it to allow you to get at the controls you need while using the Treo. Missing holes can mean that you can't use the case in certain situations. For example, the case that comes with your Treo doesn't have a hole for the headphone jack. If you want to listen to music or talk on the phone while leaving the Treo clipped to your belt, you can't do it without resorting to a hole punch to make the necessary cut out. Some vendors have also completely forgotten that the Treo has a camera in it and have failed to provide a cutout for the camera lens. If you want to snap a quick shot, you have to remove your Treo from the case first.

- **Belt clips**   Some cases come with belt clips; some do not. If you prefer to carry your Treo in your pocket, purse, briefcase, or portfolio, then having a belt clip isn't important to you. However, if you like to have your Treo clipped to your belt, then a good belt clip is essential. Most case vendors offer both clip and nonclip versions of their cases. Some vendors, such as Piel Frama, even offer a case with a removable belt clip so that you can use the case with a clip and then unscrew the knob from the case to keep it smooth when you don't.

- **Cradle compatibility**   If you use a cradle, some cases allow you to leave the case on the Treo and still plug the Treo directly into the cradle for charging and syncing. Others will only allow you to sync with a cord. If you like to use the cradle, you might find it a pain to take the case off every time you want to charge or sync. If you are a noncradle user, then this is a nonissue!

- **Storage**   If you like to carry extra storage cards for music, pictures, or other reasons, look for a case with the ability to store the cards right in the case. Some cases can also carry paper money and a credit card so that you can leave your wallet at home!

- **Personalization**   A number of case vendors allow you to further personalize your case by choosing the material, color, and other features of the case. In addition, some will emboss your name, your company name, or your company's logo on your case.

A full listing and description of the cases that we are currently aware of is in Chapter 16, along with information on what key features they offer and our opinions of the overall quality and usability of the case.

Cover Up the Screen

One way to tell a new Treo from an old one is by how scratched the screen is. Inevitably, sometimes as you use the tool you won't bother to pull the stylus out of the back when you just want to tap something really quickly. Instead, you will use your fingernail, a pen with the lid on it, or some other object. There are other things that may come in contact with the screen as well. For example, if you wear earrings, you might accidentally scratch the screen while talking on the phone.

A popular product for protecting your screen is a clear adhesive screen protector that you can apply to the screen of your device. Once a screen protector is on, it is very hard to tell it's there. It forms an extra physical layer between you and the screen. The stylus works as easily as before, and the screen is just as bright. You lose nothing by applying a screen protector, and you gain a screen *saver,* so we highly recommend adding this accessory to your arsenal of Treo tools. There is a full list in Chapter 16 of providers of these protectors. Some work better than others as far as being truly invisible and for adhesiveness. The ones that we have been using on our Treos are from BoxWave (www.boxwave.com) and are very reasonably priced.

These screen shields last a very long time; if you see that one has gotten scratched or dirty, you can simply peel it off and apply a new one.

Wrap It Up

Once you have begun using your Treo, you will continue to find more and more ways to improve your productivity and your fun with the device. The information in this chapter hopefully has empowered you to get the most out of these productivity and personal-life enhancements.

Chapter 10

Use Productivity Applications

How to...

- Make appointments in your Calendar
- Manage your Contacts
- Take notes and memos
- Convert measurements and weights with the Treo Calculator
- Manage your shopping list
- Track and protect your credit card numbers, frequent flyer numbers, and more

Depending on which model of Treo you own, and what carrier you are with, you will likely find that there are some slight variations in which productivity applications come preloaded on your device. This is because the Treo is also your phone; and the carrier, or wireless service provider, that provides you with your mobile phone number and access might choose to configure the standard software on the Treo differently, due to marketing differentiation. Also, as the Treo has matured with each subsequent model, generally the on-board applications have also become more capable with each iteration.

You will find little variance in the standard applications for managing your Calendar, Contacts, and Notes, as all of the Treo devices (600 through 700p) are based on a version of the Palmsource 5.*x* operating system, but beyond that there will most certainly be differences. A number of the Treos have been shipped with versions of the SplashData products, so we will cover those in this chapter. For applications that you may have custom-loaded, you can refer to the manufacturers of those applications for additional information on how to use their software. Chapter 16 covers some of those vendors and tells you where to learn more.

Stay on Schedule with the Calendar

The built-in Calendar application that ships on the Treo is essentially the same calendar application that has been shipped with Palm devices since the beginning of time (although Palm has modified it slightly). If you are familiar with using the Calendar on previous Palm or Handspring devices that you have owned, you might want to just skim this section and read about the features of this version of the Calendar that are unfamiliar to you. If the Treo is the first Palm OS device you have owned, this section we will show you how to create and edit appointments in your Calendar. The Treo Calendar has some unique and powerful features that you may not have seen before in other applications, such as the ability to have floating appointments and a built-in daily journal.

Navigate Through Your Calendar

You can launch your Calendar application by pressing the button immediately to the left of the five-way navigation control. This button has an icon on it that looks like the pages of a calendar. This will open the Calendar to your default view. Unless you have changed it in your preferences, the default view is the current day view (the Day view), as shown in Figure 10-1.

FIGURE 10-1   The Calendar application allows you to track your schedule, appointments, and activities.

The date you are viewing will appear on the top left of the screen with the day of the week highlighted in the appropriate box on the top right. You can move immediately to any day in the same week by tapping on the appropriate day box on the top right of the screen. Tapping the arrows to the right or left of the day boxes will advance you forward or backward one week. You can also use the five-way navigation control to move ahead or back a day by tapping the RIGHT or LEFT button on the control, respectively. Tapping the UP or DOWN button on the control will scroll you up or down through your list of appointments, as will tapping the up or down arrows on the bottom right of the screen with the stylus.

You can select any individual appointment or event in the Calendar by tapping it with the stylus or moving the cursor to it with the navigation control. Once you have selected an event, you can view its details, as shown here, by tapping the DETAILS button at the bottom of the screen or by pressing the CENTER button on the navigation control twice.

This pop-up screen allows you to see all the details of the event and navigate to any notes that you have stored for the event, as shown in this example, by tapping the Note button.

The bottom-left corner of the Calendar screen contains four boxes (see in Figure 10-1, shown previously) for the Treo 650 and 700p, or six boxes if you have the Treo 600. Tapping a different box displays a different view of your Calendar. On the Treo 700p and 650, the leftmost box displays the "today" view, which is designed to show you a summary of what is on your plate today, including appointments, tasks, and e-mail as shown in the following illustration:

Tapping on any of the line items in this view will take you to either the day view of the calendar (in the case of a calendar event), your task list, or your e-mail.

On the Treo 600, the leftmost button will show you the Day view. This is the second button from the left on the Treo 650 and 700p. This box contains a single dot in it representing a view of a single day. An example of this view was shown in Figure 10-1. The next box displays the Week view:

In the Week view, the gray boxes represent events in your Calendar. Tapping on an event will cause a pop-up window to appear, showing the event details, as shown in Figure 10-2. This pop-up window will stay visible for about two seconds.

Tapping on the gray box again while the details are being shown will take you to the day view, where you can choose to view the extended details of the event or edit them.

FIGURE 10-2   In the Week view, you can see an event's details simply by tapping on the event.

In the week view, you can also reschedule an event by dragging it with your stylus to a new date and time. You can navigate through weeks by tapping the arrows at the top right of the screen or by using the navigation control to move left or right.

On the Treo 600 only, the third box at the bottom-left corner of the Calendar screen will take you to the Agenda view of the week:

This view gives you a little more detail on each appointment. Each box contains the day of the week and the date in the bottom right-hand corner. Tapping on this date will return you to the Day view for the current day. Tapping on any specific appointment will also return you to the Day view with that appointment selected. This is not a very commonly used view and was replaced by the today-style view on the Treo 650 and 700p models.

At the very top of the screen, you will notice a small number 2 in a box. Tapping this number will show you two weeks in the Agenda view instead of one, as shown in the following illustration. Tapping the number 1 box at the top will return you to the Agenda view of the week.

Any time you view a multiday view, the current date will appear, in bold (or on some models flashing on and off or highlighted) to help you to identify it.

The fourth box at the bottom left of the Calendar screen will take you to the Month view, as shown in Figure 10-3.

This view is fairly self-explanatory except for the symbols that appear within a given date. On the Treo 650 and 700p you will see squares appear to the right of the date if you have appointments on that date. Squares on the top are appointments in the morning and on the bottom, the afternoon. The color of the square will tell you if it is a business event (green), personal (blue), travel (gray), or unfiled (gray). On the Treo 600, the rectangles on the left of a date box are appointments in the morning. The bigger the rectangle is, the longer the appointment is. Rectangles on the right side of the date box represent events in the afternoon. On all the platforms, a dot in the middle represents a task, a floating untimed event, or a journal entry for that date.

There is also a Year view, which allows you to see the entire calendar year at a glance. This is accessed by selecting Year View from the menu in any of the views, or by tapping the Year button

FIGURE 10-3   The Month view lets you see your entire month at a glance.

in the Month view. On the Treo 600 model specificaly, the fifth box on the bottom left of the Calendar screen launches you into the Year view of your Calendar:

The current date will be shown in bold on the Treo 650 and 700p. On the Treo 600 specifically, any date on which you have an event will show with a dark circle inside the date. The date you are looking at will flash on the screen, and the first event from that date will show up in the title area at the top of the screen. The arrows on the bottom left will move you forward or backward within the current year one day at a time. The arrows at the top right will leap from year to year.

On the Treo 600, the sixth and final box in the bottom left of the Calendar screen shows a view of your Calendar called the List view. It generates a list of all of your appointments from the current date you have selected and beyond. The up and down arrows in the top right of the screen allow you to move ahead or back in the list. If you tap the up arrow, you can select from a pop-up window to move one day, one week, or one month, or else to pick an item.

You can set preferences from the menu by chosing Preferences, where you can set what time you want your standard day to begin and end. The Display Options menu item allows you to customize how the display appears for the Agenda, Day, and Month views as shown in Figure 10-4. Note that on the Treo 600 you have different menu items for each of the views preferences.

FIGURE 10-4   You can customize how your events are displayed through the Display Options window.

When you start creating a New event, you will need to select the start and end times for the event using the Set Time window.

Create a New Entry

There are four ways that you can create a new event in your Calendar. You can tap the New button at the bottom of the Day view, select New Event from the menu, tap on a blank space on your Day view for the time slot you want and begin entering details, or simply begin typing for a new event to be created as an untimed event.

With the Treo 650 and 700p, when you start creating a new event, the first thing you will have to do is select the start and end times for your event, as shown in Figure 10-5.

From this window you can choose your start and end times, or choose to make your event an untimed event by tapping the No Time button, or make it an all-day event by selecting the All Day button. The untimed event appears at the top of your Day view much like a to-do list reminder. This is very handy for things that you need to remember or do on a given day that don't have a specific start or end time. The All Day option will set up an event that starts at your day beginning time (as you selected in your Preferences), which defaults to 8:00 A.M., and ends at your day ending time (again as defined in your preferences), which defaults to 6:00 P.M.

 Never Miss Another Birthday or Anniversary

If you set up all of your important birthday and anniversary dates as events in your calendar that recur once per year, and then set an alarm to give yourself a few days warning, you can make sure that you always have time to book a restaurant, buy a gift/card, and arrange for a babysitter. Your Treo can make you a hero!

Things are slightly different on the Treo 600 model. When you create a new event from the New button on the Day view, or from the menu, you have to identify in advance what kind of event you are creating, either by selecting a menu item or choosing an option from a pop-up screen that appears when you press the New button. The event types you can choose from are Appointment, Floating Event, To Do, and Journal Entry.

New Appointment

When you choose to create a new appointment, you will be prompted to set a time for the appointment, as discussed earlier, unless you started your new appointment by tapping an empty time slot in your Day view, in which case you have already selected your time.

You can select the Start Time or End Time field and type in the time using the keyboard or select the time using the selection boxes on the right of the screen.

Not every appointment will have a precise time, so you can also choose All Day or No Time using the buttons on the screen. Once you have entered your time, tap the OK button to continue.

You will be returned now to the Day view with an empty appointment line into which you can begin entering your appointment description. Once you have done this, you can tap the Details button to set the other information about the event:

On the details screen for this event, you can change the time and date by tapping on the respective fields. Tapping the Time field returns you to the time entry screen that was shown in Figure 10-5. Tapping the Date field takes you to the Set Date screen, where you can choose a date by tapping on it:

10

Months can be selected by tapping them, and the year can be changed by using the left and right arrows beside the year. You can immediately select the current date by tapping the Today button.

On the Treo 600 you can also move one day forward or backward by using the arrows to the immediate right of the Date field on the details screen. These arrows have been removed from the Treo 650 and 700p versions. Selecting the Alarm check box will cause an alarm time to be displayed. An alarm will be raised before the time of this event to warn you that the event is near. You can set the alarm by putting in the number of minutes, hours, or days that you want to be alerted in advance. The unit (Minutes, Hours, or Days) is selected from the drop-down list to the right of the numeric field.

The next field, Repeat, allows you to specify if this event is recurring by defining when it repeats. By default, the Repeat field starts at None. Tapping this field opens a pop-up box where you specify how this event repeats.

On this pop-up box you select the repeat cycle (daily, weekly, every other week, monthly, annually, or other). For some of the repeat cycles, you must enter additional information in order to complete the necessary information to schedule the recurring event. For example, if you selected Daily Until, this would take you to the Set Date screen, where you would select the end date when you wanted this event to stop repeating. My daughter has a soccer game every Wednesday from 6:00 P.M. to 7:00 P.M. from May 1 to June 30, so I would enter June 30 for the "until" date.

The Other option in the repeat cycle pop-up box will open a detailed window where you can set up more complex repeat logic for an event, as shown in Figure 10-6.

For example, if you had a meeting scheduled to meet with the Vice President of Sales, Judy Smith, every Friday at 9:30, you would select Week, specify every 1 week to recur, select No End Date for the recurrence, and select the *F* box for Friday in the Repeat On field.

FIGURE 10-6 The Change Repeat window allows you to set up the repeat pattern for an event that recurs.

Did you know?

Keep Your Private Records from Being Displayed

When you see a gray box with a lock beside it anywhere on your Palm, this indicates that there is a private record there that is currently masked from view. To learn how to view these records or set up this security feature, refer to the section "Secure Your Data" later in this chapter.

Once you have your schedule defined properly, you tap OK to return to the details screen. If you had to meet twice per week, say Tuesdays and Fridays, you could pick both the T and F box to accomplish this.

Below Repeat in the Event Details screen, you can define the event as private by selecting the Private check box. This means that if you have security assigned to mask or hide private records, this event will show up as a gray box in your schedule.

To delete an appointment, you simply select the Delete button from the details screen.

You can add a free-form note to the event by tapping the Note button and entering any text you would like to attach to the event. If you are meeting Judy, as in our example, in the note you might add a description as to where you are meeting and what you need to bring.

Tapping OK completes your work in the details screen and returns you back to the Day view of your Calendar.

Edit and Delete Entries

To delete an event from your Calendar, you open its details screen and tap the Delete button. When you do this, you will be presented with a pop-up screen that will ask you to confirm the delete and ask if you want to save a backup copy on your PC:

On the Treo 600, you can also designate whether or not you want to be prompted when you delete by changing the Confirm Each Deletion check box on this screen. This option has been removed on the Treo 650 and 700p.

10

Jump to a Date

If you are at your dentist and are scheduling your six-month checkup, it is easier to jump to the future date than to use the regular navigation to try to get there. You can jump to the date by tapping the Go button on the bottom of the Day view. You can then use the Go to Date screen to select a year, month, and specific date to bring up:

	Go To Date				
◀ **2006** ▶					

Jan	Feb	Mar	Apr	May	**Jun**
Jul	Aug	Sep	Oct	Nov	Dec

S	M	T	W	T	F	S
					1	2	3
4	5	6	7	8	9	10
11	12	13	14	15	16	17
18	19	20	21	22	23	24
(25)	26	27	**28**	29	30	

[Cancel] [Today]

This window operates the same as the Set Date window, the only difference being that the current date is shown in parentheses instead of in bold. If you are already looking at some date in the future or past, you can return quickly to the current date by tapping the Today button at the bottom of the Go to Date screen.

Send an Entry to Someone Else

Sometimes you want to share an entry in your Calendar with someone else. You might have a family get-together that you want your spouse to have in his or her Calendar. Perhaps you have just made an appointment to see someone, and you want to make sure you both have the details in your calendars.

You can send an appointment to someone by beaming it through the infrared port of the Treo, sending it via Bluetooth (if your Treo is equipped with it), or by messaging it through e-mail.

On some older Treo models, when you try to send appointments or other data to someone, in addition to the e-mail option you will see an option that says MMS, for the Multimedia Messaging Service. This is a bug because you cannot actually send this type of data through the MMS service. If you try, you will see an error message. This isn't your fault, just the imperfect world of software! This glitch has been fixed in all of the newer Treo models.

To beam the appointment to someone, you must be in close range so that the infrared ports on both of your devices can see each other without obstructions. With the record you want to share selected in your Calendar view, select Beam Item from the Record menu.

A pop-up window will appear to show that your device is searching for another device with an infrared port to receive the transmission. This can include any number of devices, including other Palm devices, Pocket PC devices, and some mobile phones.

Once a device is located, this screen will change to show the event that is being transmitted. When the other device acknowledges receipt, the two devices disconnect from each other.

If the person you want to schedule the appointment with isn't standing right by you or doesn't have a handheld device, you can send the event through e-mail.

To send the contact by e-mail, you must select Send Event from the Record menu (this is Send Item on the Treo 600). When you do, you will see a small pop-up asking you which messaging system you want to use. The two standard choices you should see are Bluetooth and VersaMail. Choose VersaMail, and you are prompted for whom to send it to using the Mail program; it will also ask if you want to attach a message. The recipient will get an e-mail with a .vcs file attachment. This is a standard format used by many calendaring programs, so it doesn't matter if people you are sending it to are receiving it on another Palm or in Microsoft Outlook. They can click the attachment and accept the appointment into their calendars.

Look Up a Contact in Your Phone Book

Sometimes when you are entering something in your Calendar, you might want to look up a name and phone number in your phone book. For example, if I wanted to schedule a phone call with Dayton Foster, I could make an entry in my Calendar that says "Call Dayton Foster" and then highlight Foster in the title and select Phone Lookup from the Options menu. This would open the Lookup screen, and the Treo would locate any records whose last name matched what I entered, as shown in the illustration. If there are no records that match, the Treo continues searching, dropping the last letter of the name to try to find a match. It continues doing this until it exhausts letters.

From the match list, you can select the phone number that you want to paste back into your Calendar event and tap the Add button to return to the event. Dayton's phone number is now pasted into my event:

 Create a category called Emergency Contacts so that you can quickly jump to key phone numbers for your doctor, poison control office, fire, ambulance, veterinarian, or any other number that you might need in an emergency situation.

View Your Task List

Although the Calendar application and the Tasks application (known on earlier Treos as the To Do application) are shown as separate views in the database, as you can see from the preceding sections, the Palm OS really treats them both simply as events to be managed. Thus your tasks will appear in your Calendar Agenda view according to their due dates. This may not always be the easiest way to work with your task list, however, so there is a separate application called Tasks that you can launch from Applications Launcher. The main Tasks screen is shown in Figure 10-7.

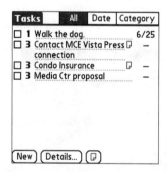

FIGURE 10-7   The Tasks screen can be a convenient way to work with your list of tasks.

By default, this view will show your Task items sorted by priority and then due date. When you complete an item, you can select the check box with your stylus, and the item will be removed from the list, if this is how your preferences are set. By default completed tasks are shown as "struck out" with a line through them, but this gets very cluttered, so you should change your preference to not show completed items. A page icon on the right side shows you if an item has an attached note. In the top right of the screen, a selection box allows you to choose to view all of your Task List items or view them by category or date. As mentioned earlier, I find it beneficial to categorize my task list items by work and personal, so I set up these respective categories.

Tapping the Details button allows you to view and edit the settings for the currently selected Task item, including its priority, category, due date, and if it is private:

From this pop-up, you can also choose to delete an item. The Note button lets you view and edit any attached note on this item.

The Preferences menu item under the Options menu (or the Show button at the bottom of the To Do List view of the Treo 600) allows you to set your preferences for what you would like to view on your list. This button opens the Tasks Preferences screen. Here you can define the order in which you want to see your items and what you want to show on the screen, including completed items, due items, record completion date, due dates, priorities, and categories:

New Task

If you tap the New button in the Task List view a new item will be created in your task list with an empty check box and a number beside it. The number indicates the priority of the item.

10

Tapping on the number causes a small pop-up window to appear where you can select a new priority from 1 to 5.

Alternatively, you can tap the Details button, and you will be presented with the details screen for the Task item, as shown in the following illustration:

Here you can change the priority and assign a category for the task to help you more easily sort your tasks. For example, I create a category called shopping, which is a list of groceries or other things I need to pick up. Then when I hit the grocery store, I simply choose the category Shopping from my view and I can see everything I need to purchase.

The Due Date field allows you to define a specific date by which this item must be done. If you tap this field, you will have options for setting the date to today, tomorrow, one week from now, a specific date, or no date.

As with the other records we have discussed, you can also choose to mark this record as private so that it cannot be viewed by others, and you can attach a note to the record.

Set Your Preferences

First, let's look at how you can set the preferred font sizes for your productivity applications. Under the Options menu, you can select Font to open a pop-up window that lets you change the size and weight of your font from among four choices, as shown in the following illustration. The smaller and lighter the font, the more information you can get on the screen, but if you find yourself squinting, then the larger, darker fonts will be easier to read.

For the Calendar application specifically the preferences are set differently, depending on whether you have a Treo 650, 700p, or 600. For the 650 and700p you choose Display Options from the Options menu to open the Display Options window shown in the following illustration:

Here you can set various options for how you want your information to display in the Agenda, Day, and Month views. You can also select the default view that you want to appear when you start the Calendar application. It is very much a personal preference if you like to see the Agenda or Day view first! For the Agenda view, you can choose if you want your Tasks and Messages to appear on the view, and you can also select a custom image to show in the background very much like the Wallpaper option discussed in Chapter 2.

For the Day view you have the option to show the Category List (which is handy if you use Categories extensively as I do, but a waste of screen space if you do not use them), Show Time Bars (the bars on the left of the screen that stretch to show you the duration of an event), Compress Day View (taking out unused time slots so you can see more on your screen), and Show Category Column.

The Month View preferences also give you the option of whether or not you want to see Timed, Untimed, and Daily Repeating events in your view.

For the Treo 600, on the Preferences screen, shown in the following illustration, you can set the start and end times for your daily and weekly Calendar display. You can also set the default duration for a new event. By default, this is one hour, but if you generally have appointments that only last for 30 minutes, for example, you can change this by tapping the Event Duration field and changing this to 30 minutes.

The Week Start field allows you to specify which day of the week you want to begin your weekly views of your Calendar events. The Initial View field lets you pick which of the six views you would like to have open by default when you run the Calendar application. By default this is the Day view, but your own choice might be something different.

The Button Views option allows you to specify which views you want the Calendar application to toggle through each time you press the CALENDAR button. You can select as many as you like by tapping them.

Secure Your Data

Overall security for your Treo is a topic that is handled in Chapter 13. Here we will look at security specifically as it pertains to the Calendar, Task List, Memo Pad, and Contacts applications. When you select Security from the Options menu of any of these applications, you will see a pop-up allowing you to change your current privacy setting:

The three options you have to choose from are as follows:

- **Show Records** This means that anyone looking at your Treo will be able to see any records marked as private in your Calendar, Contacts, Memo Pad, and Task List. If you are the only one who uses your Treo and if you have a password set for the whole device, then this is acceptable.

- **Mask Records** Your private records in these four applications will show as a gray bar with a lock icon beside them. Tapping the record will require the user to be prompted to enter the Treo password in order to view the record.

- **Hide Records** Any records you have defined as private will not show up in your screens. If you regularly pass your Treo off to others to use, this may be the setting you want to have.

If you do make a change in this field, and you have a device password set on your Treo, you will be prompted to enter the password to authorize the change.

In general, it can be rather a burden not to be able to see what is in your own schedule. Unless you have reason to be particularly paranoid, we would recommend that you implement some of the device-level security discussed in Chapter 13 but leave the personal productivity application security settings set to Show Records.

Synchronize Your Calendar with Your Desktop

All of your Calendar, Contacts, and other information are synchronized with either Outlook, Palm Desktop, or another third-party application, depending on how you have set up your HotSync settings. This topic is covered in Chapter 3.

Carry Your Contacts with You

In addition to your Calendar and Task List information, your Treo will store all of your contact details in its phone book. On the Treo 600, there is no icon on the Applications Launcher to open the phone book Contacts application; instead, you must navigate to your phone Dial Pad screen. From there, you can press down on the navigation control to open the Contacts main screen. Luckily this oversight was corrected on later Treo models, where you can select the Contacts application from the Applications Launcher or from the Favorites button on the Dial Pad screen opening the Contact main window, as shown in Figure 10-8.

Navigate Your Contacts

By default, you will be viewing all your contacts when you first open the Contacts screen; but like other records, you can categorize your contacts to make them easier to sort through. Tapping the drop-down selection list in the top-right corner allows you to choose different categories to view or to edit your categories.

For each contact, you will see a phone number. Tapping on a phone number will open a pop-up window with the number displayed, and here you are asked if you would like to dial the number now. If you tap OK, you will be immediately connected to that phone number.

FIGURE 10-8   The Contacts application contains all of your phone numbers and addresses.

Tapping on the name line will open up the contact details:

If you want to edit the details for this contact, you can tap the Edit button to be switched to an editable screen.

You can navigate through your list of contacts by

- **Using your stylus** You can scroll using the up and down arrows on the bottom right of the screen and select any contact or phone number by tapping it.

- **Using the five-way navigation control** You can scroll up and down using the control. Pressing the CENTER button on the control is the same as tapping a record. Pressing the LEFT or RIGHT buttons will switch from navigating the list to navigating the buttons on the bottom of the screen (in this screen there is only one button, New Contact).

- **Using the keyboard** You can begin typing the name of the contact on your keyboard. The letters will appear on the top left of the screen. With each keystroke, your Treo will search to find all the matches in your list and will display them on the screen. Keep typing more letters to narrow down your search. You can type the first name or last name because the Treo will attempt to match either one. Pressing the RETURN button produces the same effect as tapping the selected record.

Create a New Contact

Tapping on the New Contact button will open a blank contact screen in edit mode. You can type all of the details into the appropriate fields. The drop-down arrows beside the different types of contact points (phone numbers, e-mail, and so on) allow you to select different contact points for this specific contact. If you have the Treo 650 or 700p, you can add a photo to each contact that will be photo caller ID when the person calls, and in the 700p you can add a personalized ringtone for each contact.

Note that there is more information than can fit on one screen, so as you enter data you can scroll the screen down to enter the additional fields that are out of view. The + button will allow you to add additional fields to your contact record such as Phone/Email, Instant Message ID, custom fields, and more.

How to ... Beam Your Business Card

As you meet people at functions, you will notice more and more they exchange business cards by beaming their cards back and forth. To set this up on your Treo, you must first set up a contact in your list with your own personal information in it. This should include all the same information you would put on your business card, including phone numbers, your e-mail address, and so on. Then, while you have your own contact open, choose Select Business Card from the Record menu. You will be prompted to confirm that this contact is the one to be sent whenever you transfer your business card:

After confirming this, a small index card icon appears in the title bar whenever you view this contact detail. Now, from any contact in your list, if you choose Beam Business Card from the Record menu, it will send this record you have just specified.

Tapping the Details button allows you to specify a category for this contact, label it as private, and enter a free-text note relating to this contact. It is here that you can also delete a contact you no longer want to store by tapping the Delete button:

If you are creating a contact that is very similar to an existing contact in your list, you can save yourself some effort by duplicating the contact and then editing what is different. You do this by opening the details screen of the original contact and selecting Duplicate Contact from the Record menu. This will create a new contact with the word "copy" appended on the end of the first name. Now you can edit the new contact to change the fields that are different.

10

Send a Contact to Someone Else

Contact records are the most common information that people like to beam between two handheld devices. Suppose you are sitting down having coffee with someone and your friend says, "I should really give Dayton a call. Do you have his number?" You can pull up Dayton in your contact list and beam Dayton's information to your friend's PDA. You do this by opening Dayton's record and selecting Beam Contact from the Record menu. Then you point your Treo infrared port at your friend's PDA infrared port, and the contact will be transferred to your friend's handheld. You can beam information between most handhelds, including Palm OS devices, Pocket PC/Windows Mobile devices such as the HP iPAQ, and even many mobile phones.

Message a Contact

Sending an SMS to a contact is as easy as dialing. If you tap on a phone number for a contact that is designated as a mobile number, in addition to the option to dial the number, you will see a button allowing you to send an SMS message:

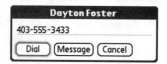

Tapping this button will take you to the SMS application (discussed in detail in Chapter 5), where you can enter a short text message to be sent to the person's mobile phone.

Take Notes on the Go

Have you ever wanted to write down something that you just heard or saw, but after quickly tapping your pockets, you realized you didn't have a pen or paper? Now you don't have to get caught without a way to take a quick note. Your Treo can serve this function for you and can synchronize these notes to your Outlook or other desktop software for easy collection of these thoughts.

Navigate Your Notes

Launching the Memos application (known earlier, on the Treo 600, as Memo Pad application) from the Applications Launcher will open the main Memo screen, as shown in Figure 10-9.

As in other screens, you can categorize your notes and view only specific categories by selecting a category from the drop-down list at the top right-hand corner of this screen. Tapping any note or navigating to it with the navigation control and pressing the CENTER button will open the note. Every note opens in edit mode, allowing you to make changes to it right on the screen.

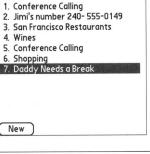

FIGURE 10-9 The Memos application is great for taking notes on the fly.

Create a New Note

If you start typing on the keyboard or you tap the New button, a new note will be started. The first line you type, in this case "My new note," will end up being the note title in the list:

The Details tab lets you pick a category as well as set the record as private. This is also where you delete notes if you no longer want them, or you can delete them with the Delete Memo menu option under the Record menu.

Send a Note to Someone Else

You can send a note to someone else by beaming it if the recipient is within range. Simply select Beam Note from the Record menu to initiate the beaming from the infrared port. You can also send a note by Bluetooth or via e-mail. If you do this, the note will be attached to your e-mail as a .txt file. Finally, notes can also be sent via Multimedia Messaging Service (MMS) if your carrier supports this. MMS is discussed in detail in Chapter 5.

Sort Your Notes

In the main Memo list, you can change the order of your notes by dragging them with the stylus within the list. If you would prefer to have them sorted alphabetically, you can change this under the Preferences menu item under the Options menu. This is the only preference that you can set for Memo Pad.

Make a Voice Note

On the Treo 700p there is an application built in called Voice Memo. It allows you to take voice recordings of your thoughts and ideas while you are on the fly. Each memo can be up to 99 minutes long and will be stored based upon the date and time of the recording. You can play them back on demand from the Voice memo application.

Convert Weights and Measures

The Treo, like many other PDAs, has a built-in calculator. What really sets the Treo calculator apart, though, is its advanced functions. It can function as a financial, statistical, logical, and advanced math calculator simply by selecting an option from the leftmost drop-down list below the display area, as shown in Figure 10-10.

In the drop-down list you will also find options for converting weight, temperature, length, area, and volume. For example, if you wanted to determine what 20 degrees Fahrenheit is in Celsius, you would enter the 20 using the keypad. Next, select Weight/Tmp from the drop-down list. Now select the units you are converting from, in this case °F. Then select the units you are converting to, °C, and you get your answer: 20 °F = −6.67 °C.

If you have large fingers and would rather just have a simple calculator where you can tap on the screen with your fingers (remember to use a screen protector, as discussed in Chapter 16!), you can toggle between the advanced calculator and a simplified calculator using the Options menu.

FIGURE 10-10   The Treo calculator provides advanced functions for finance, statistics, weight and measure conversions, and more.

Organize Your Shopping Trips

Depending on where you bought your Treo, it may have come equipped with versions of productivity software from SplashData (www.splashdata.com). One of these applications is SplashShopper. This is a very useful application. I am sure everyone reading this has made a trip to the grocery store and then been unable to find the shopping list. Going from memory, you do your best, but you always forget items you meant to pick up. Also, often you will be somewhere and think, "I need to remember to buy light bulbs," but since your shopping list isn't with you, you forget. With SplashShopper, you have your shopping list conveniently right on your mobile phone!

SplashShopper can track your shopping lists for a wide variety of goods, including groceries, books, clothes, take-out food, gifts, movies, music, wine, and any other category you might choose to create. For each category, you have a screen with two tabs, All and Need, as shown in Figure 10-11.

On the Need tab, you have what you currently are planning to purchase. As you cruise the aisles in the grocery store, you can check off each item as you place it in your cart. The All tab contains the list of all the foods that you normally buy, so you can easily move them from the All tab to the Need tab when you need to. Selecting an individual product in the list opens the details screen for that product:

10

FIGURE 10-11   SplashShopper lets you track your shopping lists for many different categories of goods, from books to groceries.

You can see and edit details, such as which store to buy the product from, the product description, which aisle it is in (if you have this level of information, you won't be running back and forth through the store), and more. You can also put in the price of the object. If everything on your list has a price defined, SplashShopper will estimate the cost of your shopping excursion so that you won't have sticker shock when the clerk rings up your total.

Tapping the Home button on the bottom of the shopping list screen switches you to the main SplashShopper screen, where you can switch among the different lists and see how many of each item you have to purchase:

The piece of the SplashData family that you don't get with your Treo is the companion desktop software. You can upgrade to this software at a 50 percent discount from the regular price at the SplashData web site at www.splashdata.com/treo. The desktop version of SplashShopper doesn't add a tremendous amount of functionality, but what it does do is allow you to enter all of your data with a nice large screen and a full keyboard, which alone is worth the nominal cost. The ability to enter all of your data on your PC and HotSync it over to your Treo makes the software much easier to use.

Store Your Credit Card, Passport, and Other Important Numbers

There are so many credit cards, ID cards, and other pieces of important information that we all receive that it becomes completely impractical to carry all of this information with us or memorize it. Yet it seems that just when we need a certain number or card, we don't have it handy. SplashID, shown in Figure 10-12, is a secure way to keep all of your personal information with you on your Treo. Your information is protected with a personal password and Blowfish encryption.

Like other software from SplashData, there is a desktop console you can purchase as an upgrade. This is handy for keeping a backup of your data and also for the ease of the initial data entry.

SplashID is a very simple program to begin to use and one that you will find extremely useful. It has thinned my wallet considerably!

FIGURE 10-12 SplashID lets you securely carry your personal information, such as passwords, credit card numbers, frequent flyer numbers, and more.

Stay on Time with World Clock

If you travel, or if your work or hobbies cause you to need to interact with people in multiple time zones, a very useful application that comes standard on the Treo is World Clock (known on earlier Treo models as City Time):

With World Clock, you can see what time it is where you are and what time this translates to for other places in the world. You can default the display to show times for four other locations in the world. The world map updates to show you what parts of the world are in light and in darkness.

Another interesting feature is that you can see what time the sun will rise and set in your home location by selecting Sun Rise/Set from the Utilities menu:

Wrap It Up

Whether you are managing your time, Task list, personal information, or something else, your Treo is your ideal personal assistant! In addition to the great personal productivity tools presented in this chapter, you can learn about others in Chapter 16. You may also want to refer to the references in Appendix B for where you can go to learn more about enhancing personal productivity with Treo.

Chapter 11

Work with Documents, Spreadsheets, and Slide Shows

How to...

- View and edit Microsoft Word documents
- Work with Excel spreadsheets
- Give PowerPoint presentations right from your Treo
- Read Adobe Acrobat files
- Open e-mail attachments
- Move files between your PC and your Treo

A truly powerful use of the Treo is to be a mobile office and PC replacement. You can read and edit Microsoft Office documents, spreadsheets, and presentations with the right software. When you receive e-mail with attachments on your Treo, you can open them right on your smartphone.

Different Treo models came with different versions of software onboard. The most recent models all contain full versions of Documents To Go from Dataviz (www.dataviz.com), which will allow you to work with Microsoft Word, Excel, Powerpoint, Adobe PDF, and text documents.

Work with Documents, Spreadsheets, and Presentations

With a converged smartphone like the Treo, it will be natural for you to receive e-mail from people with attachments you would like to read. You also may find that you want to have certain documents with you when you travel, and that are accessible on your device whenever you need them.

In order to do this, you can take advantage of software that comes preinstalled on your Treo. This chapter will focus on the Documents To Go package, but solid offerings from other vendors will be mentioned as well, a full list of which can be found in Chapter 16.

Start Documents To Go

Your Treo comes equipped with a product called Documents To Go from DataViz (www.dataviz .com), which allows you to view Microsoft Word and Excel files on your Treo. On all the new Treo versions it is already preinstalled on your device. With older Treos, it must be installed from the companion CD the first time you sync your Treo. The new Treos have fully functioning versions of the product, but the older devices are limited in that the software doesn't allow you to actually edit or compose documents. However, you can upgrade to the Professional or Premium version of Documents To Go at their web site link, www.dataviz.com/. The enhanced versions allow you to not only view but also edit and create documents and spreadsheets. In addition, you can view and edit PowerPoint slide shows and read Adobe Acrobat PDF files.

When you launch Documents To Go, it will open to the document that you were last working on, or if it is your first time running the program, you will see a list of documents currently on your Treo, as shown in Figure 11-1.

The list will show all the documents on your device, including Word files, PowerPoint presentations, image files, and spreadsheets. The icon on the left side will allow you to distinguish between the different types of files. If you tap on the icon with your stylus, a pop-up menu will appear that lets you choose from the following options:

- ■ **Details**   Lets you view and edit information on the file, including the name, where it's located, the category, format, size, and time it was last modified.

- ■ **Delete**   Allows you to remove the document from your Treo. You will need to either confirm or cancel the action before the file is permanently deleted.

- ■ **Beam**   Transfers the file to another computer, smartphone, or handheld through the infrared port.

- ■ **Send**   Allows you to e-mail the file to another person using your mail program.

- ■ **Print**   Allows you to print the document you selected if you have third-party printing software installed on your Treo (it doesn't come preinstalled). PrintBoy from Bachman Software is one of the current preferred applications for printing directly from your Treo. You can learn more about PrintBoy from the link on the DataViz web site at www.dataviz.com/print.

- ■ **Move to Card** or **Move To Handheld**   Allows you to move the file from the built-in memory of your Treo to an external Secure Digital card or, if the file is currently on the card, move it to the built-in memory of your Treo.

The name and size of the file will be shown, and on the right side of the screen you'll see a column with either a HotSync symbol or a dash. If there is a HotSync symbol, this indicates

11

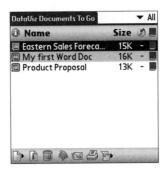

FIGURE 11-1   The documents that you can work on will be shown in the list view that appears when you open Documents To Go.

that the file will be synchronized with the file on your desktop using Documents To Go DocSync technology. This is a great feature that incorporates any changes you make on the Treo back into the original file on your PC. If you do not want your changes synced back to your PC file, tap on the HotSync icon to make it switch to a dash. The dash indicates that the file will not be synced.

The final column on the right will have an icon of a storage card if the file is located on the card. If the file is in the memory of your smartphone, the column will be blank.

You can filter the list to only show documents of a certain category using the category drop-down in the top right-hand corner of the screen. You can choose to filter for only a certain type of document using the Show drop-down at the bottom of the screen. Your filter options are to show all supported formats or any single format.

To open a document for reading or editing, simply tap the filename.

Compose Documents with Word To Go

When you move a file from your desktop to your Treo through the Documents To Go conduit, it will, by default, convert it to a lighter format called Word To Go—however, you *can* select the format you would like to work with, as explained later in this chapter. The primary advantage of the Word To Go format is that it takes less memory on your handheld to store. Just the same, you may want to keep documents in your native format if you plan to send them direct from your Treo using e-mail or beaming. Both formats show up in the document list with an icon depicting a page of paper with a small blue *w* on it. Tapping the icon will open the document in the Word To Go application, as shown in Figure 11-2.

The document will be formatted to make it as readable as possible on the small screen of your Treo, but you will notice that much of the desktop formatting has been removed or modified out of necessity.

FIGURE 11-2   Word To Go is the document-editing software where Microsoft Word files can be viewed and edited.

Count the Words in Your Document

If you need to know how many words are in your document, this is easily accomplished using the Word Count menu option under the File menu. Before you choose the menu item, you should either select the text you want to get the word count for, or if you want the count for the whole document, make sure that no text is selected.

Word Count
Paragraphs: 0
Words: 4
Characters: 9
Characters (with spaces): 12
[OK]

The resulting pop-up window will tell you how many words, characters, and paragraphs are in your document.

Edit Your Document

When you have opened a document, you can edit the content using your stylus and keyboard. The five-way navigation control allows you to move the cursor throughout the document. Pressing the CENTER button will move the focus to the toolbar at the bottom of the screen, where you can now navigate between the buttons and select the action you want. Pressing UP on the navigation control will return you back to the text of the document.

If you want to make changes to a block of text such as deleting it, copying it, or changing its font, you must first select it. You select a block of text using the stylus. Place the stylus at the start of the text block, and then drag the stylus to the end position. This will cause the text to be highlighted in yellow. If you type anything, the highlighted text block will be deleted and the new text that you type will replace it. You can also cut, copy, and paste text as you do on your desktop, using the appropriate options under the Edit menu. If you happen to make a mistake and want to return to the state you were in before, there are also Undo and Redo menu options under the Edit menu.

You can change the format of the selected text in two ways. First, you can use the formatting buttons that you will see in the toolbar on the bottom of your screen (or if you have an older version of Docs To Go, on the top-right corner of the screen). You will see icons for *B, I,* and *U* that will toggle the text into (or out of) bold, italic, and underline, respectively. If the text is currently formatted with any of these properties, the buttons will appear with a dark gray background. If the text does not have that property, the button background will be the light gray of the standard toolbar.

11

The next button, with an icon like lines on a sheet of paper, is used to change the justification of the text (to left, center, right, or full justified). Following that is an icon to toggle normal bullets on or off. A small right-arrow icon will open a pop-up list of other menu icons for toggling numbered lists, spell checking, bookmarks, zooming, indenting, inserting hyperlinks, and undo/redo options. You can customize your toolbar in Word To Go so that any of these icons can take the place of the regular ones that you find you don't use as often.

The second way to change the formatting of the selected text is to use the menu items under the Format menu to change the font, paragraph formatting, or bullet and numbering style.

The button with the capital *A* character will open the Font screen, where you can set the properties for the font of the selected text.

In the Font drop-down list on this screen, you can choose from Arial, Courier, Courier New, Helvetica, Symbol, Times, and Times New Roman fonts. The Size selection will let you pick appropriate font sizes from 8 up to 72 points. The Underline option will let you select from none, single, double, dotted, wavy, and word-only underlining of the selected text. You can also turn on bold, italic, strikethrough, superscript, subscript, and all capitals using the check boxes. Tapping the Color box will let you select the color for the text from a pop-up color tablet that fills your entire screen. The Highlight box performs a similar function, allowing you to choose a color for the highlighting of the selected text. When you are finished setting the properties for the font, you can select OK or Cancel to close the Font screen and return to the document editing.

The Paragraph option under the Format menu will open the Paragraph formatting screen.

On this screen, you can select the alignment (or justification) of the text. You can also set indenting (both left and right) as well as any "special" or "advanced" indenting (different settings for the first line or a hanging indent). Finally, on this screen you can set your line spacing options.

If you select Bullets & Numbering from the Format menu, you will be able to adjust the characteristics of how the current paragraph or selected text is numbered.

This works very much the same as it does in the desktop Microsoft Word software. You will select whether the text is to be bulleted or numbered. There are only two options under Bullets, On and Off. However, under Numbers, you have several options as to the style of the numbering, which you can select on the screen using the appropriate button. You can also choose if you want to restart the numbering, or continue the numbering from the numbered paragraphs previous to the current text.

Although there may have been images in your document when it was put onto your Treo, you can't use Word To Go to insert images into the document. You can, however, insert a page break or table from the Insert menu:

- ■ **Page Break**   Inserts a manual page break into the document.

- ■ **Insert Table**   Opens a pop-up window allowing you to define the number of columns and rows for the table that you want to insert into the current document.

The table will be inserted where the cursor is in the document. You can then enter the information into the table. When you have finished entering information into the table, you can tap the left arrow at the bottom of the screen to return to editing the document. From that point on, you will see the words "Edit Table" above any tables in the document. Tapping the Edit Table label will open up the table so that you can change the information in it.

- ■ **Add Bookmark**   Allows you to define a name for the current position of the cursor. Then at any future point if you tap the Bookmark icon (on the bottom right of the screen), you will see a list of defined bookmarks. Selecting a specific bookmark will scroll you immediately to that point in the document. This can be very handy for moving around quickly within large documents.

11

Bookmarks can also be added right from the Bookmark icon's pop-up list. If you want to rename or remove a bookmark you have defined, you can choose Edit Bookmarks from the pop-up list.

■ **Insert Hyperlink**   Allows you to insert a *hyperlink,* which is a line of text that appears underlined, and when the reader clicks or taps it, it links the user to another file or resource. These resources are usually on the Internet.

For example, you could define a link for the name of a company you are referencing in your document. You could have the text show "Palm Website," and create a link that says www.palm.com. The text Palm Website will show up in the document underlined in blue (by default). When the user taps on "Palm Website" or selects it with the navigation control, it will open up the web browser with the home page of Palm showing.

Start a New Document

To begin creating a new Word To Go document, you must return to the Documents To Go list by closing the current document you are in. This is accomplished by tapping the Exit icon button in the lower-left corner. If you have unsaved changes, you will be prompted to save the document as discussed in the next section.

Spell-Check Your Document

You might think that you have to give up spell checking on a smaller platform like the Treo. Not so! Word To Go contains its own mini-spell checking utility to help you out (although this feature is only available if you upgrade to the Premium Edition!).

To launch the spell checker, select the Check Spelling menu item under the File menu. It will search any text you have selected, and then prompt you to see if you want to search the rest of the document.

If it finds a word it doesn't know, it will open up a section at the bottom of the screen with the unknown word highlighted. You can correct it right on the line, or you can ask the spell checker to make recommendations. This is different from desktop word processors, which will automatically make recommendations. On the Treo, searching the dictionary can be a little slow, so it won't search for recommendations until you ask it to. Recommendations will appear in the box below and can be selected with your stylus.

After you have either made changes or chosen not to, you can use the buttons at the bottom to change this word once, or throughout the entire document. You can also choose to add the word to your standard dictionary. You can also ignore this instance of the word or all instances of this word in the document.

Tapping the left arrow on the bottom left of the screen will exit the spell checker and return you to editing the document.

In the document list screen, you can select the New button on the bottom left. Notice that this button has an arrow on it. This is because the button will open a pop-up menu where you must define what kind of new document you are going to create.

11

Save Your Document

When you are working in a document, you can save that document either from the menu options (Save or Save As) or by tapping the Exit button on the bottom left of the screen. If the document is a new document, you will see three options in a pop-up window after pressing the Exit button:

The three options are Save Document, Return To Document, or Delete Document. If the document is an existing document, you will have four options: Save Changes, Save As (a new file), Don't Save Changes, or Return To Document:

Change Preferences

You can tweak the behavior of Word To Go so that it better fits the way you work. This is accomplished by opening the Preferences screen from the File menu and choosing Word To Go from the drop-down list of applications you can set the preferences for

There are two check boxes on the top of the screen that you can toggle on and off:

- **Include in Global Find** This option will search any documents on your Treo for text entered using the find/search function on the Treo. It allows you to search for text in documents, but does make the find process take slightly longer.

- **Always Search for Supported Files When Opening Documents To Go** When you first start Documents To Go, it will be default search the device memory and any inserted storage card for documents. This is useful if you add and remove storage cards and want to see the current list of documents. The downside of this is that it slows down the opening of the application. If you rarely switch your storage cards, you might find that unchecking this option will speed up your access to the Documents To Go application.

Work the Numbers with Sheet To Go

Being able to open and work with spreadsheets on your Treo is extremely valuable. Whether you are scoring your golf handicap while on the course, converting exchange rates, tracking expenses while traveling, or marking off an inspection checklist, spreadsheets are something that virtually all of us can put to use.

Spreadsheets and workbooks show up in the Documents To Go list with an icon of a green grid with a pencil, or in the case of a native Excel file, as a green box with a .XLS inside. You can tap the document, or select it with the navigation control to open the spreadsheet.

Navigate a Workbook

Once you've opened the worksheet, you will see the first page of the workbook displayed, as shown in Figure 11-3.

If your workbook has multiple sheets, each sheet will be shown as a drop-down option in the top-right corner. In Figure 11-3, the sheet that is currently being viewed is titled Sheet1, the default name. You can move between sheets by selecting the sheet you want from this drop-down.

FIGURE 11-3 Sheet To Go lets you work with your Excel spreadsheets right on your Treo.

You can navigate around the current sheet by tapping the arrows at the bottom center of the screen. You can use the navigation control to move the currently selected cell one cell at a time in any direction.

The Go icon (which is in the list of extra icons you access by pressing the right arrow icon on the toolbar) will allow you to jump to a specific location in your sheet. Tapping this button opens the Go pop-up window.

You can enter a specific cell address in the Go To Cell field, or you can jump to any cell that has a bookmark or comment by selecting it from the list and tapping Go.

Editing

To edit the contents of a cell, you must first select it. This is best accomplished with the stylus by tapping it or using the navigation arrows on the bottom of the screen to move to the right cell. The selected cell shows up with a dark outline around it. The contents of the currently selected cell are shown on the dotted line immediately below the cell display area. Tapping the line will allow you to use the keyboard to enter text and numbers on the line. If you need more space to enter your value for the cell, you can tap the down arrow to the right of the entry line. This will open a pop-up window that expands the entry line to a full screen.

You can also enter formulas in the same way you would in Microsoft Excel on your desktop. If you haven't memorized all the formulas that you can use, there is a convenient way you can enter them. If you tap the *fx* toolbar button, you will be taken to the Insert Function window.

Use the Global Find Feature

One invaluable feature of the Treo is the ability to search all applications, contacts, and more for a particular block of text. To launch this feature, press the OPTION button on your keyboard plus the SHIFT/FIND button (which has a small magnifying glass icon on it to symbolize the Find function). This will open the Find pop-up window.

Enter the text you are searching for and tap the OK button. Your Treo will now search through everything in its memory looking for the text you entered. If it finds it, the display will show you the application the information was found in. You can tap on the line or select it with the navigation control to be taken to the information. It will show only one page of results at a time. Once the first page is full, it will wait for you to select one of the matches, or you can tap Find More to search for more matches.

The Insert Function window is the holy grail of function tools. It contains a list of all of the functions you can use in your formula. The list will also show you how the arguments need to be entered into the formula.

By default, all formulas are shown; however, you can select a subgroup of functions from the drop-down list at the top of the screen. After selecting the function that you want, tap the OK button to paste the function back into the cell value line.

You can use the two buttons to the immediate left of the entry line to accept your entry (the green arrow icon) or cancel (the red *X* icon).

An important part of editing spreadsheets is the ability to insert new rows, columns, and sheets. You can do all of this from the Insert menu by selecting the type of object you want to insert. If you select Row or Column, you will be prompted to enter the number of rows or columns you would like to insert.

If you select Sheet, you'll need to specify where you want to insert the new sheet. You can place the new sheet at the end of your workbook, before the current sheet, or after the current sheet.

Under the Edit menu, you'll find standard options for cut, copy, and paste, as well as menu items for clearing a cell, or deleting cells, rows, columns, or sheets.

Another key editing feature is the ability to change the formatting of your cell or sheet. This is done through the Format menu. The Cell menu item (or alternatively, pressing the Cell Format toolbar icon, which appears as the letter *A* underlined) will open a pop-up screen where you can change the alignment of the cell, as well as change the font to bold or normal. The Locked check

How to ...   **Set a Column Width**

By default, columns are created with a standard width. If the standard isn't appropriate for what you are entering, you can use the stylus to change the width of the column. Tap and hold the stylus on the line on the right of the column whose side you want to adjust in the column header. The normal dotted line in the sheet will be replaced by a solid vertical bar. Now drag your stylus left or right to make the column the size you would like.

box allows you to set the cell so that someone looking at the workbook is unable to edit that cell. Finally, you can set the color for both the cell and the text in the cell using the two color buttons. The currently selected colors are shown to the right of the button.

You can also control the formatting of numbers in a cell or range of cells. To change the formatting, select the cell, or cells, that you want to modify. Then select Number from the Format menu, or press the $ icon on the toolbar. The current format for the cell will show up in the Format pop-up screen that appears. If the format you select has additional options you can define, they will appear in the pop-up screen. For example, for some formats you can choose how many decimal places of precision you would like, and how you want the number to appear if it is negative. By default, negative numbers will be shown with a minus (−) sign in front of them, but you can change this to show negative numbers with parentheses such as "(1.25)," which is a standard for financial information. You can also choose to have negative numbers show up in red.

11

The default format is General; however, you can change the format to:

- **Fixed**   With this option you can define how many decimal places you want to display, how you want negative numbers to be shown, and if you want a separator for numbers greater than 1000.

- **Scientific**   Displays the number in a standard scientific format with a specified number of digits of precision. For example, a value of 125.35 in scientific notation to four digits of precision would show as 1.2535e+02. This format is normally used for displaying very large or very small numbers.

- **Currency**   This is for handling financial numbers. In addition to the standard formatting, you can also select the currency type, including the U.S. Dollar, Canadian Dollar, Euro, Japanese Yen, British Pound, and many others—from the Australian Dollar to the Thai Baht. Selecting a currency changes the symbol that appears next to the number to the correct symbol for the currency.

- **Percent**   Shows decimal numbers as a percentage with the percent sign (%) beside it. For example, 0.12 would show up as 12%.

- **Text**   Shows the number as a text label instead of a general number.

- **Date**   Displays the number as a date field. You can further define the format of how you would like the date to appear.

- **Time**   Displays the number as a time value. You can also define the format that you like your time to be displayed in.

Column, Row, and Sheet Menus

When you want to take an action that is to affect an entire row, a column, or the whole worksheet, you can take advantage of the row, column, and sheet menus. These menus appear when you tap either a row number, column letter, or the small arrow that appears on the top-left corner where the row number and column letters meet, as shown in Figure 11-4.

FIGURE 11-4   Tapping on the row, column, or sheet header will open a menu for actions you can take that will affect the relevant item you have selected.

The Column Header pop-up menu has eight options you can select from, as shown here:

- ■ **Freeze (or Unfreeze)**   Allows you to fix the current column plus all columns to the left of it in place. When you scroll the spreadsheet, the frozen columns will stay displayed. This is very handy when the left column of your spreadsheet contains labels that you want to be able to see as you scroll to the right. If you already have this column frozen, then the menu will show an Unfreeze option instead of Freeze. Selecting Unfreeze will remove the current column freeze.

- ■ **Fit**   Causes the column width to resize to fit the widest text in the column.

- ■ **Home**   Returns you immediately to column A, regardless of what column you are currently viewing.

- ■ **Select**   Causes the entire column to be selected. This is so you can perform an operation on the entire column, such as cut, copy, or format.

- ■ **Insert**   Allows you to insert columns before the column whose header you tapped. You will see a pop-up screen prompting you for how many columns you want to insert.

- ■ **Delete**   Allows you to select the current column (or more). A pop-up screen will allow you to confirm that you want to delete the column and will also allow you to delete multiple columns if you choose.

- ■ **Hide**   Hide allows you to make the column invisible. Once a column has been hidden, it can be made visible with the Unhide menu item that appears in the column to the immediate right of the hidden column. Selecting this will make the hidden column visible. Alternatively, the sheet header pop-up menu contains an Unhide All option which will make all hidden columns and rows visible.

- ■ **Sort**   Allows you to re-sort all the selected columns by specific criteria. Note that you must select the columns in advance of pressing the Sort button. Any data outside the selected area will not be shuffled with the sort.

11

The Row Header pop-up menu contains a subset of the items from the Column Header pop-up menu. The two excluded functions are Fit and Sort, which aren't relevant to rows. The difference, of course, is that when you select any of the actions on the row header pop-up menu, it will affect the row, not the column. For example, selecting Home returns you to Row 1 but doesn't change your column.

The Sheet menu contains some different options that impact the current worksheet you are working with:

■ **Find** Allows you to enter text that you want to find in the current workbook or sheet. You can limit the search to only the current sheet if desired.

- **Find Next**   Allows you to search to the next instance of the text you entered in the Find pop-up screen.
- **Home**   Returns you immediately to column A and row 1 of the current worksheet.
- **Unhide All**   Makes all hidden rows and sheets visible.
- **Reset View**   Returns all column widths to their default setting. This isn't something you should do often, so if you hit this by accident, remember that there is an Undo menu item in the Edit menu. If you select Undo, you can return all your column widths to their previous settings.
- **Format Sheet**   Allows you to change the name of the current sheet and also to protect the sheet. Protected sheets can be viewed but not changed.

Create a Chart

A picture can be worth a thousand words, particularly when you are looking for a summary of information such as financial results, polls, or other numerical data where comparing multiple fields is important.

If you have upgraded to the Premium Edition of Documents To Go, you can create charts on the fly in Sheet To Go using the Chart button, which is the small bar chart icon in the toolbar. Before tapping this button, select the data in your spreadsheet that you want to make a graph out of.

After tapping the Chart button, you will be taken to the Chart Wizard, which is a series of screens that will define the properties of your chart.

First, you must define the type of chart you want to create. There are many varieties to choose from, including pie charts, columns, stacked columns, lines, bar charts, and more. The data range field is the set of cells that you want to include in the chart. If you selected a range before tapping the chart icon, this will already be populated for you. Tap the Next button to move to the next screen, or the Finish button at any time to jump right to viewing the chart.

The next screen in the wizard lets you define if your chart series is in rows or columns. You can also define a different label for each series in the chart.

The final screen lets you define titles for the chart and the chart axis. You can also choose not to display the axis titles if you prefer.

The Finish button will cause your finished graph to be displayed. You can tap the Details button to return to the wizard and change information. The Legend button will open up a legend showing you each of the graph series labels. You can also tap any data point on the graph to see its precise value and details.

Tapping the Done button will prompt you to either save the chart, or not. If you decide to save it, the chart will be saved as a new sheet in your workbook. Afterward, you can open it using the sheet selection drop-down in the top-right corner of the Sheet To Go main view.

Start a New Spreadsheet

To begin creating a new Sheet To Go workbook, you must return to the Documents To Go list by closing the current document you are in. This is accomplished by tapping the Done button in the lower-left corner. If you have unsaved changes, you will be prompted to save the document as discussed in the next section.

In the document list screen, you can choose the New selection button at the bottom left. You'll notice that this button has a right-facing arrow in it. This is because the button will open a pop-up window where you must define what kind of new document you are going to create.

For a new spreadsheet, you will select either Sheet To Go or MS Excel as the document type.

Save Your Spreadsheet

As with documents, when you're working in a spreadsheet, you can save that document either from the menu options (Save or Save As) or by tapping the Exit button on the bottom left of the screen. If the spreadsheet is a new document, you will see three options in a pop-up window after pressing the Exit button.

The three options that appear are save the document, return to the document, or delete the document. If the spreadsheet is an existing document, you will have four options: Save the Document, Save as a New Filename, Don't Save Changes, and Return to Document.

Change Your Preferences

You can tweak the behavior of Sheet To Go so that it better fits the way you work. This is accomplished by opening the Preferences screen from the File menu and then setting the options in exactly the same way you did with Word To Go. You can choose if you want to include Sheet To Go documents in the Global Find feature, and you can also choose if you want Sheet To Go to search for supported documents on your Treo every time it starts.

Present Like a Pro with Slideshow To Go

A lot of business people give presentations while on the road, and this has generally required hauling around a bulky laptop with you when you travel. Now you can carry, edit, and present your PowerPoint slide shows right on your Treo! In order to accomplish this, you will have to use a combination of third-party software and hardware. You can load, edit, and view PowerPoint files right on your handheld with just software, but to connect to a projector or monitor, additional hardware is needed.

Slideshow To Go is the third component of the Documents To Go suite. With it, you can view, edit, and compose slide shows right on your Treo. Native PowerPoint slide shows are not editable on the Treo, but you can display them.

A Slideshow To Go file is opened right from the main Documents To Go screen. It appears with an icon next to it that looks like an orange box with a stylus. Native PowerPoint shows will have an icon with .PPT inside a box.

Navigate a Presentation

Once you've opened the presentation, what you will see next depends on whether your file is a native PowerPoint file, or a native Slideshow To Go file. If it is a native PowerPoint file, you will see the Outline view of your presentation and you will see the titles of the individual slides and the text from each slide, as shown in Figure 11-5.

Slideshow To Go format files will open to the Slide view instead of the Outline view.

In addition to Outline view, Slideshow To Go also has a Slide view and a Notes view. The three buttons on the bottom left in the toolbar (just to the right of the Exit button) will let you switch between Outline, Slide, and Notes views, respectively. The drop-down arrow in the top-right corner will let you jump to any slide in your slide show. The up and down arrows in the bottom-right corner will let you page through your slides one at a time. In Slideshow view,

FIGURE 11-5   Native PowerPoint files will open in Outline mode in SlideShow To Go.

there is a button on the toolbar that looks like a magnifying glass with a plus (+) sign on it. This button will zoom in on the slide to make it easier to read any small details. While zoomed in, this button changes to a minus (−) sign, which will return you to a normal view when tapped.

To begin displaying a slide show, choose the View Show menu item from the Slide Show menu or press the Slide Show button on the toolbar (this appears as a projector screen with a pie chart on it. This will let you move through the slides in a presentation mode and advance the slides by tapping the slide with your stylus. You can time your presentation by tapping the Start Timer button on the bottom. This lets you rehearse your slide show and see how long you are spending on each slide. While timing, a stopwatch with appropriate controls will appear at the bottom of the screen.

Editing

To edit the contents of a slide show, you must be in Outline mode. In Outline mode, you can put the cursor right into the text with the stylus and add, modify, and delete any of the text information on the slide. You cannot change any graphical information such as background, colors, or images on the slides. To do these advanced functions, you will need to sync the slide show to your desktop and modify it with the full version of PowerPoint.

The toolbar buttons with green arrows pointing to the left or right only appear when you are working on bullets in the slide. With these arrows, you can promote or demote any bullet.

From the Edit menu, you can perform standard cut, copy, and paste functions with the text. You can also delete the slide from this menu, or launch the slide sorter where you can reorder your slides by dragging them with the stylus.

To create new bullets for your slide, select New Bullet Item from the Insert menu or the toolbar icon with a picture of a round bullet with a green plus (+) sign. On the Insert menu, you can also insert a new slide into your show or create a duplicate of the current slide.

11

The Notes view is specifically for viewing the written notes associated with a slide in the slide show.

Start a New Slide Show

To begin creating a new Slideshow To Go presentation, you must return to the Documents To Go list by closing the current document you are in. This is accomplished by tapping the Exit button in the lower-left corner. If you have unsaved changes, you will be prompted to save the document, as discussed in the next section.

In the document list screen, you can select the New Selection button on the bottom left. You will notice that this button has a right-pointing arrow in it. This is because the button will open a pop-up window where you must define what kind of new document you are going to create.

For a new slide show, you will select Slideshow To Go. When you start from scratch on a new slide show right on the Treo, it will be the very basic black text on a white background with very little formatting. If you want to create slide shows with more pizzazz on your Treo, try loading a few base template shows with some initial formatting on your Treo, and then doing Save As to save the file with a new name.

Save Your Slide Show

As with documents, when you are working in a slide show, you can save it either from the menu options (Save or Save As) or by tapping the Exit button on the bottom left of the screen. If you are working in a new slide show, you will see three options in a pop-up window after pressing the Exit button.

The three options are save the document, return to the document, or delete the document. If the slide show is an existing document, you will have four options: Save Document, Save as a New File Name, Don't Save Changes, or Return To Document.

Change Your Preferences

You can tweak the behavior of Slideshow To Go only slightly. To make changes, open the Preferences screen from the File menu.

There is only one check box on the top of the screen that you can toggle on and off. This check box is Include Slideshow To Go in Global Find. This option will search any Slideshow To Go files on your Treo for text entered using the find/search function on the Treo. This allows you to search for text in slide shows, but it does make the find process take slightly longer.

On the bottom of the screen, you can select your preferred save mode. The default option is Confirm Changes. In this mode, you will be presented with the options discussed in the "Save Your Slideshow" section earlier. In the AutoSave Changes mode, you will not see these options. Instead, any changes to the slide show will be automatically saved when you tap the Exit button.

Hook Up Your Treo to a Projector or Monitor

To use your Treo to drive presentations, you will need add-on hardware. Although there used to be a few different vendors offering solutions to do this, it appears that your options have been narrowed down to one. iGo, with its Pitch Duo product, seems to the only current and active vendor in this market.

The Pitch Duo from iGo, available through the Palm store (store.palm.com), is an incredible device and an absolute must-have for the business traveler who has to frequently give presentations while traveling. It is a stand-alone piece of hardware, shown in Figure 11-6, which connects directly to the monitor or projector being used for the presentation.

The Pitch device connects directly to the monitor. Your Treo then connects with the Pitch device via Bluetooth. Then, from the Treo, you run the supplied iPresent software to select a preloaded PowerPoint presentation. One of the great features of the Pitch product is that it runs through Bluetooth (or the sync cable if you have the older Pitch Solo product) instead of having to plug into the SD slot. This means that your SD slot is free for storing your presentations. As part of my work, I give many graphic-intensive PowerPoint presentations. To store them all in the internal memory of the Palm would be impossible, so the ability to load the presentations onto an SD card is absolutely critical.

11

FIGURE 11-6   The iGo Pitch Duo allows you to run high-quality PowerPoint presentations on a projector or monitor, right from Bluetooth-equipped Treo.

Once you have opened the presentation you want to give, you can view the outline or notes views, but to get right to the most important function, you can tap on the presentation icon on the bottom and your presentation will now begin on the monitor you are plugged into! Using the up and down arrows on the bottom right of the screen will advance you from slide to slide, or you can pick a specific slide from the list and jump right to it. You can also use the navigation control to move through the slides by tapping up or down.

When you use the provided software on your desktop to move your PowerPoint presentations onto your Treo, you will select the resolution that you would like to use and the format that allows you to choose quality over file size, or vice versa. Unfortunately, the Pitch product doesn't support the fancy transitions and animations that PowerPoint is capable of, so keep this in mind with some of your sophisticated slide shows.

Another fantastic feature of the Pitch product is the capability to display the screen of your Treo live through an external monitor or projector. To give you a real-world example, my company develops software that runs on the Treo. We can give live demonstrations of the software to groups by using the Pitch to display those screens on a large monitor. This is a much better way to give demonstrations than asking people to try to gather around our Treo and look at the tiny screen while we try to show our software! Another method for showing live Treo screens is PDA Reach from June Fabrics (www.junefabrics.com), which is discussed in Chapter 16.

Read Acrobat Files

Another very popular format for files is the Adobe Acrobat standard. Though these files have the .pdf extension, you can view them on your Treo using third-party software. For example, the Documents To Go software that we have been profiling in this chapter allows you to sync PDF files to your Treo through their standard interface. PDF files that are stored on a storage card or sent to you via e-mail can be viewed right on your Treo as shown in Figure 11-7.

FIGURE 11-7   Documents To Go also gives you the power to read Adobe Acrobat PDF files right on your Treo.

Read E-Mail Attachments

One of the powerful and compelling features of the Treo is its capability to keep you connected not only to your important e-mail, but also to the attachments within an e-mail. Most common e-mail attachment formats can be opened and viewed right on your Treo, including Microsoft Word and Excel files, images (JPEG), and more. For detail on this capability, refer to Chapter 6.

Move Files Between Your PC and Treo

To read and work with documents on your Treo, you must get them onto the device either by receiving them as an e-mail attachment, or by syncing them over from your PC. This latter task is accomplished with the desktop companion software for the productivity tool that you have chosen to use with your Treo. With Documents To Go, this is accomplished by using your mouse to click the Documents To Go icon on your computer desktop. This opens the window shown in Figure 11-8.

FIGURE 11-8   The Documents To go desktop application manages the synchronization of your documents between your PC and your Treo.

You can drag and drop files from your desktop into either the Handheld or Expansion Card pane. Files dropped in the Handheld pane will be converted and synchronized into your Treo's internal memory. Files dropped in the Expansion Card pane will be synced to the SD card in your Treo.

Each pane will tell you the details and status of the file. First you will see the filename and an icon indicating the desktop file format. The Type column will tell you what the file format will be on the handheld device when the file is synchronized, while the Size column displays the size of the file after it is converted. The software will attempt to make the file as small as possible given the limited storage capabilities of mobile devices in general. The Status column will tell you if the files on the handheld and the desktop are current, or in need of synchronization to bring the handheld up-to-date.

When you select any particular file, the details of that file will appear in the box on the right. Here you can change some of the characteristics of the file to control how it is synced to the Treo, its format, and so on.

Syncing your Treo will bring any new files over to your smartphone and will also update any desktop files with changes you have made on your Treo. This last feature is a great tool, since it allows you to ensure that both your desktop and smartphone files are always in sync.

Print from Your Palm

It is only natural that once you start carrying and working with documents on your Treo, at some point you will want to be able to print a document out. In order to do this, you will need third-party software that will function as a print driver and allow you to connect to a printer. There are various ways to connect your Treo to a printer, including the following:

- **HotSync** Files can be queued up to print from your desktop-connected printer when you HotSync your handheld. This has a somewhat limited value for the mobile traveler, since you could then just print any synced files from your desktop.

- **Infrared** This is a much more functional model for the Treo user, since it allows you to use the Treo's infrared port to beam a printed document to a printer with a similar infrared port.

- **Bluetooth** This wireless technique allows you to print from your Treo within 30 feet of the printer.

- **Data connection** Through the data connection discussed in Chapter 5, you can connect to your office network with a VPN and print to any printer on your office network.

Once you know which form of connectivity you will be using to print, you will need the software to support your printing in that format. A full listing of Treo-compatible software is provided in Chapter 16; one type of software that is fully compatible with the Documents To Go software discussed in this chapter is PrintBoy from Bachmann Software (www.bachmannsoftware.com). It supports printing to most of the major printers on the market today through all of the techniques just mentioned. It also conveniently allows you to print using the Send function in many of the built-in Treo applications.

Wrap It Up

The software solutions discussed in this chapter are an absolutely essential component of turning your Treo into a fully functional mobile office. The ability to work with the same kinds of files that you work with every day at your desk will greatly enhance your mobile productivity. Although we focused on one primary software product in this chapter, there are many excellent products you might consider for your needs, including QuickOffice, WordSmith, and others. Please refer to Chapter 16 for more details on these alternatives.

11

Chapter 12

Manage Your Finances with Your Treo

How to...

- Download and install mobile financial management software
- Manage your accounts
- Work with the account register
- Manage your investments
- Categorize your financial information
- Manage your payees
- Protect your information with passwords
- Synchronize with desktop Quicken or Microsoft Money

This chapter will focus specifically on what you can do on your Treo with financial management software such as LandWare's Pocket Quicken software. It is not our intention to teach you how to use products like Quicken, but rather to show you how your Treo can factor into your personal financial management.

Chances are that you use either Quicken, Microsoft Money, or an alternative financial package on your desktop. To make it easier, we've divided this chapter into two parts. The first part focuses on mobile software for Quicken users given that they make up the majority of personal finance users, while the second section looks at other financial software.

Before you install Pocket Quicken, you must have already installed Quicken on your desktop PC; otherwise, the two programs will not synchronize properly. Once you have successfully installed and synchronized them, you are ready to go.

Account List

The primary window of Pocket Quicken is the Account List, as shown in Figure 12-1. In the Account List screen is a list all of your accounts with their current or ending balances showing. (You can choose between Current and Ending Balance using the drop-down selection box in the column header.) The net balance of these accounts is displayed at the bottom of the window, which, if you have every account entered, will be your approximate net worth. Tapping on a checking, savings, or credit card account will highlight that account. Then tapping the Register button (the second icon picturing a check book register) at the bottom of the screen will take you to the Register for that account (see the next section, "Account Register"). If you tap the Register button without selecting a specific account, you will see the consolidated Register for all the accounts. Tapping the Accounts button (the first icon showing a picture of a page with a list of lines on it) at the bottom will allow you to toggle back to the Account List screen.

If you wish, you can select in the drop-down account type filter at the top right of the screen to view in the list only a subset of accounts. You can choose among Bank Accounts, Credit Cards, Cash Accounts, Assets, Liabilities, and Investments. This can be very helpful if you have a large number of different accounts and complex personal finances.

Accounts ▼ All Types

Name	Ending Bal
Chequing	$4,768.75
Investment Account	$10,000.00
Savings	$3,432.98
Visa	$-43.76

Balance Total   **$18,157.97**

Edit...

FIGURE 12-1   The Account List window lists all your accounts and their current balance.

At the far right of the screen, you will notice a striped arrow pointing upward. Tapping this arrow will open a pop-up window, shown next, allowing you to change the sorting of the Account List screen to sort by name, type, or preferred; or you can choose Display Preferences to open the Preferences screen (discussed later in this section).

Accounts ▼ All Types

Name	
Chequing	Sort List by Name
Investment Acc	Sort List by Type
Savings	Sort List by Preferred
Visa	
	Account Preferences

Balance Total   **$18,157.97**

Edit...

Tapping the account name in the list will open the Account Overview screen, shown next, where you can see more information about the account in general, such as the account number and the contact information for your banking representative. Tapping the Edit button will take you to a screen where you can update the information for this account. You can also select the Preferred check box to set an account as being preferred, a category that can be used to sort the accounts in the Account List screen. Note also that, if you have entered a phone number for your account representative, you will have a Dial button enabling you to place an immediate phone call to your contact.

Account Overview

Savings
Derek Piggy Bank Bank Account

Ending Balance	$3,432.98
Current Balance	$3,432.98

Main savings account
Account Num: 12-345678
Contact: Kirsten Jones Ph:
555-555-1234

Done   Edit   Dial

12

When editing the Account Overview in the Edit Account Details screen, you can view a summary of the account balances by tapping the Balances box at the top of the screen. In the Account Balances screen, shown next, you can view the ending, current, and minimum balances of the account. You can also see what currency this account is in. If your desktop version of Quicken is not set for multicurrency support, this field will show as None Selected.

Tapping the Sync box will open the Edit Account Synchronization settings screen, where you will be able to view and adjust how this specific account is handled during the synchronization process. By default, the account will be set to the Send & Receive option to send and receive transactions, which means that it will be kept in sync with the account in your desktop Quicken. In some situations, you may not want an account on your handheld to sync at all, or you may only want to put transactions you enter on the handheld into your desktop Quicken, without pulling new transactions down. You can do this by changing the Transactions drop-down to No Transfer or Send Only, respectively.

There is a fourth box entitled Notes in the Edit Account Details screen where you can add any particular comments or free-form notes that you would like to store.

You can toggle between any of these four views using the boxes at the top of the screen, and you can tap the OK or Cancel button to return to the Account List screen. This is also the screen where you can delete an account by tapping the Delete button.

New accounts cannot be set up on your Treo. To create a new account, you must create it in your desktop version of Quicken and then sync it over.

Account Register

The Register screen, shown in Figure 12-2, can be accessed by highlighting any account in the Account List screen and then tapping the Register button at the bottom of the Account List screen. Every transaction in Quicken has an associated Register entry. The default view of the Register will show the date of the transaction, the payee, the category, and the amount of the transaction.

You can change the center column to display different information as suits your particular preferences. You do this by clicking the column header and selecting what you would like to see from the pop-up list. Following are the items you can choose to view:

- Account
- Payee
- Account and payee
- Reference number and payee
- Memo
- Category
- Class
- Payee and category
- Reference number, payee, and category
- Payee and memo
- Payee, category, and memo

12

FIGURE 12-2   Manage individual transactions in the Register screen.

The top-right drop-down behaves a little differently from what you might be used to. It allows you to change which transactions you are viewing in the Register screen. When you tap it, a new pop-up screen will appear, as shown here:

In this screen, you can pick All Accounts or a specific account from the list to view. There are also tabs on the left side of the pop-up to allow you to see subsets of all the accounts by account type. This can be very handy if you have a large number of accounts in your Quicken file.

The bottom of the Register screen shows, by default, the ending balance in your account. If you prefer, you can use the drop-down selection box on this line to change the view to the current balance or the available credit.

Enter a New Transaction

Tapping the New button at the bottom of the Register screen will open a pop-up screen containing three options to specify what kind of new transaction you wish to create: Payment, Deposit, or Transfer.

If you choose Payment, you will be taken to a blank Edit New Transaction screen to enter the details of your new transaction, as shown here:

Being able to enter new transactions on your Treo is extremely handy. You can record transactions while you are at the grocery checkout, gas bar, movie theater, or wherever, instead of trying to remember them all later! The details you need to fill in including the following:

- **Ref**   This is the reference number or text. This might be the check number, or it could be text that will remind you of how it was paid. For example, EFT stands for electronic funds transfer. If you tap the drop-down selection arrow, you will be presented with a list of predefined references you can use. If you don't remember what your next check number is, you can choose Next Check Num and it will fill in the number for you!

- **Pay**   This is the payee, or who you are making the payment to. You can fill in the name of the payee; or if you have memorized transactions with them, you can access the transactions by tapping the drop-down selection arrow. The curved arrow on the right of the entry field will cause Pocket Quicken to attempt to fill in the rest of the blanks based on the payee name you entered and the entries in your memorized transactions list. (See the section "Memorized Transactions," later in this chapter.)

- **Payment**   This is the amount of the transaction.

- **Memo**   Any notes you want to record about the transaction go in this field.

- **Cat**   This is the category for the transaction. Quicken uses categories to help you track where you spend your money for budgeting and planning purposes. If you tap the drop-down selection arrow, you can find the category in your category list.

Tapping the Split button allows you to define multiple categories for the payment. For example, imagine that your cable TV provider is also your Internet provider. You can then break down the amount of the bill that is related to your cable TV charge and the amount that is related to your Internet service.

- **Class**   This field allows you to specify a class for the transaction. For example, you may have classes defined to track how you spend (essential, discretionary, emergency), or perhaps to differentiate between personal and business expenditures.

12

The Details button at the bottom of the Edit Transaction screen opens a Transaction Details pop-up screen, as shown here, that shows you the status of this transaction—whether it has been cleared, when it was created, and if it has been synced to the desktop yet.

Even if the transaction you are entering is not a payment, but a deposit, the screen will look very similar to a payment screen. The only difference is that in the Payee field you will enter who the money being deposited came from.

If the new transaction is a transfer, you will need to enter the Category field as a "transfer" category. Transfer categories are indicated by the prefix Txfr: and are followed by the name of the account you are transferring funds into. For example, to transfer an amount from your checking account to your savings account, you would create a new transaction in your checking account as a Transfer. You would fill in the amount of the transfer, and under Category you would select Txfr:[Savings] to complete the deposit into your savings account.

Categories

Categories are an important part of Quicken and therefore have been fully implemented in Pocket Quicken. Categories are used in new transactions, as discussed earlier; and when transposed back to your desktop Quicken, they allow you to better manage your finances through budgeting and planning.

The Category & Transfer List screen can be opened from the Lists menu. On this screen, you can see all of your categories and subcategories, as shown in Figure 12-3.

FIGURE 12-3 Display all the categories and subcategories available to you in the Category & Transfer List window.

The Edit button will allow you to edit a category or add a new category to Pocket Quicken as required.

The Transfers button scrolls the list to the end of the categories and the beginning of the transfers.

Investments

Unfortunately, Pocket Quicken features only very limited support for your investment accounts. If you invest or trade regularly in the stock market, the ability to manage your portfolio from your Treo would be invaluable. Until LandWare adds this feature to the product, you must content yourself with checking your portfolio on your Treo using your broker's online interface.

Investment accounts in Pocket Quicken only show you their current market value as per your last synchronization.

Memorized Transactions

Pocket Quicken keeps track of historical transactions (transactions you've made previously). You can reference this historical list and reuse the transactions as you need them. You access this list by choosing the Memorized Transaction option from the Lists menu. This opens the Memorized Transaction List screen shown in Figure 12-4.

In this list, you can see the names of your payees and also the amount and category of a transaction. You can select any individual transaction from the list and tap the Use button to create a new transaction using the same information. You can then edit the information before saving the new transaction. For example, I could reuse my Shaw Cable memorized transaction, but perhaps this month my bill is slightly more or less. All I have to do is edit the payment amount and save it as a new transaction.

Tapping the Delete button after selecting a memorized transaction will delete the transaction from the list.

12

FIGURE 12-4   Memorized transactions are historical transactions that you have entered in Quicken.

The Built-in Calculator

Even though your Treo has its own built-in calculator, if you want to use it you have to exit Pocket Quicken, make your calculation, and then get back into Pocket Quicken to enter your calculated value. To save you from this frustrating process, Pocket Quicken has its own built-in calculator that can be accessed at any time with the Use Calculator option on the Activities menu:

Work Your Budgets

Budgets are a core feature of Quicken, but Quicken users don't often use them. Because of this, the budget functionality of Pocket Quicken is hidden until you enable it in the general preferences, as described in the following section, "Quicken Options."

Once budgets are enabled, you will have a Budget button on the bottom of your Account List and Register screens. Tapping this button will open the Budget screen, where you can see for each expense and income category the amount of your monthly budget and the amount remaining in your budget. If you like to consult this before making purchases, it is very handy to have this in your Treo when you need to decide if you should buy that new pair of jeans or not!

Quicken Options

There are many places in Pocket Quicken where you can make adjustments to the default behavior of the program to make it better match how you like to work.

General Preferences

When you choose Preferences from the Options menu, you will be taken to the Preferences screen, where you can toggle between Accounts, Budget, General, Register, Security, Sync, and QuickFill preferences using the boxes at the top of the screen.

In General Preferences, shown in this illustration, you have the ability to define which screen you want to open first each time you start Pocket Quicken. You can choose between Account List, Register, Budgets, or whatever you were looking at last when you exited.

You can also set a home currency, but LandWare recommends you let this be set by your desktop version of Quicken to help prevent any accidental conflicts of information.

If you like, you can set an option that will open the calculator whenever you double-tap with your stylus on a entry field.

If you select the Global Find check box, the information in Pocket Quicken will be searched when you use the global find function in the Treo applications.

12

Accounts Preferences

The Accounts Preferences screen is where you can adjust what you want to show on the Accounts screens and how. You can select different font sizes, sort orders, and shading options; set a default account; and choose to view account type, hidden accounts, and currency symbols, as shown here:

To help make the Register easier to use, you can define row shading. This is an option we highly recommend. It will cause every other row in the Register to appear with the background color you specify. This makes reading the Register much easier. Note that not only must you check the Use Row Shading check box, you must also pick a color by tapping on the Pick Color box; otherwise, you won't see the rows being shaded any differently because the default color is white!

Budget Preferences

The Budget Preferences screen, shown in the following illustration, is similar to the Account Preferences in its ability to define what you see and the font size it is displayed in.

Register Preferences

Also very similar to Account Preferences, Register Preferences will let you display the data in the Register screens in different font sizes, notify you if a transaction is uncategorized, and control if synchronized transactions and dates are displayed or not.

Security Preferences

The Security Preferences screen provides you with options to secure your Pocket Quicken information. You can set options for the handheld and the desktop. On the handheld you can

- Hide account numbers.
- Set a four-digit PIN code that must be entered when the application is launched.

The desktop component is where you will set the Quicken password that you have set on your desktop version of Quicken (if it is password protected). Without this, Pocket Quicken cannot synchronize information. More detail is provided on this in the later section "Set a Quicken Password."

QuickFill Preferences

The QuickFill Preferences screen is where you can change how Pocket Quicken attempts to speed your data entry by completing some fields for you.

In the Data Entry section, you can choose whether to have Pocket Quicken attempt to complete the field into which you are currently entering data by looking up what you have typed and comparing it with previous entries you have made. For example, if I enter **Sh** in the Payee field, Pocket Quicken will see that I have previously made payments to Shaw Cable and will fill in the rest of the field for me. If I keep typing, it will continue to try to match up previous entries for me. If I like what it has recommended, I need only tap the next field and continue. This can speed data entry in Pocket Quicken considerably.

If you select the second check box in the Data Entry section, Pocket Quicken will automatically enter the Pocket Quicken tag into the Memo field of all new transactions. This means that it will insert "PQ:" at the start of the Memo field of each new transaction, which can make it easier to identify transactions entered from Pocket Quicken later, when you are looking at your desktop Quicken register.

Selecting the third check box on this screen causes Pocket Quicken automatically to add all new transactions you enter into the historical list.

Sync Preferences

On the Sync Preferences screen, shown in Figure 12-5 you can choose what information you want to synchronize with your desktop Quicken.

You can toggle between the Receive and Send option settings using the two boxes at the top of the screen. In the Receive options, you can choose what you want to pull down from Quicken on the next sync. This includes the Account, Currency, Category, and Class lists. If, for any reason, you don't want one of these lists, you can deselect corresponding relevant check box.

12

FIGURE 12-5   You can control what is synchronized with the desktop version of Quicken on the Synchronization Preferences screen.

The next two options are designed to limit how much historical data you cache on your Treo. Memory space is always at a premium, and your Quicken files can quickly grow very large. In order to keep the data on your handheld optimized, you can limit how far back transactions are synchronized by setting the historical time period of transactions you want to receive.

The Send options, shown next, are very brief. The only things you can elect to do here are to send your new transactions or not or to export your transactions to a QIF file. The latter option would allow you to have Quicken itself do the importing, but the PocketQuicken sync makes it all automatic, so I expect you would only choose this option if you have problems with your PocketQuicken sync functionality.

Manage Data Volume

As mentioned in the preceding section, it is important to make sure you don't let your Pocket Quicken data grow too large, lest it impair the functioning of your Treo. Another tool for monitoring this is the Quicken Data Summary screen, shown here, which you can open by selecting Data Summary from the Options menu.

At the bottom of the screen, you can see the total amount of data Pocket Quicken has loaded on your Treo, along with the amount of free memory currently available on your Treo. You can see a breakdown of these records in the information at the top of the screen.

Tapping the Trim Transactions button takes you to a screen where you can remove historical records from Pocket Quicken. These records will remain on your desktop version of Quicken; you just won't be carrying them around in your Treo any longer.

You can specify to remove records from all accounts or from specific accounts. You can then specify which records you want to eliminate by indicating any record before a specific date. Alternatively, you can elect to remove records with any date but with a specific status. You can choose statuses of Uncleared, Cleared, Reconciled, Cleared or Reconciled, or Any Status. These two options can be combined to eliminate only records before a specified date and with a specific status.

Set a Quicken Password

Your financial information is private and sensitive information. If you have not already secured your Treo from unauthorized use by employing a device password or one of the other techniques described in Chapter 13, you can add a password specifically to the Quicken application to prevent unauthorized access. (Or if you are particularly paranoid, you can use all of the above for extra levels of security!)

12

To set a password for Pocket Quicken, select Security from the Preferences menu. The Security Preferences screen will appear, in which you can set and confirm the launch PIN you want to use. From this point on, you will be asked to enter the PIN whenever you start Pocket Quicken.

On this screen, you can also set an option to hide account numbers in your records so that in the event that someone gets into your financial information, it will be impossible to extract your account numbers.

In the desktop version of Quicken, you can also specify a password to open the file on your desktop. If you have this option set on your desktop, you must set a matching password in Pocket Quicken in the Quicken File Password field or Pocket Quicken will not be able to synchronize the financial data.

Other Mobile Financial Software

There are literally hundreds of other mobile financial software packages that you can load on your Treo. They range in cost from free to expensive. You can find many of them by referring to the Palm OS software sites mentioned in Appendix B. Here are a few that you might want to take a look at:

- **SplashMoney from SplashData (www.splashdata.com)** A full-featured financial application with many of the same functions that are addressed in this chapter. It has the ability to track all of your accounts, enter transactions, and work with budgets. It can also upload transactions into Quicken or Microsoft Money; however, this is not a smooth and seamless process as it is with LandWare's Pocket Quicken.

- ■ **Ultrasoft Money by Ultrasoft Limited (www.ultrasoft.com)**   A great fit for people who prefer to use Microsoft Money. It synchronizes fully with Microsoft Money and allows you to perform virtually all of the same functions that Pocket Quicken does, except with Microsoft Money instead. If you don't use Quicken or Money, then Ultrasoft's CheckBook product may be just what you're looking for.
- ■ **Expense-n-Go by Solid Rock Software (www.budgetprogram.com)**   A handy tool for tracking the expenses for your business.

There are hundreds of other software programs for managing personal finances on your Treo. Check out the sources in Appendix B to find the product that meets your specific need!

Wrap It Up

The bottom line for managing your finances on your Treo is that there are solid solutions available for both Intuit Quicken and Microsoft Money users, with the restriction that we haven't yet found one that will update stock prices in your portfolio through the Treo's Internet connection. However, given the rapid growth of the Treo platform, we anticipate you will see this feature appearing in these products in the very near future.

In closing this chapter on mobile financial software, we would like to add that it would be nice if Intuit, the manufacturer of Quicken, would provide Treo-compatible Quicken software to all Quicken users for no additional cost, but this seems unlikely in the immediate future.

12

Chapter 13

Secure Your Treo

How to...

- Identify security risks
- Take precautions to minimize security risks
- Use third-party software to secure your Treo data and connections

This chapter discusses both personal and corporate security. You will notice that some topics in this chapter are directed toward individual users, while others are directed toward the individuals responsible for corporate data and network security. It is a good idea to understand both the risks and the steps that you can take to reduce the risks.

Why Worry about Security?

Portable mobile wireless devices like your Treo continue to be hot topics in the press, and not all of the press is positive. Interestingly enough, the primary qualities that make mobile devices like your Treo so useful and convenient are the same attributes that make them open to security risks. For example, mobile devices such as your Treo are small and portable, meaning that they are also easy to misplace. Your Treo is capable of storing large amounts of personal and corporate information, meaning that the consequences of losing it can be significant if it gets into the wrong hands. The tremendously useful wireless connectivity that allows you to send and receive e-mail, browse the Web, play games, and perform countless other tasks also means that there is a relatively unguarded path for malicious programming code to get onto your Treo, and possibly onto your PC. There are two general categories of security risks:

- Damage caused by viruses
- Damage caused by personal or corporate information falling into the wrong hands

The Risk of Data Falling into the Wrong Hands

Your Treo is a compact, powerful device with enough memory to store at least 24MB of data; it can store much more than that if it contains a Secure Digital memory card. This is a significant leap ahead in mobile computing, but it also means that if your Treo is lost or stolen, your e-mails, documents, and pictures are in grave danger of being misused.

Your Treo has the powerful ability to transmit messages and data using wireless networks. Wireless connectivity is an extremely useful feature that allows you to stay connected and stay mobile. But this also means that there are many ways a virus can be transmitted to your Treo—through the voice phone channel, the GPRS data channel, the infrared port, and even infected memory expansion cards. Wireless data is easy to intercept, and your information may be scanned right out of the air.

So what's the big deal? Most of us feel that our personal data would not be very useful to anyone else or damaging to ourselves, but personal information can be very damaging if it gets into the hands of people who know how to use it for their benefit. If you use your Treo for work as well as for personal data, the security risk can be many times higher than the risk for someone who uses the Treo strictly for personal data; the level of risk depends on the nature of your work.

The risks involved with losing your Treo or having it stolen are listed later in this chapter, in the section "Risks of Your Treo Being Lost or Stolen."

The security risks are much greater for companies, and these risks, as well as preventive measures that should be taken, are presented later in this chapter, under the heading "Corporate Security."

The Risk of Damage Resulting from Malicious Code

You are likely familiar with viruses that spread through the Internet. Examples of well-known viruses include "Mydoom," "Chernobyl," and "Anna Kornakova," but new viruses are released many times a day. If you have ever had the misfortune of having your PC infected by a virus, you can identify with the amount of inconvenience that can be caused. For example, I was sitting in an office with a coworker who had his entire hard drive erased by a version of the "Chernobyl" virus. It is an understatement to say that it was not a fun day for him. In fact, he permanently lost a significant amount of data, not to mention the lost time it took him to rebuild his laptop. In addition to the inconvenience factor, viruses can be very expensive for the organizations that fall victim to them. This topic is covered in much more detail under the heading "Corporate Security," and your antivirus options are listed later in this chapter. Fortunately, viruses that target the Palm Operating System have been rare.

Risks of Your Treo Being Lost or Stolen

As stated earlier, the two primary qualities that make mobile devices like your Treo so useful and convenient are the same attributes that make these devices possible security risks. Unless you attach your Treo to your hand with duct tape, which is not recommended, by the way, there is always a risk of losing it or having someone pick it up when you are not looking.

Research information collected by David Melnick, Mark Dinman, and Alexander Muratov for the book *PDA Security: Incorporating Handhelds into the Enterprise,* (McGraw-Hill, 2003) reveals the types of information that are commonly stored on wireless mobile devices. Based on feedback from executives around the U.S., those types of information are the following:

13

- ■ **Network passwords**   Obviously, your Treo is a very convenient place to store those hard-to-remember usernames and passwords. The risk is that if the wrong person gets hold of this information, there can be a gateway into your entire network, critical data, and systems to which you have access.

- ■ **Customer information**   According to many executives, customer information getting into the wrong hands is a public relations nightmare and possibly a lawsuit waiting to happen. In the financial services sector, if customer data leaks, the company is legally obligated to contact every customer to inform them that their personal information may have been compromised. Or wouldn't it be less than ideal if a competitor somehow got your customer list and contact information?

- **Press releases**   If your organization routinely shares prepress release information via e-mail, or if an employee works on public relations documents on his or her Treo, there is the risk that private information is released to the public long before it is intended to be released. Having this happen is especially risky if your company is publicly traded. In the U.S., the Securities and Exchange Commission (SEC) has very strict rules about releasing information before public distribution. Remember Enron and Martha Stewart?

- **Bank account numbers and credit card information**   This type of information is commonly stored on mobile devices, even though many of us know better. But it is just so darned convenient. A user is even more likely to store this information as Internet purchasing and banking transactions become more common. The risks here are relatively obvious; if an unscrupulous person gets your credit card number, there is a good chance that you may be financing something like a world-class collection of a rare Beanie Babies for someone you don't know.

- **Corporate financial information**   E-mail is generally the way most organizations share information. Users routinely exchange spreadsheets and other documents as attachments. You may be surprised at just how much inside information you keep in your e-mail Inbox. Whether it's an in-progress annual report or the internal projections for next quarter's sales, the inadvertent leak of financial data may have a serious and long-lasting impact on your organization.

- **E-mail**   Again, there is no telling what kind of information mobile device users have conveniently stored in their e-mail. When most of us stop to consider it, there is likely a significant amount of information that we would prefer to keep private.

- **Intranet access**   Are you familiar with the term "The keys to the castle?" Users who work for companies that have corporate intranets—web sites not meant for use by anyone outside the company—often store username and password information on their mobile devices. This risk is relatively obvious, but the other risk is that many web browsers allow cache login information. So a person who picks up a Treo may be able to access a corporate intranet by simply choosing a shortcut or web favorite and clicking "log in." This provides an ultra-convenient way for someone to gain a lot of insider knowledge about an organization.

- **Price lists**   Consider this scenario. Your best salesperson just finished a meeting with a valued long-time customer, and when she left, she forgot her Treo on the boardroom table. The customer picks up the Treo to return it and notices some interesting information on the screen, the prices that a major competitor has been paying your company for products. "My largest competitor is getting a better deal!" This situation may cause irreparable damage to the relationship and cost the organization dearly.

- **Employee information**   Privacy legislation does not look favorably on an organization publicly sharing employee information, whether it was intended disclosure or not. If employee information is publicized, the potential costs include litigation and the significant negative impact of bad publicity.

■ **Medical (HIPAA) information**   This point is aimed directly at organizations that are involved in health care. The U.S. Health Insurance Portability and Accountability Act of 1996 (HIPAA) deals with the privacy of patient records and other health care information. Palm-powered devices are very popular for doctors and health care workers, because there are many applications designed specifically for medical information uses. If a mobile device containing patient information is lost or stolen and HIPAA rules are violated, the fines can be upward of $50,000. The negative backlash that could occur because of a security breach could be devastating for a health care organization. After all, if you can't trust your doctors and nurses, who can you trust with your private information? More information about HIPAA is available at www.cms.hhs.gov.

See the heading "Treo Authentication and Encryption Solutions" for solutions to help minimize these risks.

Precautionary Steps for Minimizing Security Risks

If your Treo is misplaced or stolen, you and your employer will be relieved that you took some important precautionary measures. Some of these precautions are included in the following list; they should not be taken lightly.

■ **Password-protect your Treo**   The steps to set your Treo security settings include setting your Treo to auto-lock after a defined amount of time has passed. After that amount of time passes and your Treo auto-locks, a user must enter a password in order to access your Treo. Defining your Auto Lock settings is covered in Chapter 2.

■ **Regularly backup your Treo**   By regularly backing up your Treo data to your PC through routine HotSync operations, you will minimize how much data you will permanently lose if you lose your Treo.

■ **Encrypt sensitive data**   Data encryption is very important for data in your Treo memory, as well as data stored on expansion cards and sent over the network. Software options to help you encrypt your data are mentioned later in this chapter.

13

TIP   *Some applications developers have taken the initiative to help you protect your Treo from prying eyes by including password protection and data encryption. Some of your options are mentioned later in this chapter under the heading "Treo Authentication and Encryption Solutions."*

Corporate Security

You are likely aware of some of the technical security risks that too often are topics in the press. This section provides an overview of the potential security risks of your Treo—and wireless handhelds in general—for companies.

Much of the talk about corporate security risks and what should be done to defend against attacks amounts to nothing more than technical fear mongering. Despite the attempts to guess dollar values for security attacks that have not yet occurred, the fact is that the actual cost of a security breach cannot be known until after it has already happened. This fact does not mean that precautions are not warranted; in fact, ideally, you don't want to ever find out how much an attack costs your organization. The best way to avoid incurring costs is to understand the risks and protect yourself and your organization.

"Inoculating the Network," a survey that was published in *The Economist* on June 22, 2002, stated that, out of 503 companies surveyed by the Computer Security Institute of San Francisco and the Federal Bureau of Investigation (FBI), 90 percent reported security attacks during 2001. The estimated average loss was $1.9 million per company. This obviously does not take into account companies that don't publicly admit to being attacked or companies that either don't know how much the attacks cost or won't say. It is clear that security breaches can be extremely costly.

In addition to the financial costs, there are some costs that are more difficult to value in monetary terms. For many companies, the costs associated with destroying the confidence of customers and business partners are devastating. The larger an organization is, the more a negative public impression will cost the company in the long run. Many organizations work hard to create positive public perception, and even a small security problem that becomes public can erase years of effort and negatively impact a company's bottom line.

The security risks associated with wirelessly connected mobile devices can be divided into a few general categories: theft or loss of a device, interception of wireless data, and the threat of damage caused by viruses and malicious code.

 Your Treo features an infrared port that is by default prepared to receive data. While it is a low-risk concern, you may want to disable the IR feature until you need it. To do this select the HOME button | System| Prefs | Power and toggle the Beam Receive option off.

Minimize the Risk Involved with Using Wireless Mobile Devices

There are specific precautionary steps that should be followed by every organization with employees using mobile devices. This section is directed at the corporate IT or security person responsible for network access and data, but the information is valuable for any mobile device user, as it can help avoid unnecessarily risking company assets.

1. **Research and understand the risks** The first step is to understand how employees are using their Treos and other wireless mobile devices. Answering these questions will allow you to understand some of the risks and the scope of any potential issues.

   ■ How many employees use wireless mobile devices?

   ■ What devices are being used?

   ■ Do the users synchronize their devices with network computers?

   ■ What type of data do users store on their devices?

   ■ What applications do users use on their devices?

2. **Create or modify security policies**   Create or modify your organization's security policies to ensure that wireless handheld devices are within the control of the organization and clearly convey the policies to staff.

   ■ Often, many of the devices in an organization are personally owned, rather than supplied by the company. It is crucial that you define policies that effectively define how these personal devices interact with corporate data and systems. The policies should include sections that cover situations in which employees have their own mobile devices. Issues like whether or not the organization will allow employees to synchronize devices with work computers should be included. Another item that should be included is a detailed list of specific security concerns regarding particular devices or software.

   ■ Convey the very important point to users that they must use the password protection that is built into their devices. Often, users turn off this protection for the convenience of being able to use their Treos without having to log in, but the cost to the organization could be significant if a device is lost or stolen. Some of the software options to help enforce this security policy are listed later in this chapter, under the heading "Treo Authentication and Encryption Solutions."

3. **Track mobile devices**   As an aspect of asset management, most organizations take time and effort to ensure that they have an up-to-date inventory record of each server and workstation being used by the company. Usually this information includes hardware and software configurations, as well as network addresses and which users are assigned to specific hardware. Doesn't it make sense to do the same thing for mobile devices? Gartner Group estimates that companies with more than 5000 employees could save between $300,000 and $500,000 per year by tracking, tagging, and storing contact information about their wireless mobile devices.

4. **Dictate standard security software that mobile users must use**   Requiring mobile device users to use antivirus and virtual private network (VPN) software can go a long way toward protecting your network assets. It is also important to ban any software that may be a security risk. For example, some organizations ban certain document applications because of the security vulnerabilities they cause.

Bluetooth Security

Bluetooth is not available on the Treo 600, but the 650 and 700p both have Bluetooth wireless capability. Bluetooth is covered in detail in Chapter 5, but it is worth mentioning here as we discuss security. Among other security risks there have been incidents of viruses being passed from one mobile phone to another via Bluetooth. While these types of attacks are rare and require that a virus author specifically target the Palm operating system, it is still worth being aware of the risk, however small.

Bluetooth is a standard that has been designed with several built-in security features such as "Pairing," also known as bonding, which is a concept that was introduced to create a first-time recognition of Bluetooth devices that are allowed to communicate with each other. The initial pairing process is required to allow each Bluetooth device to recognize the other and begin communicating. It is a security feature embedded in Bluetooth that effectively prevents unauthorized Bluetooth device from connecting to your Treo.

Some Bluetooth settings that you should be aware of include the ability to keep your Treo from being "discoverable." This means that if one Bluetooth device is scanning an area for another Bluetooth-capable device, the first device will not identify your Treo as a Bluetooth device. The simplest method is to turn off Bluetooth completely, but if you prefer to keep it running, follow these steps to access and change the discoverable mode:

Treo 700p

1. Press the HOME button; you may need to press it more than once to get to the applications screen.

2. On the applications screen find and select the Bluetooth icon. You will see the Bluetooth screen as shown in Figure 13-1.

3. With Bluetooth turned On, change the Visibility option to Hidden. A feature that is unique to the 700p is the ability to make visibility "Temporary." which makes your Treo visible to other Bluetooth devices for two minutes before turning visibility off.

Treo 650

1. Press the HOME button; you may need to press it more than once to get to the applications screen.

2. On the applications screen, find and select the Bluetooth icon.

3. Change the Discoverable menu list to "No" (you will have to remember to turn this back on if you want a device to be able to discover your Treo).

FIGURE 13-1   Treo 700p Bluetooth settings

Third-Party Security Software

The Treo has some valuable built-in security features, such as Auto Lock and password protection, but some enterprising software developers are also sensitive to the unique security requirements of mobile devices. The software listed in this section allows you to enforce passwords and encrypt data on your Treo; it also facilitates secure network connections through authentication and network data encryption.

Software for Enterprise Device Support and Security

As mobile devices like your Treo are adopted by organizations and corporations, it has become increasingly clear that supporting, managing, and securing these devices can be a significant challenge. Some software vendors are meeting that challenge head on.

SonicSentinel (www.Avocent.com) and Handheld Manager (www.LANDesk.com)

Avocent has been providing software that allows systems administrators and IT professionals to manage back-end computer systems and network infrastructure using wireless mobile devices. Avocent is leveraging its experience with wireless technologies to help organizations effectively manage their mobile devices. The company uses the technology in two products called Avocent SonicSentinel and LANDesk Handheld Manager, and are designed to help enterprises and wireless service providers support, manage, and secure their wireless mobile devices. The key functionality is listed here:

- **Device monitoring** Information about specific devices is sent back to the central server, including connection status, battery levels, location, and other asset management and user statistics.

- **Alerting** Based on device feedback and configured alert thresholds, alerts are generated to ensure that the correct people are made aware of changes requiring attention.

- **Real-time visual monitoring** The server console features a graphical interface that allows a support person to see the status of a device at a glance.

- **Real-time control** The challenges associated with supporting mobile devices are similar to the challenges of remotely managing any network node (that is, server, workstation, router, and so on), you need to ensure that the device is working properly and that it is connected, secured, and running the correct software and patches. Real-time control of mobile devices generally falls into two broad categories:

  - **Support** An example might be a user experiencing difficulty receiving e-mail, so a support person accesses the device from the SonicSentinel server to diagnose the problem and change settings to get the user up and running again.

  - **Security** An example might be when a device has been lost or stolen and a support person wipes the data to prevent unauthorized access.

- **Security** The mobile agent may be configured to enforce security standards—for example, each device must be password enabled, meaning that the user cannot disable the password lock functionality.

- **Asset management** The application maintains up-to-date records of each mobile device, including ownership, owner contact information, physical location (using GPS), installed software and hardware configurations, and so on.

Afaria Security Manager for Handhelds by XcelleNet, Inc. (www.xcellenet.com)

The Afaria suite has a lot of functionality and features a handheld security-specific application called Security Manager for Handhelds that features

- Power-on Passwords with configurable password levels and formats, password change frequency, and lock-out behaviors

- On-device data encryption to protect data using a choice of AES, TripleDES, RC2, and Blowfish

- Centralized security policies

PDA Defense (www.pdadefense.com)

PDA Defense by Asynchrony Solutions, also discussed under the heading "Treo Authentication and Encryption Solutions," is mentioned here because of its specific value to companies. This type of software helps defend your Treo data against unauthorized access by enforcing password protection, encrypting data, and managing connection types, such as the ability to disable the infrared port on a Treo. Some of the features of PDA Defense are given in the following list. This software is a cost-effective way—about $20 for a single-user license—to help ensure that your data is protected in the event that you lose or misplace your Treo.

- 128-bit-512-bit encryption
- Card encryption support
- Encryption of databases
- Password encryption
- Bitwiping (deletion of data based on defined rules)
- Admin IrDA disabling
- Password history tracking
- Password masking
- Temporary unlock password

- Application launch protection
- Admin application lockout
- Custom splash screens to display your corporate identity
- User-specific policy settings
- Enterprise-wide policy settings

Antivirus Software to Protect Your Treo, Your PC, and Your Network

The Internet is an extremely effective way to distribute software viruses that are aimed at disrupting services, causing user frustration, and inflicting financial pain on people and organizations all over the world. This fact is great if you are a hacker or virus programmer but not so great if your organization is vulnerable. The Internet is a public network and therefore results in inherent security and privacy concerns. Computer viruses have unfortunately become commonplace. Most viruses target specific application weaknesses in places like operating systems, databases, web servers, and e-mail servers. For the most part, mobile devices have not been popular targets yet. But you can bet that this will change as mobile devices become more popular and hackers and virus programmers become motivated to attack devices such as your Treo. After all, your Treo is connected to the Internet just like any home PC or corporate web server.

Fortunately, there are companies that offer software to help protect your Treo from malicious virus attacks. Antivirus software that you can use falls into one of two main categories:

- Software that runs on your desktop PC and protects your PC and network by scanning files for viruses during and after a HotSync operation
- Software that runs natively on your Treo and operates in the background to scan for viruses and malicious programs

Each type of software offers protection and, if you can, it is a good idea to run antivirus software on both your PC and your Treo. All of the major software companies that offer antivirus virus protection for PCs will detect known viruses if they are found in your Treo HotSync files.

Antivirus Software for Your PC

The first type of antivirus protection is the most common, software that runs on your PC to prevent viruses from infecting your computer and the network and to prevent viruses from spreading to others through your computer. When you synchronize data from your Treo to your PC, the files will be scanned to prevent malicious programs (programs you may have picked up from e-mail or Internet activity on your Treo) from infecting your PC or network.

13

Antivirus Vendors for Windows PCs

Following is a cross-section of antivirus vendors, but there are many more to choose from, and some, like AVG Control Center, offer free versions to noncommercial users.

- McAfee, a Network Associates Company (www.mcafeeb2b.com)
- Symantec (www.symantec.com)
- Aladdin Knowledge Systems (www.ealaddin.com)
- FRISK Software International (www.f-prot.com)
- F-Secure Corp. (www.f-secure.com)
- GFI Software Ltd (www.gfi.com)
- Panda Software (www.pandasoftware.com)
- Trend Micro, Inc. (www.trendmicro.com)
- AVG (www.grisoft.com)

Antivirus Vendors for Macintosh PCs

A cross-section of vendors that provide antivirus software for Macintosh personal computers is listed here, and there are also others.

- Norton AntiVirus 9.0 (www.symantec.com)
- Sophos (www.sophos.com)
- Intego (www.intego.com)

Antivirus Vendors for Linux PCs

While Linux is not a common platform for desktop computers, it is worth mentioning that companies such as AVG (www.grisoft.com) and Alwil Software (www.avast.com) offer antivirus software for Linux systems.

Antivirus Software That Runs on Your Treo

As mobile devices like your Treo are becoming more popular, more software vendors are offering virus-scanning and other security products designed for them. The two largest companies in the antivirus protection market are Symantec and McAfee, and both offer antivirus software that runs on your Treo to scan for viruses and other malicious programs.

The products listed here run natively on your Treo and run in the background to scan your Treo files, looking for signatures of viruses and Trojan horses and worms; they also prompt the user if malicious code is detected. Depending on the product, updated virus definition files are either loaded to your Treo during synchronization with your PC or sent over the air directly to your Treo using the wireless Internet connection.

- Symantec AntiVirus for Palm OS (www.symantec.com)
- McAfee Anti-Virus Resident Scanner (www.mcafee.com)
- McAfee VirusScan Wireless (www.mcafee.com)
- F-Secure Anti-Virus for Palm OS (www.f-secure.com)
- Trend Micro PC-cillin for Wireless Version 2.0 for Palm OS (www.trendmicro.com)
- Computer Associates InoculateIT (http://ca.com/)

Treo Authentication and Encryption Solutions

Authentication and encryption have been mentioned several times in this chapter because they are so important. There are software products in the marketplace that allow you to protect the data on your Treo by enforcing password authentication and encrypting the data stored on the device. Both of these are extremely important for protecting your personal and corporate information. *Authentication* simply means that a user needs to enter login credentials to access the Treo applications and data, while *encryption* means that even if a person steals your Treo and is able to move the data off of the device, the data will be encrypted and therefore unreadable.

A cross-section of the products that are available for your Treo is listed here. Expect many other products to enter the market as the Treo becomes even more popular.

- SplashID (www.splashdata.com)
- Chapura Cloak (www.chapura.com)
- Certicom movianCrypt (www.certicom.com)
- Asynchrony PDA Defense Enterprise (www.pdadefense.com)
- Credant Technologies Mobile Guardian (www.credant.com)
- TealPoint Software Corporate TealLock (www.tealpoint.com)
- Trust Digital PDASecure (www.trustdigital.com)
- Kasten Chase Assurency SecureData for Palm OS (www.kastenchase.com)

TIP   *If you have a Treo 600, it ships with a trial version of SplashID available on the companion CD. SplashID is a great application that is designed to store your passwords, bank account numbers, and other private information in an encrypted format. If you like the trial version, you can easily upgrade to the full version over the wireless Web.*

VPN Solutions

Virtual private networks (VPNs) are valuable tools, especially for wireless use, because they allow you to securely connect to a remote network and encrypt all of the data that is passed between your Treo and your network. This is extremely important when you are connecting over the public wireless networks because data is easily scanned out of the air. If the information is encrypted by a VPN solution, the data packet will appear as a bunch of scrambled random characters that are useless to the would-be hacker. Some examples of vendors that provide VPN solutions for the Palm platforms are listed here, but expect more to enter the marketplace as devices such as your Treo become more popular and the market grows.

- Certicom movianVPN (www.certicom.com)
- V-ONE Corp. SmartPass for Palm (www.v-one.com)
- SafeNet SoftRemotePDA (www.safenet-inc.com)
- Mergic VPN for Palm OS (www.mergic.com)

Enterprise Network Authentication

Many organizations are understandably concerned about the risks associated with allowing a wireless mobile device to connect to the corporate network over a wireless network. Some of the solutions that address these risks are mentioned in the preceding section on VPNs and in other parts of this chapter. One of the ways to help ensure that users who are attempting to remotely connect to the corporate network are really who they claim to be is by using one of the sophisticated user authentication solutions. These products use more than just a username and password to authenticate a user, which makes unauthorized access very difficult even if someone has stolen your Treo. A cross-section of some of the products that are available for your Treo is presented here:

- **RSA Security SecurID (www.rsa.com)**   SecurID on your Treo is used in conjunction with a RSA ACE Server, and it works by using a one-time-use SecurID access code that automatically changes every 60 seconds.

- **Trio Security Trio VAULT (www.triosecurity.com)**   Trio VAULT combines three-factor user authentication, a single-sign-on solution, and access management.

Wrap It Up

This chapter was not designed to scare you but to make you aware of any possible risks and the best ways to minimize those risks. Of course, any risks are generally more significant for some groups of users than others and are dependent on how you use your Treo and who you work for. Clearly the FBI is more concerned about security than many of us need to be, so it is only necessary to take precautions where appropriate.

Chapter 14 Navigate with GPS

How to...

- Use GPS to determine your location
- Navigate to anyone in your Contacts list
- Find a restaurant, gas station, bank, or other site in any city
- Play team sports with GPS

Have you ever wished someone were beside you in the passenger seat, guiding you to an unfamiliar address? Or perhaps you've been in a strange city and were trying to find the nearest restaurant or gas station?

Figuring out where we are and where we are going has always been cumbersome and often inaccurate. You can buy a map for a city, but as time passes and things about the city change, it gets less and less accurate. Well, navigational tools have been greatly improved courtesy of Global Positioning System (GPS) technology.

What Is GPS?

GPS is a network of 24 satellites around the globe that broadcast radio navigation information you can use to determine your exact position anywhere. These satellites act as reference points to determine any position within meters. Actually, these satellites can be used to determine location down to centimeters, but that level of accuracy is only accessible to the U.S. military, who designed and created the system (at a cost of over $12 billion).

Initially, GPS devices were expensive and only practical for large businesses and the government. However, continued advancements have reduced a complete GPS system to a few miniaturized integrated circuits, dramatically shrinking its cost and size. GPS has become available to just about everyone and has found its way into cars, boats, planes, construction equipment, and farm machinery. It can even be attached to your Treo. (Who knows? Maybe future Treo versions will fully integrate GPS.)

How Does GPS Work?

GPS works by comparing the signals from multiple GPS satellites (at least four are required for this process to work). A GPS receiver accurately measures the distance from four or more satellites whose positions are known, and then uses this information to compute its precise location.

The explanation of GPS used here is simplified. For a more technical understanding of how GPS works, refer to www.trimble.com/gps for an excellent tutorial.

What Do We Use GPS For?

GPS can be used in a wide variety of ways. The possible uses fall into one of five general categories:

- **Location-based services**   To determine where you are. If you are a hiker, you could use GPS with your Treo to find your current position. GPS could also be used with a wireless service to deliver *location-based services,* services that combine your current location with other information and software you load into your Treo, which can then feed you information relevant to you for your current location. For example, suppose you are looking for a particular type of shoe. You could use shopping software loaded on your Treo to indicate you are in the market for these shoes. Then, when you walk past a shoe store, your Treo's location-based services software could determine if that store has your shoes on sale, in stock, and in your size.

- **Navigation**   To get from one location to another. This is why you find GPS systems (such as the Hertz Neverlost system) in more and more rental cars and available as options on many new vehicles. Now you can have this functionality in your pocket everywhere you go. If you like to fish, you can use your GPS to locate and easily return to your best fishing holes!

- **Tracking**   To monitor the movement of people or things. Many trucking companies have adopted GPS to help their central dispatching keep track of where all their vehicles are. This has also been used effectively in the fields of law enforcement and security.

- **Mapping**   For cartography. Almost all modern maps are created using GPS technology for precision.

- **Timing**   To accurately determine the time, GPS satellites can be used as a form of atomic clock, allowing you to get very precise time on your GPS receiver. Every GPS satellite has its own atomic clock on board.

14

Emergency 911

A little-known secret is that CDMA versions of Treo, like those offered by Sprint and Verizon, have a GPS chipset and antenna in them. See http://www.verizonwireless.com/b2c/aboutUs /wirelessissues/enhanced911.jsp for details why. Unfortunately the GPS information can only be used for emergency purposes and is not available for general-purpose uses.

GPS on Your Treo

Your Treo will not come installed with a GPS solution. If you want to perform GPS functions with your device, you will need to acquire both a GPS receiver and software. Some sources for this equipment are listed at the end of this chapter, in the section "GPS Hardware and Software." For the purposes of this chapter, we will use a generic Bluetooth GPS receiver as an example. This device connects to your Treo using a wireless Bluetooth connection as described in Chapter 5. There are a wide variety of Bluetooth GPS receivers on the market, most of which are very compact, are easy to use, and usually come with a vehicle power adaptor for powering the receiver while you are in your car. Keep in mind you may need two power sources so that you can power the GPS and the Treo if you are navigating for an extended period of time. For software, we will use NavCard for Palm OS 5 from Mapopolis (www.mapopolis.com) as an example in this chapter. You can use any vendor's hardware (check to make sure it conforms to the NMEA standard) or software you like; the techniques discussed in this chapter can be applied to most GPS software packages.

We will not be teaching you every function of Mapopolis, but rather focusing on the most common GPS navigation activities that a Treo user might want to accomplish.

 If you are driving a car, never attempt to interact with a GPS navigation system while the car is in motion. If you need to change an address, you should pull over or allow a passenger to update the information for you. Most GPS software packages will give you audible instructions through your Treo's speaker when you need to turn or perform some other action.

The main interface of your GPS software will likely contain a large map-viewing area, along with a menu or control buttons on one edge, as in Figure 14-1. In Mapopolis, you have some other common interface elements:

- **Compass** The lower-right corner contains a compass that shows you which direction is north. North isn't always up, and the map will rotate to face the direction you are going if you have it set to Auto Rotate. If the top of the map is indeed north, then the compass box will disappear.

- **Scale indicator** The lower left of the map area contains a box with a line in it that indicates the scale. The size of the line represents the distance indicated by the number to the right (in Figure 14-1, it is 10 meters).

- **Menu buttons** The menu buttons are used to interact with the Mapopolis map, open the menu, zoom in and out, and more.

Note that touching the Menu button on the far right of the button set will open the main Mapopolis menu, shown in Figure 14-2, which will get you into the other parts of the software discussed in this chapter.

FIGURE 14-1   The Mapopolis interface contains a large map-viewing window with additional controls at the bottom for changing the view and other options.

Check GPS Status

Before you can use your GPS, you need to make sure it is working properly. To ensure that the GPS is indeed communicating, select the GPS button from the menu shown in Figure 14-2. This is where you can configure your GPS settings, start and stop your GPS, and find out GPS-provided information such as longitude, latitude, elevation, and speed, as shown in Figure 14-3. The graphical readout at the very bottom of the screen will show you how many satellite connections the GPS unit currently has, and the strength of the signal. A full bar indicates a stronger signal than a half bar. You must have at least four full bars for the GPS receiver to be able to relay accurate information. Incidentally, the GPS transmissions are "line-of-sight," so there cannot be obstacles between you and the satellites. Because of this, your GPS generally doesn't function indoors, in parking garages, or in other such locations.

14

FIGURE 14-2   The main Mapopolis menu is where you go to enter destinations and manage your navigation.

FIGURE 14-3   The GPS status screen will tell you the details of your connection with the GPS satellites as well as your current location information.

In this example, we are currently connected to four satellites (the minimum). The lines connecting to each satellite indicate the strength of the satellite signal. You can also see your current latitude, longitude, altitude, and velocity (if you are moving!). With some GPS software, you can also see the date and time. This is an extremely accurate date and time because it is based on the atomic clocks aboard each of the GPS satellites you are communicating with. If your software shows a number beside each satellite readout, this is the unique identification number of that particular satellite vehicle (SV).

If you are running your GPS with software and hardware from different vendors, you will need to tell them how to talk to each other. To do this, press the Settings button on the menu screen shown in Figure 14-2 and select GPS from the drop-down in the top right of the screen. This will open the configuration information, as shown in Figure 14-4.

FIGURE 14-4   The configuration screen allows you to set up how your software communicates with your GPS receiver.

On this screen, you can specify the type of connection that your GPS receiver has. This is done with the drop-down selection box at the top of the screen, where you can choose between serial ports, infrared, SDIO (refer to Chapter 15 for details on Secure Digital Input/Output), or Bluetooth connections. After connecting to a new GPS unit, you may need to return to the main GPS status screen and manually start the GPS. Now that you have the hardware and software talking, you are ready to start using your GPS!

Other options that you can configure on your Settings screen drop-down options include:

- **General: Use Finger Data Entry**   This option makes the buttons on the screen larger so you can tap them with your finger instead of a stylus.

- **General: Keep Device Power On for 1 Hr**   Prevents the Treo from turning off even if it is set to auto-power off to conserve battery power. If you have a power source for your Treo 600 model specifically, while using GPS, you are better off to set the Power On in Cradle option in the general Treo preferences.

- **General: Regenerate Route at Start**   This option is very useful if something interrupts you in the middle of navigating to a destination (for example, taking a phone call). When you go back to Mapopolis, it will automatically regenerate the route plan for your current trip.

- **General: Display Metric Units**   Allows you to switch to metric from Imperial measurement units.

- **Display: Display City/Town Names**   This causes the map to display city and town names and boundaries on the map.

- **Display: Display Landmarks**   Will display icons for key landmarks on the map (such as airports, schools, etc.).

- **Display: Set Colors**   This option provides a tool for changing how colors are displayed for many different items, such as primary roads, secondary roads, water, planned route, and so on.

- **Display: Set Font**   Allows you to choose what font Mapopolis uses in the display. As Mapopolis is designed for generic Palm OS devices, different font styles may be more appealing to you on your Treo.

- **Navigation: Highway Preference**   Here you can set Mapopolis to favor or avoid highways, or be neutral with regard to highways when planning routes.

- **Navigation: Voice Prompts**   You can select between full voice prompts, minimal voice prompts, or no voice prompts for navigation instructions.

- **Navigation: Save Directions to Memo Pad**   This option will save navigation directions to the Memo Pad application, enabling you to beam them to others, print them, or save them on the Palm Desktop.

- **Navigation: Scroll Map to GPS Location**   As you progress on your route, Mapopolis will keep the GPS current location in the center of your screen, which is very advantageous.

14

■ **Navigation: Rotate Map to GPS Direction**   As you drive, the map "up" direction will always be the direction you are headed. If this option is deselected, the up direction will be north, which can be somewhat disorienting if you aren't accustomed to it.

■ **Navigation: Display Pilot Data on Map**   This causes a small window to be displayed in the upper-left corner of the screen with current bearing, range, heading, and speed information.

Find Your Current Location

Finding out exactly where you are can be useful if you get lost, if you are hiking in the backcountry, or if you work in a situation where your physical location is important to coordinating your work activity, such as is the case for bicycle couriers in large metropolitan areas, for example. Most GPS software will provide you an option for finding your current location, often with the precise street address. Mapopolis will show your current location on the map as soon as you start your GPS receiver. The GPS screen will also give you your precise location in longitude and latitude.

Navigate to a Destination

The most common use for GPS capability on a Treo is to help you find your way from one place to another. We find this particularly useful when we are traveling and have appointments all over town, in a city we are unfamiliar with. To navigate to a destination, you must tell your GPS software where you wish to go. You can do this by providing an address, specifying an intersection, or selecting a specific point on a map. In addition, you may have a set of favorite addresses for places that you go to often, or you can look up a particular contact in your address book. Mapopolis also features a powerful Points of Interest feature that allows you to get a list of the closest restaurants, banks, gas stations, and many other useful destinations. If you find yourself in an unfamiliar location and want to see all the restaurants within three miles, you can find that with the Points of Interest feature.

Specific Address

One of the most common ways to navigate is to enter the address of the location you are going to. Mapopolis offers a variety of ways to do this, all of which give the same result. Each method simply starts with a different piece of information—the address, the street, the city, a place, or an address from your Contacts. For example, if you wanted to search for an address, you would check the Address check box and then begin entering the address information on the line below the check boxes. As you enter the data, Mapopolis matches what you are typing against its database of addresses for the map you have loaded. Matching results will be displayed in the box, as shown in Figure 14-5.

If you change the drop-down selection list at the top of the screen to Street Intersection, you can navigate to a specific intersection of two roads. You enter the name (or a part of the name) of the first street in the first line. Then you can enter the name (or part of the name) of the cross street on the second line. Tapping the Find button will cause the software to find any streets in

You can enter a specific address to navigate to with your GPS.

its currently loaded map that match your 1st Street selection. They will appear in the first box. When you tap the street you want in the first box, it will then match your 2nd Street entry and populate the second box with streets that match and intersect with your 1st Street selection.

After using any of the preceding methods, you can press the Go To button to calculate the best route from where you are to where you want to go. Your next turn or instruction will appear in the box at the bottom of the map area, and your path will be outlined on the map with a green line and arrows indicating the direction of travel. As you begin to drive, the maneuvers you need to complete will be displayed one by one at the bottom of the map-viewing area until you arrive at your destination. If you have your Treo sound turned on, you will also receive verbal instructions on when to turn and what maneuvers to make.

Get There by Pointing

You don't always have to enter specific street information to get to where you want to go. If you can visually locate where you would like to end up on the map, you can simply point to your destination using the stylus and the software will determine where that is. You access this functionality by choosing the Navigation button from the Mapopolis menu. This will open the Navigation screen, shown in Figure 14-6.

Using the map to point at a destination on the map is another way to tell Mapopolis where you want to go.

On this screen, you can set the start and end points for your navigation. For either point, you can use the On Map button to open the map and select a specific point with your stylus.

You can use the zoom controls (the set of boxes on the bottom left of the screen between the plus and minus signs) to move around the map and also use the navigation control to scroll around. Once you identify where you would like to go, simply tap the location with the stylus to begin navigation.

Favorites

You might find that there are particular destinations you need to get to often, such as your home, office, day care center, or other location. You can set the software to remember a group of "favorite" destinations. With the Mapopolis software, this is called a Geomark. I find this useful when traveling in an unfamiliar city, and I often drive between a variety of meeting locations and my hotel. After picking up my rental car, I instruct the GPS to navigate to my hotel. I then make the hotel a "favorite" destination so that I do not have to reenter the information every time I want to return to the hotel.

To create a new Geomark, you select Geomark from the Mapopolis menu, and then tap the location on your map. Recently entered destinations are automatically added as Geomarks. To begin navigating to a Geomark, you select the button with the down arrow on the lower right of your map view.

Contacts

Many of the destinations to which you might want to navigate are contained within your contacts on your Treo's Contacts application, discussed in Part I of this book. You can select from your list of contacts by choosing Find from the Mapopolis menu, and then using the Address Book check box.

FIGURE 14-7   You can navigate to the address of any of the contacts stored in your Treo's Contacts application.

As you enter a part of a name in the entry field, Mapopolis looks up the matching people from your contacts. You will then see a list of your matching contacts, as shown in Figure 14-7.

Place By Category

The Place By Category feature of Mapopolis is a wonderful, extremely useful feature. It allows you to find the nearest destination from a given category. Imagine you are in an unfamiliar city, and you need to find a gas station or a bank machine. When you select Place By Category in the Find menu, Mapopolis will populate categories of points of interest in the upper box; and when you select any of the categories, the matching destinations appear in the lower box (see Figure 14-8). This makes it easy to find your way to common destinations.

FIGURE 14-8   It is easy to find the nearest hospital, gas station, bank, restaurant, or other key location with the Place By Category feature.

Load and Switch Maps

Your Treo has a limited amount of memory, and GPS maps are very detailed, meaning that they require a lot of storage space. If you plan to do a lot of traveling and need to have a number of maps with you, buying a 256MB or larger (Secure Digital) SD card is highly recommended. If you travel to only one destination at a time, always returning home in between, you can load and unload the maps you want as you need them.

Mapopolis has a complete application for loading and unloading maps. You simply have to download the map you require from the Mapopolis web site, and then sync the .pdb file to your Treo.

You can load multiple maps onto your Treo and also your expansion card. To see which maps are on your card, you will need to tap the Go To Card button at the upper right of the window.

GPS Hardware and Software

In addition to the GPS receiver and Mapopolis software used in the preceding examples, you should consider many other vendors and configurations of hardware and software for your Treo GPS needs. The GPS units come in one of four formats:

- **Serial cable** These GPS units connect into the Treo via the serial port. Power is usually not drawn directly from the Treo to power the unit, so an external power source such as a vehicle cigarette lighter is usually required.

- **SDIO card** SDIO GPS receivers use the SD slot on the top of the Treo to connect to your smartphone. These units usually draw their power directly from the Treo or through an external adapter.

- **Bluetooth** This is one of the newest types of GPS. It is essentially the same as a serial port unit; however, it makes its serial connection with the Treo via a Bluetooth connection and thus is wirelessly connected instead of needing cables.

- **Stand-alone** Stand-alone GPS receivers are units that can function with or without the Treo (although the Treo usually extends the receiver's functionality and usability). These receivers tend to connect to the Treo through the bottom serial port. One nice feature about this type of receiver is that you can use it alone, with a Treo, or with a laptop.

More detail on alternative GPS hardware and software is contained in Chapter 16 of this book. You can find a wide variety of Palm Treo-compatible GPS receivers and software at Semsons (www.semsons.com).

Other Software

In addition to the GPS vendors listed earlier, you can consider a few other pieces of software for personal navigation- or location-related applications.

MapQuest

If you aren't in the market for a full-fledged GPS solution, you can take advantage of offerings from MapQuest (www.mapquest.com). At MapQuest's web site, you can look up maps and create driving directions prior to leaving on your trip. You can then download those maps to your Treo through an AvantGo (www.avantgo.com) sync conduit. Now when you are traveling around, you can pull up these maps on demand to help you navigate.

TomTom CityMaps

One concern about GPS systems is the lack of maps available if you are traveling outside North America. A few software companies support maps for non-North American cities. TomTom (www.tomtom.com) has a database of more than 100,000 cities across Europe that ships on a CD-ROM. (Some of the larger cities are available in electronic downloads from the TomTom web site.) This software is well designed and very user-friendly.

Treo Traffic

This slick application will give you up-to-date traffic information in many U.S. cities allowing you to plan your route and avoid congestion, accidents, and construction delays. You can find this application in the Palm store at www.palm.com.

Wrap It Up

In this chapter, we wanted to introduce you to the world of personal navigation with GPS on your Treo. It isn't possible to give you a detailed analysis of all the features, software, and hardware products in this space. The vendors listed in this chapter can provide a great deal more detail on their products and features.

In addition to basic personal or business navigation, GPS is rapidly catching on for location-based services. An example of a location-based service might be a vendor providing you with information when you are near its facilities or an airport telling you, when you arrive in the airport parking lot late for a flight, that it can automatically rebook you on the next flight or possibly hold the airplane. A popular new recreational sport has even popped up around personal GPS navigation. It is called *geocaching*. It involves groups of people hiding or "caching" something in a location and then identifying where these caches are with their GPS coordinates. For more details on this sport, check out www.geocaching.com.

If you would like to dive a little deeper into the technology underlying GPS, we recommend an online tutorial put together by Trimble, one of the major GPS vendors. You can find it at www.trimble.com/gps.

14

Part III

Select Essential Hardware Accessories and Software for Your Treo

Chapter 15

Store Information and Go Further with Secure Digital Cards and MultiMediaCards

How to...

- Add storage memory to your Treo
- Format a storage card
- Use storage cards to swap files between your Treo and your PC
- Use SDIO cards to add capabilities to your Treo

There is a saying in the high-tech world, "You can never be too rich, too good looking, or have too much storage space." This cavalier, off-the-cuff comment is particularly true when it comes to mobile devices. Rarely do the devices have sufficient on-board memory to accommodate all of your needs. This is one of the reasons why your Treo comes equipped with a slot for external memory and hardware expansion. As you begin to use your Treo for more advanced functions like GPS, photo albums, and MP3 and video entertainment, external expansion cards will be an absolute necessity.

What Are SD and MMC Cards?

The Treo can use both Secure Digital (SD) and MultiMediaCard (MMC) formats for storing information externally. These storage cards are extremely small, about the size of a postage stamp, and currently have the ability to store up to 4GB of information. This is about 40 times the memory currently available to you on your Treo. That represents a lot of music, documents, and other files you can carry with you. A Secure Digital card is shown in Figure 15-1.

These memory cards are *nonvolatile*. This means that they do not require any power to maintain the memory they contain. You can remove the card from your Treo, and it will keep the information stored on it ready for you when you need it next. This type of storage is also called *solid state*. This means that it has no moving parts to skip or break down. It transfers data very fast, which makes it an ideal storage medium for your smartphone.

Although SD and MMC cards are very similar, there are differences you should be aware of when selecting one or the other to store your information:

- **Size** The MMC card is marginally thinner than the SD card, but both will work just fine in your Treo expansion card slot.
- **Speed** SD cards transfer data faster than MMC cards, which is important when loading large files such as GPS maps from the card into the Treo memory.
- **Durability** The extra thickness of the SD card makes it somewhat more durable than MMC.
- **Write protection** SD cards have a small switch on the side of them so you can make them read-only. MMC cards do not have this. This is useful if you want to prevent accidental overwriting of important information on a storage card.

FIGURE 15-1   The Secure Digital card allows you to store a tremendous amount of extra information on your Treo.

- **Copyright protection**   The SD card has additional capability for enhanced copyright security, although this may not be relevant for the average consumer.
- **Cost**   MMC cards are usually a little less expensive than the comparable SD card.

So which card you pick will depend on what you need it for, but it is safe to say that Secure Digital is becoming a much more common standard than MMC, and in fact, you might have difficulty finding MMC cards in your local retail stores any longer.

Use the Treo Card Slot

The Treo contains a slot on the top of the unit for inserting SD and MMC cards. When your Treo shipped from the factory, a fake SD card was inserted in the slot to keep out dust and other foreign objects. When your expansion slot isn't in use, you should reinsert this dummy card to protect the slot from damage. The dummy card serves no other purpose.

To remove cards from the slot, you simply push down on the card that is in the slot and it will eject with a spring-loaded push. A new card should be inserted far enough until you feel it lock into place. The card is inserted into the slot with the card label facing the front of the Treo 650 or 700p, and to the rear of the Treo 600.

When you insert a storage card into your Treo, it will open up the card's contents with the Applications Launcher, showing you any applications installed onto the card, as shown in

15

the following illustration. Your card can also contain other nonapplication files. Unlike your desktop PC, you cannot simply browse the files on the SD card; you must use applications to move to the files stored on the card.

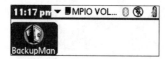

You can find out all about the card by running the Card Info application, shown here, when a storage card is inserted:

This will show you the type of card, its size, how much memory has been used, and more. This is also where you can use the Card menu to rename or format the card. Renaming the card, as shown here, simply changes the name that appears in the drop-down list of categories when the card is inserted into the Treo:

Formatting a card is rather more severe because it will erase all of the data on the card. This can be a quick way to prepare an old card when you no longer care about the contents of the card. Although most computing devices format SD cards the same way, there are some devices that format SD cards in a nonstandard format, requiring them to be reformatted before they can be used in your Treo. For example, my MP3 player can use expansion cards to store extra songs, but the cards are formatted in such a way that they cannot be read by my home computer or my Treo.

Watch Out for Counterfeit SD Cards

Did you know you can void your warranty by using cheap expansion cards? In our modern era of cheap, knock-off products, it is possible to purchase noncompliant SD cards if you're not careful. These cards can actually damage your Treo, so when buying them, ensure that they contain the SD logo, have a notch on the card opposite the write-protect switch, and only have the angle notch on one side. (Some fake cards are angled on both sides.)

Storage Capacity and Cost

Storage cards represent a very low-cost way to store more information on your smartphone. The price scales up along with the storage capacity, but you will find that the storage capacity gets larger and the price per megabyte gets lower every day. I have recently seen 1GB cards available online for less than $20. This means that for the price of going to the movies and popcorn, your Treo can have more on-board memory than the Spirit and Opportunity rovers that NASA put on Mars!

You can buy these cards at virtually any computer or photo store (many digital cameras use the same kind of cards for storing digital pictures), or you can find them online. The online sources include the manufacturers themselves, as well as online retail stores:

- SanDisk (www.sandisk.com)
- Kingston Technology (www.kingston.com)
- Lexar Media (www.lexarmedia.com)
- SimpleTech (www.simpletech.com)
- Delkin eFilm (www.delkin.com)
- Mobile Planet (www.mobileplanet.com)
- Amazon (www.amazon.com)

15

TIP *Prices for storage cards are falling all the time. If you are buying online, you can check some of the large price comparison sites to find the best deal. Sites such as PriceGrabber (www.pricegrabber.com) and CNET Shopper (http://shopper.cnet.com/) can be good sources. At these sites, you can select the specific product you are looking for, and they will search dozens of online vendors to find the best price. These sites also provide information about the reliability of the vendors in the list.*

Move and Launch Applications from the Expansion Card

After you insert a new storage card into your Treo, if there are any applications loaded on the card they will appear in the Applications Launcher. You can launch any of the applications on the card by tapping the application's icon on the screen with your stylus or highlighting it and pressing the center of your navigation control. You will notice that the name of the card appears in the drop-down selections at the top-right of the screen. These selections allow you to switch between viewing applications on the card and applications installed directly on your Treo.

As you load more applications on your Treo, you may want to conserve some of your precious internal memory by moving some of your less-used applications to a memory card. If you do this, be careful to make sure that the applications support Palm OS 5.2; otherwise, they may not execute properly when moved to a storage card. To move an application to the storage card, you must be in the Applications Launcher. From the App menu, choose Copy. This will open up the Copy screen, as shown in Figure 15-2.

After you have moved the application to the expansion card and confirmed that it works properly, you can delete the application from your Treo by selecting Delete from the App menu.

This will open the Delete screen, from which you can select and delete any applications that are loaded, as shown in the following illustration. You must first specify if you are deleting the applications from the Treo or the storage card. If you are deleting from the Treo, you set the Delete From field to Phone. To delete from the storage card, you select the name of the storage card in the drop-down list in the Delete From field.

Note that applications that are loaded on an external storage card must be copied to the local memory in your Treo before they can run. This means that you must leave sufficient memory empty on your Treo to allow programs stored on a card to be loaded locally as needed.

FIGURE 15-2 You can use the Copy function in the Applications Launcher to move applications onto storage cards.

Use Storage Cards to Swap Files

The ability to move files quickly from your PC to your Treo can be very handy. Perhaps you want to move a collection of your favorite MP3s from your hard drive to your Treo so that you can listen on the go (or use them for ringtones, as discussed in Chapter 4!). Maybe you have a number of Microsoft Word documents that you want to take with you in case you need to reference them on a business trip.

You could sync these files to your handheld using your appropriate desktop application, but it is often faster and easier to move them directly onto your storage card. In order to accomplish this, you must have a storage card reader attached to your PC. Many laptops and printers today have storage card slots built right in, but if yours don't, you can buy storage card readers as external accessories (not to mention the fact that the dedicated card readers tend to be much faster than those added to printers or other accessories). My Fujitsu laptop has a convenient SD slot where I can insert the cards from my Treo directly into my laptop. My HP 7350 PhotoSmart printer also has a card reader built into it. When I insert a card into either of these slots, the SD card appears as a new drive letter on my system, allowing me to read and write files to the card.

You need to be careful when moving files onto your storage card. Your Treo will expect your files to conform to a specific format; if they don't, you run the risk that the files you copy over will be ignored. In Figure 15-3, you can see the file structure for a sample SD card from the card reader in my laptop. Your Treo will expect to see a folder in the root of the card called Palm. Inside that folder, it will expect to find two subfolders, Launcher and Programs. The Launcher folder is for applications that are loaded on the card and that appear in the Applications Launcher on the Treo. The Programs folder contains data for specific programs that use card storage. In Figure 15-3, you will notice subfolders for the applications BackupMan and Documents To Go, which are discussed in Chapters 9 and 11, respectively.

15

FIGURE 15-3   Storage cards used in the Treo conform to a specific file structure you should adhere to.

The SD card listed in Figure 15-3 is called Revio SD and has been given the drive letter F: on my laptop. In the root directory of the card, you will see two folders called DCIM and PALM. The first one, DCIM, is from my digital camera. It contains all the photos from my camera. The second folder, PALM, contains all the information relevant to my Treo. This shows how the same card can be used in two different devices without the information conflicting.

In the PALM directory, there are two subfolders. The Launcher folder contains any applications that have been loaded on the card. The Programs folder contains any program-related information. The BackupMan subfolder contains the actual .prc file for the BackupMan application, which allows me to restore my backed-up files from the card, even if my Treo has been wiped out. (Refer to Chapter 9 for more information on this important use of a storage card.) The Programs folder also contains a subfolder called DXTG. This is my Documents To Go folder. If I want to copy a group of documents or spreadsheets onto my card, I can copy them directly into this folder. Then, when the card is inserted in my Treo, the Documents To Go application can find them using its Search For Files feature.

Use SDIO Cards to Add Hardware Features to Your Treo

Your Treo expansion slot is capable of delivering much more than just extra memory for your smartphone. It also supports the Secure Digital Input/Output (SDIO) spec, which means that it can be used to drive actual external hardware. We have already discussed some of this hardware throughout the book, but we will reference it here for your convenience. There are many SDIO products; however, not all will have drivers for Palm OS products, so if you see something you like, make sure there is an appropriate Palm OS driver before purchasing it!

Biometric Security

To further enhance security, biometric fingerprint scanners are being released now that adhere to the SDIO standard. As these products become available, you can further enhance the security of your Treo by requiring it to recognize a fingerprint or thumbprint that you swipe across the top of the expansion card slot. Without the appropriate recognition, biometric security will prevent access to your Treo files.

Barcode Scanning

There are many commercial applications where Treo devices can be used to scan bar codes for inventory management, medical uses, and much more.

TV Remote Control

Imagine turning your Treo into your universal remote control for your TV, stereo, and all of your other home entertainment devices! You can do this with the NoviBlaster SDIO card for your Treo. Now you can control everything right from your smartphone.

Wrap It Up

The ability to insert storage cards and expansion cards into the top expansion slot of your Treo opens up whole new worlds of what you can do with your smartphone. For example, you now can carry a street-by-street map of the world with you everywhere you go or keep an extensive music collection for your entertainment. Libraries of important documents are at the ready.

In addition, the future is unlimited when you consider what kinds of hardware expansions might soon be developed for this flexible tool. Watch for more exciting innovations that you will be able to leverage with your Treo in the near future!

Chapter 16

Explore the Peripheral and Software Jungle

How to...

- Expand your Treo with new hardware
- Choose software that adds value

The Treo by itself is a powerful and useful tool, but it was also designed to be adaptable and expandable. Many companies are creating products to enable you to get even more out of your Treo, and new items are appearing on the market all the time. In this chapter we examine some of the products that are available and give you our impressions of their value to you, the Treo user.

In each section we have tried to set up a standard format to help you compare the products and select the one that might best fit your needs. We have not tested all of the products listed. If it is a product with which we have direct personal experience, we review the product and share our opinions.

Hardware Accessories

As the Treo has grown in popularity, the number of hardware accessories has grown considerably. We have attempted to cover the most important of these in this section.

Headsets and Car Kits

In this section we look specifically at audio accessories and related equipment for your Treo. This includes telephone headsets, in-car kits, and mounting brackets.

When looking for a new headset to use with your Treo, you have a very wide selection from which to choose. You will need to decide which style of headset you prefer. The standard headset styles include

- **Over-the-head**   These headsets usually cover one ear and use a plastic "headband" to go over the top of your head.
- **On-the-ear**   These headsets have hooks or loops to hang on the ear, and these hooks and loops position the speaker to cover the ear.
- **In-the-ear**   This style is often referred to as an "earbud," and the speaker goes right in your ear. One advantage of this style is that it blocks out more of the ambient noise, usually making it easier for you to hear the caller. This is a very popular style because of its small size and low cost.
- **Behind-the-neck**   These headsets rest on the back of your neck, much like popular headphone styles with portable music players. One of the prime attractions of this headset style is that it doesn't interfere with hats, helmets, or fancy hairdos!
- **Binaural**   These headsets cover both ears, allowing you to focus more on the caller but not allowing you to hear any of the other sounds in your immediate vicinity.

A good source for the hundreds of different headset combinations is www.headsets.com. You can generally use any headset with a standard 2.5 mm headset plug. On the Treo 650 and 700p, Bluetooth is a very popular headset option that eliminates the cable of a traditional headset, but you may experience static or interference from time to time. We generally prefer a corded headset for sake of call clarity.

TIP *If you plan to use your Treo and headset in a noisy environment or in a car with the windows open, you might want to consider investing in a noise-canceling headset, which can help to filter out background noise so that your caller doesn't hear it.*

Palm Ultra Light Wireless Headset

Palm's top-of-the-line headset offering is a Bluetooth wireless headset that retails for $129.00.

Product	High-Performance Headset
Manufacturer	Palm (www.palm.com)
Web link	http://web.palm.com/products/Product.jhtml?id=560001&cat=280012
Description	An ultralight in-the-ear style wireless headset powered by a single AAA battery giving three hours of talk time.
Price	$129.00

Palm Wireless Headset

Palm's standard wireless headset features an over-the-ear style clip and connects with Bluetooth wireless.

Product	High-Performance Headset
Manufacturer	Palm (www.palm.com)
Web link	http://web.palm.com/products/Product.jhtml?id=210003&cat=280012
Description	This over-the-ear style headset features a rechargeable battery that uses the same charger as the Treo 650 and 700p, eliminating the need to travel with multiple chargers. Controls right on the headset make it easy to answer/end calls, control volume, or mute your microphone.
Price	$79.00

16

Palm Stereo Headphones

Of course, the standard headset that comes with the Treo doesn't let you listen to music or other sounds in stereo because it only has one earbud. Palm's solution for this is its Stereo Headphones.

Product	Stereo Headphones
Manufacturer	Palm (www.palm.com)
Web link	http://web.palm.com/products/Product.jhtml?id=80018&cat=280012
Description	Classic earbud-style stereo headset that plugs directly into the 2.5 mm jack of your Treo. Allows you to listen to music, streaming audio, and other sounds from your Treo. The built-in high-quality microphone also allows you to use it for your telephone headset.
Price	$29.99

Palm Stereo Headphone Adapter

If you would like to use your standard stereo headphones with your Treo, you will find that the plug will not fit into the smartphone, but Palm offers this adapter from its web site.

Product	Stereo Headphone Adapter
Manufacturer	Palm (www.palm.com)
Web link	http://web.palm.com/products/Product.jhtml?id=80006&cat=280012
Description	This adapter plugs into the 2.5 mm headset jack of your Treo and allows you to use any standard set of 3.5 mm headphones to listen to the sounds from your Treo. Similar adapters are available from a variety of sources such as RadioShack (www.radioshack.com), so check around for your best price.
Price	$9.99

Seidio Hands-Free Stereo Headphones

Palm doesn't have the market cornered on stereo headphones. Luckily, the Treo has a standard size and style of headphone port (conforming to the 2.5 mm standard) that allows you to use products like ones from Seidio.

Product	Hands-Free Stereo Headphones
Manufacturer	Seidio (www.seidioonline.com)
Web link	http://www.seidioonline.com/index.asp?PageAction=VIEWCATS&Category=935
Description	Seidio has a wide variety of headphone offerings compatible with the Treo line, from stereo earbuds to over-the-ear models.
Price	$16.94 to $54.95

Jabra JX10 Wireless Headset

For the ultimate in wireless headsets, our current favorite is the lineup from Jabra. They feature both wired and wireless headsets with built-in noise cancellation and a very comfortable in-the-ear gel bud which makes wearing these headsets a dream. The JX10 is their latest offering and lives up to everything we have come to expect from Jabra.

Product	Jabra JX10 Wireless Headset
Manufacturer	Jabra (www.Jabra.com)
Web link	http://www.jabra.com/JabraCMS/NA/EN/MainMenu/Products/WirelessHeadsets/JabraJX10/JabraJX10.htm
Description	Over-the-ear style wireless Bluetooth headsets.
Price	$179.00
Review	This product is the top of the line in Bluetooth wireless headsets both in style and in function. It is very reliable and features a rechargeable battery. Controls on the headset make answering calls and adjusting volume very straightforward.

ZipLinq Retractable Earbud Headset

For the road warrior who hates cables, ZipLinq offers a retractable headset.

Product	Hands-Free Headset with Universal Jack
Manufacturer	ZipLinq (www.ziplinq.com)
Web link	http://www.ziplinq.com/retractable-cable-handsfree.html
Description	An earbud-style headset with an answer/disconnect button mounted on the microphone. This headset is unique in that the cable retracts on a small spool; this makes for very easy storage and long life.
Price	Not priced
Review	This product is very handy for people like me who tend to snag their headset cords on every object within three feet. In fact, I usually ruin two or three corded headsets a year, just walking around with them. I also find that the cords are always tangled up in something, making it awkward to pull out and use when you want to. The retracting feature is a wonderful option. The only drawback to this unit is a merely mediocre microphone. This product would work much better with a higher-quality microphone, preferably with noise-canceling features.

16

There are many other compatible headsets that will work with your Treo that you can choose from as well, including products from Plantronics (www.plantronics.com),

Motorola (www.motorola.com), and many other vendors, but we have found the preceding products to work well with our own Treos.

Cases

In Chapter 9, you were introduced to some of the important aspects of cases to protect and personalize your Treo. Some case vendors you can look to are listed in this section. Cases tend to be one of four primary styles:

- ■ **Holster**   This style stays on your belt like a holster, and your Treo comes out of the case whenever you want to use it. This is our preferred style of case for the Treo, but this is very much a personal preference. When the Treo is out of the holster, there are none of the extra protective benefits of the flip-top or glove-fit styles.

- ■ **Flip Top**   The flip-top case stays on your Treo all the time and has a cover flap that covers the front of the Treo to protect it. You have to flip this cover back in order to use the Treo. We find this style to be somewhat bulky when trying to hold the Treo to your head for a phone call, but it does provide the maximum amount of protection for your Treo if you tend to carry it in your briefcase or purse.

- ■ **Glove Fit**   This style of case, as you could surmise from the name, slides over your Treo like a glove or second skin. It stays on your Treo at all times and usually features either a cutout or clear plastic screen protector over the Treo screen and keyboard. The ones with the plastic covers help to keep your screen and keyboard clean and free of debris, but they can make typing on the keyboard or tapping the screen with the stylus more challenging. The advantage over the flip-top style is that there is no extra flap to hold in place while making phone calls.

- ■ **Flexi Case**   Similar to a glove-fit style of case, the Flexi Case is made from an alternative soft material such as high-grade silicone that will provide for a slip-resistant grip and extra cushioning in case you should drop your Treo. There is very minimal bulk added to the phone, and many feature an anti-glare screen protector to save your screen from scratches and dust.

- ■ **Folio**   The folio style tends to be more like a wallet and holds your Treo on one side while offering storage space for credit cards, money, or perhaps a writing pad on the other side. Not useful if you want to have your Treo on your belt, but quite handy if your Treo's regular home is in your briefcase.

Bellagio (www.bellagiodesigns.com)

Bellagio features several cases covering three styles of cases for the Treo, holster, flip-top, and glove. All of the cases are made of Italian leather, are available with or without a spring-loaded swivel belt clip, and provide all the right cutouts for accessing your Treo controls. The cases can also be personalized with your name, company logo, or other information.

Product	Treo Leather PDA Case
Manufacturer	Bellagio Designs (www.bellagiodesigns.com)
Web link	http://www.fortte.com/scr/showcategory3.php/63
Description	Bellagio has produced good-quality cases right from the early days of the Treo and has continued to refine their designs with each successive generation of cases.
Price	$24.99 to $44.99 depending on style
Review	This is a well-made case that offers solid protection. It features all the appropriate cutouts for the camera, speakers, headphone jack, microphone, and sync cable.

Covertec Cases (www.covertec.com)

Covertec has a reputation for being one of the highest-quality PDA case manufacturers in the market. Having had first-hand experience with their top-end product, we can personally vouch for the fine workmanship, quality stitching, and practical functionality of their cases. They are focused primarily on two case styles, the holster and the flip-top. They also have a tremendous range of colors to choose from to really make your case fit your personality!

Product	Treo Holster and Flip-Top cases
Manufacturer	Covertec (www.covertec.com)
Web link	www.covertecstore.com
Description	Horizontal pouch-style cases and one-piece, always-on flip-top cases. Both styles are available in a wide variety of eye-catching colors. Overstitching is available in different colors, which adds style and class to the cases. The pouch has a built-in belt clasp, while the one-piece model has a removable swivel belt clip.
Price	$24.95 to $39.95
Review	The Covertec case is my current case of choice for my Treo. It is without question one of the highest-quality cases that I have seen on the market. It is a distinctive and classy case that looks good in both business and casual environments.

EB Slipper Case (www.ebcases.com)

E&B Company is another popular case vendor that makes a product for the Treo. They are primarily focused on flip-top and glove-style cases. They do have one holster style case, but it doesn't rank at the top of comparable holster offerings from other vendors.

16

Product	Treo Cases (various models)
Manufacturer	E&B Company (www.ebcases.com)
Web link	http://www.ebcases.com/Categories.bok?category=SmartPhones%3APalm
Description	Primarily focused on flip-top and glove-style cases.
Price	$32.95 to $69.95

Palm Cases (www.palm.com)

Palm offers a half-dozen interesting case designs for your Treo. Among the more standard leather holster offering, you will find a unique hard case ($39.99) made of durable polycarbonate, as shown in Figure 16-1. This hard case is great if you are particular hard on your Treo!

You will also see on the Palm web site an interesting silicone form-fitting case that turns your otherwise slippery Treo into something much easier to hang onto ($29.99).

Product	Holster, Hard, and Silicone Cases
Manufacturer	Palm (www.palm.com)
Web link	http://web.palm.com/products/Category.jhtml?id=290003&cat=270008
Description	A half-dozen cases are available from Palm with some very unique offerings. The biggest limitation of Palm's case offerings is the lack of color variety. Through Palm's web site you can also order cases from other manufacturers such as Vaja, discussed later.
Price	$29.99 to $39.99

FIGURE 16-1   The Palm hard case is extremely valuable if you find that you are very rough with your Treo.

Krusell Cases (www.krusell.se)

Krusell is a world-class case manufacturer that has a great deal of experience making high-quality cases for a variety of handheld devices. One of the particularly unique features that they offer is their "Multidapt" system, which allows you to take your standard case and also turn it into a rigid bicycle or car mount for holding your Treo while cycling or driving. Krusell also offers a folio-style case.

Product	Handit, Horizontic, and Calandaric Multidapt Cases for Treo
Manufacturer	Krussell (www.krusell.se)
Web link	http://www.krusell.se/searchResult.php?brand=Palm&model=TREO+700P%2FW&x=16&y=5
Description	Krussell, a popular worldwide case manufacturer in Sweden, has delivered cases including one-piece, flip-top, holster, and folio styles. These cases are generally available though online retailers, such as Incipio (www.incipiodirect.com).
Price	Not published
Review	One of the fantastic features of the Krussel cases is their Multidapt clip style. This is unique among all the cases we've reviewed. It allows you to easily adapt your Krussell case to attach to a variety of surfaces. The clips can attach as a simple miniclip, a spring-loaded clip, or a twist-on clip. There are also full-swivel clips in four different formats that you can try out to find the one that fits your preference. The same Multidapt clip can also be used with a Krussell car mount, or one of my favorites, a bike holder that attaches your Treo to the handlebars of your bike. This is handy if you like to use GPS with your Treo and also for bike commuters.

Nutshell Cases (www.tuff-as-nuts.com)

Nutshell has a reputation for cases that are simple and functional.

Product	Treo Natural Leather Case
Manufacturer	Nutshell (www.tuff-as-nuts.com)
Web link	http://www.tuff-as-nuts.com/treo-700p.html
Description	Nutshell makes a vertical, pouch-style case with options that include belt loop style (leather or stainless steel), a choice of colors, and storage slots.
Price	$349.95

16

Piel Frama Cases (www.pielframa.com)

Piel Frama's cases are considered to be some of the higher-end cases in the marketplace. They have great material options, including combinations of cow leather, ostrich, and crocodile. For the people looking for a very tough case, they also have an aluminum option!

Product	Treo Leather and Aluminum PDA Cases
Manufacturer	Piel Frama (www.pielframa.com)
Web link	http://www.pielframa.com/menu_palm_treo_700w.htm
Description	Piel Frama makes an extremely high-quality, executive-style case. The leather Treo models are all flip-top models. The leathers are patterned and come in either a pure cowskin, cowskin-crocodile (black), or cowskin-ostrich (brown) style. The magnetic closure strap is a nice feature. The case also includes a money pocket and two slots for SD/MMC cards. An ABS plastic insert also protects the front screen from impact.
	The aluminum model is a very robust hard case that will protect your Treo from a great deal of abuse. Our only concern with this case is that it obstructs most of the keyboard, requiring you to open the case (easily accomplished) in order to type a message. It does provide the extra protection, but at the cost of usability.
Price	45 Euros for the aluminum model or 90 Euros for the leather (approximately $112.00 U.S.)—includes courier shipping from Spain

Proporta Side Case (www.proporta.com)

Proporta's cases feature a soft leather construction in a flip-top style.

Product	Leather, Aluminum, Waterproof, and Silicone Cases
Manufacturer	Proporta (www.proporta.com)
Web link	http://www.proporta.com/F02/PPF02P05.php?t_id=314&t_mode=cat
Description	The Proporta leather cases are made in Brazil out of soft leather. They come in flip-top and holster styles. There is also an aluminum hard case and silicone glove-style cover for your Treo. If you like watersports and would like to keep your Treo with you in your boat, Seadoo, canoe, or other place where it might get wet, Proporta has some interesting offerings in the area of watertight bags and cases for your Treo.
Price	$19.95 to $39.95

Seidio (www.seidioonline.com)

Seidio has multiple different styles of cases for your Treo, including an executive pouch-style case, silicone skins, and swivel holsters.

Product	Swivel Cases and Holsters
Manufacturer	Seidio (www.seidioonline.com)
Web link	http://www.seidioonline.com/index.asp?PageAction=VIEWCATS&Category=933
Description	The swivel clip holster is a very useful product that allows for quick and easy access to a ringing Treo. The face of the Treo faces in to protect it from scratches while it is in the holster. This case is made out of high-impact plastic. The other Seidio offerings are more like the commonly seen leather holster belt cases and the executive leather pouch.
Price	$19.95 to $39.95

Sena Cases (www.senacases.com)

Sena Cases has quickly become a dominant case vendor in the mobile device market. Their flip-top style leather case for the Treo is unique in that it is hinged from the bottom instead of the top (does this make it a new category, the flip-bottom?). The also have glove-style cases and leather holsters. The two-tone leather styling options make the Sena case very unique and one of our favorites.

Product	Treo Flip "Bottom," Glove, and Holster Cases
Manufacturer	Sena Cases (www.senacases.com)
Web link	http://www.senacases.com/catalog/Palm-Treo-700w-700p-Cases-p-1-c-386.html
Description	Quality leather cases with magnetic enclosures and unique two-tone color options.
Price	$39.99 to $49.99
Review	The Sena cases have long been some of our favorites because of their high-quality leather, fine stitching, and stylish looks. Given Sena's long history of quality, we have no hesitations recommending this product.

Leather International (www.leatherintl.com)

Leather International manufactures a Treo 600 case that uses the "holster" style.

Product	Horizontal Holster for Treo
Manufacturer	Leather International (www.leatherintl.com)
Web link	http://www.leatherintl.com/products/products.asp?id=118
Description	A very stylish leather holster (pouch style) in a vertical format. You can customize the product with your own logo or image.
Price	Not published

16

Vaja Cases (www.vajacases.com)

Vaja is the Cadillac of case manufacturers for PDAs and mobile devices. Its Treo cases are great examples of its artistic work. Vaja offers three styles, the one-piece iVolution the flip-top Classic, and the extremely distinctive glove-style T7.

Product	iVolution T6 for Treo
Manufacturer	Vaja Cases (www.vajacases.com)
Web link	www.vajacases.com
Description	The iVolution T6 is a one-piece leather case with a swivel belt clip.
Price	From $90.00
Review	The iVolution T6 is a unique case offering for the Treo. It is a semi-rigid, one-piece design that is extremely durable and that acts like an extra layer of armor for your smartphone. It features all the appropriate cutouts to ensure that you can charge and sync your device, as well as use the headphone jack, volume controls, camera, and SD slot.
Product	**Classic 797 for Treo**
Manufacturer	Vaja Cases (www.vajacases.com)
Web link	www.vajacases.com
Description	The Classic 797 is a flip-top case made of fine-quality leather.
Price	From $75.00
Review	The Classic 797 is another example of fine Vaja craftsmanship. The leather is of the highest quality, as is the stitching. The case fits the Treo extremely well and can be customized with embossing and other personal features.
Product	**T7 Crystal or Silver for Treo**
Manufacturer	Vaja Cases (www.vajacases.com)
Web link	www.vajacases.com
Description	The T7 Crystal (or Silver) is a one-piece glove-style leather case with sparkling Swarovski crystals embedded into the case, giving a very distinctive and swanky appearance!
Price	From $340.00
Review	If you want to make an impression on the red carpet in Hollywood, this is the case for you! An extremely unique offering available in many different colors. We guarantee that you will get noticed with this, the highest of the high-end cases.

And finally, although it is not really a case, we have to mention an amazing product called eGrips. These are stick-on adhesive grips that you can put on your Treo to keep it from slipping out of your hands. They are inexpensive and come in a wide variety of styles to personalize your device. They are available at www.egrips.com.

Chargers, Cradles, and Cables

Every mobile device faces challenges with power consumption. If you are a traveler or a heavy user of your Treo, you will need to think about how, where, and when you will recharge your device. In this section we will look at some options for powering and syncing your Treo.

Small Sync/Charge Cables

There is a host of very small cables on the market that will charge your Treo from the USB port on your computer. Many of these are actually manufactured by a single company and are just resold under different labels. With every sample mini-sync cable that we tried, we were able to charge our Treos but never successfully initiated a HotSync with one of them.

One of the primary vendors of these mini-sync cables is ZipLinq (www.ziplinq.com). The cable retracts to a very small size and is highly portable. This is a great way to recharge while on the road. The size makes it easy to carry in a pocket.

Another mini-sync vendor is BoxWave (www.boxwave.com). BoxWave also offers a car adapter and wall adapter that can be used to charge your Treo with the mini-sync cable. You may think the tiny cable would break easily, but we found it to be very durable and strong. The cable measures 35 inches when fully extended.

Pocket PC Techs (www.pocketpctechs.com), a vendor that you will see referenced a few times in this chapter, also offers a version of this sync cable called the Lil-Sync.

You can generally get the mini-sync cables from any of these vendors, and your local computer store also probably stocks the cables.

Of course, there is a multitude of power and sync accessories available right from Palm (www.palm.com). These include spare batteries, travel chargers, cradles, universal power products, sync cables and more.

The universal power products that Palm offers are from the iGo family. We are very big fans of the iGo Everywhere and iGo Juice products from Mobility Electronics (www.igo.com). These are universal adapters for charging all the devices that you carry. They allow you to charge your laptop, Treo, and other accessories. You can charge them from an outlet, auto power adapter, or airline power port. We travel frequently and tend to carry many different devices because of our line of work, and with the iGo we significantly lighten our travel load.

Alternative Chargers

In addition to the standard electrical chargers in the preceding section, for those folks to travel a little further afield and may not have access to an electrical outlet, there are some alternatives to consider.

First let us introduce you to the Solio Universal Solar Charger (www.solio.com) shown in Figure 16-2. This device, only slightly larger than a computer mouse, opens up like a fan to expose three solar panels. You can stick this device with a suction cup to a window and it will store electricity generated from the sun internally until it is needed to recharge your Treo or other mobile device (interchangeable tips make this equally good as a charger for your

16

FIGURE 16-2   The Solio solar charger allows you to charge your Treo from the energy of the sun!

Treo, iPod, or other mobile device). Eight hours of direct sunlight will store enough energy to fully charge your Treo once. The lithium-ion battery inside the Solio will hold its charge until you need it, for up to a year. Not only is this incredible useful if you are anywhere without regular electricity, it is also very environmentally friendly! The Solio product starts at $89.00.

Another alternative way to charge your Treo when you don't have access to power is the Seidio Emergency Charger, which will charge your Treo from a standard 9-volt battery. A single battery will charge your Treo to about 50 percent of its capacity. Seidio isn't currently listing the product on their web site; however, you can purchase it through the Treo Central web site at http://store.treocentral.com/content/accessories/5-58—193.htm.

External Keyboards

Many vendors make external keyboards for mobile devices; three of whom are now offering products specifically for the Treo. As always, Palm has an option available at www.palm.com. The Palm folding external keyboard ($69.95) is well constructed and is provided by a major manufacturer that also builds external keyboards for other vendors, such as Dell. It collapses to a size that easily fits into a jacket pocket. The web link to learn about this product is http://web.palm.com/products/Product.jhtml?id=80007&cat=280011. This keyboard works via the infrared port on the top of the Treo. The only caution that we would provide with regard to this product is that it sometimes doesn't work well with third-party software. For example, when we tested the product with the GoodLink push e-mail product from Good Technologies, the keyboard was all but unusable.

You can also get an infrared keyboard from ENR Tech, and you can order it at www.pocketirkeyboard.com for $54.99.

There are Bluetooth wireless keyboards for the Treo 650 and 700p available from ThinkOutside (www.thinkoutside.com) for $129.00 and Freedom (www.freedominput.com) for $99.95. Both of these units are full-sized keyboards that will bond with your Treo through a Bluetooth wireless connection as described in Chapter 5.

GPS Systems

The GPS system you might select will depend on your Treo model, as the options available for the Treo 650 and 700p are much more extensive given their Bluetooth capabilities. We will look at the Treo 600 first.

We found two GPS systems that you can connect directly to the serial port of your Treo 600. The first is the iTrek Mouse. The iTrek Mouse is manufactured by Semson's & Co. (www.semsons.com). This GPS functioned flawlessly in our trials. It was quick to acquire the GPS satellite signals and maintained a strong lock throughout our tests. This unit ships with software from Mapopolis.

Semons also sells Bluetooth GPS units for your Treo 650 anf 700 such as the iTrek M5, which we tested with our GPS software in Chapter 14 with a great deal of success. A second GPS option is available directly from Mapopolis (www.mapopolis.com). This is a similar hardware option that will connect to your Treo 600 through the serial port and will plug into the power outlet in your vehicle.

For a Bluetooth-equipped Treo, you have an extensive list of GPS vendor options. Sometimes the GPS receivers will come with software from a particular vendor, and other times not. If the receiver is NMEA compatible, it should function with most vendors' software. For GPS receivers you can look at

- Semsons (www.semsons.com)
- GlobalSat (www.usglobalsat.com)
- Pharos (www.pharos.com)
- Emtac (www.emtac.com)
- Palm GPS Navigator (www.palm.com)

For software for GPS navigation on your Palm Treo you can look at

- Mapopolis (www.mapopolis.com)
- TomTom (www.tomtom.com)
- CoPilot (www.copilot.com)

Palm's GPS Navigator product comes bundled with the TomTom navigation software.

Memory Cards

You can purchase SD and MMC memory cards from a variety of vendors; however, you will see some quality differences. One of our preferred memory card vendors is Kingston (www.kingston .com). We have found this company's cards to be well built and durable, and we have never experienced any issues with them. Cards from SanDisk (www.sandisk.com) have also held up very well to our abuse.

We strongly recommend buying name brand-quality memory cards; imitation cards run the risk of not only losing your data, but damaging your Treo and voiding your warranty.

16

Screen Protectors

Screen protectors are simple, transparent semi-adhesive pieces of plastic that stick right to the touch screen of your Treo. They allow you to use your Treo as normal but protect the screen from scratches and dirt. These are highly recommended and inexpensive accessories that no Treo owner should be without. A single protector can last for a very long time and is disposable; if it becomes scratched, you can simply peel it off and apply a new one. Some users have expressed concern about these protectors potentially reducing the sensitivity of the touch screen, but we can tell you from experience that with the higher-quality screen protectors, this is not an issue.

There are many vendors offering screen protectors that fit the Treo, and you can likely find the protectors in your local computer store. Some of the vendors are listed here:

- **Boxwave Clear Touch (www.boxwave.com/products/cleartouch/index.htm)** Adhesive screen protector.

- **G2 Screen Protectors (www.pdascreenprotectors.com/)** Adhesive screen protector.

- **Javo Screen Protectors (www.javoedge.com/)** Adhesive screen protector.

- **Martin Fields Screen Protectors (www.overlayplus.com)** High-quality, adhesive protectors; very clear and durable.

- **NuShield Screen Protectors (http://www.nushield.com/products_pda-phones_treo.htm)** This protector is nonadhesive, so it slips under the edges of your screen border, instead of relying on mild glue to hold the protector to the screen, as other models do. If you are leery of putting anything adhesive on your screen, then this is the screen protector for you!

- **Palm (http://web.palm.com/products/Category.jhtml?ID=280010)** Of course, Palm offers its own version of this product.

- **Pocket PC Techs (www.pocketpctechs.com/ws.asp)** Its WriteShield product comes in two kits, standard and deluxe. WriteShields are also nonadhesive. The protectors in both kits are the same; the difference is the accessories you get with each kit. The standard kit comes with three screen protectors, four cleaning cloths, six applicator/remover picks, and a high-quality microfiber cloth for cleaning your screen. The deluxe kit comes with everything the standard kit does, plus it comes with a two-ounce pump bottle of screen cleaning fluid.

- **PurpleMoo Screen It (www.purplemoo.com/)** Adhesive screen protectors.

In-Car Accessories

The hands-free audio equipment mentioned earlier in this chapter could follow as part of the in-car accessories group, but there are some other products that you should be aware of as well.

Please note that you should never operate your Treo while driving a car, and attempting to do so could be extremely dangerous. Only operate your Treo if your vehicle is stopped, or have a passenger work your Treo for you.

FIGURE 16-3 The Palm Comfort PLUS Handsfree Car Kit can make using your Treo in your vehicle a much safer proposition.

One of the products that you can consider if you use your Treo in your car is the Treo Comfort PLUS Handsfree Car Kit from Palm (www.palm.com), as shown in Figure 16-3.

This kit includes a cradle for securely holding your Treo, a microphone, an external antenna, and a wiring kit and charging adapter for keeping your Treo charged in the vehicle. The audio components include built-in echo and noise cancellation to make your Treo more usable for voice calls while in your car.

There are also other vendors that provide general car mounts for holding your Treo in your vehicle. These types of kits are not full hands-free kits but will provide a stable platform for operating or viewing your Treo. The advantage of these kits is that they can be used with external GPS solutions that plug into the serial port. The vehicle mount kits that we use are from ProClips (www.proclipusa.com). They have mounting kits for most vehicles, the majority of which are very easy to install and make no permanent attachment to your car (meaning that you don't have to screw plates into your dashboard or other parts of your vehicle to make them stable). The ProClip Swivel Mount has been very useful for working with GPS in our vehicles.

You can also find mounts that will attach to your windshield with a suction cup like the Slim Line Universal Mount Kit for Treo found at Seidio (www. seidioonline.com). However, we have had limited success with the windshield mount versions, because they never seem to stay adhered to the window, no matter what we try.

Styli

If you need to replace your stylus for your Treo, you can do that directly through Palm, or you can look to third-party providers for some interesting stylus upgrades.

Pocket PC Techs has a great addition for your Treo stylus. Their custom stylus includes a built-in pen. No longer do you have to search for a pen to write with, because there is always one tucked conveniently inside your Treo stylus. This product can be purchased directly from Pocket PC Techs (www.pocketpctechs.com) for $12.99. You can also order pen refills at this site.

Stylus Central (www.styluscentral.com/) also has a stylus with a built-in pen for your Treo.

16

Software

Throughout the book we have referenced various software programs that can add value to your Treo. Here we will provide a quick summary of some of the software products we covered, as well as some others that are recommended by Treo users. This section also tells you where to learn more about the products. Remember that there are more than 20,000 commercial software applications available for the Treo, and this is just a set of the software that we use, as well as software that has been recommended by other Treo users.

Communications

You will find a wide range of communications software products for your Treo, including the following:

Product	Description
TreoGuard from Geakware (www.geakware.com)	TreoGuard is a utility for Treo smartphones that can prevent the SPACEBAR and RETURN buttons from answering phone calls. It also has a feature that allows you to turn off the screen when a call is answered, thus saving valuable battery life. ($8.99)
Chatopus (www.chatopus.com)	Chatopus is a Palm OS instant messaging (IM) client for the Treo that allows you to instantly communicate with other people via instant messaging.
	Chatopus allows users to communicate with Jabber contacts. What's more, it also supports the transport aspects of Jabber, allowing users to establish links to other IM solutions, including MSN Messenger, ICQ, AIM, Yahoo! Messenger, and others. ($14.95)
GoodLink from Good Technologies (www.good.com)	A high-end enterprise, real-time push e-mail delivery product that enables real-time e-mail delivery, as well as wireless calendar and contact synchronization with your enterprise. (Price is negotiated based on enterprise deployment.)
Hand RSS News Reader from Stand Alone Inc. (www.standalone.com)	RSS News feeds are the newest way to download and read news stories on a variety of subjects, from all over the Internet. Handheld Headlines/RSS for Palm OS allows you to download these news feeds to your Treo via HotSync or wirelessly; you can then read them later. Use it to keep updated with the latest news, sports, and financial updates and to read your favorite web sites!
	Hand/RSS for Palm OS is preconfigured for a variety of news feeds, including BBC News, Boing Boing, CNet News, Fark.com, MSNBC, Salon.com, SlashDot, The Register, Wired, and more.

Product	Description
	Additionally, you can add any new feeds quickly and easily from other RSS sources. ($14.95)
PocketExpress from Handmark (www.handmark.com)	This useful product will wirelessly download useful information to your Treo on a scheduled basis or on demand. You can keep on your handheld the latest news, sports scores, weather forecasts for multiple cities, and much more. In addition, this product gives you the ability to look up phone numbers (including reverse lookup) and to locate addresses on maps and download them in real time to your Treo. This is a tool that no Treo should be without! ($69.90/year)
Mergic VPN from Mergic (www.mergic.com)	Allows you to establish a virtual private network (VPN) or secure connection to a corporate network for the purposes of e-mail access, systems management, intranet access, and more. ($29.99)
Mobile TS from DDH Software (www.ddhsoftware.com)	Mobile TS allows you to use your Treo to make a Microsoft Terminal Services or Remote Desktop connection to another computer and see the screen of that computer right on your Treo; it also allows you to have your keyboard commands and mouse commands (screen taps) sent back to the remote system. ($39.99)
PDANet Modem from June Fabrics (www.junefabrics.com)	This handy program allows you to use your Treo as a wireless modem for your laptop. By connecting your Treo to your laptop with a HotSync cable, you can now wirelessly connect to the Internet to download e-mail and surf web sites. Remember that this is a wireless connection and will not run at the speed of the broadband connection you are likely accustomed to! ($34.00)
Radio Control from Chris Hobbes (www.clanhobbs.com/treo)	A useful utility for automatically turning the radio of your Treo on and off at predetermined times (like when you are sleeping). This helps to prevent interruptions and also conserves battery power. (Free)
SnapperMail from SnapperFish (www.snappermail.com)	One of the most popular e-mail programs for the Palm platform. It includes attachment support and automatic mail fetching. ($24.95 to $59.95)
TAKEphONE by ShSh (www.shsh.com)	TAKEphONE is an add-on utility for improving the usability and integration between the Treo contacts application and the phone. It helps you find phone numbers and create and edit contacts. ($19.95)
VeriChat from Intellisync (formerly PDAApps) (www.pdaapps.com)	An instant messaging (IM) client for your Treo that allows you to have online chats with Yahoo, MSN Messenger, ICQ, and AOL Instant Messenger users. ($24.95 to $39.95 per year)

16

Multimedia

The Treo is growing in capability as a multimedia device thanks to some of the following software packages:

Product	Description
Kinoma Player/Producer from Kinoma (www.kinoma.com)	Kinoma Player 3 delivers full-screen, full-motion, full-color, high-resolution video on your Treo. The Player only plays back files that have been encoded with the Kinoma Producer software, which can convert your DivX, MPEG, AVI, and other file types. (Player is $19.99; Producer is $29.99)
MM Player (www.mmplayer.com)	MM Player (short for Multimedia Player) allows you to play back a variety of audio and video file types on your Treo, including MPEG, MP3, WAV, and AVI, among others. ($17.95)
Pocket Tunes from NormSoft (www.pocket-tunes.com)	Pocket Tunes turns your Treo into a portable audio player. You can play compressed audio files (.mp3 or Ogg Vorbis) or uncompressed .wav files from a flash memory card, or you can stream .mp3 files live over your wireless Internet connection. This is one of the most popular audio players available for the Treo. ($14.95 to $61.80)

Productivity

A key goal of most Treo users is to increase their productivity. The software featured here can help.

Product	Description
Documents To Go from DataViz (www.dataviz.com)	Treo version of popular Microsoft Office programs for working with documents, spreadsheets, and presentations. ($29.99 to $89.99)
QuickOffice from Mobility Electronics (www.quickoffice.com)	Allows you to create and open native Microsoft Office documents on your Treo. ($39.95)
WordSmith from BlueNomad (www.bluenomad.com)	A full-featured word processor for the Treo. ($29.95)

Security

Mobile device security is a very significant problem, and Treo users, particularly in a corporate environment, should understand how they are protecting (or should be protecting) their devices.

Product	Description
SureWave Mobile Defense from JP Mobile (www.PDADefense.com)	Encrypts and protects data on your Treo from being accessed by unauthorized people.
SplashID from SplashData (www.splashdata.com)	Allows you to encrypt and store important numbers in one place, such as credit card numbers, membership numbers, bank accounts, and more. ($29.95)
3nity Password Keeper from Smart Mobile Applications (www.smart-mobile.net)	Also allows for encrypting and storing your important numbers. ($14.95)

Utilities

These are valuable software products that can help you make your Treo function even better.

Product	Description
Backup Buddy from BlueNomad (www.bluenomad.com)	A backup utility for backing up and restoring data from your Treo, right to your SD or MMC memory card. ($16.95)
BackupMan from Bits & Bolts (www.bitsnbolts.com)	This is the backup software covered in the Backup and Recovery section of this book. It allows for full backup and restore to and from your SD or MMC cards on an ad hoc or scheduled basis. ($14.95)
BatteryGraph from Jeroen Witteman (www.jeroenwitteman.com)	Allows you to monitor and graph your battery strength and usage. If you want to see how various applications and actions impact your battery, this is a very useful tool. (Free)
HandZipper from HandWatch (www.handwatch.com)	Most Palm applications on the Internet are stored in a WinZip (.zip) file. With this utility, you can easily unzip and zip files right on your Treo without having to use the HotSync application to load them. It also works for attachments you may receive that are in a .zip format. ($9.99)
HiLauncher from RaNo Software (www.hilauncher.com)	Creates a Windows-like Start menu for your Treo. An easy and useful way to launch your most popular applications. ($14.95)
KeyCaps600 (not for Treo 650 or 700) (www.geekandproud.com/software)	A utility that makes text entry easier. By holding or double- tapping a key, you can select uppercase, lowercase, or special characters. This is a must-have software for the Treo 600 user. (Free, but a $10 donation is appreciated)

16

Product	Description
mCamLock from MotionApps (www.motionapps.com)	Allows you to disable the camera on your Treo. This is a concern for many organizations where privacy could be compromised with a camera-equipped device, such as at a hospital. ($29.99, and enterprise licensing is available)
mLights from MotionApps (www.motionapps.com)	Gives you control over backlight settings to better conserve your battery power. ($7.99)
Skinner from 79b Media (www.79bmedia.com)	Allows you to change the appearance of your Treo with downloadable "skins." ($14.99)
Today from Jonas Lindstedt (nikman.k2.net/today/)	Gives you a Pocket PC-like Today screen upon startup of your Treo. (Free)
TreoButler by Hobbyist (available from PalmGear www.palmgear.com)	A utility for managing alarms, alerts, navigation, application launching, LED control, Keyguard, and more. ($6.00)

Wrap It Up

As the Treo devices continue to be among the top sellers in the mobile communications market, we are seeing more and more third-party accessories and applications showing up. Being able to personalize your Treo to your own tastes with a case and other accessories helps when integrating your smartphone into your mobile lifestyle!

New products are being announced every day, so watch the web sites referenced in Appendix B to find out about new product announcements for useful accessories and software for your smartphone.

Part IV

Appendixes

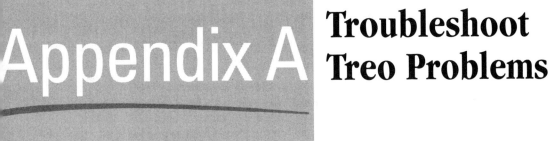

Appendix A

Troubleshoot Treo Problems

How to...

- Overcome the most common Treo user problems
- Overcome the most common technical issues

Palm has designed and engineered your Treo with the utmost attention to detail to ensure that your experience with your Treo is as painless and trouble-free as possible. That said, there are a few user and technical scenarios that may cause problems for you, your Treo applications, or the Treo itself. This chapter serves to help you overcome the most common known issues that you may encounter. The chapter is divided into functional categories to help you quickly locate answers to the most common questions.

Error Messages and Troubleshooting

Many computers and applications log "events" to make the task of finding out what happened a little easier. Event logs create paper trails so that when a computer or application misbehaves, you can track down the problem. Your Treo has the same type of log. When your Treo crashes, it resets itself and stores the reason for the crash in an error log. Often, when your Treo crashes and resets itself, the issue is automatically resolved; however, if your Treo is resetting itself more often than you would like, you can access the error log to help you find out what is causing the crashes. The steps to get to the error log are a little different depending on what flavor of Treo you have, GSM or Sprint. The steps you should take to find the error log are listed in this section.

GSM/GPRS/EDGE Treo

If you have a GSM/GPRS/EDGE Treo (in the U.S. any non-Sprint Treo and in Europe any Treo on the Orange network), follow these steps to find the error log:

1. Press the PHONE button on the keyboard.
2. Dial #*377 on the dial pad on the screen, or type #*377 on the keyboard; then select Dial.

A dialog box appears, displaying the date of the last crash, the application running at the time of that crash, and if appropriate, the error message that resulted from the crash.

Sprint CDMA Treo

If you have a Sprint CDMA Treo, follow these steps to find the error log:

1. Press the PHONE button on the keyboard.
2. Dial ##377 on the dial pad, or type ##377 on the keyboard; then select Dial.

A dialog box appears, displaying the date of the last crash, the application running at the time of that crash, and if appropriate, the error message that resulted from the crash.

There are many types of possible errors. There is an extensive list of these error messages and the most likely cause of each one on the Palm support site (www.palm.com).

It is also worth mentioning that the Palm support web site lists general desktop errors, Windows errors, Macintosh errors, and HotSync log errors.

Third-party applications are commonly the cause of errors. If a particular application name shows up in the error log, you may want to consider deleting that application. The steps for deleting an application from your Treo are covered in Chapter 3.

Treo Battery

Your Treo has a removable (700p/650) or built-in (600), state-of-the-art lithium ion battery that generally doesn't require maintenance; but just in case, a few tips can help you troubleshoot battery challenges. This section lists some potential battery problems and their solutions.

My Treo battery doesn't seem to charge.

Is the power adapter plugged in correctly? Make sure that it's hooked up to an active power outlet and that all connections are tight. If the connection to your Treo seems a little loose, try disconnecting it and reconnecting it again. To check to see if your device is charging, open the Applications Launcher screen by pressing HOME on the keyboard. Then look at the battery meter at the top of the screen. You will see a lightning bolt symbol over the battery when it is charging properly.

Sometimes the charging light can malfunction, in which case you will need to perform a reset to bring your Treo back to normal functioning.

- **In-cradle reset**   (Treo 600 only) This may be necessary to "reboot" the charging circuitry. The steps for performing an in-cradle reset are covered later in this chapter under the heading "Perform an In-Cradle Reset."

- **Soft reset**   Steps for performing a soft reset on your Treo are covered later in this chapter, under the heading "Perform a Soft Reset."

My battery loses its charge very quickly.

Your Treo has a lithium ion battery (nonremovable in the Treo 600) that will eventually wear out and that you will have to replace, but there are a few things that you can do to maximize your battery life:

- Recharge your Treo battery before it drains completely.
- If you can, charge the battery often, even before it gets low.

Tips on how to maximize your battery life are included in Chapter 9.

A

Treo Sound and Speaker

Your Treo has a built-in speaker on the back of the device. It also has a jack for an earbud or headphones to allow you to listen to music and the sounds of games, video, and so on.

Why does my Treo speaker buzz when I play music loudly?

The Treo speaker is designed to play system sounds such as ringtones and applications "beeps." It is not designed to play loud music, and if it is buzzing, you likely have the volume too high. Like any other speaker, it can be damaged if too much volume is being pushed through it. Here are some steps to help you avoid damaging the built-in speaker:

- *Use headphones.* Using headphones with your Treo is covered under the next heading, "My stereo headphone cable doesn't fit into the earphone jack on my Treo."

- *Don't use MP3 volume boost.* Some MP3 encoders allow you to boost the volume of a song by as much as 15 dB. If you are encoding MP3s for use with your Treo, don't boost the volume when encoding. More information should be available from the company that developed your MP3 or in the documentation.

My stereo headphone cable doesn't fit into the earphone jack on my Treo.

The headphone jack is designed to be used with the included Palm headphone cable. This cable is a mono headset with a call-control button and microphone meant for telephone use. It allows you to talk on your Treo phone in a hands-free mode. You can use a stereo headset to listen to music and other sounds, but the Treo only works with a 2.5 mm stereo headset plug or a standard 3.5 mm stereo plug with a 2.5 mm to 3.5 mm adapter. This type of adapter is sold by Palm and other Treo accessory vendors, and most consumer electronics stores will likely have an adapter that will work.

The Treo Screen

Your Treo has a 320×320 pixel (160×160 on a Treo 600) bright, color TFT screen, and a few tips for troubleshooting Treo screen issues are covered in this section.

Why does my handheld screen flicker or shimmer?

You may have noticed faint white lines that appear diagonally when you are scrolling quickly in an application. This is normal behavior for your Treo, but there are some known application conflicts that increase screen flickering. The most common applications that may cause flickering are some games, launchers, and theme applications, because they tend to change the display settings to suit their needs. If this flickering problem just began happening, consider if you recently installed an application. If you think you know which application may be causing the flickering, uninstall it to see if the problem is resolved.

There are also some types of third-party applications that are more likely to cause flickering. These include applications that were initially designed for previous versions of Palm OS and were later updated to run on OS 5 or later.

My Treo is looping, flashing, or frozen on the Palm Computing Platform logo.

If your Treo encounters a system extension that is corrupted or isn't working properly after a device reset, it will automatically reset and try to load the corrupted extension again, which causes it to reset again. This creates an infinite loop situation that your Treo can't break out of.

A system extension is a software program that is loaded the first time your device starts after a reset. System extensions add to the functionality of your device. An example of a system extension is the software that allows your device to send data through the infrared (IR) port.

If your Treo is stuck in an infinite loop, try performing a soft reset on your Treo, which is described later in this appendix, under the heading "Perform a Soft Reset." If this doesn't help, you may have to perform a hard reset, as described under the later heading "Perform a Hard Reset." Note, however, that performing a hard reset means that you will lose all of your data, so use it as a last resort.

Synchronization with HotSync

Your Treo is best used in conjunction with a PC to allow you to synchronize data between the two. Synchronization is covered in Chapter 3. Before you can synchronize your Treo with your PC, you need to install the Palm Desktop and HotSync Manager software on your PC. This software is included on the CD-ROM that came with your Treo and is also downloadable for free from Palm (www.palm.com).

I keep seeing the error "Unable to HotSync due to system error" when I try to HotSync.

This error may occur when you try to perform a HotSync operation at the same time your Treo is on an active call of any type. Possibilities include making a voice call, sending or receiving e-mail, browsing the Internet, or downloading files from the Internet. There are a few options for overcoming this error:

- ■ *Ensure no active Web operations are occurring.* Ensure that you are not making a voice call, browsing the Web, or downloading files from the Web, and then try to HotSync again.

- ■ *Disable automatic e-mail checking.* Another reason this may happen is that some e-mail applications check your e-mail in the background. This means that you may not always know when your Treo is checking for e-mail. If this error seems to happen irregularly, this may be the problem. You can disable automatic e-mail checking in your e-mail application, perform the HotSync operation, and then turn automatic e-mail checking back on. You may have to check the documentation of your e-mail application to find out where to change this setting.

A

■ *Turn off Wireless mode.* If the two previous suggestions don't work, turn your Treo Wireless mode off, perform the HotSync operation, and then turn it back on again. With the Wireless mode off, there is no chance that an application is performing Internet functions without you knowing about it. You can turn Wireless mode on and off by pressing and holding the END/POWER button.

Treo Phone

Mobile phone technology has been mainstream for many years, and the technology is relatively mature. However, problems can still arise.

I am having trouble dialing phone numbers with the keyboard.

Your Treo is likely set up to start a Contacts search when you type rather than dial a phone number. One or the other of the settings must be active, but not both. The steps for toggling to the option for typing a phone number are listed here:

1. Press the PHONE and then the MENU button on the keyboard.

2. From the Options menu, select Phone Display Options (Treo 600-Display Preferences).

3. In the menu that appears, select the second of the following two options:

   ■ **Typing Starts Contacts Search**   When this option is selected, any typing you do in the Phone application will cause the Treo to try to find the contact that matches the letters you type. So if you are trying to type a phone number, your Treo will behave strangely.

   ■ **Typing Dials Phone Number**   When this option is selected, the number pad on the keyboard is active and you can type a phone number.

I'm not happy with the sound quality on my Treo phone.

There are many factors that can cause problems with the sound quality you hear, or that the person you are speaking to hears, when you are talking on your Treo phone.

These factors include

■ The phone of the person you are talking to

■ The signal strength and the quality of the connection between the phones

■ The environment: weather, background noise, solar flares, and so on

■ Wireless network problems

Some things you can do to maximize the sound quality of your phone conversations are listed here:

■ *Hold your Treo correctly.* Position the Treo handset closer to your ear to prevent sound from leaking back to the microphone. Be sure you're holding the Treo so that your hand is not near the microphone hole on the back. Your hand, or any other reflecting surface, tends to conduct the speaker sound down to the microphone and cause echo on the recipient's end.

■ *Turn down the phone volume.* Try decreasing your Treo volume to avoid *coupling,* or feedback, on the receiver's end. (Coupling occurs when the receiver hears his or her voice as it goes through your speaker, is picked up by your microphone, and gets sent back with a slight delay as it travels through the network.) This applies to both the speakerphone and the built-in ear speaker.

■ *Turn your Treo over.* If you are using the speakerphone functionality, try turning the Treo over so that the screen is facing down.

When talking on my Treo, I hear echo, echo, echo!

If you are hearing your own voice echo when you are talking, the echo is originating from the other person's phone, not yours. You can ask the other person to either turn down the phone volume or to hold the speaker closer to the ear to minimize feedback.

I hear static when I talk on my Treo phone.

Static is generally caused by a barrier between your Treo and the cellular tower to which your Treo is connected. For example, a barrier exists when you get into an elevator while talking on your phone. There is not too much you can do except to be aware of barriers and avoid talking on your phone when you are in an elevator or driving though a tunnel, for example.

Wireless Connectivity

Your Treo, as you know, is equipped with wireless radio components to allow you to make wireless phone calls and send and receive wireless application data. Due to the complexity of this feature, and depending on whether or not your Treo arrived perfectly configured, you may need to do a little troubleshooting to ensure that your Treo is set up correctly.

Why does my GPRS/EDGE or PCS Vision service disconnect periodically?

You may have already experienced intermittent service as you move around within your city, state, or province. Wireless networks do not yet cover every square mile of surface area, and many areas have better connectivity than others. So if you are disconnected, it may be because you are in an area without wireless coverage.

Some mobile service providers log wireless users off after a given period of time—from hours to days, depending on the carrier. This is another explanation for unexpected disconnections. You may be automatically disconnected regardless of whether you have been using your connection during the defined time period.

A

How do I reestablish my wireless connection?

Provided you are in an area with wireless coverage, launch an application that requires a data connection, such as a web browser or an e-mail application. Your connection should be established automatically, but you may have to approve the connection when prompted.

What should I do if I can't connect to the Internet at all with my GPRS/EDGE/EDGE Treo?

If wireless applications such as e-mail and the Web will not work, here are some things to try to help get you going:

- *Turn your Wireless mode off and on again.* When you do this, your Treo will try to reauthenticate with the network, and that will often fix a broken connection.

- *Be sure that your username and password are correct.* Some wireless service providers require that you enter a username and password to allow you to connect to their wireless network. This information is stored in your Network Preferences settings, and your Treo should have been preconfigured with this information. If it wasn't, your Treo will not be able to authenticate with the wireless network.

- *Check your wireless service contract.* If you have never been able to use e-mail or have never had access to the Web on your Treo, check to see whether your wireless service contract includes GPRS/EDGE data services. Not all service contracts include data services by default, and it is possible that you are only covered for voice data and not other forms of data. To make sure your GPRS/EDGE service is enabled, contact the company that holds your contract. Contact information for major carriers that host Treo service is listed at the end of this chapter. If you have your service contract handy, the contact information should be provided there as well.

- *Find out if GPRS/EDGE is provided in your area.* GPRS/EDGE networks do not offer coverage everywhere, and it is possible that GPRS/EDGE is not provided in your area. This may not seem like a particularly useful point, but sometimes a user buys a device from a source other than from the local service provider. For example, I bought my Treo on eBay because the carriers in my area are not selling them yet. Obviously, you can't use GPRS/EDGE if it is not supported in your area.

- *Contact your wireless service provider for assistance.* If none of these steps helped, contact your wireless service provider directly for assistance. Sometimes, problems originate with the carrier rather than directly with you or your Treo.

Troubleshooting Bluetooth Issues

Bluetooth capability is not available on the Treo 600. Bluetooth short-range wireless is covered in detail in Chapter 3, which provides a lot of information about Bluetooth, but here is some more information to help you troubleshoot.

My Bluetooth headset quit working.

If your Bluetooth headset suddenly doesn't work, you will want to go through the pairing steps once again, covered in Chapter 5, and the first thing you will need to do is delete the headset from the Trusted Devices list on your Treo. To do this, launch the Bluetooth application, select Setup Devices, select Trusted Devices, and delete your headset from the list.

I can't get my Treo to connect to my PC using Bluetooth.

This is one of the most common Treo Bluetooth problems and may have one of several causes relating to configuration on the PC. Chapter 5 deals with Bluetooth, and you may have to consult your PC documentation to correctly configure it for Bluetooth, but here are some things to check:

- Is the PC Bluetooth enabled?
- Is Bluetooth on?
- Is Bluetooth in discoverable mode?
- Is the Treo farther than 30 feet away from the PC?
- Are you entering the correct Bluetooth passkey for the PC, on your Treo?
- On your Treo, are you using the Camera or Camcorder application? Bluetooth is disabled when the Camera/Camcorder applications are running.
- Are you connected with Bluetooth but find that it doesn't seem to be working? You must configure how your PC interacts with your Treo (for example, file transfer, Internet access, etc.). Check your PC documentation to configure your PC Bluetooth application.

More about Bluetooth Configuring and Connecting—Bluetooth is not available on the Treo 600.

Your Treo user documentation covers a lot of ground regarding Bluetooth, so we'll just talk about the things you are most likely going to need to configure.

If you know that the Bluetooth device that you want to connect to is within the 33-foot range and you still get the Devices Not Found error message or no devices show up in the Bluetooth browser, the device may not be in discoverable mode. If it is in discoverable mode, there is a small possibility there is interference from other radio devices using the same radio frequency. Devices such as microwave ovens, some cordless telephones, and certain wireless LAN products, among other things, can interfere with Bluetooth. If you can, turn off these devices and try the discovery again.

- *Put your Treo into discoverable mode.* It is a good idea to leave discoverable mode turned off on your Treo to help avoid unwanted connections. However, if you need to turn discoverable mode on, open the Applications launcher by pressing the HOME button and then Find, selecting the Bluetooth icon, and changing the Discoverable drop-down list to Yes.

A

■ *Change the Bluetooth device name on your Treo.* You want to use a different name for Bluetooth than your Treo device name. To change it, open the Applications Launcher by pressing the HOME button and then Find, selecting the Bluetooth icon, selecting the Device Name field, and typing in a new name. Finally, select OK. That's it. Now that name will show up when another Bluetooth device detects your Treo.

Browse the Internet

The ability to browse the Web is one of the most interesting features of the Treo. Even if you are a seasoned Internet veteran and are already familiar with PC-based web browsers, there are some differences between PC and Treo web browsers that you should be aware of when browsing the Web on your Treo.

I'm having trouble downloading a specific file with the Blazer Web Browser.

Your Treo will not download any file type that is not supported on your Treo. That is, unless an application on your Treo can read or use the file, it is unsupported. The types of files that can be downloaded by default include the following:

■ **PRC files** (*filename*.**prc**)   Palm application files

■ **PDB files** (*filename*.**pdb**)   Palm database files

■ **MIDI/MID files** (less than 64KB) (*filename*.**mid**)   Sound files commonly used for ringtones

■ **JPEG/JPG files** (*filename*.**jpg**)   Image files, the same format the Treo saves files in

—as well as files with extensions of JFIF, JPE, OPRC, TXT, and VCF.

If a file cannot be downloaded, you may see one of the following error messages:

Download Error: The file type you are attempting to download is not supported on your device.

Data Timeout: The page download could not be completed. Please try again later.

If the file you are trying to download is one of the supported file types, the following are some of the other reasons you may be having trouble downloading the file.

Did You Lose Network Coverage?   If you lose wireless network coverage at any point during the download, the download will not be completed. This is more likely to occur with large files that may take several minutes to download. Also, if you are moving in a vehicle while downloading a file, you may lose your connection to a cell tower as the signal is handed off to another tower. Staying in one area with good wireless coverage while a file is downloading tends to offer the best results.

Did the Connection Time Out?   Your Treo web browser may time out while waiting to hear back from the Web or another server along the way. If this happens, you may see this error:

`Data Timeout: The page download could not be completed. Please try again later.`

The time-out could be due to web congestion or a slow connection. Try again later.

Do You Have Enough Free Memory on Your Treo?   Your Treo must have enough space to store the file that you trying to download. If there is not enough space to store the file, you will see this error message:

`There is not enough memory available on your device to download this file.`

If you see this message, then you are running out of memory and will need to remove some files. This topic is covered in this chapter under the heading "What can I do if my handheld is running out of memory?"

I can't connect to the Internet at all.

See this topic under the heading "What should I do if I can't connect to the Internet at all with my GPRS/EDGE Treo?"

Why does my Treo 600 Web Browser crash when I try to enter a URL?

If the Blazer Web Browser is consistently crashing or resetting whenever you try to enter a web site address, you may see an error message similar to this:

`A reset was caused on 05/19/2004 at 11:13 while running "Web": Fatal Exception,`
`Datamgr.c, line:6341 invalid unique ID passed.`

This type of error is known to occur if the "predictive text database" in the Blazer browser becomes corrupted and is therefore unusable. To resolve this issue, follow these steps:

1. On your desktop PC, go to the web site http://nosleepsoftware.sourceforge.net and download a file utility called "FileZ." This utility allows you to delete the database on your Treo that is normally a hidden and undeletable file. There are other utilities that allow similar functionality, but FileZ is sanctioned by Palm, so we know it works.

2. Once you have downloaded FileZ to your PC, install it on your Treo using HotSync. Chapter 2 details the steps for installing applications.

3. Once FileZ is installed, open the Applications Launcher screen by pressing HOME on the keyboard. Find and launch FileZ.

4. In FileZ, choose the View and Edit Files option.

5. Locate and select the file named Web Find AutoFill.

6. Press MENU on the keyboard and select the Delete option from the menu.

7. Select Yes when the file delete confirmation screen appears.

A

8. Now, locate and select the file named Web URL AutoFill.

9. Press MENU on the keyboard and select the Delete option from the menu.

10. Select Yes when the file delete confirmation screen appears.

Now you should be able to enter URLs into the browser to view web pages without experiencing any problems.

E-Mail

A few tips for troubleshooting Palm Mail are included in this section. Many other e-mail software options for your Treo are available, however, and they are covered in Chapter 6. If you have trouble with one of those e-mail applications, you can find answers by consulting the vendor's product documentation or by contacting the software company directly.

I am having memory issues with e-mail.

Many of us tend to use e-mail more than even the phone, and we get many messages per week. It is important to be conscious of how many e-mail messages you are storing on your Treo. E-mail messages can eat up a lot of memory and can affect other applications. Storing too many e-mails can cause a painfully slow HotSync process as well.

Refer to your e-mail documentation to learn how to archive or delete older e-mails (not applicable to web-based e-mail). Palm provides technical support for VersaMail on the Palm web site (www.palm.com).

VersaMail e-mail regularly times out.

If you are experiencing a scenario where you are checking an e-mail message and VersaMail times out, and from then on whenever you check your mail you get a time-out, then VersaMail may be trying to download a message that is bigger than the maximum message size that you have configured on your Treo.

To overcome this problem, raise the maximum message size in VersaMail. Launch VersaMail, press the Menu button, select Options | Preferences | Delivery Options, and increase the Maximum message size to something more reasonable, such as 2 Megabytes. Of course, you may need to keep a closer eye on your memory usage.

MMS

Chapter 5 discusses Multimedia Messaging Service (MMS) and provides some tips for troubleshooting MMS problems, but here are some additional tips. Note that the Treo sold by Sprint in the U.S. does not support MMS but offers similar functionality with its Picture Mail application. Sprint Picture Mail is covered in Chapter 5.

I can't send an MMS message.

Are you talking on the phone when you are trying to send the MMS message? Your Treo doesn't allow you to send an MMS message and talk on the Treo phone at the same time, so you will need to wait until you are finished talking on the phone to send the message.

MMS freezes my Treo, and then I can't turn it off.

If this happens when you are trying to send an MMS message, this is a sure sign that you don't have MMS activated on your mobile account or your manually entered MMS settings are wrong.

The first step toward working through this problem is to perform a soft reset on your Treo; see the section titled "Perform a Soft Reset," later in this chapter, for tips on how to perform a soft reset. Then you should contact your wireless service provider to ensure that you have MMS capability active on your account and that your MMS settings are correct.

SMS

This section provides tips for troubleshooting some common Short Message Service (SMS) issues. (The Treo's SMS application is discussed in Chapter 5.)

My SMS application crashes when I import messages.

If you haven't used the SMS application before, you may find that when you first launch the SMS application, your Treo resets itself. If this is happening, check the error log to find out if a fatal error occurred. Error logs were covered at the beginning of this chapter, under the heading "Error Messages and Troubleshooting."

If a fatal error occurred, a likely cause is that you upgraded to your Treo from a previous Treo Smartphone and didn't install the Treo software from the CD included with your Treo. When you install the desktop software on your PC, it filters out incompatible applications that won't work on your new Treo Smartphone. If you don't install the desktop software, the incompatible applications will not be filtered out and the incompatible applications may cause your Treo to crash or cause other unexpected behavior.

What should I do if my SMS application crashes when I am importing messages?

Install the software from the CD that came with your Treo Smartphone. When asked if you want to quarantine (filter) incompatible content, choose Yes. Perform the HotSync operation as directed, and let the installer finish its job. Then launch the SMS application on your Treo Smartphone. This should return it to normal.

A

Camera

Your Treo camera is very easy to use, but as with anything technical, you may experience challenges.

Why won't an image transfer from my desktop to my Treo with HotSync?

The first step is to make sure you are following the correct steps for performing a HotSync. Consult the Treo user guide for the steps. If you are sure you are doing everything correctly, the most likely reason the picture is not being transferred correctly to your Treo is that the picture is too big.

If the picture you are trying to transfer is larger than 2048×2048 pixels, the HotSync application will not transfer it to your Treo. Before transferring it, you will need to reduce its size with an image-editing software package. Digital photo editing, including resizing images, is covered in Chapter 7.

I am having display problems caused by third-party software.

Some third-party software can cause interference when displaying pictures on the Treo screen. Essentially, the problem stems from software that changes the screen color settings for the application's own purposes. The result of the modifications is that some images won't display correctly. Butterfly and Psycho Path are applications known to have this effect on the Treo 600.

I performed a HotSync operation, but I can't find my Treo pictures on my PC.

When you perform a HotSync operation on a Windows PC, your images are transferred to the following file location:

- **Treo 700p**   My Documents\My Photos\Palm Photos*username*\Internal (or the "Expansion Card" folder)
- **Treo 650**   My Documents\My Pictures\palmOne Photos\ *username*\Internal (or the "Expansion Card" folder)
- **Treo 600**   C:\Program Files\Handspring\Treo Pictures*username*

All images will be in JPEG format, which is one of the most common formats for images on the Web.

If you have a Macintosh, there are four ways you can transfer pictures taken with your Treo camera to your Mac:

Copy to Mac Using a HotSync Operation (Treo 700p/650)   When you perform a HotSync operation with your Mac, your Treo photos are backed up to a folder on your Mac.

- Photos stored in your Treo internal memory
  - Treo 700p: Mac HD/Users/*Mac username*/Pictures/Palm Photos/*Palm device name*/Internal
  - Treo 650: Home/Pictures/palmOne Photos/(Palm device user name)/Internal
- Photos stored in your Treo memory expansion card
  - Treo 700p: Mac HD/Users/*Mac user name*/Pictures/Palm Photos/*Palm device name*/Expansion card
  - Treo 650: Home/Pictures/palmOne Photos/*Palm device name*/Expansion Card

- Videos stored in your Treo internal memory
  - Treo 700p: Home/Movies/Palm Videos/*Palm device name*/Internal
  - Treo 650: Home/Movies/palmOne Videos/*Palm device name*/Internal
- Videos stored in your Treo memory expansion card
  - Treo 700p: Home/Movies/Palm Videos/*Palm device name*/Expansion Card
  - Treo 650: Home/Movies/palmOne Videos/*Palm device name*/Expansion Card

Using an SD/MMC Card   To do this, you need a Secure Digital memory expansion card and an SD card reader. This is covered in more detail in Chapter 7.

By E-Mail   To do this, e-mail the picture as an attachment to yourself, and open it when you check your e-mail on your Mac. Then save the picture to your hard drive.

With Missing Sync   You can also use third-party software called The Missing Sync from Mark/Space (www.markspace.com) to transfer the pictures to your Mac.

Why does the Treo camera preview image look funny?

Your Treo camera was designed to allow you to take quick, easy-to-use digital snapshots. On its web site, Palm says "We'll be the first to admit that while it's a great little camera that most people are happy with, it's not the same as a professional-grade 8-megapixel digital SLR. The pictures taken with a Treo are more like those taken with a 110 instamatic camera, although the Treo 700p takes pretty decent photos: consumer-level quality in a small, accessible format." See the picture-taking tips for using your Treo camera in Chapter 7.

Why do my Treo pictures have blue spots on them?

If you have light blue dots on your images when viewing them on your Treo screen (the dots are likely more obvious in the darker areas of the image), it is usually an indication that the picture was taken under poor lighting conditions. Chapter 7 provides steps for getting the most out of your Treo camera, including tips for improving the quality of your pictures and image editing.

Media: Music, Nonmusic Audio, Video, TV, and Streaming Media

The Treo 600 does not play music right out of the box, unless you count MIDI ringtones as music. The good news is that there are many third-party applications that allow you to listen to music or watch video with sound. If you don't already have a music player for your Treo 600, some options are discussed in Chapter 8.

All Treo models: If your Treo seems to be functioning properly except that it can't play media, contact the vendor that produces the software you are using to find solutions to problems specific to that software. See also "Reset Your Treo," later in this appendix, for a possible solution.

A

The types of music files that can be played on your Treo depend on the media player that you are using. Consult the user guide for the media player, such as RealPlayer, iTunes, MobiTV, etc. It is important to know that there are many files that need to be converted by the Palm Desktop Media application for playback on your Treo.

Third-Party Applications

One of the many great things about the Treo is that a lot of new applications, games, and utilities are being developed for this popular platform. Yet while software seems plentiful, many of these applications are not much more than hacks. (A *hack* generally refers to software written by an individual for a specific purpose that may do what it is designed to do but is not thoroughly tested.) Use software hacks at your own risk. If your Treo or your data is damaged as a result of using a hack, you don't have any recourse. In fact, many developers honestly call their own programs hacks. Some of these less-tested freeware and shareware applications may cause problems with your Treo hardware or software or may interfere with other applications.

How do I figure out whether a third-party application is causing trouble on my device?

Since there are so many applications available for your Treo, it is best to get support from the author or vendor of the third-party software that you installed on your device. There are a few of steps you can try to do to troubleshoot a problem with a third-party application on your Treo:

1. If your Treo is resetting, look in the error log to see if the log names a specific application. Viewing the error log is covered earlier in this chapter, under the heading "Error Messages and Troubleshooting."

2. Next, try a soft reset, which is covered in this chapter, under the heading "Perform a Soft Reset."

3. If the problem continues after a soft reset, continue to Step 4.

4. Try a system reset, which is covered in this chapter under the heading "Perform a System Reset." A system reset can be very helpful if a third-party hack is causing the problem.

5. If you have tried a system reset and are still encountering the problem, you can try disabling all hacks in any third-party extensions manager you may have installed (HackMaster, X-Master, TealMaster, and so on). You may have to look at the extensions manager's documentation to find out what you have to do.

6. If none of these steps has solved the problem, you may need to try a hard reset, which erases all data and returns your device to its factory state. This is covered later in this chapter, under the heading "Perform a Hard Reset." The good news is that if a hard reset fixes the problem, it indicates that the problem was caused by a third-party application or a corrupted file.

If you now know which third-party application is causing the problem, it is a good idea to delete that application. Chapter 3 gives instructions on deleting applications from your Treo.

Security

If you are experiencing problems with third-party security software, contact the software vendor or use the vendor's online support services. The item listed here is related to the built-in security features of your Treo.

My Treo used to auto-lock but doesn't anymore.

If you have recently performed a hard reset on your Treo, that is likely the problem. Performing a hard reset erases your password, and without a defined password your Treo won't lock. This is because, of course, you wouldn't be able to log in without a password. To reenable the auto-lock functionality, you will have to go back to the Security Preferences screen to reenter the password you want to use to log in to your Treo when it auto-locks.

Expansion Cards

Your Treo supports SD (Secure Digital) cards and MMCs (MultiMediaCards) only. So when you decide to buy an expansion card, be sure that it is an SD or MMC card. There are many types of cards for specific purposes, such as extra memory, applications, games, and so on. If you are sure that you have the correct type of card for your Treo but are having difficulty, contact the card vendor directly.

Memory

A Treo 700p has 60MB, a Treo 650 has 23MB, and a Treo 600 has 24MB of user-accessible memory. This may sound like a lot of memory, but you may be surprised how quickly you will fill it up as you add applications, capture digital pictures and video, and receive e-mail, etc. To keep your Treo running at its best, you need to be conscious of how much memory is available.

What can I do if my handheld is running out of memory?

There are several things that you can do to reduce the amount of memory you are using. These are explained next.

Purge and Archive Old Records   The built-in Treo applications, such as the Calendar and Contacts, To Do List, and Memo Pad, retain data until you delete it. One way to minimize the amount of unused data on your Treo is to purge and archive the application data.

You can archive your application data on your Treo by simply moving unused data to your PC during a HotSync operation so that you retain a copy of it on your PC and delete it from your Treo. This frees up precious memory.

Purge or Archive Your Old Palm Mail Items (Treo 600)   To purge or archive your old Palm Mail items, follow these steps:

1. Launch the Palm Mail application.
2. Press MENU on the keyboard and select the Purge Items menu option.

A

3. In the Purge screen, which appears next, select the parameters for which data you want to purge, including the Before date, which allows you to define the calendar day that splits your mail into what you will keep and what you will purge. In other words, any mail older that this date will be deleted.

> **NOTE** *If you want the data to be backed up to your PC when it is deleted, make sure the Save Archive Copy on PC option is checked.*

4. When you have defined the parameters you want, press OK. The next time you perform a HotSync operation; old items will be purged from your Treo memory. If you are using VersaMail to send a receive e-mail, there is a purge function within the application that helps clean up memory.

Purge or Archive Your Old Calendar Items   To purge or archive your old Calendar items, follow these steps:

1. Launch the Calendar application, ensuring that it is in Day View—the screen should show only one day at a time.

2. Press MENU on the keyboard and select the Purge Items menu option.

3. In the Purge screen, which appears next, select the parameters for which data you want to purge, including the Before date, which allows you to define the calendar day that splits your Calendar items into what you will keep and what you will purge. In other words, any Calendar items older that this date will be deleted.

> **NOTE** *If you want the data to be backed up to your PC when it is deleted, make sure that the Save Archive Copy on PC option is checked.*

4. When you have defined the parameters you want, select the OK button on the screen. The next time you perform a HotSync operation; old items will be purged from your Treo memory.

Clear Your Blazer Web Browser Cache or Memory   To make your web browsing experience faster when you return to previously viewed web pages, the Blazer browser stores web page information and images in a memory location known as the *cache*. This memory can get large, so it's a good idea to delete the cache regularly and set a lower limit for it. To clear the Blazer cache, follow these steps:

1. If Blazer is not currently running, press HOME on the keyboard to open the Applications Launcher screen. Find the web icon and launch Blazer.

2. Press MENU on the keyboard, select Blazer Preferences on the screen, and then select Advanced.

3. Change the Cache Size to a lower setting. (If you change your mind later, you can change the setting at any time.)

4. Tap the Clear button to delete the Blazer cache, and then select OK.

Move Files to an SD / MMC Card   If you have a memory expansion card for your Treo, it is a great place to store data without slowing down your Treo. You can even run applications right off of the card; and cards, like any technology, are coming down in price all the time. Be sure you get a Secure Digital card or a MultiMediaCard (MMC) because these are the only formats your Treo supports.

Reset Your Treo

A Treo reset will fix many problems you may be experiencing with both software and hardware. A reset is conceptually similar to rebooting a PC. There are a few different types of reset actions that you can perform, and these are explained in this section. There are several types of resets. Some should only be used in specific circumstances, and some only work on specific Treo models. These are the resets available:

- Soft reset
- Battery reset
- System (warm) reset
- Hard reset
- In-cradle reset (Treo 600 only)
- Battery disconnect (Treo 600 only)
- Zero Out (Treo 650 only)

Be aware that a "hard reset" will erase all data on your Treo, including your auto-lock password and network and connection settings, so use it only as a last resort.

Perform a Soft Reset

A soft reset can fix a variety of problems and is similar to rebooting a desktop computer or server. A soft reset tells your device to stop what it is doing and start over again. All records and entries stored in your handheld are retained with a soft reset.

Performing a soft reset does not usually affect the personal data on your Treo, but it is a good idea to perform a HotSync operation before you perform any reset to your Treo. This will help to ensure that if you do lose any data during the reset process, it will be easy to restore that data from your PC.

Follow these steps to perform a soft reset:

1. Locate the reset button.

   a. Treo 700p/650: Remove the cover on the back of the Treo; it is to the left of the removable battery.

   b. Treo 600: It is on the lower-right side on the back of your Treo.

A

2. Treo 700p/650: Use the stylus to gently press the reset button.

Treo 600: Unscrew the point of the stylus, or straighten a paper clip and gently press the reset button.

 Do not perform a soft reset if you are receiving warnings that your battery is low.

What if a soft reset deleted my data?

If you perform a soft reset and you lose data, then your Treo may have a more serious hardware issue. Contact the company from which you bought your Treo or contact Palm to find out where to take your Treo to have someone evaluate it.

Battery Reset—Treo 700p and 650 Only

Another way to get the same results as a soft reset is to a battery reset. This is just another way of saying: remove the battery. Palm recommends that, when you perform a battery reset, you turn off the screen first to reduce the risk of data corruption.

Perform a System Reset

Why would you do a system reset? A system reset bypasses any third-party extensions that may be causing problems and bypasses the Palm OS system extensions that enable your handheld to beam and perform other functions.

 Once you have identified and removed the software that is causing the problem, remember to perform a soft reset (see the section "Perform a Soft Reset") to restore these functions. Certain features of your device such as HotSync and some wireless communications will be disabled after the system reset, but a soft reset will restore them.

A system reset tells your Treo to stop what it is doing and start over again. No records or entries stored in your device are deleted when you properly perform a system reset. You can perform a system reset by following these steps:

1. Remove the back of your Treo 700p/650 so that you have easy access to the Reset hole. If you have a Treo 600 you don't have to remove the back.

2. Press the UP button on the five-way navigation control.

3. Locate the reset button

   a. Treo 700p/650: Remove the cover on the back of the Treo, it is to the left of the removable battery.

   b. Treo 600: It is on the lower-right side on the back of your Treo.

4. While pressing the UP button on the five-way navigation control, gently press the reset button.

   a.   Treo 700p/650: Use the stylus to gently press the reset button.

   b.   Treo 600: Unscrew the point of the stylus, or straighten a paper clip and gently press the reset button.

5. The Palm Computing Platform screen appears. Release the UP button when you see this screen.

6. Once you've tested that the system reset worked, be sure to perform a soft reset. Otherwise, some functions, such as infrared beaming (covered in Chapter 2), will not work properly.

Perform a Hard Reset

The explanation for performing a hard reset is provided in this section; however, please read the following Caution before you do this.

A hard reset will erase everything on your Treo, including configuration settings. All your personal data and third-party applications will be deleted. Do not perform a hard reset unless you have backed up your data to your PC or you are willing to lose all of your data, preferences and settings.

Follow these steps to perform a hard reset:

1. Remove the back of your Treo 700p/650 so that you have easy access to the Reset hole. If you have a Treo 600, you don't have to remove the back.

2. Hold down, and keep holding, the power button (For the Treo 600, this button is also known as the Wireless Mode button and is to the right of the antenna if you are looking at the top of your Treo from the front of the device.)

3. Locate the reset button

   a.   Treo 700p/650: Remove the cover on the back of the Treo; it is to the left of the removable battery.

   b.   Treo 600: Look on the lower-right side on the back of your Treo.

4. While continuing to hold down the power button, turn your device over so that you can see the back of it. Press the reset button.

   a.   Treo 700p/650: Use the stylus to gently press the reset button.

   b.   Treo 600: Unscrew the point of the stylus, or straighten a paper clip and gently press the reset button.

A

5. When the Palm Computing Platform logo is displayed on the Treo screen, release the power button.

A warning appears on the screen to advise you that you are about to erase all of your Treo data.

6. Press the UP button on the five-way navigation control to complete the hard reset or press any other button to perform a soft reset and leave your data alone.

Your device then takes you through a series of screens to walk you through initial setup.

Recover Your Data after a Hard Reset

The good news is that even if you perform a hard reset and later regret doing so, your data and applications will be loaded from your PC the next time you perform a HotSync operation. This is one of the reasons why performing a regular HotSync operation of your Treo with your PC is a good thing to do; that is, it allows you to keep up-to-date data backups for your Treo.

Perform an In-Cradle Reset—Treo 600 Only

The major reason you would need to do an in-cradle reset on your Treo is to help your battery recharge correctly if you find that your Treo turns off as soon as you turn it on and won't charge in the cradle. The reset will reboot the recharge circuitry. Here's how to perform an in-cradle reset:

1. Connect your Treo to its charger. If you are using a powered cradle, make sure the power adapter is attached to the cradle or cable and plugged into a live power outlet.

2. Without lifting the Treo off the cradle or cable, perform a soft reset, as explained in the earlier section "Perform a Soft Reset."

Battery Disconnect (Treo 600 Only)

A battery disconnect reset is a last resort that results in cutting battery power, which deletes all data and settings and returns your Treo 600 to a factory-fresh state. It is essentially an extended type of hard reset.

1. Disconnect your Treo 600 from the charger.

2. At the same time, hold down the K and BACKSPACE keys.

3. While holding down the K and BACKSPACE keys, press the reset button on the back of your Treo with the reset tool (unscrew the tip of the stylus) or a straightened paper clip. This is awkward on purpose so that it is unlikely to happen by accident.

4. Continue holding down K and BACKSPACE until the screen briefly flashes white and then turns black. Release the K and BACKSPACE keys when this happens. Your Treo should appear to be dead and the screen should not turn on. If you see any activity, the reset was unsuccessful, so try the process again.

5. When you have successfully killed your Treo 600 with the reset, connect it to the charger and plug the charger into a power outlet. The screen will be blank for several seconds (as long as 30 seconds) before turning on.

Zero Out (Treo 650 Only)

A Zero Out operation is an extreme special case that completely rewrites your device's internal memory with zeros and ones and returns it to a factory-fresh state. An example of when you might want to use it is if you are selling your Treo or sending it for service and want to ensure that no data will be shared. If you are sure that you want to perform a Zero Out on your Treo 650, follow these steps:

1. Remove the back of your Treo 650 so that you have easy access to the Reset hole.

2. Connect your Treo to the HotSync cable or cradle (the HotSync cable does not need to be connected to a PC or connected to power).

3. Press and hold the POWER button and UP on the five-way navigation button.

4. While continuing to hold POWER and UP, press and hold the HotSync button on the cable. As you press HotSync, ensure that your fingers are not touching any other part of the five-way navigation tool; you must only press the UP button during the entire process.

5. As you continue to hold POWER, UP, and HotSync, press and release the reset button, release POWER, UP, and HotSync.

6. If the reset was done correctly, the screen of your Treo will go blank and you will not be able to turn it on.

7. Your device will appear to be dead for several minutes—up to ten minutes. During this time, your device's internal memory is being reformatted. If your device doesn't appear dead for several minutes, then the Zero Out reset was performed incorrectly; try again.

8. When your Treo does wake up and you see the Palm and Palm Powered logos on the screen, you will eventually see the Welcome program that allows you to calibrate the touch screen and set the date and time.

TIP   *Another way to do perform a Zero Out reset that requires less manual dexterity is to set a password in the security app and then perform a hard reset. This technique works on the 650 and 700p as well as the 600.*

Traveling Outside Your Country of Residence

By design, wireless connectivity means mobility, but that doesn't mean you won't experience some challenges if you move around a lot. A few tips for troubleshooting connectivity issues if you are traveling outside your home country are listed in this section.

A

Can I use a GSM Treo in countries other than my own?

Your GSM Treo is a quad-band device and is capable of running on 850/900/1800/1900 Mhz networks, so provided that you have a roaming contract that covers the countries in which you are traveling, you can use your Treo.

Can I make calls with my Treo from outside my country?

To make calls outside of your country with your Treo, you will need to activate international calling and roaming with your mobile service provider. Talk to your carrier if you need additional information about international roaming.

What countries have GSM coverage?

GSM is a well-defined and supported standard for communications. You can confirm coverage for GSM networks in a specific country by using the official GSMWorld web site (**www.gsmworld.com/gsminfo**). In many cases, several GSM carriers are located in an area. To be sure there is GSM coverage in the area in which you will be traveling, contact your wireless service provider.

Find More Information about Troubleshooting

There are many places where you can find information about troubleshooting Treo hardware and software problems. If you are having trouble with a particular software application, search the program's help files or contact the application vendor directly.

- **Palm**   The support site at Palm (www.palm.com) is a great place to search for troubleshooting tips.

- **Treo user groups**   Appendix B provides sources for more information on resolving user and technical problems. Many of the Treo fan web sites, such as www.treo.com and www.treocentral.com, have user groups where you search for topics and answers or post questions to other users. Often, you can get answers to your questions within a short time.

- **Ask your wireless service provider**   Contact your wireless service provider's support department for assistance. Following is contact information for the largest providers:

  - AT&T Wireless (www.attws.com), 1-800-888-7600

  - Cingular Wireless (www.cingular.com), 1-866-246-4852

  - Sprint PCS (www.sprintpcs.com), 1-800-974-2221

  - T-Mobile (www.tmobile.com), 1-800-937-8997

  - Orange (www.orange.com), +44 (0) 207 984 1600

Appendix B

Find More Information

How to...

- Locate web sites about the Treo and mobile computing
- Find magazines for Palm OS users
- Get up-to-date information on mobile computing at conferences

You can explore many sources of interesting information about your Treo, and the amazing (and not so amazing) things you can do with it. Given the relatively long history of the Palm operating system (Palm OS), you will find many web sites containing large databases of software and information. The tremendous popularity of the Treo device has also lead to a great number of Treo-dedicated web sites on the Internet, which are a great source of information. In the references provided in this appendix, you will find information ranging from the practical, such as troubleshooting tips for when your Treo won't power on, to the zany, with some bizarre and unusual uses for your smartphone.

We have categorized the information sources by type and given a brief description of what you can expect to find at each of these sources. The number of potential information sources is growing so fast that we cannot possibly list them all here, but we will take as thorough a cut at the Treo space as possible.

Web Sites

In this section, we focus on Treo-specific web sites first and then follow with some general Palm OS- and mobility-related web sites that have useful information for the Treo owner.

Treo-Specific Web Sites

The following sites are primary sources of information on the Treo:

- **Palm (www.palm.com)** Palm will always be a great source for information on your Treo. Here you can expect to find information on accessories for your Treo, special offers from the carriers, news about the Treo, and tips and tricks. You can even sign up for the Treo newsletter.

- **Treo Central (www.treocentral.com)** Treo Central is one of the main Internet sites for Treo owners. It addresses issues of owners of all Treo models, not just the Palm OS Treo, so you will find software and other information that doesn't necessarily apply to your smartphone. The site does include Palm OS Treo-specific sections, however, where you will find forums and plenty of information on accessories, software, news stories, and more. Treo Central also has a mobile browser-friendly version of their site that you can connect to at http://treo.tc/.

You Can Find Your Own Answers on the Treo 700p!

In the Treo 700p a new application called My Treo was included that allows you to gain access to the knowledge base tech support articles from the web as well as an on-device user guide.

- **treo1.com (www.treo1.com)**   This site is very similar in structure to the Treo Central mobile web site mentioned previously in this list. It is formatted for your mobile screen and is easy to browse. It contains information on mobile accessories, software, news, ringtones, weather reports, and more.

- **PalmSource (www.palmsource.com)**   Just prior to Palm's merging with Handspring, it spun off its Operating System Group as a new company called PalmSource. Subsequently, PalmSource was acquired by Access and now is a division of Access. PalmSource produces and markets Palm OS, the operating system used in your Treo. There is a great deal of useful information on this web site, both for developers of Palm OS applications and for people who use the devices for personal and business purposes.

- **TreoAddicts (www.treoaddicts.com)**   Although not the most up-to-date of the Treo web sites, this is another source of news and reviews for the Palm Treo owner.

- **MyTreo (www.mytreo.net)**   This is an excellent web site and forum with news, discussion groups, software downloads, and an online store.

- **TreoMB (www.treomb.com)**   A new web site with news, reviews, and user discussion forums for the Treo. The content doesn't seem to update as frequently as other sites, but this site still contains some interesting nuggets.

Treo Users

There are a number of dedicated Treo users who post their experiences, their favorite software, and more on the Internet. You can learn from these users by visiting their sites or weblogs:

- **TreoNauts (www.treonauts.com)**   Andrew is a walking Treo knowledge base and an excellent source of top software and accessories for the Treo. Andrew travels extensively, often hitting many of the top industry-related tradeshows and posts the things he finds most interesting on his blog.

- **The Shifted Librarian**   Jenny is a technically savvy librarian who uses her Treo 600 to the max. Learn how she puts it to use by reading her weblog at www.theshiftedlibrarian .com/stories/2003/12/04/whatsOnMyTreo600.html.

B

Other Web Sites

A large number of other sites we wanted to list have relevant information for the Treo owner, and more such sites seem to appear daily. These sites may be more general than the ones previously listed—related more to Palm or mobile computing than specifically to the Treo—but nonetheless may have useful information for the Treo owner.

General, News, and Reviews

These web sites focus on general information, news, and product reviews relevant to either the Palm world or to the world of mobile computing in general:

- **Brighthand (www.brighthand.com)** Probably one of the most active and popular mobile discussion forums. Information on new devices, rumors, and other assorted news often appears here long before it does anywhere else.

- **Palm Blvd (www.palmblvd.com)** A very active collection of news and discussion forums, and a vast library of downloadable software for your Palm device. Be sure to check compatibility to make sure that software you download will run on your Treo.

- **Palm Infocenter (www.palminfocenter.com)** A chat board with active news threads and discussion forums.

- **PalmStation (www.palmstation.com)** A Palm news and ramblings site.

- **The Gadgeteer (www.the-gadgeteer.com)** A massive set of reviews of just about every high-tech gadget that Julie and Judie, the site authors, can get their hands on. Material useful for the mobile enthusiast often shows up here.

- **PalmLoyal.com (www.palmloyal.com)** Software, links, and Palm discussion.

- **EuroCool (www.eurocool.com)** A Palm news and discussion forum with a European flavor.

- **MobileTech Review (www.mobiletechreview.com)** Formerly the PDA Buyers Guide, this site has reviews of all different types of software and accessories for your Palm OS Treo.

- **Handheld Computing (www.handheldcomputing.com)** This is a general site discussing mobile computing, although it has separate sites for Treo-specific accessories.

- **PhoneScoop (www.phonescoop.com)** This is a general information site about wireless products, but as the name states, it prides itself in sleuthing out new, unreleased phones. They also provide information about phones, such as tear-down information and links to the FCC web sites. You can find most Treo products here, even those that Palm is not ready to launch. Sometimes the info they report is just rumors, but this site is enjoyable to read, to find out about the latest and greatest phones in the wireless industry.

Software

The following sites are focused solely on software. Some are for Palm only; others offer software for a variety of handhelds and mobile devices. Most of the sites advertise a mixture of freeware, shareware, and trial software. Sites like Handango actually sell the software, and CNET has free downloads.

- ■ **Handango (www.handango.com)**   One of the most popular mobile software sites.
- ■ **FreewarePalm (www.freewarepalm.com)**   A host of free applications for your Treo.
- ■ **VersionTracker (www.versiontracker.com/palmos)**   The latest Palm software, with optional e-mail updates.
- ■ **PalmGear (www.palmgear.com)**   Palm software, accessories, and more. Tens of thousands of software titles are available for downloading. At PalmGear, you'll also find active discussion forums and knowledge bases for learning more about your devices.
- ■ **CNET Download.com (www.download.com)**   Downloads of all shapes and sizes, but if you select Palm OS applications specifically, it will filter for you.
- ■ **Tucows (http://www.tucows.com/Windows/PDA/PalmOS/)**   Many shareware applications for your Palm OS device.

Magazines

There are a variety of both print and electronic publications for the Palm OS, although so far, no magazines have surfaced that are dedicated to just the Treo! Web sites and e-zines have for the most part killed off the technology print magazine market. A couple of the surviving publications are listed here:

- ■ *Palmtop User* **(www.palmtop.co.uk/palmuser)**   A bimonthly print magazine with lots of useful information for all Palm OS users.
- ■ *Palm Tipsheet* **(www.palmtipsheet.com)**   A free monthly electronic newsletter with useful information on the Palm platform and tips for how to use it better.

Conferences

Conferences are always an interesting place to get up-to-date information on the mobile computing world and meet other enthusiasts who use Treo and Palm devices. Conferences can be a little expensive, but if you learn of a conference in your area, the exhibit halls are usually free.

PalmSource Developer Conference

The PalmSource Developer Conference is an annual conference geared primarily toward developers of Palm OS accessories and software. However, this is often the place where new leading-edge products that may be useful to you on your Treo are announced. Full information can be found on the PalmSource web site at www.palmsource.com.

B

Mobile & Wireless World

Owned and produced by *Computerworld* magazine, this conference focuses specifically on how wireless and mobile technologies are affecting, or in the future may affect, the enterprise workspace. More information is available at www.mwwusa.com.

CES

For a more consumer-oriented look at the mobile space, you will find there is a lot to see at the Consumer Electronics Show (CES) held each year in Las Vegas. This is an extremely large show, with over 100,000 attendees annually and over 2,000 exhibitors. It focuses on all aspects of computer electronics, but Palm OS applications and hardware are part of the action. For more information, visit www.cesweb.org.

3GSM World Congress

The 3GSM World Congress conference in Barcelona (it can move from site to site in Europe) is one of the main forums where new mobility products and technologies are discussed and introduced. Not only the Treo, but certainly the Treo 600 and related products, will be there. With over 26,000 attendees from 154 countries and almost 600 exhibitors, this is a very large event. More information can be found at www.3gsmworldcongress.com/congress.

CTIA (Cellular Telecommunications Industry Alliance)

CTIA has two events every year, one is focused on Information Technology and Entertainment and is usually held in the fall. The other is focused very much on the nuts and bolts of the mobile communications industry and is held in the spring. More information can be found at the CTIA web site at www.ctia.org.

Index